HAVE YOU FORGOTTEN YET?

HAVE YOU FORGOTTEN YET?

THE FIRST WORLD WAR MEMOIRS OF

C. P. BLACKER MC GM

EDITED BY JOHN BLACKER

Pen & Sword
MILITARY

First published in 2000 by Leo Cooper
and republished in 2015 by
PEN & SWORD MILITARY
An imprint of
Pen & Sword Books Ltd
47 Church Street
Barnsley, South Yorkshire
S70 2AS

ISBN 978 1 78346 167 7

A CIP catalogue record for this book
is available from the British Library

Printed and bound in England
By CPI Group (UK) Ltd, Croydon, CR0 4YY

Pen & Sword Books Ltd incorporates the Imprints of Aviation, Atlas,
Family History, Fiction, Maritime, Military, Discovery, Politics, History,
Archaeology, Select, Wharncliffe Local History, Wharncliffe True Crime,
Military Classics, Wharncliffe Transport, Leo Cooper, The Praetorian Press,
Remember When, Seaforth Publishing and Frontline Publishing

For a complete list of Pen & Sword titles please contact
PEN & SWORD BOOKS LIMITED
47 Church Street, Barnsley, South Yorkshire, S70 2AS, England
E-mail: enquiries@pen-and-sword.co.uk
Website: www.pen-and-sword.co.uk

CONTENTS

EDITOR'S INTRODUCTION

In 1963, when he was 67, my father, Carlos Paton Blacker (known to most of his family and friends as 'Pip' or sometimes 'CP', and to whom I shall refer as CPB), started to write what he called his autobiography. After a preliminary chapter on his school days, he launched into an account of his experiences in the First World War, which started as soon as he left school. For this he had much material to draw on: he had written to his parents almost every day and they had preserved his letters; he also had the diaries which he had kept at the time, and many of the large-scale, cloth-bound maps, often showing the trenches and strong-points, which had been issued to officers, and one or two of which were still stained with his blood.

But as his account of the war became longer and longer, members of his family expressed the hope that his 'autobiography' would not be confined to this relatively short period of his life. His war experiences, we pointed out, were far from unique, and such as had already been vividly described by others, notably Robert Graves and Siegfried Sassoon. On the other hand his later life had held much of unusual interest: he had qualified in medicine and then specialized in psychiatry, so that he had seen the development of that subject from early days; he had also played a pioneer role in the birth control movement, which had likewise undergone enormous changes during his lifetime. But these suggestions met with a firm refusal: his 'autobiography' would go no further than November 1918. Eventually it took him longer to write than the war had lasted, and when finished it ran to some nine hundred pages of typescript. He took no steps to publish any of it.

He died in April 1975, aged 79. Soon after his death, one of his colleagues from the Maudsley Hospital, Dr Denis Leigh, visited our family home to collect material for an obituary of my father which he was writing for one of the medical journals. We showed him the nine hundred pages. He took one look at them and said: 'It's not an autobiography; it's a catharsis.'

The literal meaning of the word catharsis is a 'cleansing', and the First World War was, in my father's words, 'a terrible period in the history of the world which cast its shadow on everyone who lived in it'. In his case the shadow was deepened by various factors. In the first place his heart was never in the war; he did not believe in Germany's sole culpability for the start of hostilities and he could not participate in the 'frenzy of hatred' against Germans which gripped the great majority of British people. Secondly he undoubtedly suffered from feelings of guilt for having survived it. Indeed one side of him clearly wanted to be killed, and this death wish remained with him for the rest of his life. Only feelings such as these can explain some of his more anomalous actions. Why, for example, did he feel a compulsion to join the army at all, given that he had no desire to kill Germans, and he had been honourably failed in his medical examinations because of his eyesight? Why did he feel the need to apply for a transfer from the 4th to the 2nd Coldstream Battalion in the spring of 1918, thereby greatly increasing the risk of his own death? The arguments which he assembled against making such a move were cogent; those which he gives in its favour seem less convincing. In seeking, in his imagination, the advice of his dead brother, was he in fact plumbing the depths of his own subconscious?

Although, as I have said, he made no move to publish it, there were strong indications that he was not averse to the idea of publication. At one point he let his imagination run sufficiently wild as to speculate as to how any financial profits which might accrue from it could be devoted to the reconciliation of British and German ex-servicemen. But any publication clearly necessitated heavy editing of the original manuscript. Apart from its excessive length, his detailed re-living of the four years comprised descriptions of events which were, as he put it, 'narrowly personal and of no interest to anyone but myself'. It has therefore been reduced by about half.

Yet what remains constitutes, I believe, a worthwhile contribution to the literature on World War I. It contains various features not readily found elsewhere: his own introspective reactions to the traumatic events in which he was involved; his shrewd character sketches of his fellow officers; his strange mystical experience on the banks of the River Somme; the poignant juxtaposition of the desolation wreaked by the war and his intense love of natural history, particularly birds and wild flowers, evoked by such places as the Clairmarais Forest and the wood on the hill above Corbie. Above all he believed that the whole war was a hideous mistake which should never have happened; if such mistakes are not to recur, nobody should be allowed to forget.

ACKNOWLEDGEMENTS

My father's original manuscript was typed by the late Mrs Peggy Hope-Jones, but attempts to read it with scanners were unsuccessful, and I am greatly indebted to Huyette Shillingford for re-typing the relevant sections in WordPerfect; without her help the whole project might never have got off the ground. I am also grateful to Evelyn Dodd who assisted with the typing of the chapter on the Canal du Nord, and to Mary Gibson for compiling the index. Thanks are due too to the Audio-Visual and Printing Services of the London School of Hygiene and Tropical Medicine for drawing the maps and reproducing the photographs. I am grateful to Lord Skelmersdale for the photograph of his father, to my cousin Alexandra Drossos for sending me copies of letters in her possession relating to Robin's death, particularly that from my grand-father, Carlos Blacker, to his sister, Carmen Devaux (Alexandra's grandmother) which I have quoted in Appendix 2, and to several people for reading the manuscript in draft, spotting typographical errors and making valuable suggestions: my sisters Carmen and Thetis Blacker, Michael Loewe, Peter Lowes and Carine Ronsmans; the last-named also accompanied me on the visit to the Somme in May 1998 when she provided valuable encouragement and support.

I also wish to acknowledge with thanks the Bernard F. Burgunder Collection of George Bernard Shaw, Division of Rare Manuscript Collections, Cornell University Library, and The Society of Authors, on behalf of the Bernard Shaw Estate, for permission to reproduce the letter from Bernard Shaw in Appendix 2. I am indebted to Major and Mrs Holt for finding and sending me the transcript of letter which my father wrote to Rudyard Kipling on 13 October 1915. Finally I want to record my warm thanks to Mr J. Robert Maguire for sending me, and giving me permission to use, the Rudyard Kipling letter in Appendix 2, for the many things which he has told us about our own family which we did not previously know, and for his encourage-ment and stimulus to pursue the task of editing my father's manuscript.

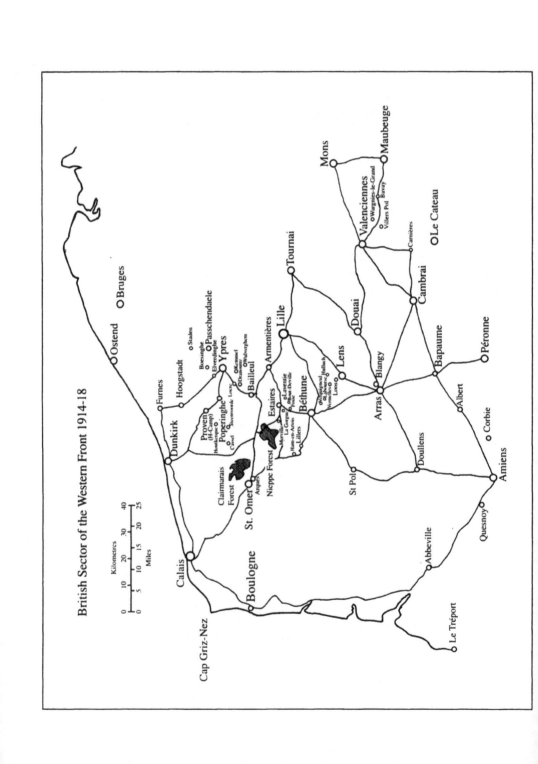

British Sector of the Western Front 1914-18

Kilometres
0 10 20 30 40

Miles
0 5 10 15 20 25

Cap Griz-Nez

Calais

Boulogne

Dunkirk

Furnes

Hoogstadt

Ostend

Bruges

St. Omer

Clairmarais Forest

Arques

Nieppe Forest

Proven (H-Camp)
Houtkerque
Cassel
Saccomverde
Lizerne

Poperinghe

Staden

Boesinghe
Elverdinghe

Passchendaele

Ypres

Kemmel
Dranoutre
Wulverghem

Bailleul

Estaires

Armentières

Lille

Tournai

Laventie
La Gorgue
Morville
Ham-en-Artois
Lillers
Fosse
Neuf-Berquin

Béthune

Guinchy
Richebourg
Vermelles
Loos

Hulluch

Lens

Douai

Cambrai

Le Cateau

Carnières

Villers Pol
Bavay
Wargnies-le-Grand

Valenciennes

Mons

Maubeuge

St Pol

Arras

Blangy

Bapaume

Albert

Péronne

Doullens

Corbie

Amiens

Quesnoy

Abbeville

Le Tréport

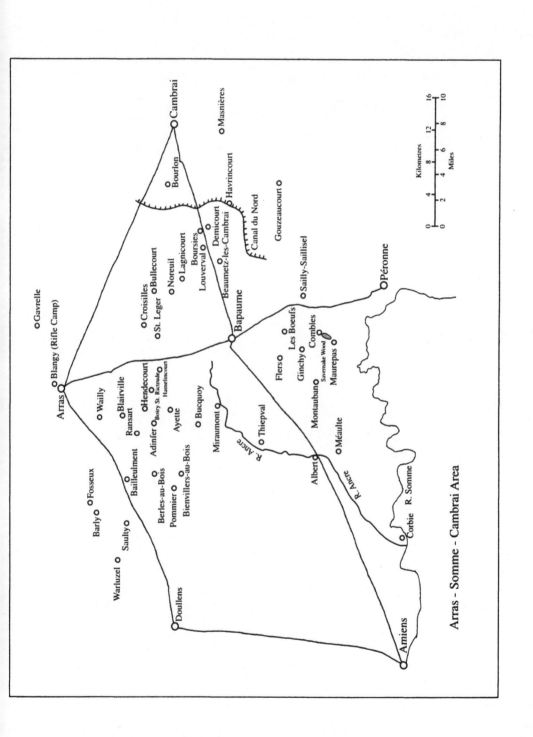

Arras - Somme - Cambrai Area

PROLOGUE

CPB was born in Paris on 8 December 1895. His father, Carlos Blacker, (who features significantly in this story) was the son of an English businessman, John Blacker[1], and a Spanish Peruvian mother, Carmen, née Espantoso. Carlos was a gentleman of leisure all his life; he never seems to have made a serious attempt to earn his living, and his only foray into the world of business was catastrophic: he lost all his money and was declared bankrupt in 1894. This disaster also led to a rupture with one of his best friends, the Duke of Newcastle, who in a fit of temper accused him of cheating at cards. The charge was wholly unfounded and years later Newcastle apologized. But in the meantime Carlos was faced with a dilemma. He was called upon to defend his honour, and since duelling was illegal he was expected to sue his former friend for libel; failure to do so was regarded as being tantamount to an admission of guilt. But not only would such a step involve him in expenses which he could not afford, the whole prospect was also totally abhorrent. Rather than proceed with it he left England to live in self-imposed exile on the Continent. Thus it was that CPB was born in Paris, and he did not in fact set foot in this country until he was nine years old. Later, when both the sons were at boarding school in England, the family moved back to this country to live in a house called Vane Tower in Torquay.

Carlos was a brilliant linguist with refined tastes and many varied interests, and counted among his friends distinguished literary figures including Oscar Wilde, Anatole France and George Bernard Shaw. He had been painfully involved in the Dreyfus Case in the late 1890's[2]. His sister, Carmen, and her husband, Charles

---

[1] John Blacker must have been a wealthy man. He spent a fortune (estimated to be £70,000 and equivalent now of several millions) on books with supposedly Renaissance bindings. After his death in 1896 the whole lot turned out to be forgeries. An account of this bizarre episode may be found in Mirjam M. Foot, 'Double Agent: M. Caulin and M. Hagué,' *The Book Collector* 1987 (Special Number for the 150th Anniversary of Bernard Quaritch) pp.136–150. Hagué was the forger.

[2] Further details may be found in the entry (by Robert Maguire) 'Carlos Blacker' in *L'Affaire*

Devaux, had taken up residence in Germany, and their son, Ernest, was an officer in the German army in World War I. Thus CPB had a first cousin fighting on the other side.

CPB's mother, Caroline, was American, the daughter of Daniel Frost of St Louis, who had been a general in the Confederate army in the Civil War. She had eloped from America to marry Carlos against her father's wishes. They were married in February 1895. Apart from CPB, they had only one other child, Robin, born in June 1897, who also features largely in this story.

CPB's aunt Carmen lived in Freiburg in south Germany, and substantial periods of his early childhood were spent there. They were happy times and they influenced his attitude towards Germans for the rest of his life, as he describes:

My father, who influenced me much in my feelings during early days and in my later sympathies, did not conceal his love of Freiburg and the Black Forest which he looked upon as a second home. Indeed, my earliest memories are of my aunt's house from which my small brother and I used to be taken for daily walks by our white-haired Irish nurse to whom, despite her occasional severity, we were devoted. Our most usual outing was a path winding up a fairly steep hill which overlooked Freiburg and was known to us as The Schlossberg. My earliest out-of-door memories are of snow-laden fir trees bordering an ice-covered rockface on our left, and of frost-encrusted railings of wire netting bordering the path. My father, walking at a faster pace, would sometimes follow us to the summit of The Schlossberg, where, close to a seat, we would prepare a low heap of snow on which a sort of fire ceremony was enacted. My father would produce from his pocket a box of elongated fusee-type matches, a few of which we would stick into the snow heap and light, thus producing a minor fireworks display. In the course of these walks Robin and I were encouraged to ask my father children's questions, mostly unanswerable – such as, why does fire melt snow? Why do some trees bear soft fruit you can eat and others dry stiff cones which you can't? On these questions my father would deliberate and give replies within the range of our understanding.

Another indoor feature of the daily routine in my aunt's house was nursery prayers, morning and evening, over which our Catholic Irish nurse presided. Robin and I knelt on each side of her by her bedside. There we recited the Lord's Prayer and said the Hail Mary. Other topics of religious or moral import were subjected to bedside discussion, including the Ten Commandments, not all of which were as immediately understandable to small children, as the one about honouring one's parents. Soon afterwards I broached the subject with my father during one of our walks up The Schlossberg. My father had a quiet

Dreyfus de A à Z (ed. by Michel Drouin), Flammarion 1994, pp.136–142. Also J. Robert Maguire, 'Oscar Wilde and the Dreyfus Affair', *Victorian Studies* Vol. 2 No. 1 (Autumn 1997); M. Hichens, *Oscar Wilde's Last Chance*, Pentland Press 1998.

voice and very gentle manners. He could attune himself to children of different ages and knew exactly how to talk to them. He dealt with our questions about the Ten Commandments by telling Robin and me that these Commandments were directed to different people. Some were specially meant for children and others were more for grown-ups, but that in due course we would understand them all and profit by them. In the meanwhile we could take it that all ten could be summed up in one comprehensive Commandment, which, if acted on by everyone, would make the world a much better place than it was. What, we asked expectantly, was this Commandment? My father hesitated a few seconds before answering. He then spoke the following two words: 'Be kind,' he said. After all these years I clearly remember the moment when he pronounced these words. It was a cold evening and we were standing near the seat at the top of The Schlossberg. My father was smiling with pleasure over what he was saying, and I saw his face in profile. His dark moustache was touched white with frost. He was wearing gloves and a cap. Robin and I wore mittens and woollen head coverings. 'Be kind to one another, especially to children younger than your-selves,' he said, and, as he spoke, my father looked to us to be the kindest, wisest and best of men. Something of this well-remembered visual impression remained with me throughout the ensuing war, and remains still.

These and other early experiences, which I need not describe, made it natural for us to regard Freiburg and its inhabitants and the surrounding wooded and hilly country as friendly. My father whose sympathies were liberal, disliked what was called chauvinism, and he regarded as chimerical the con-viction held by some of his English friends that Germany was determined to go to war against England and that such a war was inevitable.

My sympathy with my father and my happy early memories of Freiburg caused my later feelings as a soldier to be stratified and ambivalent. I never overcame these early sentiments to the point of hating and wanting to kill Germans. I also absorbed some of the religious sentiments earlier conveyed at the bedside. During bayonet-fighting training, I was sometimes uneasily aware of my father's maxim about kindness being an essential commandment and duty. At instructional sessions and demonstrations, the following question would disquietingly formulate itself: 'What would Jesus Christ, who had told us to be kind to our enemies, have said if instructed to kick a prostrate man in the face or genitals, or to go for his eyes with his thumbs, or to plunge six inches of bayonet into his soft parts?' I may at this point say that I was never involved in hand-to-hand fighting. Indeed I do not know for certain that I ever killed or wounded a German. But I may have done so without knowing it. More than once I fired a Lewis gun at shadowy figures distantly seen at dawn or dusk moving along roads or duck-board tracks within the range of visibility. I recall firing a few bursts of Lewis gunfire at a relieving party proceeding along the top of a communicating trench near Hamelincourt. I was conscious at the time of an unmilitary ambivalence, wanting at the same time to hit and not to hit those just-visible figures who were not threatening or attacking us. This ambivalence formed part of a mental balance-sheet on one side of which was the necessity of winning the war which involved killing and maiming. The physical sufferings entailed by wounds and mutilations were a part of the effects of what we were being trained to do; but also to be taken into account in the balance-sheet were the reactions of the near relatives of the killed, their parents, wives, sisters and children. By 1918 I knew what it meant to lose a brother and to participate in the grief of parents, and I also had the experience of a platoon or company officer of writing letters of condolence to the next-of-kin of killed men and of acknowledging their replies. It was obvious that near relatives of killed Germans felt exactly as did the relatives of our killed. The mental sufferings of bereaved civilians formed no less a part of the balance-sheet of war than the physical afflictions of maimed and crippled combatants. It was in 1915 when, as told below, I was working as a non-combatant at the Belgian Field Hospital into which had been admitted a severely wounded German officer, that I realized how pleased I was to be in a position to do something for this man.

★   ★   ★   ★

In September 1905 CPB was sent to a boarding school in England, Cothill near Abingdon, of which the headmaster was M.J. Dauglish, generally known as 'Doggie'. It was the first time that he had come to England. Apart from initial home-sickness, CPB appears to have been happy at Cothill, except for one feature, the French classes.

My main dread each day was the French lesson. I was placed by Doggie in the second class (there were five) with boys much older than myself because he knew I could speak French. Doggie himself took this class. He could speak no colloquial French, and when, later (in 1920), he came to stay with us in Dinard, he made it a condition of his coming that he would not be expected to speak French. But he knew how to teach French grammar, which was the basis of the curriculum, much as was Latin grammar for that language. I well recall my first lesson. I had got to know the small boys who were my contemporaries in the classes for Latin, arithmetic, etc. But here I was among bigger boys, strangers who out of school would have taken no notice of me. After we had got into our places at our desks we were given certain pages to learn from a book. The book was a French grammar and the pages were headed 'syntax'. I wondered what syntax was. Could it be something about a tax on sin? I could not understand a single word of the pages we were expected to learn. The dread moment came when we 'went up'. We took our places on a form and were asked questions. You went up or down the row depending on whether you correctly answered or failed to answer the question put to you. I was at the bottom of the form. Apprehensions mounted as my moment approached.

When it came I stood up. 'Blacker,' said Doggie, 'do the past participles of verbs conjugated with *avoir* (pronounced avouah) agree with the subject or object?' (That is how I recall the question.) Not knowing the meaning of a single word contained in this question – participles, conjugation, subject, object – I said I did not know. 'Oh yes you do,' said Doggie. 'How would you say this in French?' He then said something in English and I said it in French. The class exploded. They leant back in their seats and guffawed with laughter. The rafters rang. The joke was my French accent. When silence was restored, Doggie questioned me about my answer. But I was speechless and on the verge of tears. He eventually gave me up, and when the hour was over I crept away feeling like a miscreant, an abject fool whom none of the bigger boys would take any notice of except to laugh at. (Yet, thinking back, I see exactly why Doggie grilled me. He doubtless felt ill at ease about the lack of contact between the French he taught and the French that was spoken, and he wanted to establish a bridge between the two. He may even have hoped that I might be of some use in the class for this purpose.) Thereafter, the class in French became the day's nightmare. It was the first thing that, with an inner sinking feeling, I thought of when I woke up in the morning. There was one day of the week on which there was no French class, and on those mornings I would wake up and my spirits would soar.

In retrospect, CPB judged himself to have been of about average intelligence when at school. He also did quite well at games at Cothill, but towards the end of his time there he started to suffer from knee trouble.

One day I tried to volley with my right foot a ball which I caught not in the instep of my boot but on the toe, thus wrenching my foot and putting a strain on my anterior thigh muscles. I experienced a severe pain just below the knee where, later, a painful lump developed. Not long afterwards I did the same thing to my left knee. Thereafter any sort of extensor pull hurt and even a light blow on the tender area was agonizing and incapacitating. I was told that the trouble was a partial detachment of the epiphysis of the tibia, also known as Schlatter's disease. My games career when at Eton (1909–14) was seriously affected by this disability. But it had practically remedied itself by 1914. The cartilage ossified and during the ensuing years of the first war I was scarcely troubled.

In the summer of 1909, CPB went to Eton, where his housemaster was Hugh de Havilland, sometimes known as 'The Man'. He was 'a strongly-built man with a straight back, grey hair and quiet manners. He believed in trusting his boys. Some of us may have thought that he carried this principle rather far.' *The trouble with his knees precluded CPB from playing either cricket or football, but he found he could box and fence. He distinguished himself in both these sports, particularly the former. He made several good friends at Eton, notably Oscar Hornung, Bartle Frere and Cecil Sprigge. Of these the first two were killed in the war; Cecil Sprigge remained one of his closest friends until his – Cecil's – death in 1959.*

In his last three terms, or 'halves' as they are called at Eton, CPB was captain of Hugh de Havilland's house. When he left at the end of the summer half of 1914 he had little inkling of what was in store for him.

1

THE OUTBREAK OF WAR

The war came on us suddenly. The half was over and members of the Officer Training Corps (OTC) were spending ten days in camp at Mytchett Farm. I did not enjoy these periods in camp. They took a bite out of the summer holidays. One slept badly in the tents on palliasses stuffed with straw, one's uniform was uncomfortably hot in warm weather, the drills and schemes bored me. The best times were the evenings. One then felt cool and relaxed, and there were sing-songs which could be enjoyable. I used to count the days till camp broke up and we could go home.

Before we left for camp, at the end of July 1914, I heard but a single allusion to what lay ahead. It was at lunch in the latter half of July. I was sitting on the Man's right, and he mentioned events in Austria. The Archduke had been murdered and the Man took a grave view. 'That,' he said, 'might lead to a war.' 'You mean a local war?' I asked. 'Something like another Balkan war, but perhaps more in the middle of Europe?' I don't remember his exact reply, but he took a grave view. I could not see how Britain could possibly be involved and hence, so far as I was concerned, the Man's anxiety was misplaced.

On Tuesday, 28 July we left Eton for Mytchett Farm. By Friday, 31 July there was considerable alarm. We were told that the camp might be broken up because the regular officers concerned with the OTC might be called up. On Monday, 3 August we were roused from our slumbers very early by CSM Carey. He walked along our lines resoundingly whacking our tents with his cane shouting, 'Up everybody. We strike camp.' My reaction was one of joy. Five extra days at home. We marched to Frimley, trained to Eton where we drew some cash and cabbed to the Great Western Railway station. At Paddington we washed, shaved and changed out of uniform. Robin and I parted from two others who had come with us and took the 4.15 train to Torquay where we arrived after ten.

We had given no forewarning to those at home of our arrival. Robin and I walked into the dining room where they were finishing dinner. Deep gloom was immediately sensed. My father was silently brooding. I asked him how serious he thought things were. He hesitated and finally said that only by a near-miracle could a general European war be averted. Would it involve us, I asked. He replied that he did not see how we could fail to be involved. For the first time I thought that it might have been better if world events had permitted us to finish our pre-arranged period in camp. I tried to comfort my father, but there was little I could say. By this time Germany and Russia were at war, Belgium had been invaded and we had sent an ultimatum to Germany saying that if she did not withdraw from Belgium, whose neutrality had been violated, we would declare war. My father said that it was impossible at this stage for the Germans to withdraw from Belgium. We went to bed full of dark forebodings. Next day, Tuesday 4 August, we were at war with Germany.

The morning papers effervesced with war and war-like spirit. Moreover they displayed notices urging men between eighteen and forty to join the fighting services. I saw this exhortation in *The Times*. I said to my father, 'This looks as if it applies to me.' 'It does,' he said. My first vision was of a life on the lines of an unending OTC camp, but incomparably worse. There would be every kind of superimposed horror. War? Till then it had been a distant word. Something that had happened far away or long ago. Now it was a burning reality. I could not picture a war against a civilized and previously friendly nation, least of all against the Germans whom I had always liked. My first inclination was to blame someone. But whom should I blame? I went over the chain reaction as I then understood it, from Serbians to our own Foreign Office. The Serbians had lit the fuse by assassinating an Archduke, heir to an imperial throne. Damn those Serbians, I said to myself as I stood on the terrace and looked out over the sunlit bay. It was at its loveliest that morning. Brixham trawlers with their chocolate-coloured sails were standing, tall and motionless, off Torquay harbour and the far coast, abruptly terminating in the sharp outline of Berry Head, was just visible through a filmy stillness. A perfect summer morning, windless and peaceful. What a contrast, I thought, to the turmoils now in the minds of men. How long would it be, I wondered, before our inner worlds could again be attuned to the scene below. And what dire changes would by then have been enacted?

On that morning there began to open between my father and mother a fissure which, imperfectly healed, remained till my father died fourteen years later. It was concerned with the Germans. My mother used to say without irony that my father's spiritual home had always been Freiburg. He had gone there during a stressful period of his life. He had taken refuge with his sister Carmen who, my mother (I think truthfully) said, understood him better than anyone else. As he walked about the streets of Freiburg and the hills round it, he would admire everything; he would point out the neatness, the orderliness, the cleanliness. Germany had caused him no stresses as France had done during the Dreyfus

Case; nor had he painful associations such as those with England. He deeply admired Germany: its science, its music, its industry, its discipline. Without much idea of what it was like from the inside and never really expecting it to be used in war, he admired the German army. The toy soldiers with which I used to play as a child were German soldiers with spiked helmets. The soldiers one saw in the streets had formed my mental picture of what a soldier looked like and was. Their parades (especially that held in the park close to our home in the Ludwig Strasse on the Kaiser's birthday), their smartness, their seeming cheerfulness and zest, the clock-work precision of their saluting, the punctilious yet friendly way the officers acknowledged their salutes, their military music (concerts with much deep brass were regularly held in the above-mentioned park), the way the army formed an integral and colourful part in the life of the town – all these things had been noticed by father. He had pointed them out to me and they had impressed me. I did not set eyes on a British soldier till I was ten.

These were the people with whom we were now at war and against whom there broke out a frenzy of hatred. To my father this hatred was incomprehensible. But not to my mother. Her reactions were in every way orthodox. She was in no way influenced by the experience of having lived (seemingly happily) among Germans. The invasion of Belgium, whose neutrality Germany had guaranteed, was a plainly monstrous act. Indeed, my father and mother felt passionately in quite opposite ways. My father talked with vehemence, eloquence and a total lack of restraint. In England there prevailed at first an extravagant and irrational optimism. Our navy was, of course, supreme, and our army, though small, was unmatched in quality. Once across the channel our troops would give the Kaiser and his hordes (latter-day Huns: the word came in quickly) what they had asked for. We were, moreover, the wealthiest country in the world and the most powerful. Aided by the French and the Russians, whose numbers caused them to be compared with a steam-roller, the incomparable British Tommy would soon settle the war. The Kaiser and Crown Prince, dubbed Big and Little Willie, were often cartooned as squealing dachshunds running away from a rampaging lion or a fuming John Bull. The war, it was confidently predicted, would be over by Christmas. If one wanted to be in time for the fun one ought to enlist at once.

The revived word jingoism entered my father's vocabulary to denote boastful nationalism. An example sticks in my memory. A musical comedy of some sort was being given at the Torquay theatre. In the third act, I think, a jingo song, sung by the blonde tenor, was introduced in a manner that had no bearing whatever on the farcical plot. The theme was the Kaiser's mailed fist, and the song ended with the words:

> 'We'll show this German bully
> That we've got a mailed fist too.'

As he sang these words the tenor looked ferocious and shook his clenched fist at the audience. Rapturous applause calling for an encore. This time the lines were sung:

> 'We'll show this German sausage
> That we've got a mailed fist too.'

As he sang the word sausage, the tenor's lips curled in contempt, and instead of waving a clenched fist at the audience he raised two fingers in a gesture then regarded as lewd. Pandemonium of laughter and applause. My father looked glum but Robin thought it funny. As we were walking out of the theatre Robin asked what sort of people we were at war with. Were they Huns or Sausages?

But the German advances into Belgium and France dashed hopes of a victory before Christmas. The initial enthusiasm was followed by misgivings which, at this stage, produced a singular reaction – faith in miraculous deliverance. This faith gave rise to two myths: the first was that a large force of Russians had been shipped from Archangel to an unnamed port in Scotland and were being secretly transported through Britain to the Western Front; the second was that, at Mons, the advancing Germans had been halted and our troops saved by an apparition of angels.

My father's feelings for Germany included a realistic appreciation of their military power. Hence he took a pessimistic view of the immediate course of the war. He would hold forth to all and sundry that a quick victory was impossible. Seeing that there was no primary dissension between Britain and Germany – both having been brought into the war by commitments to allies – the sensible thing to do was to try to put an end to it as quickly as possible. Both sides should be invited to declare their war aims and an effort should be made to reach an accommodation. This was what two sensible individuals would do if they had been brought into conflict by a chain reaction which neither had started and which neither had been able to control. Little need, perhaps, for such exploration if the war was to be short and victorious; much need if long and of uncertain issue. A little reason was called for and less emotion. The alternative course, involving a prolonged holocaust the outcome of which was at this stage unpredictable, was surely unthinkable in a civilized world. But few people shared his views. It took him some time to realize that the events which filled him with horror were accepted by others with mixed feelings which included a sort of pleasurable exaltation. The story about Russian troops landing in Scotland and passing through England on their way to the Western Front was, he declared, ruled out by the poor railway communications between central Russia and Archangel (at which place the Russians were said to have embarked) and by the inadequate harbour installations of that arctic port. But the rumours thickened and at least one person told my father that his scepticism in the face of what was by then overwhelming evidence amounted to defeatism. I recall how a lady to whom one evening my father had explained his reasons for disbelief triumphantly burst into his study the day after with conclusive proof. A relative in the House of Lords who was at the hub of events had told her in strict confidence that the rumour was perfectly true. When my father politely maintained his position the lady lost her temper. She asked if he was implying that she was telling lies. Later the rumour was officially denied. But this same lady declared that the denial was made in the national interest, to put the Germans off the scent.

The story of the angels of Mons, though never taken as seriously as the other, provided a good outlet for my father's bitterness, which became increasingly focused on organized religion. You would have thought, he said, that Christians who took seriously the commandment 'Thou shalt not kill' would have felt it their duty to stop the war. But no. Both sides beseech (or instruct) the same deity to lead their armies to victory, a victory to be attained by the maximum slaughter of the people on the other side. A pity that the two sides could not at least agree to spare the deity these confusing stresses. It was reassuring and comforting to our religious leaders, he would say in one of his many ironical moods, that the angels of Mons had left us in no doubt on which side the deity's sympathies lay. The miracle should provide a heartening theme for sermons in many churches and would certainly lead to a speedy victory. The fact that the churches on both sides vociferously supported the war, he would say when in another mood, involved a regression from Christianity to militant Jahve worship, from the New Testament to the Old. This was what civilization had come to. My father would quote bloodthirsty passages from the books of Joshua and Judges.

On the other hand my mother's conventional reactions and her credulity of atrocity stories which were soon in lively circulation were entirely spontaneous expressions of her character and feelings. She did not weigh or question what was said in the press. She believed almost everything she read, and she reacted with an indignation which was shared by most English people including all her relatives. Indeed, hers was a familiar reaction to stories of German atrocities. These, she said, would not have been so shocking if they had been perpetrated by a less civilized people. She had held the Germans to be no less civilized than ourselves; that made it all the worse that they should descend to such barbarities. My mother's almost unqualified indignation and credulity puzzled and pained my father. He once said to me that he did not understand them, seeing that, unlike most English people, my mother had lived in Germany where she had received much kindness. I also found my mother's violent feelings difficult to understand except in so far as they were prompted by a solidarity with her family, all of whom adopted just the same attitude. My mother was intensely loyal to her family. Indeed, loyalty was one of the most prominent features of her character.

A further source of stress for my father was the predicament of my Aunt Carmen who had not moved from Freiburg and whose son, Ernest, was an officer in the German army. Communications with her had been cut off and such news as came to us was via my grandmother who was in Montreux, for Switzerland, being neutral, maintained communications with both sides. It transpired that, *mutatis mutandis*, Carmen's reactions were much the same as my father's. Rumours of atrocities by British and other allied troops and by Belgian and French civilians were, it appeared, rife in Germany. They matched the rumours and stories current here. Carmen said she didn't believe them. She knew the British: they did not do that sort of thing. This was conveyed to my grandmother in letters charged with distress and apprehension. My father well recognized that Carmen's position in Freiburg was incomparably more difficult than his at Torquay.

Singularly contrasting with the views of my Aunt Carmen were those of my Aunt Dolores, my father's other sister. She was possessed by an even bitterer hatred of the Germans than my mother, and this my father found even more difficult to understand. Indeed it seemed to him that the world had suddenly gone mad. (The rift between my two aunts was never healed.)

These domestic frictions put an end to the carefree home life we had always enjoyed before. Breakfasts were apt to be bad times. My mother, by this time tense and nervous, would read something in the morning paper which would kindle her indignation. She would then round on my father as if the newly announced outrage or atrocity were his fault. The spirit of the ensuing alter-cations sharpened rather than healed the differences. One felt a continuous subterranean tension and there were few days when there were not eruptions. But my parents continued to entertain as lavishly as before. The same guests came to stay, the same local people would come in to meals.

My father's reading reflected his mood. He turned back to J.G.Frazer whose accounts of primitive rites and superstitions provided ironical comparisons with contemporary aberrations. He also read Reinach, Anatole France, Loisy, Voltaire and others in whose scepticism he found support for his feelings about the war. He also took a keen interest in documents bearing on the origins of the war – or rather on the events leading up to the war – on which he became quite an authority. It was useless to try to discuss these subjects with my mother. But he liked to air them to me. At this time I felt deeply sorry for my father, whom the war had scarified in his most vulnerable places. He had been a cosmopolitan liberal for whom progress in internationalism provided a guarantee of peace. Suspicions of Germany's intentions had begun in Tory circles when she proceeded to enlarge her navy. Indeed, there were some who had declared that war against Germany was inevitable. Such arguments my father dismissed as inapplicable to the twentieth century. Why, he had asked, should the Germans want a war? They were doing very well without one. The German people were prospering and, except for a minority, were peaceably inclined. This was the line taken by my father before August 1914. He later contended that if a plebiscite had been held in Germany, say, in June 1914 as to whether they wanted or did not want a European war, they would (except for a numerically insignificant war party) have opted for peace, as England would most certainly have done if, at that time, the same question had been put to us. But by 30 July, worked up by events in Russia, the Germans would have opted for war, much as we would have done for other reasons six days later on 4 August. If you say that a nation 'wants a war', you have to say what elements in that nation want it, against what country it wants it and (important) at what moment of time it wants it.

The events of August 1914, by most regarded as abundantly justifying the forebodings of jingo xenophobes, had proved my father majestically wrong. Not only was he disillusioned in his humanitarian idealism, he felt personally discredited as an authority on international affairs. Germany, moreover, was the home of his favourite relative and the scene of the happiest days of his life.

All this I understood. Both Robin, my brother, and I sympathized with him, and he freely unburdened himself to us, especially to me. The war brought me closer to my father and somewhat estranged me from my mother.

It was, I think, during the summer holiday of 1914 that my father met Bernard Shaw. I recall how it happened. We were bathing at Meadfoot beach when Jack Warren, from whom we hired bathing cabins and boats, pointed to a bearded man swimming towards the raft which was moored some fifty yards out. He swam vigorously, using an effective side-stroke. 'That,' said Warren, 'is a well-known man. He's staying at the Hydro.' I told my father who was much interested and introduced himself. They had several friends in common, including Norman Forbes Robertson. The Shaws came to tea and, thereafter, were regular visitors. My father found him a congenial companion with whom he discussed, among other things, the events leading up to the war. At the end of 1914, GBS published a booklet called *Commonsense about the War* which owed something to my father to whom he later gave the script, mostly in short-hand. I found Mrs Shaw easier to talk to than GBS and we became friends. The Shaws came back to Torquay in 1915 and GBS was with my father when he received the news of Robin's death. He was characteristically kind.[1]

About joining the army Robin and I felt somewhat differently. From the very first Robin was inflexibly determined to join at the earliest possible moment. But he was then but seventeen and two months (having been born on 13 June 1897) and well below the age-limit. He therefore did two further halves at Eton (winter 1914, spring 1915) before leaving some two months before his eighteenth birthday. He was killed three months after his birthday.

I did not share his single-mindedness about military service. Indeed, I found myself now and then meditating on the theme of moral versus physical courage. Which would make greater demands – to get killed as a combatant or to refuse to take part in the war as a conscientious objector? I came to the conclusion

[1] See Appendix 2.

that the answer depended on how you had been brought up. For someone who had been to a public school the moral pressure to 'join up' was well-nigh irresistible. For any of my contemporaries to refuse on grounds of conscience would have called for enormous moral courage, provided that he had normal awareness and an average sensibility to public opinion. But for a recent immigrant to the country living, say, in the east end of London, it might be the other way round.

A further thought occurred. Though I had been weakening on Christian doctrine, the Christian ethic had gained force. What would Christ have taught? He might have declared in incisive words that the kingdom of heaven was not gained by wars between nations and that there could be no wars without combatants. The path to the kingdom was straight and narrow, and persecution was the lot of all who followed it. No man need be a combatant. Wars were of Caesar, not of God. At this time I knew nothing of Quakers. There were none among my parents' friends.

I once broached the question with my father. I asked him whether, if he were my age, it would enter his head openly to stay out of the war. He told me that the issue had arisen for him during the Boer War for which he had felt little enthusiasm. There had not then been a recruiting drive like the one then in spate. He had finally offered his services to the War Office as had done two of his friends at the same time. But his services had not been called on. The Boer War, however, was not a life-and-death struggle as this one was going to be. 'So that if you were now in my place,' I asked, 'I take it that you would join up?' Rather hesitantly he said yes. But I then saw that it would call for more moral courage to stay out openly than to plunge in and get killed like everyone else who shared my background. I always had a deep respect for the genuine conscientious objector.

The summer holidays in 1914 were not particularly notable. My first thought was to join the Devonshire Regiment, and I made some inquiries. I was told to produce a certificate of medical fitness. All went well till my sight was tested. Without glasses I could read none of the test letters. That, for the time-being, settled things. Several of my school friends went into the army: Oscar Hornung into the Essex Regiment, Bomba Oldham into the Seaforth Highlanders, Bartle Frere into the Bedfordshire Regiment. I decided to stay at Torquay till October and then go up to Oxford. Robin and I had some pleasant times bathing and fishing. I bought an aquarium which I kept in the loggia and which I stocked with anemones, gastropods and crustacea, including a small lobster. These I collected at low water from the rock pools at the eastern end of Meadfoot beach. I spent much of my time alone in what was my favourite area – the promontory of Hope's Nose which juts out towards the Orestone Rock and forms the northern arm of Torbay. There I found a family of ravens which frequented the cliff on which they had built their nest, a massive structure of sticks piled up on an inaccessible ledge and used from year to year. They seemed on friendly terms with a nearby colony of noisy jackdaws. On the rocks exposed at low water were oyster-catchers and turnstones, and on the gorse-covered slopes were stonechats and linnets. The Orestone was a favourite perching and nesting place for cormorants. A drain which issued from the tip of the Nose attracted numerous herring gulls. Here it was that I first became acquainted with kittiwakes which nested on the Flat Rock. I loved the clamour of these birds. We used to fish in the bay for mackerel and, along this rocky stretch of coast, for pollack and conger.

Among my father's guests at Vane Tower was a Swedish ex-Officer called August Schwan who knew a lot about the German army and had, I gathered, passed through a Prussian staff college. He gave details about the Schlieffen Plan and I recall his telling us that Hindenburg, acclaimed as the victor of the Battle of Tannenberg, was a figurehead; the strategist with the real drive and initiative was General Ludendorff. That was the first time I heard of Ludendorff. I recall conversations between Schwan and Bernard Shaw and was struck by GBS's capacity to listen. He sat in a garden chair, his left elbow on the arm of the chair and his fingers to his cheek. He remained in this intent position, motionless except for an occasional short nod, during a prolonged exposition of which I understood nothing. His immobility struck me as statu-esque and, having a camera in those days, I tried to photograph him without his noticing. But the thing did not come out. GBS later warned my father about Schwan. He thought he might possibly have connections with Germany. My father, who could never think ill of his friends and who had mocked at the prevalent spy mania (espionitis), dismissed the possibility saying that if Schwan were a spy he would not talk so freely. I never heard of him after 1914.

I recall the impact of the first reported death. On 14 August 1914, ten days after we had entered the war, R.A. Compton-Thornhill (Scots Guards: left H. de H.'s in 1910) was killed. The first of a numerous company. I remember feeling absurdly incredulous: 'That can't really be true.' This reaction to the deaths in battle of contemporaries and friends did not outlast 1914. Of this more later.

*   *   *   *

In October 1914 CPB went up to Oxford, where he started to read zoology but stayed for only one term. He was clearly restless and anxious to be more closely involved in the war.

We went down from Oxford on 8 December 1914 – my nineteenth birthday. Christmas was spent at Vane Tower where I recall the atmosphere was calmer. By this time the Town Hall was turned into a war hospital for surgical cases. John and Sylvia Payne (both doctors) had beds and encouraged me to help the nursing staff. I spent most mornings there. I also was allowed to be present during operations and, on one occasion, to help at one. I recall watching a difficult operation on an arterio-venous aneurism in the neck which involved ligating the carotid artery. I came home rather excited and smelling strongly of ether. There had arrived for a short stay that afternoon Robbie Ross[3] whom I met for the first time. I was at once charmed by him. He inquired with close interest about my reactions as a spectator in the operating theatre. He was a small bald man with a low, asthmatic but beautifully modulated voice and a most engaging smile. His views about the war were close to my father's and he would listen with amusement to my father's vehement talk. My mother's reactions to my father also amused him. His sympathy for my father and invariable courtesy to my mother eased things between them and life was definitely pleasanter for us all when he was with us. He regarded the war as a sort of national – or international – aberration which was reflected in people's vocabularies. The conversion into an adjective of the word Hun – someone had spoken of a German piano as a Hun piano – struck him as comically indicative of the nature of the aberration. My father used to draw him out after dinner about Oscar Wilde. He talked quietly and without a trace of personal bitterness about the hatred which had ensued from that affair. Indeed, my father was the one who became indignant and voluble, and the intensity of his feelings was a measure of his admiration for Robbie's poise, of his capacity to accept as tragic but inevitable the events which led up to Wilde's imprisonment and followed his release. One's admiration for Robbie's equanimity was enhanced by his physical frailty; he then suffered from asthma from which he died in 1918.

CPB made two more attempts to join the army, but was rejected because of his bad eyesight on both occasions. The second of these had taken him to Wareham in Dorset, where he met an Eton master called E.J.Churchill, who put him in touch with an organization called the British Field Hospital for Belgium, or, for short, the Belgian Field Hospital, which had originated in the wave of sympathy for Belgium which swept the country. Churchill had heard that the hospital needed a courier to go between the committee in London and the commandant at the hospital, which position CPB secured.

[3] Robbie Ross (1869–1914) was a literary journalist and art critic who had been one of Oscar Wilde's most intimate and loyal friends.

2

THE BELGIAN FIELD HOSPITAL

The London Headquarters of the Belgian Field Hospital was in Suffolk Street, and its secretary was an old Etonian called Baillie Hamilton. I did several journeys from London to Belgium, spending most of my time in Belgium. At its beginning the hospital had been in Antwerp. It was said to have had a narrow escape from capture. Thereafter it established itself in the township of Furnes situated some ten miles east of Dunkirk and some four miles east of the Franco-Belgian frontier. Furnes had been intermittently shelled and the place had been a good deal knocked about. Some time in January 1915, not long before I arrived, the hospital had been hit and a nurse of the name of Rosa Vecht killed. The hospital building had been so damaged and was held to be so dangerously situated that it had been decided to move. The new site was an empty 'hospice' outside a village called Hoogstadt on the Furnes-Ypres road, about two miles south of Furnes through which, during my attachment, I was to drive many times on my way to and from Dunkirk. Only once during these transits was Furnes being shelled.

Though it was well within the range of fire, the hospital at Hoogstadt, unlike Furnes, was never shelled – at least it wasn't while I was there – though near-by crossroads were. Hence we felt pretty safe though the line was but five miles away. We were thus in what was called the front-line zone; the sound of gun-fire was never long unheard by day and at night the eastern sky flashed and flickered in a tempo of which the accompaniment varied between an occasional mutter, which was almost comforting in its remoteness, and a pulsating din like the rhythmical beating of a Cyclopean drum. At one period the Belgians, or it may have been the French, placed a battery of long-range naval guns west of the hospital. (The line lay to the east and south-east.) These guns seemed to shatter the building as they hurled their massive projectiles over our heads; and at least once the battery drew counter-fire. As they passed over the hospital in their westward course, the German shells were on their downward trajectory, so that their sound was a crescendo and definitely frightening. We did not therefore much like these naval guns.

The departure time of ships from Dover varied with the tides and with miscellaneous man-made rules and precautions. If the ship left early in the morning, I would go by train to Dover the night before and stay at the capacious but seemingly sepulchral Lord Warden Hotel. My first transit was on 3 February 1915. The day before I had been introduced in the London office to a new Matron, Miss Davis, for whom during the journey I acted as escort. Miss Davis was a very tall, thin and severe-looking woman whom I made it my business to look after during the voyage. She was amiable then and thereafter. I had the impression that shyness (perhaps connected with her embarrassing tallness) was responsible for a somewhat frosty manner. I wondered how she would go down as Matron in the informal conditions of this largely improvised hospital. In the event she proved an excellent matron, though she did not stay long.

Our sea passage on Wednesday, 3 February 1915, from Dover to Dunkirk was calm and uneventful. We had spent the night of Tuesday 2 February at the above-mentioned Lord Warden Hotel and boarded the boat early, a fine sunny crossing during which I wrapped up Miss Davis on deck and sat with her. We arrived at Dunkirk at about eleven in the morning. My first impression was of an untidy but colourful medley of uniforms – French, Belgian and British. No sooner had we crossed the gangway than an air raid alarm sounded and approaching German planes appeared as enlarging specks in the distance. They seemed untroubled by widely dispersed puffs of smoke – erratic anti-aircraft fire. (It was for the first time borne home on me how anti-aircraft gunners were at a disadvantage compared with ordinary gunners whose targets are mostly out of view. The whole world could see how bad was the former's shooting.) The planes came near enough for me to recognize the black crosses on the wings. They seemed to be making straight for the harbour where Miss Davis and I were standing. Their approach provoked a train of thought which must, I suppose, have occurred to everyone who is bombed, shelled or shot at for the first time: there is a most vital difference between reading a war story and having a taste of war oneself. You know, when you read a story, that, however perilous the hero's adventures, however tremendous his ordeals, he will survive. He may perhaps be wounded or incapacitated. But it would spoil the story if he were killed. Not so the first-hand experience. This was brought home as I stood on the Dunkirk Quay and saw the German planes coming up, as if the airmen knew that Miss Davis and I were standing there. 'There is no reason,' I said to myself, 'why, in the next few seconds, a bomb or a piece of shrapnel should not fall on this precise spot thereby inscribing finis to this hero's story.' I was aware of a not entirely unpleasurable tension. I might be killed, certainly, which would be a pity. But this was what, with a bit of a stretch, could be called a baptism of fire, of which noble experience I had read somewhere that after it your life was never quite the same as before. This was quite a stimulating thought. I asked Miss Davis if this was the first time she had been in 'war danger'. She said it was. However, the German planes changed direction and everything quietened down. (These German machines were called taubes or doves, someone then told us. I was incongruously reminded of Lohengrin's farewell in the opera's last act: '*Alljährlich nacht von Himmel eine Taube um neu zu stärken seine Wunderkraft.*' These 'doves' scarcely came from heaven.)

Nowhere could we find the car by which we expected to be met. Leaving our luggage in the care of someone on the quay, we sought a port control officer, who turned out to be a Frenchman. He had never heard of the Belgian Field Hospital and advised us to inquire at the British Consulate. To no purpose. We felt lost and time passed. The town was busy, shops open and a mixed crowd in the streets. Finally I spotted a truck with our markings. Pedley and Step greeted us and said that no message about our arrival had been received by Perrin, the Commandant. Everything seemed disorganized and casual. After a lot of delay we took to the road and crossed the Belgian frontier where there was a French and Belgian post. The sentries knew the vehicle and smilingly waved us through. From the truck I looked out on a flat and drab countryside plunged in midwinter, bleak but not unfriendly. On the straight poplar-lined road was a mixed assortment of human beings and vehicles. Peasants, men and women, mostly in black and wearing scarves, mingled with scruffy-looking French troops and rustic carts were mixed up on the roads with military vehicles. Everything seemed leisurely. The war was static and life easygoing, with no discernible sense of danger or tension in the air. We stopped at Furnes where there were more signs of war than in Dunkirk. No shops open. Streets deserted. Many demolished and half-demolished houses stood amidst rubble. I noted and liked the stepped roofs. It was dark when we drove through the small village of Hoogstadt, beyond which, approached by a short semicircular drive leading out of the main paved road, stood the hospital. That there was little fuss about lights was my first impression. We ate supper sitting on benches in a sort of refectory. The cook that evening was Miss Barron, dressed in a sort of brown smock – rather attractive. No servants and no discernible hierarchy. In an off-hand way people were mildly inquisitive but welcoming. I was assigned a bunk in a dormitory and made my first contact with the padre, S.F. Streatfield.

As I settled down my job took shape. Or rather it differentiated into several jobs. My duties were set out on paper by both Baillie Hamilton and Hodge. There had earlier been a good deal of lack of coordination about the ordering and supplying of stores. It appeared that the people at the hospital sometimes did not realize till the last moment that supplies were running out. A sudden clamour would then be raised and the London office would be put to much trouble. My job was to keep a watch on all stores and notify London well before replenishments were needed. Before my time it had been decided that the hospital should establish a store depot in Dunkirk. This manoeuvre was adopted lest the hospital were destroyed (as had more or less happened in Furnes) or lest the hospice had to be evacuated at short notice because of a change in the military situation.

The depot was located in an empty house in a suburb of Dunkirk called Rosendael. A Belgian soldier by the name of Joseph van den Briel was placed in charge. He was a most likeable man and he could not have been more meticulous and conscientious at his job. We became friends and a regular feature of my periods in Dunkirk was to visit this man in Rosendael. Clearly a man in his position, if dishonest and unsupervised, could have found the job profitable. He could have kept his relatives and friends supplied with miscellaneous goods, including food, of which there were shortages, or he could have sold the stuff and pocketed the profits. There probably was a black market in the French and Belgian towns. But if there was, we knew little of it. Indeed, I don't remember the term 'black market' being used during the 1914–18 war. When the decision was taken to keep most of the hospital stores at Rosendael and to put a Belgian in charge, the absolute necessity must have been realized of finding a reliable and honest man.

We worked out and followed a good system. The miscellaneous stores were classified under about half a dozen main categories and kept on separate shelves and compartments corresponding with these categories. Van den Briel and I each kept loose-leaf books which had to tally exactly showing what stores and in what quantities were in possession under these categories. To each article a separate page was assigned showing at the top the quantity in possession on a given date. On successive lines were shown the dates of removals, the quantity removed, and consequently the quantity remaining in store. In this way I could tell the Commandant or the London Office at any time exactly what items and in what quantities were in stock and how much of each item had been consumed within any period.

When I visited Dunkirk the first thing I usually did was to visit Rosendael and give to van den Briel a list of the stores I wanted to take back to the hospital; and I would leave my loose-leaf store-book within. On our return in the afternoon, van den Briel would have the needed stores neatly packed in a wooden box or crate, which, with the minimum of delay, we would heave on to the truck, and he would have made the necessary entries on his and my sheets. Each day I would arbitrarily select one or two items in the store and verify that the quantities corresponded with the last entries in our two books. I did not go through the whole store each day. This arrangement was welcomed by van den Briel who naturally left the store locked up when he went out. The danger of thefts in his absence was ever-present in his mind and he developed a mild anxiety state about this possibility. One day, after there had been thefts in the town, he formally asked me if he could have an assistant. Thus aided, he pointed out, the store would never be left unguarded. This request was met after I had left. I add the obvious fact that the differing items in our store were consumed at varying rates. At the top of each page was entered a figure which we called a low watermark or *basse marée*. This signified that, when this figure was reached, replenishments were needed. This low watermark figure was not always easy to fix, for one had to allow for sudden and exceptionally large demands (as occurred when there was a rush of wounded) and also for fluctuations in the time needed to acquire the replenishments. I recall discussing these low watermark figures with various people including the Commandant, with Baillie Hamilton and with the heads of departments such as the matron, the number one in the kitchen, the operating theatre sister (Cora Mayne), the transport staff (Batten, Hay, Bert Bloxham, Hammond) and others. There were no 'Stores Crises' or even 'Supply Crises' during my period with the hospital. But there was one minor crisis. Van den Briel went on leave for ten days and his place was taken by another Belgian soldier. On his return van den Briel was aghast at the muddle of his store. Items had been mixed up and, after things had been sorted out, there were some minor shortages. Van den Briel suspected the honesty of his replacement, but did not want the man (whom he personally knew) charged. I discussed the matter with Sir Bartle Frere, the Commandant, (a distant relative of my Eton friend of the same name) and he thought that more harm (in the way of friction with the Belgians with whom friendly relations were essential) than good would be done by making a row. His policy was '*glissons*' – let things slide. He told me to tell the man about the shortages and to use my discretion about what else to say.

I used to follow a routine drill for the rest of my shopping activities at Dunkirk. I quickly found that I was in a position to make myself popular with both patients and hospital staff, for I could do commissions for them in Dunkirk and also during my short visits to London. The favours asked mounted and finally became embarrassingly numerous. My technique was to do two circuits in Dunkirk. I soon got to know the shops and the people in them. I was a good customer and I could speak to them in French. I also knew the geography of Dunkirk's streets and the locations of the shops. Before leaving the hospital in the morning I would prepare a shopping list with, attached, separate lists in French for each shop. I would prepare the shortest itinerary depending on what places had to be visited. I was always accompanied by one of the transport staff or drivers – usually Batten, Hay or Bert – for whom I acted as pilot. In the course of the morning circuit I would distribute at each shop, depot or other place on my itinerary the relevant lists, and I would forewarn them about when, in the early afternoon, I would come back to pick up and pay. The morning circuit over, we would repair for lunch, usually at the Chapeau Rouge, where I was on good terms with the manager and waiters. (Part of the morning itinerary would include stopping at the restaurant, reserving a table and perhaps ordering a meal.) Then, in the afternoon, we would reverse the circuit. We would pick up and pay for the things ordered in the morning which by then were packed up and waiting; and we would collect receipts. My main difficulty was not with the job. It was to get myself paid back by the people for whom I had done the commissions. Some (I quickly got to know them) were slow to pay back and wanted me to open an account with them, saying that they had not got the cash just then but would have it next week, etc. Batten, who had a fiery temper, used to get furious with these people and once or twice dealt with them on my behalf.

Looking back, I realize that there was nothing in the least creditable to me in these store-keeping and shopping exercises. They are probably performed by every housewife once or twice a week. But nevertheless, I thought out the drill on my own and it saved the drivers a lot of trivial bother. Before I came they were asked to do the commissions which were dealt with one by one – they went to a shop, explained verbally what was wanted (none could speak French), waited for the things to be done up, paid for them and left. Time-wasting and laborious. My system went down well with the drivers and shops.

Thus the days passed pleasantly. The shopping exercises and the store worked like clockwork and the drivers were glad to have their daily programmes so arranged that no time was wasted. All they had to do was to follow my instructions.

We would often get back to Hoogstadt by teatime and, as the spring advanced, I would go for walks during the evening or withdraw with a book. It was pleasant, too, to enjoy the changes in the countryside. In April the poplars bordering the roads came into bud and green appeared in the fields. The frogs in the numerous dykes and canals – the Yser lay eastwards towards Poelcapelle and Dixmude – came to life so that, at dusk, there would arise a raucous but pleasing din reminiscent of Aristophanes. Swallows arrived. So did nightingales, chiffchaffs, willow warblers, whitethroats. The evening chorus of these birds was delivered against the distant mutterings of artillery. Two worlds. The dawn chorus was also good. During my last six weeks I used to sleep out of doors on a stretcher below one of the outside wards which was built on short pillars of brick. I would wake up as it was getting light and listen to the dawn chorus for a few minutes before going to sleep again.

I had forgotten what a happy period this had been with the Belgian Field Hospital. Not long before I left I made an entry in my diary that, if I survived the war, I would surely look back on these months as exceptionally happy. Present were all the necessary ingredients except one. I was doing the job I was expected to do competently; I was living among people I liked; the daily tasks were pleasant involving for the most part no frustrations or stresses; the rural surroundings were agreeable and I had plenty of leisure. What disturbed me was a sense of self-disapproval that I was there at all. I ought to be doing some-thing else. The mutterings of artillery during the day and the gun flashes at night were telling me where I ought to be and what I ought to be doing.

But this almost idyllic life had interruptions which, while painful and (in my then callow state) sometimes horrible, helped to assuage my secret discontent with myself.

At times the war would flare up. There would be systematic bombardments and local attacks followed by rushes of wounded. The slight cases were sent on into France. We kept the worst cases. This put a strain on everyone, especially the surgeons, and it caused our mortality rates to be high. We would then have long sleepless nights. In the dark hours I jotted down some notes of which a few have survived. They are almost illegible, but here is a transcription of one or two.

Tuesday 27 April 1915. A big bombardment started four days ago. The noise fluctuates. It sometimes mounts to a continuous roar which makes me think of Niagara. The wounded came in driblets at first and then in a fairly continuous stream. They are taken straight to the X-ray room where one of the dressers examined their wounds. Thence they are if possible evacuated. We keep the worst cases. The thing began on Friday 23 April and an imaginative Belgian said that Hindenburg must have come to the Western Front where he was making a big drive to end the war. Jackson (one of the dressers) got me out of bed early on Saturday morning (24 April) and we went down to the operating theatre where two operating tables were in use. Brilliant light and a smell of ether. On one of the tables was a young Belgian soldier of about twenty. A piece of shrapnel had gashed his right lung and opened his abdomen. His extruded entrails had been powdered over and painted with iodine. He was coughing up blood and occasionally groaning for which he apologized. As I held up to his mouth a basin for him to spit and vomit into, he whispered '*Je vais mourir.*' I half-heartedly tried to reassure him. '*C'est bon que vous parlez le français,*' he said. We carried him upstairs and put him in one of the beds. As he was being lifted from the stretcher he held on to me with his arms round my neck. I asked him if there was anything I could do. '*Oui,*' he said, '*mon chapelet. Dans ma capotte.*' Two hours later he was dead with the rosary in his hand. He was just about my age.

Later a man was brought in with a deep gash in his back and both legs smashed and gangrenous. He had lain untended for a long time. After the wound in his back had been dressed, he was given a spinal injection which produced anaesthesia of the lower half of his body. Shaw then proceeded to cut off his left leg through the thigh while at the same time Saner cut off his right foot above the ankle joint. I held his left leg while Shaw sawed through the femur. His right foot fell on to the floor. The man died on the table and his mutilated body, with its bleeding stumps, was carried to the mortuary. The butcher's work and the smell of the gangrene sickened me, but the grim drama was redeemed by the obvious decency of everyone in the theatre. The gruesome features originated elsewhere: the people in white were concerned to mitigate and save.

I sat up the whole of that night and in the intervals of performing the duties of stretcher-bearer (*brancardier*) and of assistant in the operating theatre, I typed out lists of stores for the London office. (I had decided to try to teach myself to type.) At first light I heard a robin singing and stepped outside for a breath of air after the chloroform and gangrene. Everything was dank and grey, like pewter. No wind, no colour. A thin mist veiled the trees and other familiar shapes which were so devoid of attributes as to make me think of the Cimmerian regions of the underworld visited by Odysseus; also of Kant's 'thing-in-itself'. With these dreary thoughts in mind I decided to get some sleep. On my way I passed a ward full of seriously wounded soldiers. One called out to me in a thin high voice. He told me that he had been shot in the rectum and the wound had been plugged so that he could not perform his natural functions which, at that moment, were pressing. I told the sister who said that nothing more could be done.

Connected with this period (I forget how) was a Belgian Lieutenant Kirsmacher. This man had a veneration for General Joffre, the French Commander-in-Chief, to whom he attributed high tactical as well as strategical genius. In particular, he knew how to use the Zouaves [a regiment of French colonial troops, mostly Algerians]. Whenever a bayonet charge was called for, Joffre would see that Zouaves were on the spot.

A few days before the local battle above mentioned, on our way in to Dunkirk, Hay and I had passed a train full of Zouaves, on their way up. Some of these were later brought in, wounded, by Colby, an American who was head of a neighbouring ambulance unit. He left one with us, a great swarthy man with a large bushy moustache. He was carried in on a stretcher, his thigh bandaged. It was assumed that his femur was fractured and he was taken straight into the theatre where an anaesthetic was begun before the wound was unbandaged. This powerful Zouave took the anaesthetic badly. He burst into scarcely intelligible blasphemy, about half of it in a language I took to be Arabic, and he became so violent that I had to help to hold him down. Dr Morris (Shaw's wife) poured on the ether and he finally quietened down enough to enable his pantaloons to be sheared and the bandages removed. There had been no fracture and there was no need for either an operation or an anaesthetic. Some remonstrance ensued with Colby who had brought him to us supposing him to be a serious case, and the still unconscious Zouave was moved to the staff sitting room which, during the rush, was used as a sort of waiting room for cases due for evacuation to Adenkirk. I was asked to keep an eye on this excitable man. As he came to he felt sick and his leg hurt him. I reassured him about his leg and told him that he had shown much military ardour and pugnacity while under the anaesthetic. '*Je regrette,*' he said. After a pause he continued in semi-soliloquy: '*Dommage que ce n'etait pas un Bosche.*'

'*Les cochons,*' he went on, '*les lâches. Mais ils en ont bien attrapé de nous hier . . . On a battu la charge, et nous avons avancé deux kilometres.*' He had been shot in the leg on a bridge: '*Mais ça ne m'a pas empeché de lui enfoncer la baïllonette dans le ventre.*' Which, he said, made up for everything. I believed the story at the time, but later was not so sure. There was much wishful feeling about bayonet charges. Apart from boozers and big talkers in bars, well out of the war, I have never met anyone who claimed that he had killed anyone with a bayonet. But this man's story was more likely to be true than most.

Over a cup of black coffee for which the Zouave asked I questioned him about the war. He renewed his verbal onslaughts on the Germans. All his section, platoon, company, officers and men alike, shared his detestation. Did they ever take prisoners, I asked. 'Never,' he replied. '*On leur enfonce la baïllonette dans le ventre.*'

Towards the beginning of April a very young German officer was brought in with a severe gunshot wound in the chest which, he explained to me, had been received in the following way. The Germans had taken a Belgian trench by assault. The Belgian other ranks retired, disobeying the Belgian Lieutenant in command who had remained in the trench. Our young German officer, finding himself confronted in the trench by the Belgian Lieutenant, told him he was a prisoner. But this did not accord with the ideas of the Belgian Lieutenant who, in reply, shot him in the chest at point-blank range. At that moment the Belgians counter-attacked and the Germans retired, leaving the severely wounded officer behind lying half-conscious in the bottom of the trench. After three days he was sent to an aid post in a half-destroyed house where he was put into a room with several Zouaves. These discovered his nationality because he could not answer their questions. Being in danger of his life, he was moved to our hospital.

I first saw him in a bed at the corner of one of our wards. He was in his early twenties, gentle, grateful for all that was done for him and nice-looking. The nurses felt sorry for him and gave him no less attention than they gave to the other wounded. He spent some of his time doing mathematical sums and he used to draw pictures of his home which he gave to the ward sister. Later an officers' ward was set up to which this German was moved. For two or three days I occupied a bed in this ward as a patient. An attack of flu. Also a patient was a Belgian officer with a lung wound. Whenever his wound hurt him this man used to sit forward and with contorted face break out into loud invectives against the Germans. '*Ces saligots qui ne tuent que des femmes et des enfants, qui leur coupent les mains et les pieds,*' etc. This was intended for the German in the corner who spoke French. After a particularly violent outburst of this sort in an otherwise silent ward, I took it on myself to remonstrate. I told him that he was disturbing the people in the other beds, among them myself. I added that his conduct was rather like kicking a man when he was down. When I had finished, a French officer on the other side of the ward said, '*Monsieur, je suis parfaitement de votre avis.'* The consensus of feeling was against the vituperative Belgian.

In the general ward into which the German had earlier been bedded on arrival was an Algerian whose arm had been amputated above the elbow. He had one of the toughest and most brutal faces I had ever seen. I thought I would find out if he was as bad as he looked, so I made friends with him. I asked him if I could buy anything for him in Dunkirk. He told me about his family. Both his parents had died when he was young leaving him and a younger brother to make their way. 'Did you feel responsible for your brother?' I asked. Certainly, he replied. *'Je l'ai fait apprendre un métier.'* What was the *métier*, I asked. *'Nous somme tous deux charcutiers,'* he replied, but added with a rueful look at his short bandaged stump held out in front of him, *'Je ne sais pas si maintenant je peux me débrouiller.'* The next day he showed me a photograph of his brother which he kept in his *capotte*. And the day after, as I was passing, he beckoned me to his bedside. *'Sale Boche là bas,'* he said pointing sideways with his thumb. I said that the man in the corner was certainly a Boche but not, as far as we could judge, a *sale* one. There were good and bad people of all nationalities – English, Belgians and doubtless Algerians. This German had a severe wound and was courageous. Life was not easy when one was surrounded by people who hated one. If he (the Zouave) or I had happened to be born Germans, or if the German officer had been born Algerian or British, our roles would have been reversed. The villainous looking character thought this over for a bit and finally said, *'Bien oui, c'est un malheureux, comme moi.'* I did what I could for this maimed Zouave till he left us. I concluded that, whatever his looks, he was a good brother and had likeable qualities.

*　　*　　*　　*

I have mentioned Colby, an American, who ran a nearby ambulance unit. This man used to drop in now and then. One day I asked him if, when he was short-handed, I could help by doing his morning round of the first aid station. The upshot was that, one morning in mid-May, Streatfield (our padre who, if I may risk the understatement, was not always unmanageably busy) and I joined forces in such a round. One of the posts was close to the line. All was quiet and seemingly safe. In front of the post we noticed a field full of cowslips. These, we thought, would look nice in the wards. They would cheer the patients and please the nursing staff. So we stopped the ambulance, got out and walked out into the field which, we later learned, was clearly visible from the German positions. We were busy picking when suddenly *crack*. The sniper's bullet seemed to pass between us. We looked blankly at each other. Without speech perfect agreement was reached. We about-turned and, at a slow double, made for the ambulance parked nearby.

The sniper gave us two more rounds having evidently decided that while it was tolerable for a Red Cross vehicle to move about the road unmolested, there was no call for its personnel to flaunt themselves in his arc of fire. But Streatfield and I felt somewhat shame-faced about the rapidity of our withdrawal from the cowslip field, though the episode was indubitably funny. We consoled ourselves with the thought that it would not have been exactly helpful to the allied cause for either of us to get shot picking cowslips.

*   *   *   *

My mother's fears about my safety at sea during the transits between Dover and Dunkirk, and on land in the zone of shell-fire, were supplemented by other fears. She thought that I would fall in love with a nurse much older than myself and contract a disastrous marriage. All three sets of fears were misplaced. Nothing happened at sea; the nearest I got to being hurt on land was being shot at as just described; and I never even got round to Christian names with any of the nurses. There was one who was young and pretty called Nurse Gray. I was slightly attracted by her, but discerned quickly that a firm bond existed between her and an older woman – Sister Chapman – who had lived in China. Sister Chapman took an interest in Buddhism, a subject we discussed on my very first evening in the hospital. Sister Gray was Chapman's preserve and nobody else ventured on the grass. Included in the hospital's staff were several third or fourth year medical students who were called 'dressers'. Not one ever made a pass at Sister Gray who never gave the slightest outward sign of being incommoded by Chapman's monopoly.

The sister to whom I became most attached was Sister Cora Mayne, a married woman in early middle age. She was dark, handsome, with a good figure, and she held herself well. People's first impression was that she was severe or even forbidding. She was the hospital's only theatre sister and ruled that key department with uncontested authority. She kept herself somewhat apart from the other staff and, I seem to remember, had a sitting room of her own next to the operating theatre. For quite a time I held this somewhat unapproachable guardian of the arcana in some awe. She mostly consorted with Dr Shaw, a good-looking blond-haired surgeon, and with his wife, Dr Morris, who usually gave anaesthetics for him.

I had two bouts of illness. On 1 May I developed a temperature and felt out of sorts. In the evening a generalized rash appeared. German measles. All right in a day. Ten days later I developed a higher temperature and felt definitely unwell. I dossed down in the loft during the afternoon and was dozing when I suddenly felt myself being kissed by someone bending over me. Opening my eyes I beheld Sister Mayne flitting out of the room. I was astonished and flattered. Thereafter we became good friends.

I also became friends with a high-spirited young Belgian woman who was attached to the hospital in some sort of clerical capacity. As the war advanced and conditions stabilized in our corner of the country, the Belgians gradually took over the administration of the hospital. Towards the end of my period there arrived an eminent Belgian surgeon by the name of Willems. I recall his first day. A casualty was brought in: Shaw and Willems exchanged politenesses, each bowing to the other and urging that the other should operate. Willems yielded and I later heard a discussion between Shaw and (I think) Atkey of his technique. My high-spirited Belgian girl, Mlle Feerich, was, I think, Willems's secretary. Willems was a shortish fat man. No Adonis. Mlle Feerich did not much like Willems, but I used to pretend that she did. One day I met her looking angry and indignant. She had had trouble with Willems. I said that she looked like Clytemnestra meditating the murder of Agamemnon in his bath. She shuddered at the idea of Willems in his bath, but thereafter I used to call her Clytemnestra. Anyhow, Mlle Feerich and I treated each other as brother and sister. My mother had no cause for anxiety.

*   *   *   *

One of the things I remember best after fifty years is how I came to leave the hospital. I have mentioned Nat Batten, one of the drivers. For a reason which I forget, this man had had both feet amputated. He was a tall rather gruff man of whom someone remarked that he meant what he said and said what he meant. When I first arrived, he questioned me in what I thought was a hostile manner. One of his questions was, 'Can you speak the lingo?' – by which he meant could I speak French. But it was not long before I began to like him. He used to conduct a running badinage with another driver by the name of Secker, a tall, handsome well-built man with a black moustache. One day Batten told me that Secker thought he could box. The upshot was that a set of boxing gloves was dug out from somewhere and Batten acted as both time-keeper and referee. I quickly discovered that Secker knew little. It was easy to draw him, make him miss and then hit him with a hook or straight left. After doing this two or three times, I found I could land easily without drawing him out. When we finished Secker said that I had the longer reach. I said not. We measured our reaches standing back to back with arms extended. His arms were about half an inch longer than mine. While we were boxing Batten hurled jeers at Secker who was as much engaged in his verbal duel with Batten as he was in his physical duel with me. I got to like Batten and used to enjoy his companionship during our drives to Dunkirk.

About the beginning of May the news broke that Sir Bartle Frere was to leave us. This he did on 7 May 1915. The reason was a mystery. I later learned that it was felt in London that someone deemed to have more business experience than Sir Bartle was needed as Commandant. We were told that the new man's name was Morrison. I had developed a considerable affection for Sir Bartle. All agreed – indeed the remark was frequently repeated – that he was a 'thorough gentleman'. Indeed true. He had perfect courtesy for all – nurses, drivers, Belgians – and charming manners. Hence there was genuine sorrow when it was learned that he was to leave us.

We were given no date for the arrival of Morrison. It was later learned that a telegram had been sent from London informing us of the time of his arrival, but as happened when Miss Davis and I first appeared, this had not been received. The consequence was that Morrison was kept waiting on the quay at Dunkirk till about 11.00am. Finally Batten turned up. According to Batten's account of what passed, Morrison was furious. He ranted at the lack of system in the hospital and blamed Batten. There ensued a considerable row. Among other things Batten told Morrison that if he treated people like that he would not stay long as Commandant.

Later Morrison seems to have had second thoughts and apologized to Batten. The quarrel was apparently made up and when, a few days later, Batten went on leave, Morrison said goodbye in a friendly way adding that he looked forward to the other's return. The duration of Batten's leave was not specified. He was told that he would be informed from Suffolk Street by what boat he would return. Time passed and he heard nothing. He finally wrote to me at Hoogstadt asking if I knew anything. On 14 June (my diary says) I asked Morrison if Batten was coming back. He said no. I felt indignant and decided that night that if Morrison adhered to this decision I would resign. I raised the question again the next day. Morrison was at first reluctant to give reasons, but finally said that Batten was insolent and did not know his place or words to that effect. I asked him if, before Batten had left, he (Morrison) had told him that he would be welcome when he returned. I forget the rest, but I recall that when I gave him my resignation he made a somewhat patronizing remark. It was to the effect that, when I grew up a bit more, I would come to see that it did not pay to be so quixotic.

By this time Morrison had become actively unpopular. He talked about members of the staff behind their backs to other members of the staff who repeated his remarks. Tom Hay, who was as indignant as I was about his treatment of Batten, left soon after I did. A month or so later Hay married Sister Storch in London. I left Hoogstadt very early (the boat left Dunkirk at 4.30am) on 17 June, and was given a warm send-off by about ten people who had got up early to say goodbye. They said they were sorry to see me go, but I doubt if they were sorrier than I was.

I reported to Baillie Hamilton in London that afternoon. He had been mainly responsible for Morrison's appointment and therefore did not sympathize. Indeed, he began by saying that he thought I had behaved unfairly to the hospital. The next morning – Friday 18 June – I had breakfast with Sir Bartle Frere who lived with three aged sisters. After the meal prayers were said. He had continued to take a keen interest in the hospital, and was not surprised by what I told him. He then rang up Lord Sydenham who was the titular head of the hospital and a busy man. An appointment was made there and then. I recall Sydenham as a courteous, good-looking rather wizened man. He listened attentively. His position was that the Commandant had to be backed up. 'Are these two men – Morrison and Batten – compatible?' he asked. He understandably showed no inclination to intervene, but I had the impression that he noted and regretted the discord.

*   *   *   *

Why did I resign like this? Ostensibly it was a protest against injustice. Yet I can see that, from Baillie Hamilton's point of view, two loyalties were involved: to an individual and to the organization. I think I made the point with him that I was in no way indispensable. Morrison had a good and loyal secretary in Mrs Winterbottom who had arrived after me. I felt sure that I could not get on with Morrison as I had done with either Perrin or Sir Bartle Frere. As regards the stores, there would be no difficulty as long as van den Briel remained in charge. The transactions between Hoogstadt and Rosendael were now subject to a routine which worked of its own accord. Yet, I now see, Hamilton could have replied that frictions of some sort were unavoidable and that, in the interests of the organization, genuine efforts must be made to surmount them.

But I now see that there was a further reason for my leaving. I was altogether too well off at this place. Inwardly I was not at ease. Sometimes during the summer nights when the sky flickered and the darkness muttered, I seemed to see to the east a sort of symbolical gateway – which now looks like the Menin Gate. It led into the active war, and through it I felt I must pass.

3

WINDSOR, FRANCE AND ROBIN'S DEATH

A period of three and a half months intervened between my leaving the Belgian Field Hospital and my departure to France as a second lieutenant in the Coldstream Guards. The period is much associated with Robin without whose initiative I would (if I could) have joined the Devonshire Regiment. I spent the first month, from 17 June till 15 July, at Vane Tower; the rest of the time at Windsor.

I must say something about Robin. He stayed on at Eton for two halves after me. Our relations had fluctuated. While he was still at Cothill, the decision was somehow taken that he should go into the Navy. How and why this move was approved I cannot now recall and, looking back, I cannot quite understand how it was reached. There are no naval traditions in my family. Anyhow, into the Navy Robin went. During his first days at Osborne, he was acutely miserable and wrote many letters to my mother begging to be removed. It is rather surprising, in the light of his later obsession about getting out to France at the earliest possible moment, how much less inhibited Robin had been about his early dislike of Osborne than I had been during my first days at Cothill. But he settled down at Osborne and proceeded to do well. He stayed for the statutory two years at the end of which he was made a cadet captain which was accounted a distinction. But round about the age of 14 or 15, when Osborne cadets, after their two years, moved on to Dartmouth, Robin began to develop short sight. He was never so short-sighted as I and never wore glasses. But the navy was strict about standards of vision. Robin may also have been coming round to the view that he would not fit in to the Navy. But by the time he left Osborne he was rather old for Eton. Moreover, his preparation for the Navy, which involved a good deal of mathematics and other subjects which were outside the Eton curriculum, had scarcely fitted him to take the entrance examination. The difficult decision that he should abandon a naval career was, however, taken when Hugh de Havilland, stretching things to their utmost, agreed to take him into his house if he could pass the entrance examinations. Robin was forthwith subjected to a rigorous discipline of coaching in subjects such as Latin which had been ignored at Osborne. Instead of sending him to a coach, as he would doubtless have been sent today, my parents had him taught at home. One of his tutors was Mr Purser who had been a master at Osborne. Mr Purser came to stay at Vane Tower and used to hold quite intensive morning and afternoon sessions in the schoolroom with Robin. Robin was an able boy and he worked hard with Purser. The result was that he passed easily into Eton and came to Hugh de Havilland's at the beginning of the summer half of 1912.

The house was physically full at that time and it was not easy to fit him in. Hence we were put into the same room on the top floor of Keates House. The room looked across the garden at the ugly red façade of Heygate's. (It was unusual for boys to share rooms, though an exception was sometimes made for brothers.) During this period of sharing a room during Robin's first half at Eton our relationship struck rock bottom. Life was not easy for Robin. His own contemporaries in the house were less mature than he; the fact that we shared a room made it difficult for him to make friends on his own; and, during his first term, there were few boys with whom he particularly wanted to make friends. He found, I think, that the life, which involved fagging after being a cadet captain, was petty and restrictive; and moreover the summer of 1912 was exceptionally hot. He was also passing through the stresses of puberty. The result was that his temper, which had always been more violent than mine, suffered; and I became the scapegoat. As the half progressed, he became increasingly disagreeable until, towards the end, he never spoke to me without what I thought was insolent rudeness. I confided my difficulties to Hillier (a contemporary of mine) who offered a suggestion which had never occurred to me. He said, 'Why don't you knock him out? It might teach him a useful lesson.' The more I thought this move over, the more it commended itself to me. But it took a week or so of increasing provocations to make me act. The crisis came early one morning while the school was in chapel from which Robin and I, being Catholics, were excused. I was writing at my desk when Robin came in and made some offensive remark. I got up and told him that I had had enough of his conduct and to look out for himself. Robin had never boxed as I had and did not know how to defend himself. I cracked his nose with a left, crossed my right and down he went. He got up with his nose bleeding and asked me how he was to go into school like that. I told him that that was his affair. This episode, upon which I now look back with some shame and remorse turned out to be the perfect solution of our troubles. Thereafter our relations became increasingly friendly both at school and in the holidays. Indeed, we became excellent friends. During my last year at Eton Robin became one of a close trio, the other two being Raymond Stephenson and Michael Malcolm. I was for three halves captain of the house where I felt isolated because, for one reason or another, all my contemporaries had left. I consorted much with Robin and the other two who constituted, so to speak, the next schoolboy generation to mine. During my time at the Belgian Field Hospital Robin and I corresponded regularly.

Robin was about an inch shorter than I but more solidly built. He was muscular and strong with a deep chest and good shoulders. When Hugh de Havilland first met him, he smiled and pointed to his chest, remarking that he ought to be good at games. Robin proceeded to do well. He was successful at Eton football during the Winter halves and, in 1915, after I had left, got his Field and his Oppidan Wall; during the Easter half he played rugger for the school and fenced for it. In 1914 he easily won the open Public School's foil championship with very few hits against him. Since the competition was open to all British schools, this was a most creditable performance. In the Summer half he rowed. In 1914 he got his Upper Boat Choices. During his last half he was in Pop[1] – the first boy in the house to do this since 1908. Hence I became proud of him.

When the war broke out in August 1914 Robin took a line which surprised me and both surprised and distressed my parents. He became obsessed with a single idea, that of getting out to France as an officer at the earliest possible moment. He held much the same views about the war as my father and myself; at least he inclined much more to our views than to my mother's. But this had no bearing on his personal ambition. It was not that he thought the war was going to be a short war. On the contrary, he talked of it as if it would be never-ending. Several times he spoke as if he knew he would be killed. The occasion I recall most vividly was on 10 July 1915 when we were both sitting in different parts of the smoking room of the Royal Automobile Club. I picked up a *Times* and saw in it a short notice that Oscar Hornung (contemporary of mine and a close friend) had been killed three days before, on 7 July. I took the paper over to Robin and, without speaking, showed him the notice. He read it and sat a few moments in silence. He then handed the paper back to me and said, 'Don't worry about this. We are *all* going to get killed. You and I and everybody else.' He was himself dead within four months.

During his last year at Eton Robin specialized in history. As soon as the war broke out, one of the history masters, E.F. Prior, later killed on 15 September, 1916, – who had tutored Robin, joined the Rifle Brigade. Like all Eton masters who had joined the army, he was on the look-out for school-leavers who would

---

[1] 'Pop' was the slang term for the Eton Society, an elite body among whose privileges and duties included the maintenance of discipline in the school; to be elected to Pop was a mark of considerable distinction in the School. 'Field', 'Oppidan Wall' and 'Upper Boat Choices' were also elite caps awarded to those who distinguished themselves in the Field Game (Eton football), the Wall Game and rowing.

make good officers. He arranged for Robin to join the Rifle Brigade. Robin left Eton at the end of the Easter half of 1915 and went straight into this regiment, joining the 8th Battalion, in which Prior was by then a company commander. This Battalion had been in training since the beginning of the war and was nearly ready to go overseas. They were a first-class Battalion in which Robin was entirely happy. He was exhilarated by the prospect of 'getting out' with them.

It must have been sometime in June 1915 that the Battalion duly went to France. But they left behind three supernumerary officers among whom, to his indignation and fury, was Robin. (He had joined the most recently and was the youngest, having been born on 13 June 1897. Hence in June 1915 he was eighteen.) Robin, left behind, was posted to the 17th Rifle Brigade. This unit had little resemblance to the 8th. It was in an early stage of training and the officers were quite different. For a time Robin lived in hopes of being sent out quickly as a reinforcement to the 8th Battalion. But as time passed his hopes faded until he made up his mind, wrongly as it turned out, that he had no more hope of going overseas than had any other officer in the 17th Battalion. He thought he was faced with an indefinite stay in England. Being both impatient and resourceful, he began to think of a transfer.

A friend of Robin's at Eton had been Willie Edmonstone. He had left at the same time as Robin and had joined the Coldstream in April 1915. (He was later killed on 15 September 1916, the same day as E.F. Prior and many others.) Robin either met Edmonstone or wrote to him telling him of his predicament and consequent frustration. Edmonstone replied that if Robin could arrange a transfer to the Coldstream he might get out to France quicker. There were many fewer Coldstream than Rifle Brigade Battalions and none in so early a stage of training as was the 17th. Edmonstone would do what he could to help the transfer. Robin's hopes soared. This happened towards the end of June, shortly after I had returned from Belgium.

*   *   *   *

On returning to England and seeing Lord Sydenham (as described above) I went to Torquay, where I was met at the station by my father and Robin who was home on short leave. Both were cheerful. The atmosphere at home was calmer. The garden was at its June best and Torbay, seen through the palms, looked lovely. I had no clear plans. I thought of enlisting in some unit where standards in respect of eyesight were sufficiently lax or perhaps of having another try at getting accepted by an infantry regiment. The Devonshire Regiment attracted me. My father thought that I had been precipitate in resigning from the Belgian Field Hospital and Robin, by now quite an ex-perienced adviser, urged me not to be in a hurry. We had a heart-to-heart talk in the course of which (I recorded in my diary) he said that it was nice to think that sometime or other we might be together at Balliol as we had been together at Eton.

We had friends at Torquay who lived in a capacious house above the Marine Drive. They were a Mr and Mrs Stovell. They had a son, Lionel Stovell, a couple of years older than me, who at Eton had boarded at Broadbent's. Lionel had joined the Devonshire Regiment and the father said that he might be able to help me into that regiment the Headquarters of which were at Exeter. The upshot was that, on Sunday 27 June, I went to Exeter where I was amiably received by the Adjutant of the Devonshire Regiment who advised me to write to a Colonel Snow, then at Wareham. I also paid a visit to the Territorial Headquarters opposite the Exeter Guildhall where the reception was likewise friendly and where I was given an application form. I wrote to Robin telling him of these moves.

Two days later (29 June) there arrived from Robin a letter begging me not to proceed further with the Devonshire Regiment and mentioning the possibility of his own transfer to the Coldstream. It might, he said, be worked that we should both join this regiment together. This seemed too good to be true. But could I this time circumvent the tests of eyesight?

Robin moved quickly. On 2 July I received a letter from him saying that he had made an arrangement for me to see the Coldstream people and that they wanted a certificate of moral character from Hugh de Havilland. Robin joined me in London on Saturday 3 July and we went together to Eton where Hugh welcomed us and gave me the necessary certificate; and the next day (Sunday 4 July) I presented myself at Regimental Headquarters, Birdcage Walk. There, after a wait, I was agreeably received by Colonel Richardson Drummond Hay who gave me various forms to fill in. The upshot was that I was posted to the regiment on 15 July on which day I reported to Windsor.

Paradoxically things worked more easily for me than for Robin about whose transfer there were difficulties. On the day I reported at Victoria Barracks, Windsor, I received a telegram from Robin saying that his 'gun was spiked' but that I was to 'carry on'. Until 18 August (when I moved into Victoria Barracks) I stayed at the White Hart Hotel, Windsor. At this place I received on 19 July a wire from Robin to say that, after all, his transfer had gone through and had been gazetted that morning. He would appear at Windsor that afternoon. This, to my delight he did. The date of his gazette was moved back to 2 May so that he had about two and a half months seniority over me.

I ought to say how I got through the medical examination in which I had been three times failed. My diary is not entirely lucid, but my recollection is that F.C.Conybeare [a family friend] had written saying that he knew of a doctor, Dr Gillett, who was 'broad-minded'. On 9 July I went to Farnham (it might just possibly be Fareham: my writing is not clear) where a rendezvous had been made at the Bush Hotel. Dr Gillett, whom I record as being most amiable, met me there and signed me up. But within the next three weeks I had a shock. On 27 July I received a letter from the Queen Alexandra Hospital, Grosvenor Road, telling me to report there the next day at 11 a.m. in order to have my sight further tested by Lieut. Heron. I thought I was done for. But I had some luck. I duly presented myself at the hospital the next day and was escorted to Lieut. Heron's room where I arrived punctually at 11 a.m. The room was full of soldiers and I had some fifteen minutes to wait. The test-letters were staring me in the face and I used the time to learn them by heart. When the charming Mr Heron tested me, I scraped through. I had a suspicion that the exercise had been tactfully stage-managed, that I had been given the time and the opportunity to do the necessary memorization. After that I had no further trouble with medical examinations. I might add that my short-sight (then minus five in both eyes) was but once a handicap to me during my active service. Of this occasion perhaps more later.

On 16 July, Friday, in civilian clothes (my uniform did not arrive till later) I did my first day as a Coldstreamer. And a surprisingly agreeable day it was. I got up at the White Hart Hotel at 6.30 a.m. and went to Victoria Barracks for breakfast where I sat next to a red-headed Eton contemporary called Harry Brierly who (I wrote) was helpful. 'So,' I added, 'was Piggott who accompanied me on to the Square.' My first meeting with Clive Piggott of whom, in the ensuing three years I became an ardent admirer. We have remained firm friends over the last half century.

Though I had passed certificate A and had been a sergeant in the Eton OTC, back I went on to the square. There were but three parades a day – from 8 to 9, from 11 to 12, and from 2 to 3. Extraordinarily easy hours. One could train up to London after three o' clock if one liked or one could go out on the river. Robin and I spent a lot of time with Raymond Stephenson and Michael Malcolm and it almost seemed that we were back at school but in such a way as to enjoy all the privileges and suffer none of the compulsions. Many were the pleasant afternoons and evenings we spent on the river. Robin and I were in a position to introduce some non-Etonian officers to the amenities of the Thames. I have notes of taking a Cornishman called Bulteel out in a sliding-seat gig, and of doing the same with C.W.Janson who had left Eton in 1897. I was to see more of him at the Havre base. Robin and I shared a room in the White Hart Hotel where we were looked after by a very old soldier by the name of Chidler who, every week, used to present enormous accounts for boot polish, button polish and other items I had never heard of. Robin was better at dealing with these types and situations than I.

I returned to Windsor on Monday 9 August to find Robin in a most agitated state. In a battle in the Ypres salient, practically the whole of the 8th Rifle Brigade had been wiped out. Most of its twenty-nine officers – nearly all those who had gone into the battle – were casualties. The names of nineteen had appeared in the previous day's casualty list. If only he had stayed where he was, Robin said, he would have been sent out, as had been the two other officers who had been left in England. Robin was beside himself and declared his intention of getting back into the Rifle Brigade. He seemed to think that the survivors of the 8th Battalion would think that he had transferred to another regiment in order to shirk the war. This was obviously idiotic, but he was impervious to reason. The upshot was that next day (Tuesday 10 August) Robin asked to see the commanding officer of the Reserve Battalion, Col. G.A.C.Crichton, who was sympathetic and asked to see the letters Robin had received from Col. McLaghlan who had commanded the Rifle Brigade. Two days later (12 August) Robin went to London and saw Col. Drummond Hay who, my diary tells me, promised to send him to France as soon as possible after receiving a letter of permission from his father. The letter must have been a difficult one for my father, but he duly wrote it, for, a fortnight later (Thursday 26 August), Robin departed, having been posted to the 1st Battalion. I got up early and saw him off by the 7.45 train from Windsor. I recall clearly the moment of standing on the platform with him and shaking hands as the train's whistle blew. I made a note in my diary that night: 'I put the chances at 4 in 10 that I never see him again.' I never did see him again.

The Battle of Loos began on Saturday, 25 September. The day after the papers were full of vague news of the big offensive. The next day (Monday, 27 September) they announced a 'big advance' with thousands of German prisoners. At this time we did not know how far the Brigade of Guards had been involved. It was not till Thursday, 30 September that we learned of the 1st Battalion's casualties. Thirteen out of the twenty-three officers were reported as killed, missing or wounded. No names were given. On the same day I was 'warned for the front'. It was not till Sunday, 3 October that casualty lists came in. I was helping myself to breakfast when an officer called Sorrel said hesitatingly that he was very sorry indeed to hear about my brother. 'I've heard nothing,' I said. 'What have you heard?' Sorrel hesitated, obviously not wanting to be the bearer of bad news. 'He's reported as missing,' he finally said. No further breakfast for me. I debated on whether to wire or telephone to my father and mother and finally decided to write. But in the afternoon they rang me up, having been informed by the War Office. I put the best face on it I could, assuring them that the chances of Robin being a prisoner were good.

I later learned that my father swung from an extreme of pessimism to one of optimism. He slowly convinced himself that Robin must be alive and a prisoner. Through his sister Carmen in Freiburg and by other means he tried to set inquiries going.

On the same day (3 October) that Sorrel told me that Robin was missing, I was myself given a day's notice to go to France. But the departure of the draft was postponed for twenty-four hours and we did not leave till Tuesday 5 October. Hence Monday was a day of idleness and waiting. I visited Cecil Sprigge, who was doing Castle Guard, in the morning and again in the afternoon, and in the evening I went for a walk alone along the river as far as Boveney Lock. I well recall that walk. It had been a fine day and the sunset was beautiful. I put myself through a sort of self-preparation. I had seen enough of the war when in Belgium to know more or less what lay ahead – what sort of tribulations I could expect. I visualized these ordeals and crises as fiery hoops which, like a circus horse, I would have to pass through. Aided by the sunset, which seemed providential (how different if the evening had been wet and windy), I conjured up the possible situations: being machine-gunned by night and by day; being sniped at; being shelled; leading a charge, as Robin had apparently done. Most daunting (and here my surmise proved correct) might be the giving of first aid to people I knew and liked who had been badly smashed. How long, I wondered, could I expect my nerve to hold out? Much would depend on myself; much also on the experiences to which I happened to be subjected. If one had luck, one might be spared the potentially shattering crisis for some months, by which time one might have become toughened or seasoned. If one had bad luck, the infliction – the concussion, the shell-shock, the horrific experience – would come early so that you would be more or less unstrung from the start. It turned out that I was lucky. My first really horrific experience did not come till September of the next year.

As the sun went down during this riverside walk, I came to feel reconciled to the future and a sense of confidence grew. I felt that I would be equal to the impending tribulations, and that, when they confronted me, I would remember the river and the sunset. This happened. Several times during crises the thought intruded: you've anticipated this and its going to be all right. The past and the future seemed like the two ends of an untied shoelace and the present was like a knot between the two.

The tension of those last few days at Windsor come back to me as I write. There were three ingredients which made the period seem like the end of a life – the life which, since nursery days, had been shared with my brother. Anxieties about him predominated. Was he alive? If yes, was life bearable as a prisoner of war? What sort of shape was he in? Was he physically intact, lightly wounded, seriously wounded or perhaps permanently crippled? These apprehensions were mixed up with feelings for my parents who, over and above their fears for Robin, would now have me to worry about. I could picture my father's alternating moods: trying to talk himself out of pessimism into hopefulness, succeeding momentarily, and then relapsing into gloom; and I could picture my mother determined to maintain an outward serenity for my father's sake, but inwardly tortured: self-sustained by continual secret prayer for Robin's safety and for strength to bear the shock of his death if he really were dead. The third ingredient was my own future. Would I be equal to what I knew lay ahead?

These inner stresses combined to produce a peculiar effect: one felt that one had been lifted clear of one's past so that the air one breathed seemed rarefied.

The period seemed to be one of transition or even metamorphosis, such as the insect larva undergoes when it emerges from its earthbound state to find itself dangerously poised in a new medium.

The next day, on 5 October, I crossed to France. It was hard on my parents and they were much on my mind during those last hours. But there was little that I could do.

*   *   *   *

Our departure was postponed a day so that we did not entrain till 8 a.m. on Tuesday 5 October. Colonel Drummond Hay, immaculate, distinguished and courteous, inspected the draft before it left the barracks. He shook hands with the officers. We were cheered as we marched out of the gates and were played to the station by a band. Having entrained we were wafted out of Windsor Terminus (where I had said goodbye to Robin a few days before) by the strains of Auld Lang Syne. A fine send-off on a sunny October morning. But the cheering and music didn't register. They scarcely penetrated an unresponding numbness.

The draft was commanded by an officer called Bert Hall. He was not among the most popular figures in the mess. But he knew that Robin was missing and, throughout the crossing, was considerate. We changed trains at Staines where we were joined by four Irish Guards officers.

We detrained at Southampton where, since the crossing was by night, there was a long wait in the dock area. As I had done earlier in the year during hours of idleness in the harbours of Dover and Dunkirk, I communed with the herring gulls, wheeling and mewing overhead. Large was the question-mark as to what awaited us on the far shore. My thoughts were much with my parents in their anxiety about Robin and now, of course, about me. What would the future disclose? The immediate future about Robin; and the long-term future, if he was still alive, for us both? This mood of contemplative uncertainty about impending events charged with menace begat an understanding of how birds were seen by Homer as vectors of omen and portent. Did Homer's birds know the outcome of men's tribulations and could they convey what they knew by a secret language of light and call? Or were the birds passive actors responding to guidance from without, unaware of the cryptic meanings conveyed by their behaviour, like mercury in a barometer or a needle registering the flow of electric current? Zeus intimated his mood and intentions to soothsayers by directing the appearance of birds, usually raptorial birds. Athene might convey her messages through owls or swallows, Hera through wrynecks, Aphrodite through doves. Mars? I could recall no bird favoured by that unestimable deity who enjoyed wars, which was perhaps as well. Poseidon? What birds would he use? Perhaps the kingfisher, for some reason connected with the sea and fine weather. Perhaps, yes perhaps, the gull.

These thoughts led to the question: how are past and future related? If they mysteriously inter-acted backwards and forwards in a manner intelligible to a small confraternity of seers, then perhaps birds were animated symbols or hyphens linking past and future – manifestations in the present of a traffic between the two. What then about those herring gulls overhead? If I were a soothsayer like Calchas could I read the future in their aerial manoeuvres and melancholy cries over Southampton docks?

By such thoughts, tensed by a sort of speculative apprehension, was my mind occupied as I sat with my draft of about a hundred Coldstreamers by the harbour-side. The upshot was that I found the gulls comforting. Perhaps that was just their message. Ever since, I have had a special fondness for gulls.

This train of thought was interrupted by an Irish Guardsman called Rews who suggested that, if we obtained a permit from the Embarkation Officer, we might do a brief shopping tour in Southampton. This we did. I bought a stick and a knife.

The ship was small. It looked little bigger than a destroyer. Into it some 500 officers and men – Guards (mainly Irish), Rifle Brigade, some Canadians and Yeomanry – were packed. The squash was forbidding and the atmosphere in the men's quarters almost unbreathable.

The ship sailed at 7.30 p.m. and I shared a cabin with Hall and T. E. Nugent, a distinguished figure in my time at Eton. The transit was eventful. During the night a boiler buckled and the oil in the engine-room caught fire. We were woken up in our bunks by acrid smoke. The ship stopped in mid-channel and rolled in a windless swell. With admirable composure and in perfect order, with jokes and bursts of ribald song, the troops filed up from below. A light shone down from the masthead on to the packed deck. What a sitter for a prowling submarine! The ship's crew turned hoses into the boiler-room and it was not long before the clouds of rising smoke and steam thinned and we were told that we could return to our quarters. Several men succumbed to the fumes and movement and asked leave to be sick over the side, and I was myself quite glad to be able to lie down again.

Next morning we disembarked at Harfleur. The weather had changed. Under a drab sky the harbour with its cranes and tall flaking houses looked dingy and dirty. Dirtier, I thought, than Dunkirk used to look. It was not long before the troops were sorted and our party moved off to the rest camp near Havre some five miles away. No interest whatever was taken in us by the civilian population which, by this time, was fully accustomed to the sight of British troops on the march; and no interest whatever was taken by the troops in the civilian population. Much had happened since September 1914 when the expeditionary force was greeted with garlands and embraces. Most of the Coldstreamers had been out before and knew what Northern France was like. To a man they preferred Blighty. It was hot and windless. Heavily-laden, they marched with downcast eyes. The change of scene from the day before seemed to affect nobody except perhaps myself. Harfleur compared badly with Southampton.

Seven days was the duration of my stay at the Base camp which was on the top of a hill near Havre. We were moved into huts, one of which I was glad to share with C.W. Janson, whom I had met and liked at Windsor. Also with a magnificently built Australian, R. S. Powell, brother of E. V. Powell, an Eton master and a distinguished oarsman. No one had heard anything of our 1st Battalion's casualties on 28 September.

On the day after arriving I was told that I had been posted to the 4th or Pioneer Battalion which, with a full complement of officers, had left Windsor on 15 August.

I should perhaps say something about these divisional Pioneer Battalions which were quite different from the Pioneers (formed into a Pioneer Corps) of the 1939–45 war. The latter consisted of men who, by reason of what was called educational subnormality and on account of other handicaps, were deemed unfitted for the requirements (more exacting in the later than the earlier war) of combatant formations. I don't know when the War Office decided to incorporate a Pioneer Battalion in every division. Presumably when it was recognized that, for an unknowable period ahead, a static trench warfare rather than a war of movement was to prevail in North-West Europe. Trench warfare had developed along the whole Western Front after the Battle of the Marne and the first Battle of Ypres; and in some parts, particularly in low-lying areas requiring careful drainage, the conditions had been terrible. Sickness rates from 'trench fever' and 'trench foot' had been so high during the winter 1914–15 that, in the ensuing summer months, steps were taken to anticipate similar conditions. If, by the second winter, the projected offensives failed, trench warfare would continue. Revisions were introduced at every level from the kit of the private soldier to the structure of a division.

It was apparently in the middle of 1915 that the War Office decided to add a thirteenth or Pioneer Battalion to the twelve Battalions of each division. In the words of the Regiment's historian of the first war, Lieutenant-Colonel Sir John Ross-of-Bladensburg:

> 'The war required a body of troops trained to construct field-works, to keep in good repair the roads and approaches at the immediate front, and to assist the Royal Engineers in the many duties that trench warfare imposed on them; and these special battalions, called 'Pioneers' were accordingly formed for the purpose.'

My feelings on learning that I had been posted to this Battalion were mixed. On the one hand I had nerved myself to the prospect of maximum activity and immediate combatancy and to the prospect of wounds or death; on the other I had no wish to kill Germans or anyone else and I knew that this posting would afford a slight relief to my parents. I had, moreover, got to know and like some of the officers in the 4th Battalion before they left Windsor in the middle of August. In October 1915 I had no more idea than anyone else how the casualty rates of a Pioneer Battalion would compare with those of a fighting Battalion. Since the Pioneer Battalion would not quite have to 'go over the top' like the others, they would presumably suffer less in such murderous offensives as those mounted at Loos. But what would life be like during the prolonged periods of more or less static trench warfare?

As things turned out, the war lasted longer than anyone expected, and I stayed with the 4th Battalion till the spring of 1918 when, for reasons I may get round to explaining later, I got myself transferred to the Second Battalion.

*   *   *   *

My days at the base-camp, where I had arrived on 6 October, passed quietly and were uneventful. They had a sort of unreality. We lived well – no less well than at Windsor.

On 13 October (Wednesday) I was told that I was to 'go up' that night. But I didn't leave till the evening of the next day. We entrained at Montevilliers. The weather was perfect with a spectacular sunset which, I decided, had no ulterior significance. I was second-in-command of a draft of Grenadiers, Scots and Welsh Guards. An Irishman called Kinahan commanded the train which was over a third of a mile long (860 yards). It moved at a snail's pace. It was difficult to stop the men running up and down the footboards and climbing on to the roofs of the carriages. We were generously rationed, especially with dog biscuits, (called Army biscuits, Mark 4). Our servants made us comfortable and the night was not entirely sleepless. We crawled through country which undulated at first and then became flat. In the autumn sunlight of the next day it looked peaceful and beautiful but again there was an element of unreality, a sort of dream-like element, about the journey. As we crawled along we passed small groups of peasants who waved and the children called for biscuits. We passed a group of German prisoners, some with heads and limbs bandaged, tramping disconsolately along a road that ran parallel with the railway. No reactions from our convoy; no reactions either when a passing Frenchman pointed at the Germans and drew his finger across his throat.

By evening, when the light was failing, we heard distant gunfire which got louder as we approached Béthune. There we detrained. A limber had been sent to meet me. It conveyed my valise to Battalion headquarters outside Béthune where I reported to the adjutant, Guy (commonly known as George) Edwards – a tall good-looking meticulous man. Little did I guess at that first meeting, when he scrutinized me closely, how fond I would become of him later. He told me that I had been posted to No. 3 company whither, in the dark, I was guided. There, in the dingy Company Mess were the four officers – Bingo (the Hon. E. M.) Pakenham, the company commander, Clive Piggott, C. M. H. Pearce and Lionel Bootle-Wilbraham – of all of whom more later. On that first evening, Bingo struck me as amiable; so that, having known and quite liked the other three at Windsor, I had the comfortable feeling of having found my way, after much winding about France, into an agreeable harbour. No news of the First Battalion's casualties in the earlier battle.

The day after my arrival I asked for, and was given, leave to pay a visit to the 1st Battalion. I bicycled round to their billets which were not far from ours, and was steered into the presence of Digby, the adjutant. He knew no more than that Robin was missing, but he did his best to help. He referred me to No.1 Company (Robin's), providing a guide to their headquarters. There I met Sutton (an Eton contemporary), who sent for Robin's platoon sergeant. Robin, the latter explained, was the company bombing officer; he had last been seen carrying a rifle and bayonet running forward well in front of his platoon. Fifty men had gone over; fifteen came back. This sergeant spoke warmly of Robin. He and Sutton both put the chances of Robin being a prisoner as quite good. I came back less hopeful.

On the evening of the day of my visit to the First Battalion, we paraded with packs and marched in the dark some eight miles to Vermelles. It was at the outset of this march that I made my first contact with No.11 platoon and with Sergeant E. Melton, my platoon sergeant. I recall my first sight of the platoon as I went on parade in the failing light. They were drawn up in line (two ranks) and I approached them from their left. The platoon had been commanded by Quincey Greene, of whom more later. Though they could scarcely have been indifferent to the fellow brought in to take his place, discipline forbade even the most surreptitious glimmer of interest. They formed a good line, standing at ease and looking stonily to the front. Their uniforms were frayed, but they themselves looked strong and tough. Sergeant Melton marched up to me, looking me straight in the eyes. He resoundingly smacked his butt and informed me that the platoon was all present and correct. Thus began a long and happy association with No. 11 platoon and Sergeant Melton.

This rather formidable NCO came from Exeter and expressed himself in quite broad Devonian. He was an effective disciplinarian with a rough tongue. He had a low gritty word of command, and it was seemingly with a rictus of contempt that he would call the platoon to attention. His 'Number Eleven' was so savagely spat out that one expected abuse to follow. But he was himself smart and his platoon (several of whom were better educated than himself) were well drilled and well behaved. He turned out good junior NCO's who served him well. Later he became No.3 Coy's CQMS; and after the war he got into trouble over regimental funds. There was a considerable upheaval, as I later learned from John Codrington who was himself indirectly involved. Melton was, I believe, reduced to the ranks which cannot have been pleasant for him. He died in 1955.

During the night-march up to Vermelles Melton was by my side in the dark. At first we marched in silence. It was satisfying that, for the first time since the war began, I felt properly integrated. Now I was a genuine participant, not an observer or helper in the back areas or standing on the sidelines as I had done at the Belgian Field Hospital. Here I was, a platoon commander, and I was on my way up to the line – no longer a zone outside my proper range. Soon the Very lights would be hovering and sputtering over my head and I would be hearing the crack of rifle and machine-gun bullets fired at close range. All very satisfying.

But after about an hour I began to feel the weight of my pack. I reflected that at Windsor we had not done much marching, heavily laden with equipment. Tugging at your shoulders, your pack makes you lean forward and look down as you march. Two additional stone of weight bear down on your insteps which begin to ache. On the pavé roads your hob-nailed boots slide over the smooth stones, invisible at night, which protrude from the surface, additionally straining your ankles and calf muscles. Nor is your vitality highest at one o'clock in the morning when habit prepares you for sleep. So that at frequent halts, when you can't sit or lie down, you bend forward and lean on whatever you are carrying – rifle or walking stick.

As the rumbling horizon, intermittently lit by gun-flashes and Very lights, drew nearer, I got into conversation with Melton. I told him about Robin. He listened politely and was sympathetic. I put to him a question which I had been asking myself. Would it be true that the longer we went without news the better would be the chances of his being a prisoner? These seemed to me to be the possibilities: if Robin had been killed, his dead body might be identifiable or it might not. It would not be identifiable if he had been blown to pieces by a shell. But most of the casualties had been inflicted by machine-gun fire. As far as we knew, the lines in that sector had not shifted. What had been no-man's land at the end of September was still no-man's-land. The more time went by, the greater the chances of dead bodies being found and brought in. All units did their best in this way. Since all or nearly all the casualties in the area were British, we would have more incentive to bring in the corpses than would the Germans. If, on the other hand, Robin had been brought down close to the German line, perhaps in their wire or between their wire and their parapet, the Germans might have brought him in to their side, and we would be circuitously informed, perhaps through a neutral country, that he was dead. There would then be a long delay in our getting to know, probably longer than if he were a prisoner.

I put the case in this way to Melton. Perhaps to reassure me, he said he agreed. The longer we went without news, the better might be the prospects. At this time I was searching for comforting things to say to my parents. I also badly wanted to comfort myself.

By mid-October the sector held by our division had side-slipped northwards. There had been heavy fighting round a place called the Hohenzollern Redoubt near the village of Hulluch about a mile and a half north-east of Loos. The village of Vermelles, our destination that night, lay about two miles west of Hulluch. (Vermelles, Hulluch and Loos form an approximately equilateral triangle, its base to the north, its apex pointing southward to Loos.) The next three days and nights were spent in dirty trenches and dug-outs in the blasted village of Vermelles. Shelling was continuous and the noise almost incessant. But most of the stuff went over our heads. Pearce, Wilbraham and I shook down in a small dug-out wherein we were tightly packed. Lionel (Wilbraham) and I suffered more from the stentorian snoring of Pearce than from the noises of battle. The snoring habit stood Pearce in good stead. At about six on one of the mornings two shells came down almost simultaneously within fifty yards of our dug-out, instantly rousing Lionel and me from our light slumbers. But Pearce was so deafened by the noise he was himself making that he never heard the explosions outside.

The houses in Vermelles had not been entirely flattened as were, during the battles in 1916, the villages of the Somme. But every house was damaged and about two in every five were gutted and without a roof. Bricks, jampots, rusty metal and refuse littered the pitted ground. Crosses here and there stuck out of the rubble. No vegetation: the only birds sparrows and starlings. Not even crows. A few disconnected incidents:

Lionel lost a man in his platoon hit in the jaw when drinking a mug of tea, and No. 11 platoon lost a man, Guardsman Andrews, when a shell landed in, and blew up, a bomb-store. At about ten o'clock on the second night our area was overrun by Fusiliers who had just come out of the line. They distributed themselves among us and one was killed when a shell landed just outside the derelict house which served as our Company headquarters. Rather a near thing for Packenham and Piggott who were dossed down in the place.

A corporal in my platoon by the name of Allen had a peculiar experience. He was the NCO in charge of a carrying party of twelve men detailed to carry up sandbags to the front line. They had to get out of a communicating trench and walk along the top. Stray bullets were flying about or perhaps it was a sniper who had drawn a bead on the point at which men were seen climbing out of the trench. Anyway, a bullet hit a compass Allen was carrying, glanced along his ribs, came out, and fell into his drawers whence he extracted it. He was able to walk and ended up in hospital. I saw him on the way back and wished him luck.

We did not go up to the line which ran east of Vermelles. But we performed some tasks and fatigues including the loading of four lorries with the newly-introduced Mills bombs when the site of the bomb-store (in which Andrews had been killed) was changed. At this stage of the war the old cricket-ball type of bomb was superseded, and several bags-full of the obsolete pattern were buried by my platoon. The weather became colder when we were in Vermelles, so that I was glad to wrap up at night in my British Warm. A fore-taste of winter.

This spell involved for me no particular stress or strain. My experiences in Belgium earlier in the year had provided a sort of inoculation. In our company pitch there was more noise than danger and the edge was taken off the hideous surroundings by the incessant din. It was a noisy, banging sort of period, sunless, with a note of artificiality. The external artificiality came from the fact that, though there went on an almost incessant two-way bombardment with now and then a few bullets ricochetting off the standing walls, much of the din was made by our guns. Most of the German stuff either fell short or went over our heads. There was also an inner artificiality: a superficial elation about being in a forward area served to mask inner misgivings about Robin. I was never in any particular danger, nor was I in the least tested or frightened.

At 2.30 a.m. on the morning of Tuesday 19 October I was awakened by the blasphemies of a Fusilier sergeant who had to get a move on two sections which occupied a trench twenty yards from our dug-out. He threatened to stamp on their . . . faces and to tear their testicles out. Half an hour later we were called by a sentry. We dressed in pitch darkness and considerable cold. We then waited for two interminable hours for the arrival of a relieving party from Nos. 2 and 4 Companies. At about 5 a.m. we started a much interrupted march of 2½ hours to the squalid mining village of Verquigneul. I have a mental picture of the October *dreariness* of this place as it appeared in the fading light of the evening. Rows of grimy little houses blackened with coal dust fronted a narrow pot-holed road. No pavement, no gardens, no greenery, nothing to mitigate the prevailing gloom. Happily the drabness made little impression on the troops (many of them miners from Yorkshire and Durham) in whom 'moving back' evoked cheerfulness. As we marched into Verquigneul they livened up and sang their way in.

Wilbraham, Pearce and I were billeted in a stuffy, shabby room with a stale smell and swarming with house-flies. The windows had long been shut. On the walls were religious pictures in crude colours. Favourite themes were a kneeling woman with uplifted eyes and a halo; a shaft of light descending from a massive bearded figure sitting on clouds at the top, with a dove fluttering round the shaft; and a bright red heart transfixed and dripping. In the next three years we were to see many such representations.

In the room beyond ours, and accessible only through ours, slept the *patronne* and her two aged parents. These would walk through our room without knocking. In the morning after our arrival I was soaping myself as I sat in a canvas bath when the old man passed through. He stopped and looked at me. He then ambled up and shook me by the hand. He then moved to the outside door which he opened, so that I was visible to the troops who swarmed in the yard, lifted his other hand and solemnly said: '*Pour la Paix.*'

During the next few days we moved about between two small villages – Verquigneul and Labourse. We 'went up and back.' I quote from a letter which gives an early impression of what movement at night in the forward area was like: 'Our starting-time was 8 p.m. Before starting we ate a sort of high tea which warmed us up. We sat in silence round a hurricane lamp as if it was a fire, and listened to our party singing – their usual practice when waiting or bored. The voices fluctuated, sometimes vigorously mounting, then listlessly sinking to a drone. We marched up five miles in two hours – slow progress. During the last hour, down came the rain. I was glad to have a trench coat which compared favourably with the ground-sheets, usable on the march as protection against rain, worn by the party. During a monotonous night-march along a reasonable surface (not pavé), there is a knack of half closing one's eyes and almost going to sleep. One's faculties subside and by imagining that one is in bed one can almost lose consciousness. But the march discipline must be good. I moved over two miles in this way and on arrival at our destination – the mouth of a communicating trench – felt quite fresh. We reached this point at about 10 p.m. and, led by a guide, wound our way up to the second line. Our task was to repair a battered communicating trench between this and the front line. During the early stage of the work most of us were in the open. The night was quiet: little shelling and but occasional cracks of small-arm fire. But when star-shells soared up, bathing the grim scenery in cold blue light – mysterious and beautiful – we had to stop dead: freeze.'

I continue the letter to my parents: 'I don't suppose that you have much idea of how difficult it can be to move troops through trenches by night. When you lead a platoon marching along a road by day, you see them in formation behind you. By night you can hear them on the road and, unless it is pitch dark, you can half-see them. Not so when you are leading in a trench at night; then you can only see the outline of the man behind you. The trenches are apt to be crossed by wires of various kinds in which you catch your foot; and whole duck-boards or cross-pieces of duckboards (often filched for fuel) may be missing. You curse and are momentarily held up. So is the man behind you and everyone behind him in turn. As soon as he is clear, each man scuttles ahead to catch up with the man in front whose outline he has seen disappearing round a bend. So that your party's forward movement is concertina-like or earth-worm like. Most of the communicating trenches are so narrow that it is a squeeze to pass someone moving in the opposite direction. The squeeze-past holds you up, as it successively does each man behind you so that your party gets still more strung out. If, instead of meeting a single man moving in the opposite direction, you meet a party of men, a general blockage ensues so that one party or the other has to get out and either walk along the top or wait outside the trench till the others have got by.

'Sometimes, if there are people in front of you, there is a halt. The reason is usually unknown. You stop and wait. The men being tired fall momentarily asleep. Then suddenly the word comes down to move on and there is a general scramble forward. The man in front of you, thinking only of not losing touch with the man in front of him, hurries on. Gaps form. Then, when no one is to be seen ahead, you reach a fork in the trench. You don't know which fork to take. You make a guess and hope for the best. So that it is easy to get disconnected and lost. The more the trenches form a network or maze, the easier it is to lose yourself.'

These were my first impressions of the difficulties of night movement along trenches. There were delays, hitches and losses of contact. I recall thinking that a unit needed appropriate training before it could move with assurance along an obstructed and muddy communicating trench in the dark. Obviously the officer in the lead should have an instinct about the people behind him. He should know when to pause or go slow so that touch is not lost. And he should drop 'sign-post men' at forks where wrong turnings could be taken. These could stay where they were posted, acting as animated finger-pointers, till the whole party had filed past when they could join the stretcher-bearers in the rear. On reaching the destination the 'sign-post men' report back to the officer who detached them. I recall the stress and confusion of this first night in the network outside Hulluch and wondering why some exercises had not been devised at Windsor. It would have been easy to dig somewhere – perhaps in Windsor Park – a ramifying imitation of a communicating trench with several possible exits, putting in obstructions, turnings and other complications (such as sending men down in the opposite direction) which could have been varied in the different exercises. Finally you put different units into competition as to which could form up intact at the selected exit in the quickest time. Such training would have been especially valuable for us pioneers who had to do more than the usual amount of night-movement along difficult communication trenches.

But the above is a digression provoked by my first reactions. I continue the interrupted letter: 'We finished our job at about 2.30 a.m. In getting back the party got split and the two parts lost touch. I searched for and found the lost rear part and did not get back till 5 a.m. Glad indeed to do so. But in the night our billets had been shifted to another village. There was a muddle about where our places were and we were kept waiting by a roadside for an hour in cold and wet. Pearce and I dozed off on the doorstep of a small wayside chapel where, having profusely sweated earlier, we nearly perished of cold. We were then directed to the other side of the village and the party was tucked into a dry barn with clean straw.'

These quick changes from one village to another, doubtless necessitated by the movements of other troops, raised a rather special problem for our particular Battalion. How far behind the line was it best to be billeted? The closer up you were the greater the discomfort of the living conditions. The further back you were the longer the march up. The issue was not entirely dissimilar from that posed to the headquarters staffs of higher formations such as brigades, division etc. For us the night marches up and down were tiring: more so for the men who had to carry rifles, picks and shovels than for the officers. After a march up which (what with the delays imposed by crowded roads and muddy communication trenches in constant use) might take two hours, you had lost some of your energy. But it was always a relief to get onto the work. You then become so taken up that, so to speak, you made friends with the spot and cared little about what, in the way of steel and lead, was coming past and over. Such casualties as we had usually occurred on the way up or down. If one was working day after day along a stretch of communicating trench, the German spotters might note the fact and in the daytime range on the next section ahead. You then caught it that night. Best then to do the job in discontinuous stretches. Later in the winter, when the Battalion was in the Laventie area, I used to try to go up on the afternoon before and decide the best programme for the night's work. This I would explain to the party when it was on parade before starting. When on the job, the officer's task was to move men about so that the task was finished as quickly as possible, avoiding terminal waits by the majority while a minority finished a section which was more difficult than the rest. It was also one's job to see that, in the darkness, men did not bury their rifles and tools.

I have mentioned Verquingneul and Labourse. They were more or less undamaged villages in which we spent occasional nights. It was at Labourse, on the evening of Saturday 23 October, that my blow fell.

The day had begun with farce and frustration. Arrangements had been made for the company to have baths at a nearby colliery which had escaped damage. The first party undressed and were ready to move under the showers when it was found that the water wouldn't run. In charge was a not unattractive French woman. She couldn't go into the shower room because of some twenty naked men. A male joiner was quickly whistled in who, in clearing the rust-blocked pipes, flooded the place. After which he triumphantly announced that there would be no water that day. We should come back on Monday. Attempts by some of our people to restore the flow were unavailing.

That evening No.3 Company Mess invited Burton (second-in-command) and Geoffrey Howard to a quite Lucullan dinner which included caviare as savoury. As we were about to eat the caviare, the post-corporal brought in the mail, the first for several days. There were several letters from mother. I opened them at random. From hers of 19 October, the day the news reached them, I learned the truth. It began:

> 'My precious boy – A letter came this morning from a Captain Boyd[1] telling us about our darling Robsie. What can I write except the infinite pity and sympathy we feel for you, my own dear Pip. Don't be unhappy about us. We are bearing the blow with courage and fortitude. Dada is taking it nobly and we comfort each other. He is wonderful and our love for each other and for you will tide us through these deep waters.'

I could read no more. I got up from the table and walked out into the dark feeling slightly dizzy. A fine drizzle. I leant my head against the outside wall to steady myself. I had the impression of being swept by translucent blue waves – impersonal but friendly. After a minute I recovered. I went back into the Mess. Noise and tobacco smoke. On my plate the uneaten caviare. The others had dined well and noticed nothing. The port was going round. They were telling funny stories. I would be easier alone, so I went to bed.

In the darkness and warmth of my flea-bag, my thoughts went to my parents. Curious how the currents and tides moved. How strange that, though within a few miles of where he died, I should have learned nothing, not even from his platoon sergeant. A wide circuit, it had made, the dire news! To the West Country of England and back to me at Labourse, not six miles from Loos. Again I felt those comforting blue waves: at one moment I was riding them as on a surf-board; then submerged in them. My mother had written that, at nights, she had somehow felt sustained; that in the mornings she woke up happy. Was this the same sort of thing? Whence these waves? And whence the blue? I was reminded of the blue light of star-shells which both revealed and menaced as they looked down on you; also of the blue-green sea at Cabourg. There, as small boys, Robin and I had played on the sands and at low water had caught shrimps in the sparkling shallows of long sandpools which ran parallel with the shore. The happy scene was suddenly before my eyes: the hot sun on one's skin, the cool water round one's feet, the semi-transparent darting shrimps. In the distance the murmuring sea. Back came my thoughts to my mother. Like her I should be grateful.

My mother's letters overflow with grief. But they are full of courage and muted by a kind of serenity. Her inner peace, underlying the grief, came, she believed, from outside herself. She writes that Robin seemed to be trying to comfort her, particularly at night, so that to her surprise she would wake up in the mornings feeling almost happy. She felt that if she allowed herself to grieve

---

[1] The name of the author of the letter was in fact Lloyd, not Boyd. The mistake is understandable since, as we may infer from Bernard Shaw's letter reproduced in Appendix 2, she had not in fact seen the letter when she wrote to CPB.

Robin would suffer: hence for his sake she must not grieve. Nothing could better reflect my mother's essential strength and goodness. It was not till eight days after Captain Lloyd's letter came that my father could bring himself to write to me.

Other thoughts came to me in my flea-bag on that Tuesday night. If he had been a prisoner, Robin would almost certainly survive the war and return home when it ended. One of us at least would have survived. My own death would then matter less. My parents' anxieties, if Robin had been a prisoner, would have been partitioned between us – perhaps less focussed on Robin (who would be relatively safe) than on me who would not be particularly safe. Now their anxieties were wholly focussed on me. It would help them to know that I was a little safer in the Pioneer than in any of the other three Battalions. I had had some qualms about this posting. These should now be eased. (They were eased, but not for long. They later became so acute that I transferred to the 2nd Battalion. Of this perhaps more later.)

*   *   *   *

Of Robin's story all I need not say is that about a fortnight after the attack on 28 September, his body was found somewhere in no-man's land by a unit of the South Wales Borderers. These had taken over the Loos chalk pits. He was brought back and such personal belongings as had been deemed of no use or value by his finders were removed from his pockets, listed and parcelled. Captain Lloyd, the Company Commander, had no difficulty in identifying Robin from his identity disk (which we all wore round our necks) and from his papers. My parents' address was among Robin's papers. Captain Lloyd wrote to them enclosing a diagram which showed the spot in what had been a wood where Robin had been buried; and he handed in the small parcel of belongings. This passed through 'the usual military channels' and, about a week after Captain Lloyd's letter reached Vane Tower, the parcel was handed to me. I recall the moment. It was late in the evening when a rather senior officer from the Division appeared at No. 3 Coy mess at Ham-en-Artois. At the door of the billet he asked for me and I came out; in the half-light I beheld him in a British warm standing in the road. He handed me the parcel expressing sympathy. I invited him in but he tactfully refused. Most of the contents I sent to Vane Tower[2].

*   *   *   *

[2] Among these effects was a notebook in which Robin had recorded his thoughts after leaving England. Some extracts from this notebook are reproduced in Appendix 1, together with his last letters and an account of the action in which he was killed

51

I jump four years. In the spring of 1919 I, my parents and my Aunt Lily motored from Dinard to Amiens. With us was Cecil Sprigge. The object of the expedition was to find Robin's grave. We had with us Captain Lloyd's letter and diagram. It showed a communicating trench running through a wood and by the side of the trench, a few yards from the wood's margin, the grave was marked. The burying party had put up a cross. Cecil and I easily found the spot. Of neither grave nor cross was there a vestige. The line had been static in this area till the end of the war and the wood had been continuously pounded and pulverized by artillery.

*   *   *   *

On Monday 25 October we marched heavily laden to Béthune. Thence, via Lillers to Ham-en-Artois, a clean and unspoiled village some 13 miles west-by-north of Labourse. The Hazebrouck/A map shows the roads in the area round Labourse as heavily encrusted with houses. These were the strung-out cottages of miners who lived in some density round the pit-heads. Ham was outside this congested area and my recollection is of pleasant open country with fields and a nearby marsh.

I needn't say much about this fortnight except that I reacted badly to the lowered tension. The stresses connected with Robin had been direfully resolved, but I often longed to see him again and the thought that I would never do so lay heavily. For the time being we were dully safe. The world looked bleak. I felt empty and irritable. I began to react badly to Bingo and the other three despite the fact that they were considerate and (I don't doubt) long-suffering. The village contained a minor château occupied by Battalion headquarters. There has stuck in my mind a distant view, beheld during a solitary afternoon walk, of its long-windowed façade on the far side of a big acreage of wet field from which, among sodden ground and elongated seed-pods, there sprouted a few failing flowers of cabbage. The seediness, I felt, was general. The floral vestiges of autumn, yellow and bedraggled, were retreating before the onset of winter; and to the winter, during a static war in low-lying country, no one could look forward.

*   *   *   *

Before leaving Windsor a few weeks before I had tried to steel myself to the 'horrors of war'. Little did I then know how differently from Robin's my course would run. In fact, there were to be no horrors for quite a few months. Till then my central difficulty was more homely: to get on with the other officers in my company. About these I might now say a word.

My first impression of Bingo, who wore medals of the South African War, was that he was harmless or even benign. He had about the same seniority as

52

the Battalion's Commanding Officer, Colonel R. Skeffington-Smyth, known to us as Skeff. Bingo had a bushy moustache, a stoop, mumbling speech, and a way of peering about, half mystified, half apprehensive. One of the first things I noticed was how badly he did Company Orders. After the charge had been made and the man, standing rigidly to attention in front of Bingo, had had his say in his own defence, Bingo's natural stoop would become more pronounced, he would mumble something inaudible and he would either let off a man who obviously deserved to be punished or else punish someone who equally obviously should have been merely cautioned. Quickly noticeable, also, was his lack of conversation, humour, initiative and originality. It was only after dinner that he became articulate. Over the meal he would drink a few glasses of *vin ordinaire* which heightened his colour and changed his furtive look to an angry glower. He would glare round the table apparently resenting most of what was being lightly said and would sometimes burst out with an offensive remark. To begin with, these rude sallies were mainly directed against Lionel and me. Lionel was better controlled than I and could pass them off, but I became increasingly sensitized and one evening answered him back. I have no doubt that the widening rift between Bingo and myself was mainly my fault. I must have appeared to him insufferable. The final break came in the following September of which more later.

It took me a few months to appreciate Clive Piggott, a tall well-built man with a slight stutter who ran a business in Birmingham. He was a keen member of the Church of England. His views on everything seemed to be wholly conventional. But I noticed soon that he dealt well with the mess staff; later that he dealt equally well with NCO's and other ranks; later still that he handled Bingo with perfect tact and consideration. Being the senior of the four junior officers – all of us ensigns at this stage – Clive would command the company in Bingo's absence. While we were at Ham Bingo went on leave. I immediately noticed how well Clive did the Company Orders. He was never harsh or censorious. If he had to rebuke or punish, he would do it gently and courteously; and he would often end by saying, 'So don't do it again,' often with a just perceptible smile of understanding. It took me longer than it should to see that Clive's strength lay not in his intellect but in his character. There were hard times for him ahead. Skeff, a shrewder judge of men than one might have supposed, tumbled early to his good qualities and, in the spring of 1916, made him Adjutant. Not everyone – Edwards, Coats, and Furze for example – applauded the appointment and Clive was put under much strain. This he stoically bore. As the months – and years – went by, my admiration for him grew, and I now see him as one of the best men I have known. But having no pretensions to being 'intellectual' Clive was reluctant to discuss general topics; indeed he tended to shun serious talk. What impressed me most during the next few months was his consideration for Bingo. Seeing how outrageous were the things Bingo could say when primed with *vin ordinaire* or over the port, this unvarying courtesy of Clive's (I am ashamed to say) somewhat irritated me.

Pearce had been to Oxford and was something of a scholar. He was witty and could be amusing so that at first I liked him. But during the physical discomforts of the next few weeks at Laventie his rather sharp temper shortened so that Lionel and I would find ourselves unexpectedly savaged or jeered at. Pearce was, I think, an inconsiderate and perhaps selfish man who liked to make people feel small. He made Lionel and me feel conscious of his seniority to us in Army rank. A few weeks later a shell burst near enough to him to damage one of his ear drums. He left the Battalion and I have not heard of him since. I felt ambivalently towards Pearce. My liking for him was strong enough to prevent my feeling unreservedly glad to see him go. We parted on friendly terms.

My fondness for Lionel took rather a long time to define itself. There were early vicissitudes which were more my fault than his. He had a habit (in no way meant to be discourteous or even provocative) of flatly contradicting people: 'Oh no,' he would say, seemingly for the fun of contradiction and sometimes when he had not properly understood what had been said. The confidence with which he would make statements on any topic bore but the slenderest relation to his knowledge of that topic. Indeed, I sometimes had the impression that the more he knew about what he was talking about the more diffidently he expressed his opinions. (In this respect he resembled many eminent scholars. Cautious – perhaps unduly cautious – in the field in which they are expert, they freely lay down the law about most other things.)

A few weeks after we had left Ham Lionel contradicted me flatly about something or other towards the end of a dinner during which Bingo had earlier sensitized me by some gratuitously offensive remark. Lionel and Bingo were sitting next to each other. I was strongly tempted to upset the table on them both. Instead I walked out and thereafter came as little as possible into the mess. When I look back on myself during the months after Robin's death, I am astonished by the tolerance with which everyone treated my touchiness, unpredictability and disagreeableness. Lionel was especially long-suffering. I recall how, one evening, he came into my room at Laventie and frankly asked me what was wrong. I feebly prevaricated. Lionel then asked if there was anything he could do. I said there wasn't and he left. I felt ashamed of myself.

To return to the narrative: our rest period at Ham-en-Artois was largely spent in practising the nightly erection of barbed wire entanglements and barriers of concertina wire. Indeed, my platoon was designated as the company wiring platoon, though why it was deemed necessary to train a single platoon in this universally necessary exercise I don't know.

It was during October that my parents decided to leave England. The decision was taken for various reasons – partly because they felt that my father's mother, then living in Switzerland, was lonely and would like to join them in Paris, partly because a change from Vane Tower, with its sad associations, would benefit my father, and partly because, if I obtained short leave or got wounded, they would be nearer. My father had, by this time, become fixed in his habits and disliked change, so that the initiative had to come from my mother. It was she who had to do the sorting and packing. They left Vane Tower on Sunday 7 November leaving Albertine (an ancient family retainer) and all the servants in the house, evidently not expecting to be very long away from England. They travelled up to London where they stayed at 40 Half Moon Street with Robbie Ross.

The day after they moved from Torquay we moved from Ham. So here is a convenient place to end this chapter of my narrative.

4

WINTER IN THE PAS DE CALAIS, 1915–16

On Tuesday, 10 November 1915, the Division 'moved up' to another part of the line. Our new front lay north of the Lens-Loos-Hulluch area where the September battles had been fought to a standstill. From Lillers and its surrounding villages, in which we had been recuperating and refitting, we were transferred to the area of Laventie, La Gorgue, Estaires and Merville. Of these Laventie, our Battalion headquarters for most of the winter, lay furthest east. It had been partially destroyed and was fairly regularly shelled. The other three places had suffered little. There were civilians and shops. Merville, the furthest back, was about seven miles west and slightly north of Laventie. It contained a fine church, little if at all damaged, with cathedral-like proportions in which, later in the winter, I spent some quiet hours.

The first fortnight of the period was spent by No. 3 Company at a farm in a hamlet called Fosse, a sort of overture to the winter. It was not an edifying period. The work allotted to the Company was not dangerous or exciting; indeed it was unlike anything we had to do during the rest of the war. It called for no skill and it did not require the supervision of officers who, on the spot, were an encumbrance rather than an asset. A word about this work.

The area was low-lying and liable to flooding. The waterlogging of the soil was partly due to the presence of a layer of thick blue clay a few feet down. But the wet and the clay did not preclude subterranean activity. Shafts were sunk and galleries dug in the direction of the German lines where similar activities were under way. I don't know how far either side had emulated the mole during the previous winter of 1914–15; nor do I know whether we or the Germans began the exercise in our new area. I would guess that they did. If I am right, we quickly reacted by taking counter-measures. Only where hostilities had become static was it worth while to start this subterranean form of warfare. If the lines moved forward or back, the culminating operation – the explosion of a mine under the enemy positions – would be misplaced. You might blow up your own side if an advance had taken place, or nothing more than a few field-mice if the enemy had moved forward. Your access-shaft, moreover, had to be sited within an 'operational' distance of the place where your explosions were planned. The distance became non-operational if your galleries exceeded a certain length, so that inordinate distances had to be travelled underground before you reached your sap-heads; and the longer your saps, the more massive became the accumulation of excavatated material round the mouth of the access shaft.

On what date mining operations on our new front began I don't know; nor did anyone I asked at the time. From the length of the gallery along which I crawled a day or two after our arrival, I inferred that the operations must have been going on for several weeks or even months. I should add that our new positions were located about the middle of the stretch between the Lens and Loos sector to our south – the area of the big battles of late September and early October – and the sector of Armentières to our north. Armentières was a bigger place than Lens, Béthune, Estaires or Merville. The name Armentières is not associated with local battles as are Loos, Festubert or Givenchy; it is associated, rather, with a girl who became legendary in a popular song. During the recent battles our new sector had doubtless been bombarded, but there didn't seem to have been major changes of position; so that mining operations begun before 25 September (first day of the Battle of Loos) could have been continued after the battle was over.

The tactics of underground warfare were explained to me by Lieutenant Bird (of whom more below) during the day I spent in his dug-out. These tactics could be offensive or defensive. An example of an offensive manoeuvre was later provided by the battle of Vimy in the spring of 1917. The attack was carried out by the Canadians for whom Vimy has remained a place of pilgrimage. The opening event was the explosion of an enormous mine under the German forward positions. The eruption and the crater were of unprecedented magnitude and the casualties heavy. The shattering detonation shocked and stunned most of the Germans in the area. How many other examples the first war produced of mining operations paving the way for local victories and tactical successes I don't know. None to my knowledge occurred in our area during the 1915–16 winter. Here the strategy was mainly defensive. If the misguided enemy starts sapping operations intending to blow up a few yards of your front line, or to undermine the morale of your front-line troops who begin to worry about what is going on under their feet, two main courses are open to you: either to withdraw your front line to a point out of the range of the enemy saps, or else to start counter-mining operations yourself. Not wishing to appear behindhand in initiative and skill, our higher command adopted the second alternative. But the object was mainly defensive. No major attack was contemplated on this low-lying front at the beginning of winter; nor was one expected. The object of the sappers was to frustrate the German sappers in whatever it was they wanted to do. When they were active in the sap-heads they betrayed themselves by noise. You could hear the sounds of pick and shovel. Your general object was to get below the other fellow. You could dig various deep and radiating saps and then lie low, establishing listening posts at key points. If the enemy then dug towards you, or, better, over you, you bided your time and then blew him up.

This was the sort of thing which was going on in our new sector. The sapper officers had maps of our own tunnels which were accurate in their proximal sections. But the longer your tunnel the less certain you became as to the exactly corresponding surface-points. Still more likely to be 'out' were your maps of the conjectured enemy saps. If your surface map misrepresented the underground position, you would be discredited if eventually your detonation produced a crater in the wrong place.

Not long before our arrival the Germans had exploded a couple of mines a long way away from our front line. The craters appeared somewhere between their own parapet and their wire. The object of this exercise, from the German standpoint, remained a mystery. Bird said that they may have supposed that these craters would additionally protect their front line from night raiders or even daylight attackers.

These mining operations created problems for the infantry normally occupy-ing the front line. The longer and more numerous the tunnels, the greater the volume of excavated debris calling for disposal at the shaft-head. In our area the stuff which the sappers sent up was a glutinous blue clay. This was shovelled into sandbags at the sap-heads. The filled sandbags were then conveyed to the foot of the shaft and hoisted to the surface by winches. They then had to be disposed of. These shafts were vulnerable to artillery. Much damage could be done by destroying the shaft-heads on the surface, thus producing massive blockages and wrecking both the ventilation and pumping machinery so that the shift below was in danger of being suffocated or drowned. Later our men were used as listeners in the galleries. On 2 February 1916 a sudden flooding drowned two. Their bodies were not recovered.

Hence efforts were made to camouflage what was going on at the shaft-head. But the sandbags of blue clay were difficult to conceal. The drill, however, was that these heavy, dripping and slippery objects should be removed by the infantry and deposited as far as possible from the shaft-head. So that quite a lot depended on the conduct and discipline of the infantry as well as on the plans for disposal. The infantry knew well enough that the shaft-head was liable to attract shell-fire from which they would be the first to suffer: they tended to overlook the longer-term consequences for the sappers below of being suffo-cated or drowned. After exposure on the surface in wet or frosty weather, moreover, the sandbags were liable to decompose and burst, smothering every-thing in glutinous mud and making the trenches well-nigh impassable. Hence the relations between the sappers and the infantry were not always of the best.

In the next fortnight my platoon was to become 'the infantry' and we did something, I think, to improve the relations.

It was surprising that the shaft-head was not systematically shelled. It occurred to me that, during this second winter of the war, the restraint of the gunners might have been the result of one of those tacit conventions as to the places shelled and the times at which they were shelled which grew up imperceptibly on both sides. 'The old Hun puts a few into the town hall round eleven on most mornings. Keep away from there about that time' was a type of remark one might hear. If the old Hun had shelled our shaft-head, the position of which he knew exactly, it would have been but a question of minutes before we shelled his. Such conventions suited everyone except the fire-eaters in red hatbands living in chateaux well back. I had been told that such tacit pacts prevailed more widely in the areas held by the French than by us. Bird further told me that something of a gentleman's code had evolved in the saps. There was even a story for which he could not vouch – it had not occurred in his unit – of how a German sapper unsuspectingly picked his way into one of our galleries where he was confronted by a man on listening duty whose unit had only just taken over. Instead of attacking each other the two astonished men shared their rations and withdrew, each undertaking not to use those particular saps again. An improbable story, yet perhaps with a substratum of truth. I asked Bird if he thought there might be an understanding between the gunners not to make life too difficult for the sappers. He said he thought it was possible. Indeed, he hoped that it was so.

On the morning of Tuesday 10 November we marched from Ham-en-Artois to the new area. The 4th Battalion brought up the rear of the entire Guards Division which formed a single column. For three-quarters of an hour we stood by a roadside and watched the march past. A fine sight. This was one of the few occasions during the war that I took in the Division as a corporate whole.

At last we started. No.3 Company led the Battalion. Pearce's platoon came first and mine followed his. We marched from 8 a.m. to 4 p.m. with the usual ten minutes' rest, with packs off, every hour. This was my first Battalion march. These could be taxing for the officers if the men fell out. A man wanting to fall out had to obtain leave from an officer. The request was passed up as a verbal message. One fell back and took a look at the man. Leave having been given, one sat by the roadside with the man and wrote out a note giving his name, platoon and company, declaring that he had leave to fall out and specifying the reason. This written permission the man presented to the Medical Officer when the latter, who marched in rear of the Battalion, came level with him. The Medical Officer would usually arrange for the man's equipment to be carried on one of the horse-drawn transport vehicles which also brought up the rear. As one wrote out this permission squatting by the roadside, one saw out of the corner of one's eye the column moving remorselessly forward so that one's position in it disappeared in the distance. Then one had to catch up at the double. Pearce's platoon in front of mine did badly. Eight men fell out. (Within the next few days, as a sort of punishment, Pearce had to take them for a seven-mile route march.) Only two of my platoon fell out and it happens that I remember their names – Kemp and Hoyle. But their reasons were good. Both had sustained leg injuries. Hoyle had had a pick stuck into his foot and Kemp had been shot in the shin. (In the Second World War, as the Second Battalion's Medical Officer, I would not have passed either of these men as A1. I would have had them down-graded by reason of 'disabilities affecting loco-motion.') In a letter I mentioned a comic incident during this march. Sergeant Melton was marching next to me. Behind us were two educated men – Sergeant Oliver and Corporal Newton – who started a discussion about the relative merits of Hazlitt and Goldsmith. To this exchange, which we could not help overhearing, Melton reacted with ill-concealed disgust. When we passed a partly-restored church Oliver and Newton discussed its date. One of them suggested that it might be six hundred years old. Melton, who had good eyesight, noticed that the restored front door had a date on it. He half turned round and, with a rictus of sarcasm, addressed Sergeant Oliver as follows: 'You great booby, how can it be that old when it has 1857 over the door?'

The day was rainless but overcast and rather cold. At about 4 p.m., when the light began to fail and wraiths of mist appeared over the fields, we reached our destination. The 4th Battalion was scattered about the area of Laventie. No. 3 Company had been allotted to a farm in a hamlet called Fosse which suggested that sometime or other it had bordered a ditch. The place appears on the Hazebrouck/A map which shows houses built round a T-shaped road-junction with some sort of station nearby. No recollection remains of the station; but I have a most vivid mental picture of the farm. This consisted of a quadrangular yard surrounded by farm buildings and a dwelling-house in bad repair. Occupying most of the yard was a massive and fuming midden on which were piled not only straw and the excrement of farm animals but refuse from the household. Before our arrival the farm had been occupied by Indian troops. Officers and other ranks eyed their new quarters with aversion and perhaps wrongly attributed the squalor to the Indians. (These formations were later removed from the Western Front. I was later told that they were clean and well-disciplined. On our march we had passed some turbaned and bearded men grooming horses. They looked haggard, cold and thoroughly miserable. For men accustomed to the sub-tropical heat and sunlight of India, the damp, mist and darkness of a north-European winter must have been a literal hell. What, I wondered, were their sickness rates?) The footway round the midden was deep in mud and fouled by effluent from the central mass on to which buckets of kitchen refuse were regularly emptied. Proposals to clean up the yard were instantly rejected by the *patronne*. How did we expect her to feed her hens? The midden was sacrosanct. A nearby well was the only source of water – brownish in tinge and faintly malodorous. We were grateful for the Battalion water-cart.

The barns which the troops were to occupy were filled with dirty straw which looked louse-infested. Happily, however, some bales of clean stuff had been dumped at the farm so that the first task was to scrub the place out and lay the new straw. There was a grimy farmer-owner and his wife (the *patron* and the *patronne*) who, I gathered, had not liked some of the habits of the Indians and were not cooperative.

I have a further mental picture of this quadrangular yard. Bingo decided that the company should do some arms drill. About two platoons paraded on three sides of the yard, standing at ease on the surrounding footway and facing inwards towards the midden. There they were drilled by C.S.M. Luck, tall, red-faced and with a small head. Standing on the fourth side of the square this fearsome man snarled, growled and roared. Commands mixed with abuse poured out in a raucous volume of explosive sound suggesting feeding time in a menagerie. The *patron* and his wife stood somewhere in the background marvelling. The *patron*, who had done his stint of military service, afterwards told me that he had never heard anything like it. Only Germans, he had thought, could make such noises.

A few further words about this billet. All five of us (Bingo, Clive Piggott, Pearce, Lionel Wilbraham and myself) slept and ate in a single square room with a leaking roof, a projecting hearth and a central round table. In this place I had a febrile attack of some sort, probably an acute gastro-enteritis tentatively ascribed to some brawn which had been sent out to Pearce and had been delayed in transit. I spent a day in my flea-bag on the floor shivering and sweating. I was better on the second day and by the third had completely re-covered. I was visited by Wilfred Raffle, the Battalion's efficient and popular Medical Officer, who first purged me and then sedated me with opium – the only time during my 2½ years with the Battalion that I bothered him as a patient. In the middle of my day on the floor a downpour of rain found its way through the roof just above my emplacement so that I had to move. There was some trouble with Bingo in which I played no part. Though he slept in a sort of side-room, it appeared that he disliked sharing accommodation with the rest of us. Without our knowing it, he tried to get at least two of us moved so that he could feel less crowded at night. His idea was that some of us could shift to another farm about a mile away. It was Pearce who took the initiative. When he indirectly heard of Bingo's plan, he remonstrated, pointing out how impracticable the proposed moves would be. They would much complicate our respective duties in the shift work which had to be closely geared. Bingo said little in reply and the matter was dropped. We remained where we were. I may add that Bingo made no effort to regulate or supervise the company's work. He never took up a shift himself, never went up to the front line where the shift-work was being done, or even inquired what (if anything) had happened when the officer returned after completing a shift. It was

Clive Piggott who buttressed him, who reported, prompted and advised.

During this period Pearce's temper shortened and we all began to find him difficult. For the first few days his and my shifts coincided. We both had to get up at 3.30 a.m., dress by candle-light, eat breakfast and set out together. At this early hour Pearce was at his worst and I found it difficult to avoid idiotic quarrels. During the fortnight at Fosse there had been an issue of rubber thigh-boots. These were sometime difficult to pull on. On one of our later mornings Pearce attacked me because I got into the things too early in the ritual of dressing. At that hour of the morning, he said, the squeaking of the rubber annoyed him. I asked him if he realized how difficult he was. The candle-light exchange was vociferously whispered because the others were trying to sleep. In Pearce's favour I should add that his attacks of ill-temper blew over quickly and he would later good-humouredly apologize.

I need say no more about the farm at Fosse or what went on in it beyond that, during our fortnight there, we did quite a lot to clean and tidy the place up. We improved our mess. The roof was mended and Lionel Wilbraham, with the assistance of a carpenter, ingeniously produced some chairs from wooden barrels. Indeed the *patronne* paid us a compliment when we left. She said we were the best *soldats* she had had planted on her and she wished that all could be like us. Our lot, she said, had not stolen her eggs – or if they had, very few. Not a single chicken had disappeared.

A word about our somewhat unmilitary activities during this fortnight. We were told at the start that our job was to help the sappers. We would be virtu-ally under their orders and they would show us what to do. They worked consecutively on day and night shifts and our shifts were geared to theirs. We had to provide two day and two night shifts, taking our rations with us. The routine was as follows. The two day-shifts would rise from sleep at 3.30 a.m. Together they would march about a mile from the farm to a place called Bout-Deville (Blue Devil to the troops), arriving there at 4.15 a.m. Lorries would arrive at about the same time. These usually appeared after we did and we could hear them grinding and sidling without headlights along the pot-holed roads for some time before their black shapes heaved up in the darkness. The two parties, destined for different mine-heads, would then separate. The lorries – usually two to each party – would take them to different points behind the line. The parties here 'de-bussed' and made their way on foot to the area of work. Their main jobs were pumping (water out of the mine and air into it) and carrying clay-filled sandbags to a place well away from the shaft-head. Dull and dreary work, calling for no supervision by an officer. The work was not continuous: turns would be taken with the pumping; and the winched-up sandbags would appear irregularly at the surface so that there were intervals of inactivity. The night shift was expected to arrive at about 5 p.m. In its return to Fosse the day-shift reversed the morning's drill.

On the first day, which remains vividly in my memory, several things went wrong. Pearce and I had been given to understand that we were going to the same destination. Hence our rations were put up together. We duly marched to Bout-Deville where we waited for the lorries. It was only when these arrived that we grasped that our destinations were different. Pearce was carrying the two parties' rations packaged together and there was trouble over dividing them. He went off with them all. We piled into our respective lorries and began the perilous transit. The road was dreadful – numerous deep pot-holes, several large shell-holes and ditches on each side. There being no lights, the driver had to feel his way. We proceeded noisily and slowly, swerving and lurching, the vehicles being top-heavy with troops. The drivers, who were familiar with the route, knew where the really bad places were; but they did not know what new death-traps might have been prepared by shell-fire since their last drive.

On arrival at the de-bussing point I was met by a R.E. Officer by the name of Percy who, it quickly transpired, had only just joined his unit and knew nothing about the sector or the routine. We could, he told me, get up to the line by a sunken road or by a communicating trench. I asked which was usually taken. He didn't know. What did he advise? Hesitatingly he recommended the communicating trench. The party was carrying planks and gun-cotton. If, he said, a machine-gun bullet hit a wad of gun-cotton, it would do more than just dust the mud off your tunic. Into the trench Percy and I accordingly led the party. Much mud. After some struggling and wallowing in the gradually waxing daylight we met a nondescript individual who, pointing backwards over his shoulder with his thumb, laconically remarked: 'Plenty of water along there.' Neither Percy nor I then grasped the full force of this remark. But as we moved forward, the mud turned into a soup, at first concentrated in pools a few inches deep then into a continuous and deepening canal. Then plop! down to over your boots and the water trickled in. (Thigh boots had not yet been issued.) Wet feet for the rest of the day. The water in the trench deepened till it was just below your knees. No joke for the carrying party with their planks and guncotton. The trench branched to the right and a current flowed downwards from in front round the bend. On we went against the current. Swoosh and I was in well above my knees. Impossible, I decided to go on. In front was a derelict house providing slight cover. Though Percy warned against the danger – a German machine-gunner took altogether too much interest in the derelict building – we climbed out and made for a wall along which ran another communicating trench with less water. This trench, into which we clambered down, later opened, like the upright of a letter T, into a trench crossing ours at right angles. In the half-light gaunt forms defined themselves. They wore woollen balaclava helmets and mittens. They were stamping and blowing with cold, flapping their arms against their sides and cursing. 'Oo are you?' 'Coldstream. Oo are you?' 'Sixtieth.' It turned out that they were a recently formed unit, far removed from the regimental fountainhead and its exacting traditions.

Percy and I had been joined by an R. E. Corporal who led us to a dug-out – or rather shelter – in another communicating trench further along. The Corporal poked his head in and addressed a recumbent figure: 'The second party of thirty men arrived, Sir.' No response. Statement repeated louder. A faint stir. 'What party?' 'The second party of thirty men, Sir, what couldn't come by road, Sir. Two officers outside now, Sir.' 'Oh damn. Tell them to come in.' In we went.

The recumbent figure turned out to be Lieutenant Bird in charge of mining operations. With reluctance he pulled himself out of a sheath of blankets and other coverings, thus causing a noisy scampering and scattering of mice. A man of about 35, face, hands and uniform plastered with mud. The dug-out, about 4½ feet high, contained a chair a table and a bed about 6 inches above the floor. On the table was a bird-cage containing a canary. The canary had a military purpose. It was used in the mine. When the air became sufficiently contaminated, it lost consciousness and fell off its perch. In the meantime it was on good terms with the mice; and so was Bird who enjoyed feeding them. Indeed, he had named two of them which would almost take food out of his hand.

Bird cannot have been overjoyed to have on his hands a foodless officer for the whole of a working day. But he did not show it. Nothing could have exceeded his hospitality. He shared his food and his tea for which there was but one mug. And he explained the system of reliefs. Why, I wondered, had not all this been made clear at the Battalion level? Doubtless a bog in the take-over.

I spent most of the day in Bird's dug-out listening to the occasional chirping of the canary. I also took a look at the main sap. Bird had gone down and, after some hesitation, I decided to follow him. I climbed down a thirty-five-foot steel ladder at the bottom of which opened a gallery about 3½ feet high and 3 feet wide. Every ten yards or so, glass-framed candles stuck into the revetted sides were guttering. Water on the floor. With bent back, stooping low, I moved along the corridor intending to catch Bird up. After covering some sixty yards, my back began to ache. I must stop somewhere to straighten up. But where? No facility visible. No stops with raised ceilings where one could stand up and stretch. No dry places where one could lie flat. For a spell I lowered myself like a quadruped on to hands and knees. My hands were under water and my knees got more wet. Impossible to proceed on all fours. I tried waddling with bent legs and body upright, like an anthropoid ape. But I could not do more than ten yards at a time. I pushed on for another forty or fifty yards till I thought my back would break. I then paused and listened. Perfect silence except for the guttering of a candle and the dripping of water. Then in the distance I heard a faint scraping sound. A long way off. More likely, I thought, to be our noise than the Germans! But in my half-broken state it seemed too far to investigate. What an ass I had been, I thought, not to have stuck closer to Bird who might now be anywhere in the underground maze. 'Go back,' I said to myself. The return journey seemed endless and at one moment I felt I was going to collapse. Was it just my spine, I wondered. Might it be the polluted air? Might I topple over like the canary from its perch? Or perhaps it was just funk. My progress became slower and more intermittent so that it was with considerable relief that I finally descried something that might be a shaft of daylight at the far end of the candle-lit tunnel. On reaching the foot of the ladder, it took me some minutes to straighten up. Thankfulness! Thank God! God bless and reward all miners!

Later I explained my tribulations to Bird who laughed amiably. He told me that at first most people found the back-bending a torture, especially if you had not begun it as a youngster. In time you got used to it. Now he could move fast and far without fatigue. Many miners, I recollected, though tough and strong, developed round shoulders from the prolonged stooping underground. By the time we parted, I was deeply in debt to Bird. In return for his shared rations and perfect hospitality I sent him some books and a hamper of food. He occupies a place in my private gallery of saints.

The night shift was due to arrive at 5.30 p.m. but did not turn up till 6.30. We returned along the sunken road (never again that communicating trench!) without mishap. The lorries were waiting and took us back to Bout-Deville, whence we marched to our farm arriving at 7 p.m.

I add that Fosse was not shelled while we were there and that, compared with Vermelles, this was a quiet sector. The trenches were much improved later when the Division had occupied them for a few weeks.

Life at Fosse strengthened earlier scruples about how different were the active-service lives of officers and other ranks. The routine during No. 3 Company's attachment to the sappers was that the officers' duties were confined to marching their parties to Bout-Deville where they saw them embussed. The officer then came back. He took no part in the working day. Indeed, he would have been *de trop* as I had been when Bird's guest. While the other ranks were pumping water up and air down, and struggling to carry slimy sandbags along squalid trenches, we officers sat back in the fire-warmed mess doing nothing. What, I wondered, did the other ranks think of the detached and pampered life led by their officers, each with a whole-time servant whose sole job it was to look after him. I tentatively asked Clive Piggott, who felt much as I did, if it would be possible for me to do a shift with my platoon. He said that it was out of the question and might be badly received by everyone – warrant officers, NCO's and other ranks. The latter, he said, did not expect – or want – their officers to live as they did. Clive was, I am sure, right – at least for that time and place. There was probably less egalitarianism in the Brigade than anywhere else in the army. Whether the same holds today I doubt. Like many other things, the relationship between officers and other ranks may have been

Americanized or, as the Americans might say, 'democratized.' Anyhow, this consciousness of inaction and non-participation in unpleasant duties contributed to my feeling that the fortnight at Fosse was an unedifying period of the war, so that I was not sorry to move.

*   *   *   *

The dreary winter months of 1915–16 evoke confused memories of featureless and misty scenery, of a struggle against stagnant and rising water, of an occasionally ice-bound countryside when the pools on the roads crackled under one's feet, of crumbling trenches and, above all else, of mud. At the geographical centre was a semi-demolished township without amenities, but offering dryness and shelter.

Few of us, I think, properly grasped (I certainly didn't till later in the war) how small was the corner of France in which we were operating. The distance between the different 'fronts' – Ypres, Arras, Armentières, the Somme – seemed vastly greater than they really were. When we were bogged down in the Ypres Salient, the rolling chalky downs of the Somme seemed way to the south – as far as, in peacetime, the Loire might seem from Paris.

The reality was quite different. After the war of movement ended in 1914, the sector held by the British army extended from Ypres (its northern-most point, where between it and the sea, it was flanked by French and Belgians) to Combles, west of the Bapaume-Péronne road in the south – a distance of some 65 miles. Laventie, where we now found ourselves, was no more than some seventeen miles south of Ypres.

A word about the geographical features and drainage of north-eastern France. If you look at a map you will see that, roughly between Abbeville and Ostend, the coast-line makes a nipple-like bulge pointing north-west into the sea. The northern-most point or tip of the bulge is Cap Gris-Nez between Calais and Boulogne. It is from Cap Gris-Nez, which confronts Dover across some 25 miles of water, that Channel swimmers take off from France.

If you are driving back to England from Belgium your course may take you to Calais or Boulogne. The approaches to these two familiar places differ. That to Calais is flat; but your road descends rather steeply into Boulogne. You cross a pleasant range of low hills. These rise out of the sea at Cap Gris-Nez, between Calais and Boulogne, and extend south-east in a wide hammock-shaped curve which enclosed a large part of the British theatre of war. This undulating belt of higher ground varies in breadth, forming throughout its course a watershed which affected the daily lives of the British soldiery. Between Arras, which has low hills to the east, and Abbeville-sur-Somme (some 50 miles to the south-west, not far from the river's estuary) the hilly belt is wide. Further to the south-east the belt narrows to about 20 miles. On and about these undulating and low hills the battles of the Somme were fought. Further to the east, the belt of higher ground rises and widens; and after you cross the valley of the Meuse, some 70 miles from Péronne, you move into the higher regions of Luxemburg.

This hammock-shaped belt of high ground, which widens and rises as you proceed south and east, determines the drainage and direction of the rivers of our theatres of war. In the lowlands west of the belt the general direction of their flow is north-westwards. The Liane debouches at Boulogne; and the Somme debouches about 65 miles further south at Abbeville. The low-lying country, intersected by canals, round the Belgian Field Hospital, my 'theatre' during the first half of 1915, lies to the east and north of the hammock of hills, and drains into the Yser which flows into the North Sea at Nieuport. The region further south – that of Laventie and Ypres – drains into the Lys and Schelde. These rivers flow sinuously through low country much intersected by canals (some navigable by barges) north-east into Belgium. They converge and join at Ghent. The Lys, a tributary, here loses its identity to the Schelde which, continuing on a north-easterly course, skirts Antwerp and debouches into the estuary of the Schelde from which our shelducks derive their name.

Hence, when at Laventie and later at Ypres, we laboured to drain the water from stagnant ditches and brimming shellholes, we were assisting the outraged river-gods to re-establish their erstwhile flow to the north-east. We were coaxing the reluctant waters to move towards a distant estuary frequented by large placid black and white birds who knew nothing of the nearby war.

On 24 November, No.3 Company was pulled back from the outlying hamlet of Fosse to the more central locality of Laventie – a place just big enough to be recorded on large-scale maps of France. It was a short march at the end of which we were relieved to find that this place was less demolished than we expected. The cathedral was mostly rubble. No priests remained; no religious offices were performed. But the surrounding streets were little damaged. There were no viable shops, but a few civilians moved about. No.3's officers' mess had been located by the Billeting Officer in quite a respectable-looking farm-house with a muddy courtyard in front, about a hundred yards from the demolished cathedral. Somehow responsible for the house was an ageing care-taker, a stooping black-clad man, who occasionally put in an appearance and with whom I later conducted friendly business dealings in French.

My narrative of the winter months is dull. I had better begin by trying to describe the conditions in which we lived and worked. The war in this sector being mainly directed against the weather and the terrain, the front line was less a system of trenches than of breastworks. It is quicker to dig a trench than to build up a breastwork, and when the area was first occupied trenches were dug. But these soon fell in and became water-logged, so that sandbags and wood came into demand. Such trenches as continued to be used either as holding positions or for communication had to be boarded underfoot, revetted at the sides and built up above ground by sandbags. There was, for the most part, a single frontal position. It consisted of a line of breastworks through which you could keep watch and shoot. The view through one of these loop-holes was not inspiring. Across a stretch of no-man's-land you beheld a conspicuous line of enemy breastworks which looked pale grey in the middle distance. This line wound its way out of sight to your left and right, sometimes approaching our positions and sometimes retreating, so as to enclose a no-man's-land of variable width. At the foot of both lines ran narrow belts of rusty wire which looked dark against the grey sandbags beyond. And between these two belts lay a mostly featureless waste, patched with dead goosefoot and docks and pocked with shell-holes, the deeper ones half-filled with slimy water. The panorama was dreary; yet it could convey a latent vitality. A confrontation, winding away into seeming infinity on each side, alive with watchfulness. There was menace in the confrontation. Death could strike you. It could come from quite near, from a visible point somewhere just beyond the goosefoot and shell-holes, in a straight beady line, or it could suddenly shriek down in a descending trajectory from beyond the range of your vision.

By day the view through the slit was static and drab, though you could feel the latent menace. But at night, when you could survey things from a standing position on the parapet, the panorama could be suddenly transformed. Far away on the horizon could appear a gun-flash, soundless and remote, shrouded by mist or reflected downwards by low-hanging cloud. Or, if moonless, the night could be abruptly transformed by a magical brightness. Our star-shells or Very lights were more rocket-like than the Germans'. Theirs would rise less visibly and less noisily, without leaving a trail of sparks. They would hover twinkling to a slow pulse. The light of star-shells was mostly welcome; more welcome than the danger they incurred was disturbing. But not always. If you were in no-man's-land, or standing on a parapet, the sudden stark visibility induced paralysis so that, if you hadn't thrown yourself down, you froze, pretending to be a tree-stump. To my knowledge I was never purposefully shot at under a star-shell. In consequence I came to regard them as almost wholly benign. I delighted in how they instantaneously banished the pall of night and threw into startling relief every feature of the surrounding landscape. Our type of star-shell differed from theirs in how it came down. Theirs would fade out in the sky and descend invisibly; ours would remain alight as they plunged and spluttered down to earth, often emitting their last flicker on the ground through a pall of ground-mist, leaving behind a sort of void.

Star-shells entered vividly into our lives till the end of the war and were taken for granted. I had seen them far off in the eastern sky when, earlier in 1915, I had been serving with the Belgian Field Hospital. But this winter, at Laventie, was the first time that I had stood below while they spired and nictitated over-head. As they looked down on you from the sky, you could, during your early acquaintance, think of them as the probing eyes of a demonic luminary or as celestial torches blessing from aloft a scarred and darkened world. It depended on your mood at the time and on whether or not they defined you as a target. I did not myself fire a Very light till I was in the Second Battalion in 1918.

But at this stage of the war No.3 Company was no less familiar with the scenery immediately behind the line than with no-man's-land beyond. Landmarks of this dank landscape were the skeletons of demolished farms lying amid torn and uprooted trees, and the jagged outlines of what had been road-side poplars.

The Battalion's main job was to keep communications in repair. Our activities were partly under the direction of Royal Engineers, upon whom many demands were made. We were liable to be disconcertingly switched from one job to another. Officers especially were moved about at short notice between the Companies for different kinds of repair work. The communicating trenches had mostly been dug in dry weather. But as the year advanced they slowly filled with water and caved in. Sandbags, wood, pickets and other ironmongery were accumulated in rear depots which looked rather like timbermen's yards. Thence they were transported by motor vehicles to dumps located as far forward as possible; whence carrying parties took them to their final destinations where they were put to use in the war against erosion and mud.

In the Loos sector, where advances had been made into German positions, the 'front line' (often a series of posts sometimes in echelon) was reached through seemingly unending communicating trenches. These formed a deep labyrinth in which one could get lost. Much of the network consisted of old German communicating trenches. But in the Laventie sector which had been static there was little behind the single line of breastworks. A few communicating trenches, long and in bad repair, led up to the frontal positions. These approaches were spaced at quite wide intervals and when you moved up and down you found that some stretches were more passable than others. All were freely used by night when the reliefs took place; several were also usable by day. Churned by many boots, the earth at the bottom turned first into porridge and then into soup till finally what had been a viable trench became a ribbon of water, which when used as a latrine turned patchily yellow.

It was no use laying wooden duckboards on such a base. You had first to drive piles of three-by-two timber into the bottom and then nail the duckboards on to the piles. Judgement was needed on how much of the pile you left above the surface. You did not want your duckboards to be submerged by further seepages and collapses of the sides. At the same time you did not want the flooring to be so high that the heads of people would be visible as they walked along.

The sides of the trenches, moreover, had to be revetted. The 'hurdles' used for this purpose consisted of uprights of three-by-two timber with boards nailed across, making flat surfaces. The lower ends of the uprights were sharpened so that they could be hammered into the soft floor of the trench on each side of, but leaning away from, the duckboards which ran between. The upper ends of the uprights were wired to 'anchor pickets' driven into the ground on each side of the trench, outside the parapet. (This lateral parapet was, as time passed, increasingly built up with earth taken from 'borrow-pits' outside.) But these anchoring wires had to run *through (not over)* the earth of the parapet. If they were laid *over*, the anchor wire, which was under tension, worked its way downwards through the heaped-up earth, the hurdle sagged inwards, and it was not long before the trench fell in.

Since the trenches had usually been dug before the revetting parties got to work, this wiring back of the hurdles could be well or shoddily done. The most laborious method was for a man to scrape with a pick a channel in the parapet to take the anchoring wire. It was also the most dangerous, for the man wielding the pick had to stand on the parapet where he could stop stray bullets. The Battalion had some casualties in this way, as mentioned below. The officer in charge who had to see that the wiring-back was properly done was especially exposed.

It called for no great stroke of genius to see how this difficulty could be solved. With the aid of a six or seven foot skewer or bodkin, pointed at one end and eyed (like a needle) at the other, you could transfix the parapet, drawing the wire through. I vaguely recall discussing this manoeuvre with Stephen Burton, our second-in-command, and also (a clearer memory) with the Armourer-Sergeant. The same idea had, I think, occurred to the R.E.s, so that I cannot claim credit. Anyhow, the needed implements were soon available. With their aid, revetting could be done more quickly, efficiently and safely. But these giant skewers were not as easy to carry up and down as picks or shovels; and they could cause accidents in the dark. I eventually came to an under-standing about a dump with such troops as were static at a nearby point, so that we could leave these unwieldy objects near the sites where they were used. Likewise with mauls – heavy, iron-bound, wooden mallets which were used for driving in pickets and stakes. These were unwieldy burdens on the up and down marches and we were glad to be able to leave them near the work-sites. None to my knowledge were lost or (to use a then current expression) scrounged.

Other troubles appeared as the winter advanced and the weather got colder. Trench braziers were improvised and the demand for fuel grew. The wooden cross-pieces of duckboards and the boarding of hurdles burned well, and once the discovery was made that these materials could be prized off, they quickly disappeared. Little could be done to stop these depredations towards which blind eyes were turned. No one would admit responsibility. It was worst in severe frosts. 'You won't suffer for this as long as the cold spell lasts,' people would be told, 'but after the next thaw these trenches will be impassable and you will have casualties on the top.' So they did. But not necessarily those who despoiled the revetments. There was talk of using corrugated iron, but I don't remember its coming to much. Metal was more used, I think, by the Germans than by us. It was exasperating to come up to a section of communicating trench on which you had put in good work to find it stripped and ruined.

In summary, the war during this winter was waged less against the Germans, who were happy enough to be left alone and who did not go in much for retaliation, as against the environment. Much of the time you were wet and there were periods of great physical exhaustion. The nights could seem endless. A bombardment, an air battle, a prolonged burst of machine-gun fire, a salvo of star-shells could mitigate the tedium. Such spasms of activity could come as a diversion and a relief.

A day or two after we had moved in, Guy Edwards, then Adjutant, paid a visit to the farm building where No.3's officers messed. He had fixed up his orderly room in a butcher's shop across the road. Guy (known to most people as George) was sensitive to cold and the empty shop had no fireplace or means of heating. One of the rooms of our farm, giving on to the courtyard, had a fireplace and the thought had occurred to George that it would do nicely as his orderly room.

George was a tall, clean-shaven, soldierly and good-looking man with a lean figure and rather square face, correct in everything. Outside England lived foreigners who, for him, were of little interest. George could speak no foreign language. His three main life-interests were hunting, cricket and soldiering. He would take a long time to dress when he got up. Overton-Jones, who later shared a hut with him, told me that first thing in the morning, before shaving, he would spend quite a time scrubbing his forehead. At first he tended to treat me as something of a comic turn. A bit later in the war I slowly read *Bleak House* – not a short book. Whenever George met me he would ask what page I had reached. In due course I acquired a considerable affection and respect for this man who showed me many kindnesses.

It was after we had arrived in Laventie that George discovered that I could speak French. He then requisitioned my services as interpreter between himself and the caretaker of our farm. The subject of discussion was the empty fireplace in the projected orderly room. Could a fire be lit? Yes, we were told, provided certain precautions were taken. Lighted fires could be dangerous in a bombardment. There was talk about buckets and sand. The upshot was that George decided to move in. To make way, I had to move out; but I could, if I liked, sleep in a local butcher's shop.

I took a look at the place. It was empty and clean. No meat anywhere. Behind the shop there was a sort of inner living-room which had been decorated with wallpaper and had some simple furniture. The main drawback was that it had no window to the outside. The room opened in a short passage between the marble-slabbed but empty shop in front and a small yard behind. No daylight and no means of heating. But it would provide peace and quiet. A good place to retire to from an uncongenial mess.

In this billet I was installed by Temple, my admirable servant, who managed to fit himself nicely into an opening from the passage. There we remained for some two months. I bought a large oil lamp which provided both light and warmth, albeit that the warmth was stuffy in the daytime when the lamp was lit and the door closed.

No sooner had I moved that I was attached to No.1 Company. I continued to live in the butcher's shop but to have most of my meals in No.3's mess. But I also became a member of No.1's mess which was located about 400 yards down the road which ran from the cathedral past No.3's headquarters.

Not long before my attachment, No.1 had been taken over by Jimmy Coats who presented a total contrast to Bingo. Jimmy was a good-looking and rich young man who had enjoyed himself at Oxford where he had done as little work as possible. He was a Roman Catholic and had been to Downside. Of light build, he was a keen steeplechaser and an outstandingly successful performer on the Cresta Run at St. Moritz. After the war he went in for and won the main event many times. He was cheerful and outspoken, liked by everyone and a good soldier. In mid-1916 he transferred to the Second Battalion and in due course helped me to do the same. For nigh on three years he was that Battalion's Adjutant in which position he was a pillar of strength.

The other officers were Geoffrey Howard, known to most people as Longshanks, W. S. B. Bosanquet (of whom more below), H.C. Thompson (later died of wounds), and E. Blundell, aged 56, and known to the world as 'The General'. This aristocratic middle-age man – he wore a distinguished white moustache – set a fine example to all ranks; but he could scarcely have been called the best platoon commander in the Battalion. His platoon was known as 'the General's Lambs'. Most sharply contrasted were the personalities of Jimmy and Bingo and the atmospheres of their respective messes. In No.1, champagne, whisky and old brandy flowed freely to the accompaniment of badinage, boisterous laughter and high spirits. In No.3 Bingo did not stint himself in *vin ordinaire*, but it did not make him cheerful. On the contrary it soured his humour so that, towards the end of a meal, his face began to turn dark red and he would silently glower round between hunched shoulders at anyone who ventured on more than a casual remark. Usually ill-humour accumulated till it burst out. Lionel and I were the chief recipients until Quincey Greene arrived in early February. He then had more than his share.

In those days I did not smoke or drink alcohol, so that I was not entirely at my ease in the ebullience of No.1. When you don't join in the drinking going on round you, you tend to get left behind and feel out of place. Bawdy stories strike you as silly rather than funny. But you don't want to be a drag, so you pretend to be amused. However, the fumes of cigars and alcohol in No.1 were preferable to the opaque gloom of No.3. But I was not at my ease at meals in either mess and so preferred the solitude of my butcher's shop where Temple would leave a cup of cocoa in a thermos. It was a difficult period and the others were forbearing. I recall Lionel coming in one evening and mildly remonstrating. Why didn't I feed in the mess? My reaction was uncouth. I just shook my head. They put my trouble down to Robin's death and up to a point they may have been right.

I well recall my first night with No.1. The communicating trenches in our sector were randomly christened. Some had English names such as North Elgin Street, Winchester Street or Rotten Row. Some had French names such as the Rue Tilleroy, Rue Baquerot, Rue Fauquisart – mostly local place-names. Rotten Row was our objective on this first night. The whole company turned out and I marched up in the rear. It was pitch dark at first on this December night, but round about seven o'clock a yellow moon headed up through the mist. The task allotted to my platoon was to relay the revetments of a section of trench which had earlier been worked on by the General's Lambs. The anchoring wires attached to the uprights of the hurdles had been laid *over* instead of *through* the parapet, so that the hurdles had already begun to sag inwards. Our job was to take out the hurdles and to re-wire them properly. (This was before the introduction of the bodkin.) Fairly soon after our arrival the moon rose and things became lively. Plenty of rifle fire and fairly frequent bursts of machine-gun fire from in front and to the right. Most of the men were working and all the officers were standing on the parapet. Towards the end of our four-hour stint the half-expected thing happened. With a soft sound a bullet seemed to stop in mid-air. A shout went up: 'Officer hit. Mr. Howard.' I thought at first that Longshanks had been hit. But it was Bosanquet, whom I found sitting on his haunches in a shell-hole clutching his stomach. Longshanks and I gave him first aid, which didn't amount to much. The bullet had hit him below his left ribs and come out a bit lower on the other side. Entry and exit wounds were clean. Little bleeding. But movement was painful enough to make it difficult to lift him on to a stretcher. When he later arrived at a hospital it was found that things could have been much worse. Eventually his recovery was sufficiently complete for him to return to duty and he put in five more months of active and creditable service before the end of the war.

Bosanquet's experience pointed to the usefulness of the bodkin in revetting operations. Don't stand about on the top more than you can help, especially in bright moonlight when things are apt to be lively. On our way back from Rotten Row on that first night a man walking close to me in rear was hit by a stray bullet in the calf. 'A perfectly delightful wound,' was Thompson's comment.

A couple of nights later I learned the hard way what a difference the weather could make. I had been told by Stephen Burton to take up a platoon of No.1 and repair as much as I could of a communicating trench which was in a bad way. A storm had broken before we started and a gale was blowing gusts of rain horizontally into us. Stooping, with heads bent forward, fronting the rain with our tin hats, we battled our way up in pitch darkness. I did not look forward to what we would find when we got there . In the event we found that much of the trench was crumbling into a morass. In the worst places the simplest locomotion – the placing of one foot into the mud in front of the other foot and then lugging out the rear foot – was a task which, laboriously and slowly repeated, somewhat reminded me of Sysiphus. The filling of a sandbag could take up to ten minutes. The glutinous clay stuck to your shovel so that you had to push it into the sandbag with your hands. After about an hour some men gave up trying to use a shovel at all. Better pick the stuff up with your hands. It was not long before my heavy rubber (Cording) waterproof had let the water through in a big way, before my glasses were opaque with rain and mud, and before my handkerchief was soaking from the effort to keep my glasses clean. By this time the men's overcoats were soaked through. As the unrelenting weather continued, the work slowed down and eventually reached a standstill. I struggled up and down trying to help the small knots of men with my Orilux torch. But after about an hour and a half the electric light began to give out; and the men would stop working when I had passed them with my torch. Good men who ordinarily worked well sat disconsolately, exhausted, shivering and coughing in the worsening conditions. I then compellingly realized how awkward the officer's task could be. I was expected to keep them at it. But you were expecting them to do more than you could do yourself. Should I give up and lead them home? You didn't want it said of you or your platoon (or, for that matter, your regiment) that they would only work in fine weather. After a to and fro argument with myself, I finally decided that it would be moral cowardice to keep them sitting about for another hour and a half in these conditions. I wished that Stephen Burton could take a two-minute look. He might be less likely to say that the officer in charge was no good. I consulted the Platoon Sergeant (Sgt. Ward, I think). His opinion was: 'We can't do no good up here in these conditions.' So I knocked them off and marched them home. Before dismissing them in the still continuing rain, I briefly addressed them. I said that they were in no way to blame. They, no more than I, liked walking away from an uncompleted job before the time was up. But the responsibility was mine, not theirs. All the more reasons for us all to do our best when, in the future, working conditions were good.

I felt guilty in leaving them to doss down in their soaking uniforms while I crept back to my warm billet. As I changed into dry things and drank a mug of hot cocoa from my thermos which was waiting for me, I felt thoroughly miserable. But there was no trouble on the morrow. Burton was not entirely pleased, but he said he thought I had done the right thing.

A consecutive account of the mostly trivial happenings which, during this winter, composed our lives would be of no interest. I shall therefore confine myself to a few events which have stuck in my memory.

One of the best remembered events was Christmas Day. I was in charge of a working party at a shaft-head called Ducks Bill to which I had come up on

Christmas Eve. Opposite the shaft the German breastworks were near enough for verbal exchange to be possible between the two sides. It was difficult to follow most of the dialogue, but I recall someone shouting across: 'What have you got for dinner today Fritz?' The reply sounded like 'a fat goose' (more Germans spoke English than our people spoke German). Fritz was invited to come over, but at this stage there was no movement. When dawn was breaking our relief arrived and I left. The relief consisted of a mixed party in which were a few men in my platoon (No. 11). That evening one of these told me what had happened. Loudening noises of shouting and singing came across no-man's-land, and when there was enough daylight figures could be seen moving about between their breastworks and wire. Our people followed suit. The Germans then came out in front of their wire. Our people did the same. No shooting anywhere. Both sides then gained in boldness until there was quite a crowd in no-man's-land. The man in my platoon told me that he had shaken hands with at least 300 Germans – doubtless an enormous exaggeration. 'Peace and Goodwill quite reigned, Sir,' he said with mock sententiousness. The two sides exchanged cigarettes and other souvenirs, including buttons and badges. My informant exchanged photographs with a German who said he was a Prussian and a sniper. The photograph, which he showed me, was of a big man in a soft cap and trench boots reaching up to his knees standing by his rifle. The Germans seemed anxious to show photographs of their families – parents, wives and children. The Germans took a lively interest in our equipment, especially in the fine leather jerkins which had been issued to all ranks not long before, and in our long rubber trench boots reaching up to the thigh. They chattered volubly among themselves as they closely examined these invaluable articles (for which someone in high authority deserved credit), fingering them, feeling their texture and comparing them favourably with their own equipment. *'Bon'*, many said, pointing at the leather jerkins, having acquired the same pidgin French as our men. I was told that a German officer came out and took a photograph of a mixed party with linked arms.

Another later informant was a Sapper officer in charge of the mining operations at Ducks Bill, all of whose men had come up from underground for the occasion. A smartly dressed German officer who looked as if he belonged to the staff appeared. (He had been described by the man in my platoon as 'a proper knut', with a turned up moustache.) This fellow was seen standing with one foot on a prostrate tree-trunk, calmly smoking a cigarette through a long holder and amusedly surveying the unusual scene. My Sapper informant, grimy with mud, approached him. The two saluted each other politely and entered into a disjointed conversation in which they were joined by another junior officer. 'How much longer,' the dapper German is said to have asked, 'is this war going on for?' 'For as long,' the Sapper replied, 'as you remain in France and Belgium. How long do you think that will be?' 'Many of us,' the German is said to have replied after a pause, 'would like to move out now. But the likelihood is that we will have to stay until you drive us out – if you can.'

The conversation, which was amiable, went on for about five minutes. It was brought to an end by a burst of shrapnel overhead. The story later current was that a British staff officer of senior rank had come up. Scandalized by what he saw, he telephoned to the gunners to take action. After the bang which hurt nobody, everyone scuttled back to their trenches. There was no more fraternization. But after dark there were sounds of jollification opposite which culminated in the short appearance on the German parapet of a feebly illuminated Christmas tree.

Most of the above reached me by hearsay and I don't know how much truth the stories contained. They sound improbable, but are, I suppose, possible. A different view may have been taken by the German higher command than by ours of truces and palavers. (My cousin Ernest Devaux who during the first war had been a staff officer in the German army – he took part in the Battle of Gumbinnen against the Russians in mid-August 1914 – told me that when he was ordered to the Western Front in 1915, he marched himself into the presence of his army commander – whom he had known personally before the war – and asked that he should not be posted opposite the British. His parents were English, he said, and he had many English relatives. The army commander fully approved of his sentiments and his application was granted.)

But to return to Ducks Bill. The supposition that this way of celebrating Christmas did not commend itself to our higher command is perhaps supported by the fact that, at the next Christmas (of 1916/17), orders went out that a lively fire should be kept up all day. But of this perhaps more later.

The impulse to fraternize was understandable. Though most soldiers were receptive to the indoctrination of hatred and had no scruples whatever about killing Germans, they knew that at bottom the men opposite were much like themselves and had to put up with the same hardships. They too had relatives at home. Both sides professed to be Christians. No harm in spending a few hours of the day held sacred by both sides in putting a little Christianity into practice. Anyhow, goodwill to all men, though unmilitary, was a change from bayonet drill and various other forms of killing, which could become tedious.

When I was beginning to get to know something about No.1 Company, I was moved to No.2, commanded by Mike Peto. But I saw little of that splendid man because the jobs to which I was assigned were put under the direction of Stephen Burton, the Battalion's Second-in-Command. Skeff, the Commanding Officer, rarely came up. Indeed he never once came near me during this stage of our work at Laventie.

It was not long before I was on quite good terms with Stephen (familiarly and, I think, inappropriately known as Boggie) Burton – a cheerful unceremonious man who had been twice wounded. (He was later killed.) He used to visit by day the places where work had been done the night before and would then decide what jobs were to be done next. I made a habit of going up with him when possible, even though this meant two visits in the twenty-four hours to the same site. Stephen would ride up as far as he could on horseback and I would go by bicycle. When on the sites I would listen to his comments on the previous night's work which, if favourable or encouraging, I would pass on to the sections concerned. And I would take note of what he wanted done on that same night. Several tasks might be assigned varying in magnitude and toughness. In this way I could decide beforehand how to instruct and distribute the men I was to take up that evening.

When, round about dusk, these were on parade I would tell them that I had been up to the site of work earlier that day and that there were several jobs to be done. (Multiple tasks were commonly assigned in this particular trench which was in fair shape.) Some of the tasks were longer and tougher than others. If a party assigned to a short job finished it before the rest, they must not feel aggrieved if they were shifted to help finish the tougher jobs. When the assignment had been properly completed all could knock off whatever the time by the clock, so that the closer together and the quicker they worked, the sooner we would all be back.

During this explanation, they would all listen attentively: and later there would be no comments such as: 'We've done our stint: why should we have to finish other people's?' And before marching them off I would form them up so that the parties detailed for each job would be in the form of a column (or file, since we would be proceeding up a trench) when the party came abreast of its working site. These parties would be successively peeled off as we moved along the trench. The results were good. Everyone worked hard and together, so that we usually finished before the statutory four and a half hours.

A word about a particular night's work which I clearly remember because of its unusual perfection. I marched up with Sergeant Padley, who had been commended to me by Mike Peto. Padley had taken part in the Battle of Mons and spoke of the Germans without animus. I noticed the quiet way he talked to his platoon wherein he was obviously respected. Indeed I received the impression that the men worked hard partly to please him. The night passed in almost uncanny harmony. A full moon poised in a cloudless sky shone down so brilliantly that my Orilux was never used. Yet there was neither small-arms fire nor gunfire. To the north and to the south a placid horizon. It was as if the war had been suspended – or had ended. Nor was there any wind. Perfect stillness reigned, the only sounds being those of digging – the occasional grating of a shovel on a stone, the breathing of the diggers as they heaved, the whisper of fresh earth falling on earth newly cast up. No words spoken. The silent diggers seemed to discover a collective rhythm which carried them forward at the same tempo, like oarsmen. Neither I nor Sergeant Padley had anything to do. We stood still on the top. The work did itself. A sense of inner well-being seemed to be communicated from the placid sky, like a benediction or like a gift which, in some mysterious way, had been earned by No.2 Company and by Sergeant Padley.

Early in December a change took place in No.3's mess. We lost Pearce. On returning to my billet one evening I was told by Temple that he had been blown up by what at that stage of the war was called a 'coal box' (a medium-sized shell which exploded noisily and emitted black smoke: other such shells were called Jack Johnsons and Hairy Marys) that had landed six feet away knocking him out and burying him. When extricated he was found to be unwounded but stone deaf. As soon as I could I went round to see him in his billet. I found him radiant. But he couldn't hear a word unless I bawled at him.

He was evacuated next day. I had mixed feelings about his departure. He was a cultivated man, a few years older than myself. He could be most charming when in a good temper and if he liked you. But he was subject to moods and when in a bad one he could be surprisingly disagreeable and, in the daily round, inconsiderate. He probably thought I was callow and pretentious and that a few snubs now and then would do me no harm. Several times he said wounding things. But I would have liked to have kept in touch with him.

On 22 December a peculiar thing happened. I put under arrest and sent back three men who were drunk on duty. I was still attached to No.2 Company and Sergeant Padley was again with me. We had been given a job of trench repair. All went well at first. But after we had been at it for a couple of hours, I noticed that in one place the work was not getting ahead. I commented on the slowness to Sergeant Padley who said that he had noticed the same. So I took a closer look. In charge of the section was Corporal Carthews, an educated man who, I thought, might have been eligible for a Commission. I noticed that a man called Wotton in his section, who was working on the parapet, could hardly stand. He kept cursing the sandbags. 'Damned slippery, these bags, bloody slippery, damned slimy.' I asked Corporal Carthews what was wrong with Wotton. Was it possible that he was drunk? Carthews emphatically denied the possibility. While he was doing so Wotton fell down flat on the parapet, and I was mystified to notice that Carthews was having difficulty in restraining laughter. I asked Sergeant Padley what he thought of Corporal Carthews. He replied: 'Well, Sir, if you ask my opinion I think he's drunk as well,' and added, 'there's another man the same way just down there: the first man you come to.' Sure enough there was the man leaning against the parapet, an empty sandbag on his shoulder, fast asleep. After a violent shaking this man (Witney by name) came to and asked in a besotted voice what we wanted to disturb him for. I moved him into a fish-tail to which I also sent Wotton, telling the two not to move. I later found another man (name of Harrison) lying on a hurdle with empty sandbags under his head. He was so pale that I thought he had been hit. At that stage of my life I thought that drunken men were flushed, not pale. At this moment a Scots Guards Sergeant passing down the trench stopped and took an interest. He bent over the recumbent man, used his nostrils, and laconically pronounced the single word 'Whisky'. The sergeant then proceeded to cuff the prostrate man's head with such violence that the sound was audible quite a way off. The drunk then sat up, buried his face in his hands and howled. He was seized by the scruff, canted on to his feet and held upright. He then tried to attack the Scots N.C.O. but fell down again.

All three were marched back under arrest and two days later – the day before Christmas – they appeared at Commanding Officer's Orders, when I gave evidence. None denied the charge. They were given 28 days' Field Punishment Number Two which was the most severe that a Commanding Officer could give. They could only get worse by being court-martialled. Field Punishment Number Two involved various unpleasant penalties including that of being roped up for an hour or two each day to a board or cartwheel.

This episode had both comic and serious aspects. A sort of military tragi-comedy. I felt sorry for the poor devils and would have got them off if I could. The cause was never properly cleared up. Almost certainly it was not whisky. They may have found a container of methylated spirits in a dug-out. The party was sober enough when we paraded and marched up. Corporal Carthews, I seem to remember, got off.

About this time something happened of which I have but the vaguest recol-lection and which I did not mention in any letters. I was myself blown up, or, more accurately, blown over. When on day work we officers would take our lunches up and eat them during a half-an-hour's break. I recall climbing out of the trench we were working on and making my way to a shallow and fairly dry borrow-pit on the left side. There I sat down and got out of my haversack the packet of sandwiches prepared by Watson, No.3's mess cook. As I was opening it, a stray shell from nowhere came down and burst quite close. I remembered nothing of the burst. But I recall a tremendous shower of earth coming down on me, and a loud singing – it almost seemed orchestrated – in both ears. This was followed by giddiness which persisted while a N.C.O. in my party clambered out of the trench, stood me up and helped me to shake off the earth which was mainly heaped on my shoulders and over one side, as if I had been blown over. The N.C.O. guided me into the trench where the dizzi-ness passed off and the noises in my ears quietened down. We expected more shells, but none came. I felt steady enough to carry on and did so, being in quite good shape when the time came to march home. Nobody else was hurt or involved in the explosion. I recall someone suggesting that it might have been one of our shells which fell short. More likely it was a German shell which plunged deep into the soft ground before it exploded. These shoot up a great column of earth, but the noise is muffled and they do little damage.

This episode somehow came to the ears of Battalion headquarters and it had something to do with my being sent about two months later to the wood-cutting detachment in Clairmarais forest – of which more later. I had no residual deafness like Pearce's and no ear noises. Next morning I was perfectly well. I decided to say nothing about it to my parents and as little as possible to anyone else.

I wrote to my parents every day and my mother did the same to me. My father wrote at intervals. From these letters, most of which I have kept, it is obvious how, as the year 1915 drew to its close, we were all three looking forward to my first leave. There had been postponements which had caused minor disappointments.

The happy day was the first of the New Year. The period lasted from 1–9 January. My parents were in Paris. Since landing in France I had written letters in something of diary form. The habit of composing a sort of narrative had, after the first few months, become so fixed that, during my leave, I kept it up. The pages then written have survived in mutilated form. They have been useful in providing vivid reminders of this happy interval.

After dining with Piggott in our billet in Estaires, to which minor but nearby town No.3 had just been moved, I set out on foot at about ten in the evening to the adjacent township of La Gorgue which was our railhead. The leave train was waiting and I passed the night in it. Next morning (Monday 2 January) I arrived at Boulogne where several hours had to be spent before a train left for Paris. During some of the morning, I sat in a church where there was enjoyable singing. 'What a good moment this is,' I then thought to myself. 'The beginning of a stressless interim period: a bumpy three months over and a serene ten days ahead.' That afternoon on the Paris train, I was joined by a dapper young Belgian officer with whom I had intermittent talk.

I decided not to warn my parents, who were staying with Grannie at the Majestic Hotel, about when I would arrive. Better ring up their apartment when I reached the hotel. I recall my arrival at the Gare du Nord. A large crowd was assembled not on the platform but in a central part of the station. Each of us was expectantly scrutinized as we emerged from the platform and I witnessed many joyful recognitions, wavings, embraces, laughter and tears. I took a taxi to the Majestic, arriving at about half-past seven, and telephoned to someone on the third floor that I was below. I have the clearest visual memory – it is one of the clearest of the whole war – of my father and mother standing next to each other on the landing when I stepped out of the lift. Pure joy was in their faces and, I have no doubt, in mine. Prolonged embraces and disjointed utterances were followed by a transit to the salon where Aunt Dolores and my cousin Nini were waiting with Grannie. More joyful sounds and embraces. After I had emerged from a barrage of personal remarks we went down to dinner where much time was spent in my refusing further helpings of food, it being Grannie's habit to show her affection for people by plying them with food.

My parents had many friends in Paris. Chief among them were the Benedicts, the Slaters, and Mrs. Jane Tiffany. The last was a handsome old lady with white hair, American, elegant, generous, rich, and rather feared because of her habit of telling people exactly what she thought of them. She did not disguise the fact that she had loved and still loved my father. She and the Slaters lived in different apartments of a house in the Rue Lincoln. My father had many friends including several Frenchmen with whom he fenced at the Sale Rouleau. Also our beloved Comte Guicciardi (called by my mother Gueech); also Robert Dell, Salomon Reinach (a friend in the Dreyfus case) and others. During my leave we saw a lot of these people, especially of Aunt Dolly and Nini, the Slaters and Mrs Tiffany. On the morning after my arrival I was taken to the Rue Lincoln where, to my embarrassment, I was shown off rather like a prize dog.

Everyone's idea was that as many theatres, music halls, and big meals as possible should be packed into the week. These festive occasions I enjoyed well enough. But the best moments were spent in wandering more or less aimlessly round Paris. Here my father was a perfect guide. He was deeply versed in French history especially in that of the revolution and Napoleon. I had seen little of Paris since I had left France to go to school in 1905. During my leave my father took me to various historical buildings, to his favourite streets and to places with fine vistas, and he would discourse on the events which had been enacted there. He had a wonderful gift for bringing the past to life. But into his talk there would sometimes enter a note of sadness; or he would suddenly fall silent. The thought had occurred of how the colourful past had culminated in the terrible present. The 'now' cast back its shadow on the 'then', altering its perspective and damping his animation. Personal memories would also intrude, particularly of the days when Robin and I were small boys dressed in sailor suits. An expression of pain would then cross his face and he would fall silent. Robin was dead and I too might soon be dead. I had not seen my father since before Robin's death and I knew exactly what he was feeling. I would try to cheer him. Sometime, I would say, the present nightmare would end and, with a bit of luck, he and I would again walk about Paris with no shadow over us. More often than not my father would cast off the mood. I asked him once, when his silence persisted, what he would now like to see happen, what, in fact, he would ordain if he were God. His response was lively, something like this: 'I would ordain that the fighting should instantly stop and that both sides should retire behind their pre-war frontiers. I would show them how everyone had blundered into a fool's war which no one had wanted; and I should make them sit down and devise means of preventing such a monstrous thing happening again.' But after he had thus delivered himself, the thought ensued of how utterly impossible it was (God or no God) for such a course to be followed, and I had quite a job to get him back to the charms of Paris.

I had several such walks and talks with my father. But I didn't want my mother to feel that she was being left out. She had, I think, been harder hit by Robin's death than my father, and I felt that she might like to talk to me about him. So together we visited the lake in the Bois de Boulogne where, some fifteen years earlier, Robin and I had admired the boats and fed the ducks. I have an uncertain memory of how, as we walked, she held my arm tightly against her side.

I felt that she wanted to evoke as vividly as she could her memories of Robin and to convey to him a message of love and faith. She was a devout if somewhat unorthodox Catholic. She firmly believed in survival after death; and after Robin's death she had felt him to be near, especially at night and in her prayers. She wanted to feel happy about him and she wanted him to be happy about her. On Christmas Eve she had written to me: 'I have a conviction that *he* is the fortunate one and that he is living a wonderful new life, full of activity and usefulness.' Having me close to her as we walked side by side along the margin of this lake, which had played such a vivid part during our childhood, could perhaps do more than confirm her faith about Robin. We both felt, I think, though nothing was said, that a memory of this hour of physical closeness during the short period we were together might help her if, later on, I too were killed.

The eight days, in a literal sense an interlude, finally drew to a close. The parting, we all sensed, would be painful. But only one of us failed in the requisite stoicism, namely Granny. 'Oh, my dear,' she exclaimed on my last evening, 'stay with us. Don't go back to that horrible war.' 'Ha ha,' said I with forced amusement, 'there's nothing I'd like better than to stay on here for another year, but . . . alas . . . if everyone did that we would lose the war.' 'If everyone did that in both camps,' said my father in an aside, 'the war would at once end. No victors and no vanquished.' My mother, who shared the French view about what the Germans must pay and restore, tried to cheer Granny by saying that it wouldn't be long before my next leave came round, and we must look forward to that. Agreed by all.

A good show of cheerfulness was sustained during the goodbyes and parting embraces. My father came to the Gare du Nord to see me off. The train left at about nine in the evening. 'Bless you, my boy,' he said as he stood on the platform, 'and come back soon.' I begged him not to wait and he left in good shape.

Shortly *before* my Paris leave No. 3 Company was moved back from Laventie to Estaires, a couple of miles further back. This small township had been little touched by opposition gunners and was relatively intact. Numerous shops were well-stocked and the civilian population carried on much as usual. The place contained quite a fine cathedral, dimly lit with an echoing vault, where of an evening an occasional hour of quiet was little disturbed by the continuous rumble outside of passing trucks and wagons.

Clive Piggott and I, at this period the only two officers in No.3, took the company to Estaires on 26 December, the day after Christmas. Good billets had been found for all ranks. The officers' mess was located in a large but rather dark room giving on to a main street. Clive gave me the job of Mess President for the time being. Watson, our cook, was clean and willing but unversed in the culinary arts.

Our labours during this fortnight consisted in draining and repairing three so called 'forts' (also called 'redoubts' and 'posts') well behind the forward area, though nearer Laventie than Estaires. They had ill-assorted names: Eton and Harrow forts and La Plinque post. They were sufficiently near each other for all three to be visited in an hour. To reach them you passed through a place called Pont du Hem which was occasionally shelled. Our three 'forts' had not received attention from the opposition, though Skeff had somehow got it into his head that they were rather dangerous. But the absence of shell-holes clearly showed that they were as safe as anywhere else at that distance behind the line. La Plinque post partly enclosed a farm, the owner of which told me that there had been no shelling for about two months. I don't recall at this stage of the war being anywhere overlooked by the observation balloons which, during the later battles of the Somme, became such ugly features of the eastern skyline.

Our three circular forts were dilapidated, waterlogged and unfinished. The ground in which they had been dug sloped back so that the water which had seeped in accumulated at the rear end – the end opposite that from which an attack was expected by whoever sited the forts. There were no duckboards, little wire in front and the parapet was too low and too thin. The first task was to get together on the spot the necessary concertina-wire, timber, barbed wire, six-inch nails and duckboards.

Work had been begun before my return from leave, and the condition of Harrow fort, allotted to No.11 platoon, had been much improved by the Battalion machine-gun officer, P.A. Shaw, known to us as Pa Shaw. (I remember asking him why a machine-gun officer was needed in the Battalion. The idea had been that parties working in advanced positions might need protection from sudden attack, especially at night. I don't think that Pa Shaw ever fired his machine-gun at the enemy. He was older than most of us and I recall him as a cheerful and pleasant man. He got on well with my platoon and did good work on the fort.)

Our job was to clean out the trench floors, lay duckboards, build up the parapet to the required height and thickness, and put up belts of wire. A lesson well learned in places like Rotten Row was applicable here: if there is seepage into a trench, never deepen it. Lay duckboards high enough to cover the mud and build up the parapet from borrow pits. This elementary drill had been fully grasped by Stephen Burton. But unfortunately he continued his supervision of the forward areas, and never came near our forts. In his place appeared Bingo and Skeff.

Bingo caused no trouble. He would appear fairly soon after the shift got down to work. Without engaging you in any sort of conversation, he would peer at what was happening at your fort and, accompanied by his orderly, race off to the second fort. Here he would take another peer and race off to the third fort, from which he would leg it back to the first fort, and, without asking a question or making a comment, repeat the exercise. He would spend a couple of hours each morning making these rapid circuits and return to the mess for lunch.

Skeff, the Commanding Officer, was different. He presented something of a problem. He was a short slightly paunchy figure, a landowner, I was told, in a fairly big way in Ireland and a keen horseman. It was said that on the hunting field he normally took no risks. Discretion was the better part of zeal. But at unexpected moments he would astonish everyone by taking the lead with a difficult jump or an ingenious short cut. His speech was racy and clipped. I particularly recall his use of the word 'fellow' which he would pronounce 'fler'. An astonishing range of animate and inanimate objects would qualify as 'flers', including not only horses and mules but also such things as shells, pickets, coils of wire and duckboards. He would also refer to the Battalion, or any part of it, in the first person singular. Later in the war I reported at headquarters after a noisy evening. 'Did they shell me?' he asked. 'Any big flers?' (He meant heavy shells). I once met him with a bodkin in my hand. 'What's that fler for?' he asked. Though he could appear boundlessly ignorant about anything which you would not expect an Irish landowner and senior officer to know about, he could also be shrewd. For example, when I returned from Paris leave, he plied me with questions, all to the point, about the French. His racy speech could be humorous and he did not at all mind seeing his respectful auditors suppressing smiles. He was keen on his own comfort, and if there was any question of being shelled at night, he would pick for himself the deepest dug-out. With Bingo he had taken part in the Boer War and he retained something likeable of the Boer War mentality. He was of about the same seniority as Bingo and would pull his leg often in our presence and to our suppressed amusement – of which Skeff may not have been wholly unconscious. Later, in 1916 in H camp, I met him when walking back from a hut where I had boxed a few rounds with Sergeant Sharp. My lip had been cut, I was wearing shorts and had a towel over my shoulder. 'What's all this?' asked Skeff referring to some blood on my face. I told him. Later at dinner in the headquarter mess, referring to me, he asked: 'Where was that fler at school?' 'Eton,' said Joe Forrester, our Quartermaster. 'Lord,' said Skeff in surprise, 'he's got funny ways of amusing himself' – as if that sort of thing would not have been done at Eton in his day. He would visit the forts most days, carrying with him a shooting stick with which he would point. Sometimes he would sit in a contemplative pose on this stick, holding it steady with one hand, the other being thrown across his chest. 'Look at 'im,' I once heard a man in my platoon say to his mate. ''E looks just like Napoleon.' Skeff, I thought at the time, might not have been displeased if he had overheard the remark.

By about the third week in January the forts were deemed to have been sufficiently smartened up and we returned to Laventie where other work was assigned. This was mostly on communicating trenches. The same sort of passive warfare had continued. The front line had been improved and the divisional casualties had been light. I need not say much more about our period at Laventie which came to an end in mid-February. During part of the month I was again attached to No.2. Most or our work was done in North Elgin and Winchester Streets. During our absence at Estaires civilians had taken advantage of the lull in artillery activity and had begun to infiltrate back to Laventie. My butcher's shop had been converted into some sort of grocery store and most of us were billeted in huts. The weather was variable and so were the nights. Some were dry and fine so that much was accomplished. Others were floundering nightmares of rain, mud and frustration. Lionel had one or two bad nights on North Elgin Street. For a short time we were under the direct orders of the R.E.s, and I was badly shaken when told to *deepen* a section of trench already deep in mud. Astonishing that, at this stage, R.E. officers had not learned that this was the surest way of ruining a trench. Happily the order was changed – I think through the intervention of Stephen Burton.

By mid-February, when we moved back, we had the satisfaction of leaving the sector's communicating trenches in definitely better shape than when we took them over.

During the month two officers joined us: Quincey Greene returned and H.E.C. Collins was posted. There were sharp contrasts between these two; also a biographical similarity. Quincey was an unusual sort of American. He was of medium height, pale, smart and handsome. At first sight you might have taken him for the sort of man who would edge his way into a staff job in the American army – some general's favourite, smart and dapper. It appeared that, on leaving school in America, Quincey had refused to settle down. He left home and wandered about the world usually earning and paying his way and always prepared to rough it as the occasion might require. He tramped long distances and sailed before the mast. How he found his way into the Coldstream I don't recall.

Below the smooth surface Quincey was restless, adventurous and buoyant. Long before 1917, when the Americans came into the war, Europe had attracted him. By the time we met he was strongly Francophile and anti-German. In August or September 1915 he had been the Battalion's bombing officer and was attached to No.3 Company. (Divisional Pioneer Battalions were established in 1915. According to the ideas then prevalent, they needed special bombing and machine-gun officers.) Quincey Greene had commanded No. 11 platoon and had been great pals with Sergeant Melton with whom perfect agreement existed that No.11 was not only the best platoon in the company, but also the best in the Battalion. Indeed, it was probably the best in the British army. His departure was brought about by an accident with a

Mills bomb. A detonator which he was treating with excessive familiarity went off in his hand. He came back minus a finger.

This man was an irrepressible talker. In the mess his uninhibited flow of breezy speech, interspersed with Americanisms, infuriated Bingo, who had earlier developed for him a dislike which (as was quickly shown by events) exceeded his current dislike of me. For, on Quincey's return, not only did Bingo refuse to give him back his old platoon; he also refused to part from Quincey's servant, Eborn, whom he had annexed for himself. It was not long before Quincey was posted to another company.

A natural but unexpected consequence of Quincey's reappearance was an improvement in my relations with Bingo. I seemed to annoy him less, and now and then he astonished me by being quite polite. Quincey had joined the regiment on 15 March 1915. Exactly three years and a fortnight afterwards (on 28 March 1918), he was killed at Nieppe Forest.

The other newcomer was H.E.C. Collins, whom some people got round to calling Harry. His earlier life had one thing only in common with Quincey's – nomadic habits. In other respects the two were widely different. Collins had nothing of the other's panache. He described himself as a rough diamond which, in a broad way, he was. He had a comedian's trick of doing the wrong thing. Like most vagrants, he disliked having his hair cut and had joined the 5th Battalion at Windsor in company with two equally long-haired characters, so that the trio were christened 'the orchestra'. He was said to have been expelled from Rugby and then to have taken to the road and the high seas. His travels had taken him to Australia. He had a slow way – as if he were suffering from the after-effects of a drinking bout – of telling stories about his adventures, mostly ending in his own discomforture or discredit. His departure from England the previous October had been ignominious. He had been warned for a draft and given three days' leave. After these had expired he returned to Windsor. Since nothing seemed to happen he asked permission to go up to London for a further night. The request was granted, but he was told to give a telephone number in London in case the draft should leave at short notice. Collins duly went to London. By the evening, there being no summons, he left the place of which he had given the number and spent the night somewhere in Soho. On returning next morning he was told that the warning telephone call had been received a few minutes after he had left the evening before. Panic-stricken he returned to Windsor. The Adjutant was not polite. Collins was told to return there and then to London and report himself to the Regimental Lieutenant-Colonel. The account of his conduct so outraged the amiable and gentle Colonel Drummond Hay that he gave Collins the worst dressing-down of his life. He was told that he was a disgrace to the regiment and ordered to follow the draft to France under his own steam. This he proceeded to do. But by then he was so disorganized that he left most of his kit behind at Windsor. On the way out, especially on the boat, he had drunk more alcohol than was wise, so that when he reported at Battalion headquarters at Verquigneul in the Loos area he was unshaved, dishevelled, wearing a gold-braided hat instead of a service cap, and feeling terrible. I had briefly seen him at this painful moment and had done what I could to fix him up with missing kit. George Edwards, then Adjutant, had been known to extend warmer welcomes to arriving officers than he gave to Collins who was promptly got rid of. The Battalion had been required to find an officer to take command of a wood-cutting detachment in Nieppe Forest and no one could then be more conveniently spared that Collins.

When he came back to us in mid-February – just about the time we were moving north from Laventie – he told me that his job in the forest had indubitably been the best in the British army, and that he could ask for nothing better than to be re-posted to a similar job in another forest in the area we were moving into.

Collins's qualities were not such as to excite Bingo's special animosities so that, on his return, despite his bad reputation, he fitted in quite well into our mess. I recall an incident which occurred a few months later when the Battalion was in H camp. Collins always found it difficult to get up in the mornings. He therefore gave firm instructions to his servant to call him in plenty of time and, more important, to see that he got up after he had been called. Dire penalties were threatened if this servant failed to get him out of bed. But when, at the appointed hour of the early morning, the man appeared, Collins would first continue to lie inertly in bed. Then, after some gentle stimulus, he would open his eyes and sleepily hurl imprecations at the unoffending man. Standing unmoved by the recumbent form, his servant would hear himself called a bastard and a son of a bitch. 'Go away . . . Leave me alone . . . Get out . . . Go to hell,' he would be told. His servant (whose name I forget but whose appearance I clearly recall: he had a slight stoop and was prematurely bald) had perfect manners. He stood his ground, relaxed, impassive and serene. After two minutes Collins would sit up and apologize for his bad language. He would commend his servant for doing what he had been told to do, and charge him to repeat the performance on all future occasions. His servant, who had looked after Collins during his absence in Nieppe Forest, fully understood and tolerated his eccentricities. This clownish farce was enacted on most mornings and became a source of amusement to whoever shared a hut or dug-out.

Collins was later slightly wounded. In July 1916 he was transferred to the Royal Flying Corps (why I don't recall) and for the rest of the war we corresponded. We lost touch after 1918 when, I think, he returned to the happy-go-lucky semi-vagrant life he had earlier led. He was a genial kind-hearted, easy-going man, well disposed to the world, and without a trace of egotism, ambition or jealousy. In situations of danger he behaved well. I rather think that among the trades he had earlier put his hand to was acting. He once said something about having played small parts – long parts were beyond him

– in a travelling company. He got on well with women and many of his stories were about women whom he had picked up in unlikely places and from whom he had always parted on friendly terms despite absurd complications and entanglements. In so far as he had an object in life, he said, it was to enjoy himself without doing harm to others. He was honest and truthful. He had told the strict and discreditable truth to Drummond Hay. Though never flush and not a sponger, he rarely borrowed money; but if he did, he was scrupulous about repaying. I once lent him a small sum and forgot about it. He later reminded me and insisted on repaying. The best life, he said, was one of *dolce far niente*, preferably in a sub-tropical island in the Lesser Antilles, for example, where you didn't have to work much, where the sun and the sea were warm, people uncensorious, rum cheap and easy-going women plentiful.

In late February 1916 the Battalion moved north from Laventie to Houtkerque, near Poperinghe on the Franco-Belgian frontier, stopping en route at a village called Les Lauriers, on the edge of the Nieppe Forest, where CPB was billeted in a farm.

It was I think on the evening of the next day that I was walking along the road from battalion headquarters to our farm. About a hundred yards away on my right, in the waning light, I saw the dark edge of Nieppe Forest. For two or three months I had scarcely seen a tree which was not smashed or mutilated. Wonderful, I thought, to breathe the evening air of early spring in undamaged woodland. So I walked down a path bordering a field and into the forest beyond. The massive deciduous trees, mostly oak, were leafless and widely spaced. The brown humus underfoot was sodden but not boggy. A few brambles trailed about. I stood still and listened. Through the windless air from far away – so far as to be almost inaudible – came sounds of gunfire. The predominating sound came from nearby. It was the calling of rooks. I looked up and saw that I had stumbled into a rookery. These birds, which are early breeders, were busy carrying up sticks and refurbishing last year's nests, placidly conversing the while.

I became aware of a sense of awe and gratitude: gratitude to the trees, to the forest, but above all to the rooks. The feeling of gratitude to rooks has often come back since. Indeed it comes back every time I hear these birds contentedly calling to each other round their rookeries in spring. It comes back now, as I type these lines. I have often thought of paying another visit to Les Lauriers. But I cannot find the place on any of my maps. It may have been obliterated, together with a lot of Nieppe Forest, during the battles of April 1918.

5

CLAIRMARAIS FOREST, MARCH – MAY 1915

Collins, whose happiness in his wood-cutting assignment I have mentioned, had been given to understand that, after the Division had moved north into the Salient, another detachment like his would be required to work in another forest. He let it be known that he would welcome a renewal of this assignment. It therefore came as a surprise to me and a disappointment to Collins that, shortly after we had arrived at Houtkerque, I was ordered to take charge of a composite detachment drawn from different battalions in the Guards Division to do in Clairmarais Forest, near St. Omer, what Collins had done in Nieppe Forest during the winter. Collins generously congratulated me but expressed envy. I remonstrated with George Edwards, pressing Collins's special competence for this kind of work. But I was told that the assignment could not be changed. I later heard indirectly that my having been buried by a shell explosion in Rotten Row a month before had something to do with this decision.

It was with mixed feelings that, in the early afternoon of 3 March, I clambered into a bus at Houtkerque with 23 men from No.2 Company. Serenity was impossible because of the feeling that I was, so to speak, abandoning ship. I comforted myself with the thought that I had done my best to get out of the assignment and that the change in my life would bring vast relief to my parents.

The bus was an antique piece described by the loquacious A.S.C. driver by my side as 'a proper old rattler'. His orders, he said, were to take the party to the crossroads at Clairmarais village and report back that evening. He therefore had private reasons for driving hard whatever the condition of the roads and however terrifying the noises made by the vehicle. There were moments when it seemed about to break up.

When we started ragged clouds were racing across a grey sky, portending rain. We first made due south to Steenvoorde. There we turned west, against a strengthening head-on wind, to Cassel which, perched on the summit of a commanding hill, looked as if it might once have been a fortified town. Unfolded on my knee was my Hazebrouck 5A map. It gave me the direction of Clairmarais. There indeed was the forest below me, a dark smudge on the landscape to the south-west.

From Cassel we lurched and clattered down the steep hill to a place shown on the map as Chau le Nieppe (no topographical connection with the Nieppe Forest) where, turning north-west, we were soon skirting the border of Clairmarais' own forest. The threatened storm had blown up. Gusts of sleet swept horizontally into the windscreen. On the far side of a stretch of black plough, steaming in the pelting rain, the dark line of trees looked forbidding, their branches and crowns flailing in the storm, as if they sensed us as enemies and were warning us to go away. As we moved westwards the margin of the forest approached and retreated; at one point came up to, and crossed, the road, so that we drove through it.

The light was poor when we pulled up at Clairmarais church which formed the centre of an unpretentious village. A few small houses nearby looked drab. Cold and stiff, we got out. I was at a loss where to report till I saw a board sign-posted 'To Lieut. Rean'. While the party took shelter near the church, I sought out this officer, who turned out to be the detachment's Adjutant. I found him in a farm sitting down to tea with another officer in a large room where a bright fire was cheerfully burning in a spacious grate. I was hospitably received. My party, I was told, was to share billets with a detachment from the 6th Corps in a commandeered monastery which we had in fact passed on the road. Rean, whose name was pronounced in two syllables, was an exceptionally tall man with nice manners. He accompanied me back to the church where I was annoyed to find that the loquacious driver had driven off without permission or even notice, leaving behind some of our kit including my valise. Probably my fault for not having thought of telling him to wait.

It was now dark. With wind and rain behind us we trudged back along the straight road we had come by. After we had covered about two miles, a faint light appeared ahead on the left of the road. It was the monastery where we were met by a sergeant of the already installed 6th Corps detachment. This N.C.O. showed my party into their billet – quite a good room, bare but dry – and he ladled out hot tea which someone had thoughtfully got ready. After the party had settled in, I set out alone for the officers' billet – a cottage further up the road. The place was sometimes called an estaminet because it sold drinks. I walked about a kilometre between tall Lombardy poplars scarcely visible in the dark, but fully audible as their up-growing branches were lashed by the gale. The storm, which had been gaining in violence, was at its worst when I introduced myself, my Cording waterproof dripping, into a well-lit room opening out of the estaminet's bar. There three officers were sitting by a stacked-up fire which was roaring in the chimney, there being no shortage of wood in these parts. Marshall, the senior of the three and a full lieutenant, welcomed me hospitably. The other two were Kirk (Lincolnshire Regiment) and Chard (Somerset Light Infantry) both second lieutenants. Room was made for me by the fire and I sat there warming and drying myself. The ice thawed quickly and I formed a pleasant impression.

At about ten I retired to my room upstairs which was better than I expected. Walls, ceiling and floor were of clean-smelling pine-wood. The amiable proprietors were M. and Mme. Leclerc who were helpful and later got on well with our servants. They had a son in the army. They had prepared for me a bed with a blanket, counterpane and – unexpected item – an eiderdown. I slept comfortably in vest, pants and shirt. As I dropped off, I contentedly reflected (not for the first time) on how life holds few better experiences than dryness, warmth and a good meal after prolonged exposure to wet and cold. Next day Temple brought up my valise and an ordered life began.

Up at 6.30 next morning and breakfast at seven. Another vile day. I walked to Clairmarais village with Marshall and was introduced to the commanding officer, Major Liddell – a man of short stature and tough build. He had light hair and a short moustache, closely trimmed. I soon discovered that, though severe when needful, he was respected and liked. He had the reputation of being a 'sportsman'. Then I returned to my billet where, my kit having been retrieved, I washed and shaved.

On the road to and from Clairmarais village, Marshall explained the routine. For years the forest had been well looked after by a French government department, for which acted three *Gardes Forestiers*. These estimable men wore green uniforms and peaked hats, their badge of office being a silver hunting horn worn above the peak. Their authority was further enhanced by numerous metal buttons down the front of their heavy tunics. There was game in the forest – pheasants, deer, hares, and pigeons – and shooting rights had been allocated to a syndicate. It was the main job of the Gardes to supervise the tree-felling, the ensuing clearing operations and the burning which were carried out according to a strict system of rotation geared to the rate of growth of the trees; it was a secondary duty of the Gardes ('*Gardes Chasse*' as well as '*Gardes Forestiers*') to prevent poaching. The forest was divided into rectangular areas or coops wherein the trees were in different stages of maturity. As far as I could make out, some of these coops had been bought by the British army and the wood was used for various military purposes. Fascines were among the products. These were tightly-bound bundles of long thin branches, those of hornbeam and beech being especially suitable, about eight feet in length. These fascines were laid down side by side in muddy areas where they formed rough tracks or even primitive roadways. This method of maintaining communications seems to have been traditional in the Low Countries where many parts had been reclaimed from marshland and where flooding could make certain areas impassable.

Our job consisted in felling trees which had reached the desired stature in designated coops, lopping the branches, and converting those of appropriate length and shape into fascines. The boles were sawn into specified lengths and carted off to a sawmill. Residues were burned, so that the pleasant smell of burning wood was always with us; the crackling fires were welcomed on cold days.

The *Gardes* were exacting about how the trees were felled. There being no mechanical saws in those days, the felling was done by axe. It was a terrible thing to leave a stump projecting out of the ground. The base or 'stool' had to be trimmed level with the forest floor, smooth and flat or else rising slightly towards the centre so that rainwater would run off. The axing had to be done in such a way that the tree was kept erect and poised till the last moment, the lower end of the bole being trimmed like a spinning top. The finished stool should have no cavities or depressions in its surface where water could accumulate and rot the wood.

The felling operation called for two different strokes of the axe: the first was an easy chopping stroke, the second a more difficult horizontal stroke which imposed on the axeman the necessity of bending down so that, when his axe hit the wood, his knuckles were touching the ground. You could tell, the *Gardes* told us, how good your men were by how far they bent down to deliver the horizontal stroke. You knew by their 'action' in the horizontal stroke what the finished stool would look like.

When felled, most broad-leaved trees, of which our forest mainly consisted, send up stool shoots. If the stool was properly trimmed these shoots would spring up below ground from roots radiating from the stool, thereby gaining support from the layer of soil covering the roots. The shoots grew quicker and straighter in this way and were less likely to be blown down in gales than if they grew out of an above-ground stump.

Coniferous trees do not usually send up stool shoots. Shortly before we arrived a party of Canadians had worked on the south side of the forest. They had set about their work as they had done in their native pine forests: that is to say in the easiest way, leaving a stump about a foot high sticking out of the ground. This habit had scandalized and horrified the *Gardes* who saw enacted before their eyes the violation of one of their most sacred rules of silviculture. One of these Gardes, describing to me the habits of the Canadians, raised his hands to heaven, wringing them in protest. It was abominable. But he could do nothing. The Canadians refused to change their habits. They knew better. The result, he said, was that some of the best coops had been ruined.

On our first day one of the *Gardes* demonstrated the correct method to my party in our allotted coop. I stood by and translated his instructions. He made most of us practise the horizontal stroke under his eye, paying particular attention to instructing the N.C.O.s. He examined our axes, advised about their care, and gave some hints about how to deal with initial blisters and cracked skin. It was an obvious relief to these three *Gardes* (whose names were

Barthelmie, Vatrin and Poulet) to be able to make themselves understood by men who were eager to learn. All three became good friends, and one of them later said that we made life too easy for him. Kirk and Chard were by then quite expert axemen.

Poaching, said M. Barthelmie (the senior, eldest and most corpulent of the three) was a problem. People of '*mauvais caractère*' from St. Omer and elsewhere would lay snares and shoot pregnant deer with silencer-fitted rifles. Troops – French no less than British – and aviators from a nearby aerodrome were among those who caused trouble. He was anxious that our men should not follow suit. Could I say a word to the detachment? (Major Liddell had mentioned the same thing.) I did what he asked, and it was flattering when, four months later, we left the forest, Chard and I received semi-formal thanks from the three. Favourable reports on the conduct of our party were later conveyed to the Mayor of the village with satisfactory results. He disliked the aviators, some of whom, he said, behaved like brigands. The Mayor, a moustached and voluble man, could not speak a word of English. Later he would sometimes ask me to help him in his dealings with British officers with administrative responsibilities in his area.

I recall the afternoon of our first day in the forest; also the evening of the same day. The weather had changed. The wind had moderated and veered to the north. Dark, compact and snow-laden clouds with comfortable rounded shapes billowed southwards in a majestic procession. Between short but heavy snowfalls about every forty-five minutes, the sun would triumphantly peep round a shining cloud-rim and emerge into a deep blue sky, magically transforming the forest and the flat landscape visible through the trees. The warm sunshine melted the accumulated snow which would begin to fall in muffled plops on to the forest floor (sometimes on to our heads) from the small branches above, or to slither down the boles and larger branches. Though the clouds moved in dignified order high up, the forest was windless and the light sparkling. The sky dispensed alternate frowns and benedictions. During the snowstorms which shortened the visibility and turned everything grey, we took shelter under the well-grown oaks, hornbeams and occasional hollies till the cloud passed over. The forest seemed to provide a protective canopy under which we felt at home and it prompted one of the new arrivals in my party to remark to me that we had come to a good place for out-of-door work in this sort of weather. I heard no grumbling and less bad language than usual. Some of the 6th Corps men, by now experienced axemen, sang at their work, punctuating their song with ringing axe strokes. It was during one of these glistening intervals that the *Garde Forestier* gave his instruction to my party. We knocked off at about four – the time of knocking-off being adjusted to the time of starting – and marched back feeling that we had come to a good place. A beautiful sunset bathed the forest in pink light.

Clairmarais Forest had reminded me of Nieppe Forest where, a few weeks before, I had accidentally found my way into a rookery. The reminder was vivified by a memorable experience later that evening. The coop in which we had been working lay some distance west of our billet. After a welcome mug of hot tea on our return I went for a stroll along a road which passed our cottage. I did not go far before I was enthralled by a sight which, at that time, I had never seen equalled. All the rooks in the neighbourhood converged in three long strings on some trees bordering the forest outside our billet. For three-quarters of an hour they poured in, cawing leisurely, until the bare branches were encrusted with their black shapes. The noise they made was as far-carrying and sustained as the breaking of waves on a distant rocky shore. At times the massed birds would simultaneously rise in the air in a resounding pandemonium, circle round once or twice in the fading light, and then stream down to their perches. It almost seemed as if they were concertedly welcoming us on our arrival. I wondered if any had come from as far as Nieppe Forest.

Marshall, who commanded the detachment, left about a fortnight later to rejoin his unit. A clean-shaven man of 24 with a placidly cheerful expression, he had been at Clifton and had taken, or was in process of taking, a degree in agriculture. We were all sorry when he left, especially Kirk who went to see him off at St. Omer.

Kirk left soon after Marshall. He was a dark-haired neatly-built man of about thirty with a trimmed moustache who had knocked about the world. He professed to take life as it came expecting little and contented with little. He declared that he had no religion. 'I've never seen a mountain moved by faith,' he remarked one evening, 'but I've seen one moved by dynamite.' He said that he had renounced Christianity because of its failure to solve the problem of evil. Being something of a musician he could talk well about music. He had travelled in Japan and commended that country's women who knew how to give you what you wanted. He saw around him no evidence of divine administration – 'unless the precise place where a 9.2 shell explodes is an example of a divine dispensation'. Kirk had no particular views on the war about which he was fatalistic. His humour could take facetious turns: he had various nicknames for Chard, one being Monkey Bill. He had a tiresome servant who could sometimes be heard talking loudly in the estaminet next door about working men's rights. Kirk said he would get rid of him when he got back to his unit but couldn't bother to take the necessary steps before. He told a peculiar story about how, when in the ranks, he had been charged with an offence he had not committed. Asked what he had to say at Company Orders, he replied as casually as possible in the formal circumstance, 'Nothing'. He was given some sort of punishment which did not incommode him. It later came out that he had not committed the offence and he was asked by his Company Commander why he had not said so. Kirk replied that the issue was too trivial. He went in for practical jokes of which the following is an example. The village of Clairmarais, where Liddell had his orderly room, bordered a sizeable area of marshy ground intersected by small canals. Liddell, our Commanding Officer, liked fishing. His orderly room gave on to one of these canals in which eels could be caught. A baited hook on a line was sometimes thrown out of the window and made fast to the window sill. Occasionally an eel was hooked, hauled in through the window and unhooked on the floor by an orderly. Kirk bought in St. Omer a toy crocodile with a celluloid window in its abdomen. He filled the crocodile with bits of brick and hooked it on to Liddell's line. When he next hauled it in, Liddell at first thought that he had caught something really big. But on the orderly room floor the celluloid window came off and the bricks fell out. Liddell laughed loudly and thought it a good joke, thereby enhancing his reputation as a sportsman. I was again sorry when Kirk left. He was later killed on the Somme. I learned of his death through M. Leclerc, the proprietor of our billet, who must have been told by Kirk's servant.

After Kirk's departure Liddell took a step which somewhat embarrassed me. He gave the command of the whole detachment to me, putting me over Chard who was about ten years older than I and had been at the job longer. I was happy enough to command the men from my own Division and Corps but I had no wish to be responsible for people from the 6th Corps or elsewhere.

I told Chard exactly how I felt and he could not have been nicer. He assured me that he did not in the least mind and ended the conversation by saying: 'Anyway you can count on me to give you every assistance and help I possibly can'. Which he certainly did in the ensuing three and a half months. He was a smallish wiry man of retiring disposition. He did not like asserting himself, but could do so when needed. He was happily married, hated the separation, and was most acutely longing for his period of leave to come round. His wife wrote to him daily and numbered her letters. Shortly after I arrived, Chard received his 217th letter. The two were manifestly devoted. But as he once told me with a trace of annoyance against himself, he was liable to short spasms of attraction to women he met casually. He wished that there were some sort of inoculation against that sort of silliness which could be a nuisance. These occasional stresses, I suggested, might be commoner than most people supposed. That could be inferred from how troops behaved in large towns. Though I did not at that time know much about what I was talking about, I think I was right. But not everyone was as frank with themselves as he was. I was lucky to fall in with such an admirable man who did more than he knew to cheer me up. After my difficulties in getting on with my fellow officers in No. 3 Company, it did me good to live so amicably for four months on end with someone with whom I had been thrown into contact by pure accident.

The forest, which we had first beheld as a dark smudge in the distance from the hilltop of Cassel and which, while skirting its northern border, we later saw waving at us to go away, suddenly disclosed itself as hospitable and benign. As week followed week it unfolded and exhibited its treasures. It burst into flower, leaf and song. In my inner ear these sylvan developments would take on musical forms – a sort of orchestration. Persistent were the familiar forest murmurs from the second act of *Siegfried* which simultaneously conveyed the caressing sounds of spring-time zephyrs blowing through northern forests and the responding pulsations of awakening life and rising sap in roots, undergrowth and the crowns of age-old trees.

Our forest's soil was adhesive but fertile. By today's standards I was poorly equipped with books for studying natural history. I made the best use I could of Edward Step's volumes from which I taught myself some rudiments. I learned how to recognize the commoner families of flowering plants. Most of the larger (non-passerine) birds I already knew. The song-birds which as an assemblage, I knew less well, were laboriously identified more by their calls and songs than by their pictures. The trees which I could not identify were named for me in French by the *Gardes Forestiers* – so that the French names of common trees have retained a charm which even today evokes nostalgic memories of this forest.

One of the earliest delights was the spangling of the woodland floor by a profusion of wood anemones. I recall watching with delight a canopy of these diffident pinkish-white flowers dipping in unison on their flexible stalks as they tuned their faces away from the gusty March wind. Primroses in almost excessive abundance followed. And bluebells. The succession was much what you would expect in an English forest. Of flowers rarely seen wild in after-years, I especially remember the geometrical herb-paris and the beautiful water violet (Primulaceae: not really a violet at all) which grew in a waterlogged ditch close to our cottage – almost below the trees in which the rooks had assembled on our first evening. On a windy morning about the middle of March a single chiffchaff feebly announced its arrival from a distant tree-top; by the same afternoon the wind had abated and the forest resounded with the simple but stirring calls of these welcome birds. The chiffchaffs were soon overtaken by others. Willow warblers, blackcaps, garden warblers and whitethroats arrived and swelled the fine evening choruses of endemic birds – robins, song thrushes and blackbirds. Later came cuckoos, nightjars and, in abundance, nightingales. On moonlit nights in May the forest would resound with the songs of nightingales of which as many as four could be heard singing against each other from different territories. In late May I recall hearing near the coop in which we were working a short but exceptionally clear fluting call which was new. My first thought was: 'Indubitably Siegfried's forest bird' which, with its intimate and personal message, burst into the impersonal forest-murmur music. The trees were by then nearing full leaf. The call was repeated, but I could not see the bird. Finally I caught a flash of yellow and recognized my first golden oriole. Later Chard and I found its hanging nest.

Towards its centre the forest rose to an eminence crowned with splendid beeches. Here had long been established a breeding colony of herons – birds we often saw lazily flying over the canals and marshy grounds to the north which were full of eels and frogs. A conveniently accessible feeding ground. Over this territory flocks of lapwings and black-headed gulls had come and gone by mid-April. Many of the men in the detachment took an interest in what was going on around them and several became keen. All nests were reported to Chard or me. The heron colony was a particular attraction, and one day it was found that three young birds had been blown out of their nest by a high wind the evening before. They were floundering helplessly on the ground. Some men appointed themselves as keepers and built on the ground a massive structure of sticks. On a sort of platform at the top, the young birds were installed. Here they were daily fed by their self-appointed keepers on frogs, fish and chopped meat. As they came to recognize their 'keepers' they would clack their bills at their approach. I was told that they were also fed by their parents, though I did not see this happen. In treeless areas these birds will build in lake-side reeds, so that it was not impossible that the parents may have continued to feed them on the ground.

In the coops wherein the trees had been felled there were few breeding sites for small birds other than the piles of brushwood and fascines we left on the ground. Many nests were found in these places including several of long-tailed tits which were much admired and carefully preserved. Two kestrels' nests were discovered in oaks; and, in holes of various trees, nests of green and greater spotted woodpeckers. A pair of the latter were remarkably tame. They would fly up to their hole and feed their young, ignoring the presence of several humans watching them at the foot of the tree. On a morning in May I was taken to see a dead roe deer lying in a ditch with a bullet wound in her belly. I reported to M. Vatrin who, examining the rigid animal, repeated: '*Ah oui, Ah oui,*' in tones of sadness and reproachfulness to the killers. '*Mauvais types. Mauvais caractères.*'

Chard went on leave early in May, leaving me alone with Temple and the Leclercs in our cottage; and I went on leave for the first nine days in June. When I returned the forest had passed from spring into summer. We were to depart in three weeks; and during this period the work slowed down. Tasks in the allocated coops were nearing completion and our tempo of work, which was a little ahead of schedule, was adjusted to the labours which remained.

During the long warm evenings I continued the habit of walking out in casual dress – strong slippers minus belt and headgear – to a point where the by-road leading past our billet slightly rose. At this point, shown on the map as Coin Perdu (when, why and how the corner was lost nobody knew) I used to sit for half an hour or so and reflect on the past, the present, and the impending future. As the light slowly failed, gun-flashes to the east would become visible and, on windless evenings, distant rumbles and detonations became audible. Coin Perdu, as later recalled, seemed to overlook the forest from which the spring bird-song rose up as if from below. But when I revisited the place in 1949, I was astonished to find that the trees about three hundred yards away were but little below my level. In my thoughts during these reflective evenings the forest in front was identified with the peaceful present; the gun-flashes and distant sounds of artillery to the east were identified with the immediate past and the impending but unknown future. A quiet mood compounded of grati-tude (mainly directed to the forest) and acquiescence would descend. During these moments of sunset it seemed probable that I would be killed as Robin had been killed. The possibility was wholly acceptable. Would it really matter? The answer depended on the level of one's thoughts. On a ground level, which involved my parents, it would matter a lot. My mother, aided by her faith and devotion to my father, would suffer much; but she would rise to the challenge. What would happen to my father? I felt that he would be submerged. In that sense and at that level my death would matter.

But on another level it would not matter. Time obliterated everything: the issues which today are charged with joy, sorrow and fear dissolve and vanish so that, if one waited long enough, no one would remain who remembered them. It was difficult to put into words the contrast between these two levels about which one could feel so differently. The ephemeral and the durable? The temporal and the eternal? Was there really a contrast? Was anything durable? Could anything be eternal when everything changes? Could your reactions to the savagery of war be muted or transcended by meditation or prayer or the influence of earlier thoughts? Could you train yourself to feel – could forces outside yourself help you to feel in mid-crisis – that violence and death did not really matter? Certain drugs could doubtless anaesthetize your feelings. Certain martyrs had so prepared themselves that they maintained serenity under severe duress. How far could the soul be fortified in advance? And by what disciplines?

These were the questions which used to occupy my mind during the last evenings of June at Coin Perdu north of Clairmarais Forest. What were the results of these communings when the issue was put to trial in the immediately following months and in the two years which were to follow? It is difficult to be certain. I would, I think, be mistaken if I said that nothing had been gained. I recall how, in several anguishing situations during the following September, the thought came, like a hand on my shoulder: think of your roadside; think of your forest.

As the months passed Chard and I became locally popular. Officers, several of quite high rank, who were desk-bound in G.H.Q. (St. Omer), would take afternoons off to visit the forest. These would call on Liddell who would escort them out to our coops. 'Show them around,' he would say.

Chard and I took turns. We would explain the system of forestry rotation and show them our work in the different coops. They would watch the axes being plied and several would take their coats off and give themselves a trial. They could manage the downward strokes fairly well, but not the horizontal.

After they had made something of a mess of the bottom of the tree, Chard or I would take over and trim the stool. They might then have another try, starting a little higher up on the bole. Some wanted natural history more than exercise. We would draw attention to the bird-calls and if possible show them the nests. The 'Tweelioo' of the golden oriole – new to all – was easy to hear and remember and they were delighted with its hanging nest. If they had time – which they usually had – we would take them to the heronry where they could see the young birds on their platforms of sticks and hear how they clattered their bills for food. We would show them kestrels and woodpeckers' nests. Some were interested in the flora. The afternoon would usually end with a cup of tea at Liddell's headquarters or in our humbler mess. Liddell was pleased to entertain these sometimes high-ranking guests and we were happy enough to show them round, having by then acquired a definitely proprietary feeling about the forest.

One afternoon towards the end of May there turned up in the forest un-announced a padre of high rank, Colonel William Drury, whom I had never met. He came straight up and introduced himself. I recall him as a tallish, clean-shaven man wearing glasses, with a slight stoop and a direct friendly manner. He began by telling me that he was essentially a townsman but had always been interested in natural history. How lucky I was to be here! How he wished that he had had a job like mine earlier in his life! I found him likeable and stimulating and when we parted I said I hoped he would come again. He took me at my word. He was stationed at St. Omer nearby and in the next month paid us three further visits.

In conversation one thing quickly led to another without loss of pressure and it was not long before I learned that he was a zealous follower of Henry George whose book, *Progress and Poverty*, Drury was surprised and pleased to hear, I had read[1]. But I confessed that I had not properly understood the implications of the Single Tax. He invited me to ask questions, which I did. These he answered so confidently that my earlier scepticism about the feasibility of the Single Tax was somewhat shaken. Drury saw me as a potential convert. He told me that he hated the war which had upset some of his Christian convic-tions – a bold confession, I thought, from a senior padre. He took an interest in everything around him and asked as many questions as I had earlier done – about the morale of the men in the detachment, how we got on with the French, disciplinary problems, Church parades and other matters. He had a chat with M. Poulet, who came up while we were talking. Drury asked him jokingly how he got on with his allies. Poulet cracked us up, saying that we made his life too

---

[1] Henry George (1839–97) was an American economist whose book *Poverty and Progress* was published in 1879. The 'single tax' was his remedy for poverty; it would be levied on the value of land exclusive of improvements; all taxes on industry and thrift should be abolished (ed.).

easy. After Drury had left Chard and I agreed that we had never met a senior officer who was less conscious of status and rank.

At our penultimate meeting Drury further expounded the Single Tax. Henry George's argument, he said, struck many people as difficult to follow and, for various other reasons, as unconvincing. A good deal of thought was needed before you could really see the point. The point? Yes. You did not immediately grasp the essential point, said Drury. Understanding came slowly. Indeed someone had described enlightenment (for that was what it amounted to) by the expression: Seeing the Cat. The cat came in, Drury said, because there was somewhere a design or drawing or tapestry (I have forgotten what the object was) which, at first sight, seemed formless and patternless. But if you looked at it long enough you gradually discerned within the figure the outline of a cat which gave meaning to what you were looking at. You 'saw the cat' as you might experience a revelation. During this conversation in the forest Drury was standing with his back to some tall trees, behind which was a bright sky. 'You suddenly see the cat,' he said with a large circular gesture which comprehended the shapely boles and the tangled crowns behind him. I retain a vivid mental picture of how Drury made this gesture. His figure was silhouetted against the sky between the boles of two of the trees.

About a week later, returning tired to our mess after knocking off work, I found Colonel Drury ensconced in a wicker chair reading one of my books. I was glad to see him. After cups of tea, welcomed by us both, I suggested a stroll. I took him to Coin Perdu. There we sat down and continued our discussion of the cat. As he described it, I said, this animal was static: something you could see in a drawing or fresco. Could not a non-static cat – an evolving cat – be disclosed in history? Or in biography? Could not the historian discern a pattern – you could call it an explanatory principle or even a theory – in historical events and processes? *A* cat? Or could historians of different schools discern different cats? Could not scientists have their cats? The so-called 'laws' which were expressed in equations, the periodic table of the elements, the evolution theory? Could Newton have perceived something cat-like in his law of gravitation? A most lively discussion followed. Rarely has communication been easier. Rarely have I felt in better gear with anyone.

The conversation turned to one's private, or autobiographical, cat. This animal's proper outline might not be finally discernible till the end of your life. Before then you don't know what (perhaps trivial) event of your past may later be recognized as having had a formative influence; and you don't know what future event may cause you to re-assess your past. Past experiences which may now seem quite unimportant – which may, indeed, have been forgotten – may be re-animated and lit up by future events. Drury agreed and gave an example of how something of the sort had happened to him. Then, I recall, I said something like this: 'If I survive the war and later in life look back, could it be that Clairmarais Forest will be seen as having contributed to the lineaments of my biographical cat? And could you, Colonel Drury, being part of my Clairmarais period, become part of the feline configuration? I would like to think that you might.' He accepted the compliment and by the time we set out for our cottage much good humour and good will had developed. We touched on the influence of early life in shaping one's habits, tastes and beliefs.

This lively and prophetic exchange at Coin Perdu had, till I re-read my letters of 53 years ago, become fragmented and mislaid in a '*coin demi-perdu*' of memory's storehouse. But the fragments, powerfully energized by re-discovery, quickly pieced themselves together, with the result that Colonel Drury himself and my conversational exchanges with him have come back with the utmost clarity; and the restoration has kindled an intense desire to see him again.

As the day of departure from the forest approached, mixed feelings were intensified. During June I had been afflicted by a dermatitis of the flexures which I had had before. I now think that the conflict of feelings about being away from my Battalion (plus the June heat) aggravated the itching which was worst at night. After I had left the forest the thing quickly got better.

We used to attend a church parade on Sundays. On our last Sunday (25 June) the service was taken and a sermon preached by a padre whose name I discovered to be Noel Rostram. He had visited us at work and tried his hand with an axe. On this last Sunday his theme was that we would all go away better and stronger men after our springtime in the forest. The 'ennobling effects of beauty', he boldly said, was a theme for poets rather than soldiers. But any soldier who had seen what war did to woods, fields and countryside and then had the luck to spend some spring months in a place like this could see what the poet was driving at. He hoped that 'the happy memories which you will take away of what you must now feel is *your* forest, will help you through whatever lies ahead till the war ends and you return to your families'. These words rang the bell for Chard and me, and, I am sure, for many others. After the parade I had a word with Rostram and told him so.

I recall one or two other trivial events of our last days. On a Saturday afternoon we were working as usual in a coop where the oldest and most corpulent of the Gardes, M. Barthelmie, was supervising the finishing touches. Four young women appeared with sacks, ostensibly to collect chips. I asked M. Barthelmie why they came. Was it really to collect chips? '*Oui et non*', he replied; '*Il y a peu à faire d'ou elles viennent*'. He said this with a sly expression as if the words '*peu à faire*' could be ambiguous. They could mean 'little to do' or 'few men to pick up'. One of the four who was powdered and looked town-bred, spent more time in badinage with M. Barthelmie than in collecting chips. He got the worst of every exchange with this sharp-witted blonde but seemed to enjoy his defeats. He would throw his head back, slap his protruding stomach and laugh hilariously. Pointing at the young woman he declared to the world: '*Il n'y a rien à faire contre ça. Rien, rien.*' And he looked towards me, grinning for confirmation. I wondered whether she was a friend of his and had come out to pay him a visit. Chard thought it more likely that all four took an interest in the troops. But perhaps they were merely enjoying the equivalent of an afternoon in Hyde Park.

Another vivid memory of the last few weeks comes back. Alone I felled an enormous beech which for perhaps two centuries had grown on a slope below where the herons bred. This huge tree had massive roots which, on its lower side, lay mostly above ground, where they had been bared by rains and erosion. One of the *Gardes* said it ought to come down because it had begun to rot in the centre. It took me over four days. I wanted to complete the job to the satisfaction of M. Poulet – the *Garde* who had earlier said that we made his job too easy. But I must digress.

When the Detachment from the Guards Division arrived in early March, it was decided that they would learn most quickly if they were distributed with men of the 6th Corps in mixed working parties. The latter, we were told, had become casual and it was thought that the newcomers would tone them up. But this is not how things worked out. The newcomers took their cue from the old hands. I therefore put in a plea for segregation which found favour. Discipline all round was then tightened up and standards improved to the point that, about five weeks later, men from the two corps were again mixed. This time there was no trouble.

I mention this because it contributes to my recollection of the fall of my mammoth beech. About five minutes before it was expected to crash, a mixed group of men from several units gathered round the bole, waiting for the event. It was then rather late in the afternoon. The fall of this great tree was memorable, but less so than how the waiting axemen fell on the prostrate tree like a swarm of bees. They plied their axes with such vigour and despatch that, amid a tattoo of crisp resounding strokes, the leaf-clad branches melted away, leaving the huge bole stripped, the thin end pointing uphill. As I watched I had mixed feelings. It was good to see men from all units working so busily together; but there was pathos in the fall of this majestic and ancient tree. As it lay mangled on the exposed slope which, for over a century, it had sheltered from rain and shaded from sun, it reminded me of an antarctic whale, lying immense and inert on a flensing platform, about to be cut up.

My feelings about the mixed party were echoed by Sergeant Sheppard (Coldstreamer) who, with M. Poulet, was standing with me watching. Most of the waiting men were stripped to the waist. 'You would not know which was which,' said Sheppard. I explained the remark to the Frenchman who agreed. '*On voit que vos hommes*' (he meant the guardsmen) '*sont en général plus grands*', he said; '*autrement on ne distingue pas*'.

The tree had had a fine life and a spectacular end. Its sacrifice was in a good cause. Nevertheless there was sadness in its fall and some act of mourning seemed due. The fall and the sadness were somehow connected with our impending departure.

I don't think that it is entirely vanity which prompts me to mention the following recollection. In my detachment was a guardsman by the name of Wells. He came from No. 2 Company where he had been well thought of but had refused promotion. I noted him on the first day as having distinction. He was well-built with light hair and a closely trimmed moustache. He was smart in his appearance and held himself well. When we got into the forest, I noticed that he was good with his axe and turned out well-proportioned and well-bound fascines. He was well-spoken with good manners. Inclined towards reserve, he had a preference for working on his own; a steady deliberate worker who never hurried. When I toured the working parties I quite often had a word with him. The officers' chores then included the unnecessary duty of censoring letters. A few days before we broke up, Guardsman Wells wrote home about his impending change of address. He mentioned that he was sorry his present mode of life was coming to an end – for several reasons. Among them was the fact that he would no longer have me as his officer. I was touched and pleased by the unexpected compliment from a man who would not have written in this way if he had not meant what he said.

The evening before we broke up Chard and I dined with Liddell. Rean and two others were with us and the occasion, which we expected to be melancholy, turned out to be cheerful. Liddell was to stay on a few more days. He said it was on the cards that the wood-cutting might start again in Clairmarais or somewhere else. If it did, he said, he would apply for the same team. We drank to a happy reunion – sometime! In the dusk Chard and I walked back along the now familiar poplar-bordered road. Our time together was about to end. We were both feeling nostalgic regrets, and there was something of an outpouring. It was remarkable, we agreed, how well things had passed. He and I had been thrown together by chance; we had lived in the closest contact for four months, and not an unfriendly word had been spoken. I felt rather awed.

The next day we were too busy with packing up to indulge in sentiment. The detachment paraded at 11.15 and ammunition was issued. Before marching off from the monastery I made a short farewell speech on behalf of Chard and myself. We could not have wished to work with better men, I said, and we thanked them. The very best of luck to all and a speedy return to their families. We echoed the blessing with which Rostram had concluded his sermon. They gave a cheer. On our way to St. Omer we stopped for ten minutes at Clairmarais church where Major Liddell came out and said goodbye. The sense of goodwill on all sides was strong.

We travelled by train arriving at Poperinghe Station (outside the town) at half past four. Quickly the detachment broke up. A hurried goodbye to everyone including Chard. All that could be said had been said the night before.

A few minutes later I was walking with Temple (my servant) and a signaller sent by Battalion headquarters along a road leading towards the town. We passed two Coldstream officers. Both looked at me intently. They were Cecil Sprigge and A.S. Rennie. Cecil who had joined the Third Battalion while I was at Clairmarais was bronzed and looked fitter than I had ever seen him. He had grown a small moustache. It cheered me to have him with me some of the way to my destination – a camp about four miles from Poperinghe. It was known as H-camp – our base for the next month. As we walked and talked, we were aware of a tremendous background noise. 'A hell of a row somewhere,' I remarked, 'how long has it been going on?' 'It began this morning', Cecil replied. The date was the first of July, the first day of the Battle of the Somme.

Though Clairmarais Forest quickly disappeared from the forefront of my mind, the place remained with me thereafter. How much I have owed to it I did not properly realize till I came to write this story.

6

THE YPRES SALIENT AND THE SOMME:
JULY – SEPTEMBER 1916.

The first of July was fateful in a small way to Chard and myself because of the break-up of our Detachment. The date was also fateful in a big way because on it the allied offensive on the Somme began. A word about this background.

The Battle of Verdun, opened in mid-February, had been raging for four months and was still continuing. Many have contended that this battle was the most terrible of the war. Rumours of its concentrated horror had reached us fairly early.

I heard stories from people at St. Omer and during my Paris leave. Much later I read General Pétain's book *La Bataille de Verdun*. The German higher command had decided (for reasons which were later questioned) that the war could be most decisively won by the defeat not of Britain or Russia but of France. The fortified heights of Verdun had both a military and a symbolic importance for France. Von Falkenhayn, who took the decision, is said to have declared that he would break France on the anvil of Verdun. The French, who were not taken by surprise, responded with the declaration: '*Ils ne passeront pas*'. Bombardments of unprecedented weight by guns of all calibres paved the way for massive infantry attacks. The contested ground became a heaving inferno into which both sides poured shells and sent up division after division. These met, grappled, and were slaughtered in a small area which remained almost static. The dead were buried as much by the earth thrown up in the ceaseless bombardment as by burying parties. I heard some terrible accounts of how the parapets, traverses and parados of trenches and the ground underfoot became filled with human corpses in varying conditions of dismemberment and putrefaction; so that the battlefield, on which a rain of shells continued to descend day and night, came to resemble an upheaved graveyard without gravestones. A French general described how he stood beside one of the approach roads to

Verdun during a relief and took the salutes of formations of cheering and singing young men who were moving up for their first taste of battle; and how, three days later, he stood in the same place to see the decimated survivors stagger out, pale and retching, looking like old men. Such scenes were described to me by French wounded whom I later met in Dinard where the largest hotel had been converted into a hospital. The Battle of Verdun differed from the battles in which the British were later engaged in that, at Verdun, there was little forward movement or change of position. In the Battles of the Somme, fought in the same year, and in those of Passchendaele in 1917, most of the attacks, though they did not break through, carried you into new ground. You left behind you a widening belt of desolation, but you gained a few yards so that you dug in and established yourself in clean soil, sometimes in a corn or beet field. Your dead and wounded were left behind, the dead to be buried either on the spot or in improvised cemeteries, the wounded to be picked up and carried away. You were spared the horrors of immobility in areas of intensified war.

For the relief of Verdun, the need for a maximum initiative by the British army had been continually pressed on our higher command by the French. But on our side there was reluctance about embarking on a most costly commitment unless substantial advantages could be gained. High hopes were raised on the first of July. The British army had been slower off the mark than the French had hoped because of the huge scale of the needed preparations. But by then the commitment was maximal in both guns and men. With the newly-formed Kitchener's army a penetration was expected on a wide enough front to enable the cavalry to break through. The war could be won that autumn. This was what many people – perhaps most people – in England believed. Whether the Higher Command at G.H.Q. shared this expectation is less certain. There were doubtless some optimists who did. But all agreed that the Battle of the Somme was necessary to relieve Verdun and to ease the pressure on France.

It did not take me long to discover that life in the Salient was going to be livelier than during the protracted winter at Laventie. For some weeks, I was told on arrival, things had been 'hotting up'. The cause was most clearly made known to us as soon as we de-trained at Poperinghe. A tremendous battle had begun to the south. During my walk from the station to H-Camp, and in the ensuing evening, a continuous roar of artillery seemed to fill the southern sky like a static thunder cloud. Everywhere was excitement and expectation. The 'big push' had begun.

During the first week of July the French newspapers bought locally and the English papers which arrived by mail had sensational headlines: trenches penetrated on a wide front; important positions captured; numerous dazed prisoners trailing back and filling the cages. Little during the first days about losses. But their dimensions slowly became apparent as casualty lists began to appear. From the start the idea was to intensify the war everywhere: make the Germans think that further attacks could develop anywhere and at any time; force them to keep as many as possible of their divisions away from Verdun and the Somme.

My first impressions on arrival were of a lush summer on the ground and of mounting tensions in the air. We would probably not be staying where we were for much longer. A crescendo could be sensed which would culminate in the autumn.

Peacetime rather than wartime conditions were recalled by my first contact with H-Camp, a large open space used both as a parade and cricket ground, surrounded by huts. When I arrived in the late afternoon, some sort of drill with shouting was going on at one end. I was led past a tent where a thick-set man with an air of authority, stripped to the waist, was vigorously washing his head and neck in a basin. As I came near he looked up sideways from his basin and scrutinized me as much as to say: who is this new arrival? He was the new Regimental Sergeant Major, RSM Ellis, who during my absence had replaced the redoubtable RSM Corner. The parade-ground voices of the two men, I was soon to learn, were equally stentorian; but that of Ellis had a shriller and more piercing quality. His voice became a familiar sound during the early mornings and evenings at H-Camp. This man seemed to have vaguely heard of my expected return. Rubbing his sunburned neck with a rough towel, he directed me to the officers' quarters in some huts on the other side of the open space.

I don't remember much else about that day beyond some affable greetings and my instalment on a trestle bed in a hut with several other officers. A hot night followed, disturbed by the whine of many mosquitoes, to which were added, not long after sunrise, loud sounds of bugles and shouting. A contrast to the peace and quiet of Clairmarais.

H-Camp, it appeared, was practically never shelled. At any given time two only of the four companies were in the camp. The other two were 'up', that is to say engaged on a spell in the forward areas. No. 3 was, at that time, 'up'. For messing purposes all the officers who happened to be in camp were thrown together in Nissen-type huts. These huts backed on to a small oak wood with hazel coppice. Yellow tormentils bordered a narrow path which led through the trees to the officers' latrines, and there was purple loosestrife in a ditch which ran through the wood. At dinner I sat with No.4's officers: Furze still in command with Alan Dickinson second-in-command, and three new men – E. Overton Jones, A.R. Kelsey and J.O. Boyson. These three made an agreeable first impression. The first two became life-long friends. I learned that Lionel, who was 'up' with No.3 and had had two 'hot' nights during which he lost twelve men. As I fell asleep I made good resolutions about behaving politely to Bingo.

The next day I moved 'up' and joined No.3. They were living in dug-outs, and in the cellars of a demolished farm. Movement about the place in daylight, while not forbidden, was discouraged. You could move about alone or in twos, but no formations must show themselves.

The composition of the mess was little changed. Bingo, Clive Piggott, Lionel and Collins figured as before. A newcomer had arrived by the name of J. L. Allan, a middle-aged, moustached and rather portly Australian upon whom Collins had conferred the name Woggs. In civilian life he was, I believe, a railway engineer. Woggs was not a colourful type. In the mess, as I recollect him, he was mostly silent. He seemed to have some difficulty in expressing himself – as if nervous of pronouncing words wrongly or of making mistakes in grammar. When out at night he would literally fortify himself by pulls from a flask of neat whisky. The confidence thus gained would now and then express itself rather surprisingly in the use of bad language. Because of his silence in the mess he did not clash with Bingo.

Collins had during my absence been wounded in the hand. The wound had been painful but not serious. But this time he was fully rehabilitated after his unfortunate arrival. He was interested to hear of my time at Clairmarais which he compared with his earlier period at Nieppe. 'Didn't I tell you,' he said, 'that you would find it the best job in the British army?' Collins's unconventional but likeable qualities had by this time come to be appreciated by the other ranks of No. 3 and by most of the officers in the Battalion. An officer by the name of Burgess, who had come from the Cheshire Regiment during my absence and had been serving with No. 2 Company, was shortly to be associated with Collins in a transfer to the Royal Flying Corps. A dinner for these two was arranged at H-Camp where nice things were said about, and by, both. In the course of evening strolls Collins and I had speculated about what we would do if we were lucky enough to survive the war. He said that one of his projects was to sail in a wind-jammer to New Zealand before the mast. Would I join him? I said I would.

Bingo was much the same. If there had been a change, it was in the direction of an increased dependency on Clive Piggott. Collins told me a peculiar story. One evening after dinner, in the course of which Bingo had drunk his accustomed bottle of *vin ordinaire*, Collins found him sitting alone in a corner of a hut sobbing.

During the first week I thought that things were going better. Then came a rude shock. During an evening march-up from H-Camp to our forward position, Bingo unexpectedly addressed me with unnecessary rudeness in front of my platoon. This so galled me that, during the ensuing night, I came to a decision. I would apply for a transfer to another Company. Next day I raised the possibility with Mike Peto who said he would welcome me to No. 2. I therefore applied to see the Adjutant – still George Edwards. I marched myself into the orderly room and saluted him. Why did I want to see him? I explained: I wanted to avoid a crisis. If things continued as they had recently begun, I would lose my temper and say or do something which would have to be dealt with by a court-martial. I could do no more than I had done since my return to avoid annoying or offending Pakenham. The obvious course was to apply for a transfer. George said that he was glad that I had raised the matter with him. He would discuss my application with the Commanding Officer.

Later that day an orderly came to the mess with a message for Bingo. The Commanding Officer wished to see him. Later I saw the two walking up and down together outside the orderly room. That evening I was sent for by George. He said that he had put my application to Skeff who had discussed it with Bingo. George then astounded me by saying that Bingo had no complaints about me and did not want to lose me from No.3. But I must do my best to be considerate and conciliatory. Bingo, I was told, would be like-wise. I thanked George and asked him to convey my thanks to Skeff, but added that I could do no more in the suggested direction than I had done since I had come back. I undertook to continue on the same lines. George repeated that he was glad that I had raised the matter with him and there things were left. It was not till much later – till after the war, in fact – that the probable explanation came to me of why Bingo had told Edwards that he did not want to lose me. Bingo's outbursts of rudeness had not occurred at any time of the clock. Almost all had been confined to the dinner or after-dinner periods. In the mornings and afternoons Bingo had sometimes surprised me by his affability. The cause, when you thought of it, was obvious. In the evenings he was uninhibited by his bottle of *vin ordinaire*, and afterwards wholly forgot what had happened when he was under its influence. When Skeff told him that I wanted to move out of his Company, his mind may have been a near-blank as to what had so often occurred after, say, 7.30 p.m. He might have been genuinely surprised to learn how difficult to endure some of us had then found him.

Bingo's failing morale was at this time still further sapped by an event which distressed us all. It was while we were in the Salient in July that Skeff promoted George Edwards to the rank of Second-in-Command of the Battalion and at the same time moved Clive Piggott into the Adjutant's chair. What Clive felt about the move I don't know. I later learned that life in the orderly room was not made easy by the attitude taken towards him by certain people, and he may have sometimes wished himself back in No.3. Everyone in the company – other ranks no less than officers and N.C.O's – were saddened by the departure of this fine man who was without false pride, pettiness, egotism or personal am-bition. No one could have felt his loss more keenly than Bingo to whom Clive showed an unvarying consideration and loyalty. Clive's perfect integrity and other solid qualities were not noticeable at first. They were, in fact, incon-spicuous and time was needed to appreciate them at their true worth. He had a firm Christian faith which he was somewhat reluctant to discuss. In his Birmingham home he was a regular churchgoer. How much, I used to wonder, had his faith fashioned his character and how much his character his faith? The truth, I think, was that faith and character grew out of each other and were part of the same thing.

Collins left us in mid-July. He was replaced by a Cornishman by the name of D.K. Treffry who had crossed the Atlantic to take part in the war. Treffry was a tall, big-boned, loose-limbed man in early middle-age. He had left Eton in 1896 and was therefore about 38. He had what I then called a soldier's face, thin, aquiline and greyhound-like in profile. He had a large bronze-coloured and side-swept moustache which he kept in military shape by a carefully adjusted band, worn at night. He had been popular at Windsor and at the base – a charming fellow according to advance rumour. Treffry was an ebullient man with some panache. He could tell good stories into which he projected himself with gesture and mimicry. He told quite a few on his first evening at dinner, eliciting premonitory glowers and scowls from Bingo. They were mostly funny stories which ended with the same mannerism: he would lift his chin and hand, half shut his eyes, turn his head away and say: 'I've nev-ver seen anything so funny in my life'. Treffry's volubility contrasted with Woggs Allan's silence. I was not sure at first how he would fit in. In fact he wore well. I soon found him likeable and came to enjoy his anecdotes which seemed better the second than the first time you heard them. When we had guests we would get him to repeat some of his stories.

I don't recall open clashes with Bingo. I remember Treffry having to control himself one evening when Bingo reacted characteristically to his third or fourth glass. I clearly remember Treffry's first night out with the company. Nothing came particularly near and there were no more than occasional rifle-shots. But Treffry felt that he had had his 'baptism of fire'. I recall his good spirits during our march home. That, he said, was what he had crossed the Atlantic for. When in California he had obviously chafed at being out of the war. By this time I had become sufficiently accustomed to war noises (below a certain modest threshold) in the forward areas not to have noticed anything in particular. It quite cheered me that Treffry was so pleased. I felt as I imagined Virgil must have felt when Dante, whom he was guiding, showed interest in some feature, familiar to Virgil, of paradise, purgatory or hell.

There has remained with me a clear mental picture of Treffry at H-Camp. After dinner we were sitting with No.1's officers. A gramophone was being played. Someone put on a foxtrot with a good rhythm. Treffry got up and, with careful deliberation and in slow time, danced a *pas seul*. His expressionless, almost mask-like, face and the way he alternately looked at the ground in front of his shuffling feet, and peered into the distance shading his eyes, reminded me of an Indian brave performing a ritual war dance. But Treffry should have had a feather in his hair and there should have been a totem pole. I asked him later if he had seen Californian Indians dancing, but I don't remember his answer.

Though it was unhealthier in the forward areas than it had been in the corresponding positions at Laventie during the winter, we spent less time in these areas. Troops were thick on the ground in the Salient where the policy was to rotate them freely and not crowd them into the zone occupied by the gunners. During July No.3, when 'up', was based on two demolished farms with cellars. These places were liable to be shelled and the companies which relieved each other made a point of leaving them better protected than they found them. No.4, which relieved us early in the month, had cause to be grateful. One night, when one of the cellars was full of men, the place was heavily shelled. A five-nine landed very close to one of the dug-outs which would have been blown in if we had not done some solid sand-bagging before they took over. The hours of warm summer darkness were short and the jobs assigned to the company as a whole, or to different platoons, were apt to vary from night to night. There were no continuous tasks on familiar ground as on the long communicating trenches east of Laventie. Rarely was it possible for the officer to reconnoitre the work beforehand. There was more repair work and less 'new' work than before.

The dug-outs and cellars in which we messed and slept were heavily infested by mosquitoes which bred freely in the damp ground – much worse than at H-Camp. I don't recall our using insect repellant as we would today. When your platoon lined up in the dusk their faces were blotched and swollen by insect bites. I have a mental picture of CSM Luck appearing on parade one evening scarcely recognizable. Both his eyes were closed and his temper was atrocious. I learned by personal experience how difficult it was to maintain good humour when you were under continuous assault by voracious insects.

I recall a particular evening. Allan and I paraded at 9.30 p.m. and marched up quietly. Our work consisted of heightening some traverses and building up the right-hand parapet of a communicating trench. Everything went smoothly until after midnight. It was a peaceful night with a clear quarter-moon veiled by horizontal clouds. Suddenly some half-dozen of our guns went off at once. The sky seemed to be seared by a volleying succession of tearing shells dropping sparks in their trajectories. Then, some 400 yards away, along a German front and support lines, as if the strings of an open piano were being struck in quick succession, appeared the flashes of exploding shells.

The Germans replied with heavy trench mortars. I had not before been near when these had exploded. Suffice it that they make a crater from 20–25 feet across. Five of these things fell uncomfortably near one end of our working party. After the first two had fallen, causing huge mushroom-shaped eruptions of earth and sandbags, like volcanos, I moved my party away from the point that was receiving attention. My recollection is that I sent a message to the N.C.O who was furthest away to lead a hundred yards down the trench and wait. A few minutes later I followed. I was shaken to discover that only about half of my party was to be found. The rest had vanished. I climbed out of the trench, raced along the parapet and caught up with the disappearing sections.

I never properly discovered what happened. I was told that the message, as received, was to move out altogether and go back to our farm.

This experience taught me first-hand how quickly rumours and contradictory orders can spread. An order passed down or along to change position tends to get misunderstood, especially when things are noisy and locally unhealthy; it becomes an order to move often into safety. Such a thing happens easily and is difficult to prevent when large parties are moving about in the dark through trenches or over uneven ground.

A quarter of an hour before we marched off, when first light was appearing, the word was passed down for stretcher-bearers. A man in No.12 platoon had been hit. When I reached him he was dead, shot apparently through the heart (Guardsman Gregory, who left a widow and two children). A rifle or machine-gun bullet. Nothing to do with the mortar.

One of the much-used communicating trenches in our area had for a long time been obliterated for a distance of about thirty yards before it debouched into the front line. Troops moving to and fro had to clamber out or otherwise expose themselves when they reached these last few yards and there had been casualties. For months this situation had been taken for granted and no one had bothered to do anything about it. To No.3 was assigned the task of digging out and renovating this 'prehistoric stretch', as it was called. I remember the occasion because of what we found. As we marched up I had a premonition that it would be something unpleasant.

Among the objects we dug out were a mail bag containing letters dated April 1915, about a dozen water tins, several bags of mouldered rations, eight boxes of bombs and one box of trench mortar shells. But the most terrible thing was the annihilating stench which, as we dug, suddenly pervaded the area. It was obvious that a mortar had landed in the middle of a carrying party over a year ago. How many had been killed we did not discover, or seriously try to discover. I have a hazy recollection of sending two men into the front line to try to find some chlorate of lime. They returned with as much as could be spared – not enough. We did not make ourselves popular with the troops on each side of the debouchment by the way we were 'stirring things up' and not letting 'sleeping dogs lie', as someone put it.

On the following night we carried up two containers of chlorate with which we did our best. We also dug out and relaid some grids which had got well buried, and we raised the right parapet from borrow-pits. This experience brought home what life must have been like in the static positions round Verdun where the parapets, parados and traverses were full of corpses. On the principle that an officer should not expect men to do things he won't do himself, I remained on the worst spot during most of the night, though I switched the working party about. This was one of the few occasions that I regretted that I did not smoke a pipe. At intervals during the following days and nights, the manifold smells of putrefaction, each more nauseous than the last, would come back. (I have since learned that the nature of the stench is affected by the part of the body that is most actively putrefying, by the amount of moisture in which the process is taking place, and by the lapse of time since death.) This turned me into an advocate of cremation as opposed to burial.

Someone (I forget who) told me that it was a recognized practice for the Germans to smash up with heavy mortars the points where communicating trenches opened into the front and support lines. The local destruction, if sufficiently thorough, compelled moving troops to get out of the demolished stretch and scuttle along the top. On the area thus obliterated a machine-gun was laid which, at frequent but unexpected moments, emitted bursts of fire. This seemed to us to be happening during our spells on this job which was therefore in a double sense unhealthy. The task was completed by a single platoon in two nights, and right glad we were to finish it. We had no casualties.

I recall a lecture-demonstration on gas. I went by bicycle to a place near Poperinghe. I quote myself: 'It had rained hard in the night. The roads were muddy and slippery. But I got there in time. Present were about twelve officers all from the Brigade or the R.A.M.C. Early in the programme came a lecture by a tall, stooping, heavily-built R.A.M.C. captain on the history, uses of, and defences against, gases. He spoke well and held his audience. The sort of man you would like to have about if you were hurt. We then moved to a nearby field where there were some dug-outs with blanketed entrances and huts with blanketed windows. Flannel gas helmets with tube mouths were then distributed. These we pulled over our heads. The flannel had been impregnated with a sticky gas-neutralizing substance with a chemical smell. Like a procession of troglodytes or outsize gnomes we then filed down the steps of one of the dug-outs and sat about on chairs, feeling as if we were participating in the rites of some secret society. Blankets were then drawn, a lamp was lit, and gas pumped in. The first effect was rather alarming. The gas – chlorine, I believe – combining with the chemicals with which the flannel helmets had been impregnated, evolved another type of gas which was apt to catch in one's throat and make one feel that one's helmet had a leak. But by sitting quite still and breathing as lightly as possible one could manage not to cough or choke.

We went through the same drill with a new kind of box helmet which was more cumbersome but better than the flannel affair because it effectively prevents you smelling or tasting anything. One wore goggles with this box helmet. We were then exposed to a lachrimatory gas (tear gas) of the sort the Germans send over in shells. It smells rather sweet, like pineapple. I lifted my goggles for a moment and it fairly stung my eyes. Funny, I thought, how it stings your eyes but not your nose. It was good to get out into the open air and take off all masks and goggles. As we rubbed our faces and straightened our hair we secretly registered the hope that we wouldn't have to wear the damned things for long periods in earnest, or have to run about in them.

I recall attending a field mass on 23 July at the Headquarters of a nearby unit of Irish Guards. I took four men and Sergeant Cairns, a squatly-built, snub-nose Scotsman whom I would have expected to be a Nonconformist rather than a Catholic.

The officiating priest, Father Leahy, a white-haired man with a voice which he could cause to boom when he wished, was clearly accustomed to preaching to uneducated people. About fifty of us, nearly all Irish Guardsmen, sat around on the grass, bare-headed.

God, Father Leahy began by gently telling us, was omnipotent. But there was one thing he could not do – make us repent of our sins. Father Leahy then pointed to some wooden crosses on soldiers' graves which were visible from where we were sitting. Each of you, he said, might be stretched out in such a grave next week. Each might now be standing at the door of death. We didn't know. Nobody knew. Only God knew. So now was the time for us to repent of our sins, thus making sure of salvation. Father Leahy then began to describe what would happen to those who cast aside the chance of salvation. Hell would be their fate. Hell, he said, was a fiery place peopled by hideous beings, half-animal, half-human, whose sole occupation was to devise and perform unthinkable tortures of which the worst feature was that they were never-ending.

It was not long before a low-pitched moaning became audible from two or three of the Irish guardsmen. As Leahy described hell in further detail, the lamentation spread until about half the people sitting round were beating their breasts and calling on the Holy Mother of God to have mercy on them. Their emotions were communicated to Father Leahy who finished his address with raised voice and threatening gestures.

I was astonished by this performance. I did not know how far the moanings and petitions to the Virgin were semi-conventionalized features, like prescribed responses, of illiterate people who felt that a religious service was incomplete without some sort of catharsis. If this was Father Leahy's view, and if he felt that a reminder about the nearby crosses and about the imminence of possible death was the best way of evoking the appropriate emotional responses, then he could certainly count the occasion a success. But I could not overcome a feeling of distaste over the picture of this group of fine men weeping and striking their breasts when what they really wanted was a renewal of faith and a message of comfort.

I recall an occasion belonging to this period when a glimmer of botanical knowledge proved useful. I was leading a couple of platoons on our way up to the forward area in fading light on a windless steamy night with plenty of midges about. We were straggled over a sedgy, churned-up field in which we had to pick our way, skirting shell-holes and avoiding wire. A message was passed up: 'Gas. Put on your gas helmets'. I had noticed no gas, so I halted the uneven column and went back to investigate. 'Where did the message come from? Who had smelled gas etc?' I was standing in rear of the by-then halted column, when I was told that, a few yards behind, there was a strong smell of gas. No one knew who had given the warning. I walked back a few yards and true enough a faint but pungent smell was noticeable which seemed to come from underfoot. My Orilux torch showed me that we were standing in a patch of flowers with white rays: these, when crushed, were emitting the alarming odour. I recognized the flowers as stinking camomile, over a patch of which we had trampled. The smell from the crushed leaves and flowers did not rise high enough from the ground to be noticed until the party had nearly passed. I picked a bunch and took it back. Thus was No.3 nearly 'hoaxed by daisies', as someone later put it.

During July, spent by the Battalion in the Salient, the distant but sustained thunder to the south formed a background to life by day and, together with the needle-like whining of midges and mosquitos, pervaded the short hot nights. Though unnoticed most of the time, the remote din was not, like the continuous noise of traffic in a town, meaningless. On the contrary, the far-away rumblings and muffled detonations and, at night, the flickering sky were meaningful in the sense that they were reminders of what lay ahead. They were components of a sort of logical anxiety state. It may have been some sort of wishful thinking or self-deception that made us feel that the region vaguely spoken of as 'The Somme' was further away – more remote somewhere in the south – than it actually was. What of the future when we got there? One's mind stopped. A fiery question mark reared up. Nothing could be foretold beyond that we would be put through an ordeal – into a crucible or through a tunnel – from which there might be no emergence. With massive inevitability the day of departure approached.

The move south began on Sunday 30 July by train. The end of July and the beginning of August were periods of sizzling heat. No.3 Company spent the late morning loading vehicles on to a train drawn up into a siding near (I think) Poperinghe. I recall the fierce heat which struck down vertically and the handkerchiefs knotted at their four corners with which the panting men protected their red and sweating necks. I thought of sunstroke and prickly heat. Belgium, I thought, was certainly giving us a hot send-off.

We started in the early afternoon. After an airless and slow journey we detrained, clammy and oppressed, at St. Pol, where dixies of tea had been made ready. Thence by lorry to Doullens where we arrived after midnight. Chaos and delay about billets were caused by Lionel having been sent ahead alone. He found and allotted the billets efficiently enough but had not with him people who could steer the companies to their widely scattered destinations. I remember philosophically dozing on a pavement using my pack as a pillow.

I recall a ten-mile route march soon after. Another windless and parching day. The road, which at first wound upwards in wide curves, had the unusual feature of being bordered by middle-sized rowan trees well-laden with berries in their early yellow stage. These trees were leafy enough to provide occasional patches of shade from the merciless sun. I recall thinking how neat and fresh they looked with their smooth boles outlined against the blue sky. Rowans are not typical products of the chalk; yet here they counteracted the dustiness and the midday heat and seemed in place. Why, I wondered, were not rowans more used as road-side trees? Beautiful in spring with their panicles of white blossom; and no less beautiful in autumn with their handsome red berries. By evening we were established in a steep, curved and semi-demolished wood called, I think, the Bois de Warnimont.

There we stayed for several days which continued to be hot. Treffry was a keen fisherman and had a rod. We both liked the undulating chalk country. Clear, briskly running streams coursed down some of the nearby valleys forming here and there pools in which there were fish. Treffry, who sometimes had moods of silent melancholy, enjoyed sitting quietly with his rod under a tree indifferent about his catch. Not all the valleys within our range had suffered from the war and by then the civilian population had begun to infiltrate back. Small boys always take an interest in fishing and Treffry would quite like to have had one or two sitting by his side. I recall spending an hour with him by some shallows where we were joined by two boys. One aged about fourteen wore a pink shirt, the other aged about eleven a white one. These two competed in telling us how they had been forced to leave their homes and how glad they were to get back. A lovely evening, warm and peaceful, which was pleasant to look back to during the bitter winter which followed. I increasingly liked Treffry.

Various units of the Guards Division, encamped round us, were being 'fattened up': numbers were being raised to full strength and they were undergoing special training which included bombing, bayonet fighting, and dealing with wire at night. We practised laying it out in belts and cutting lanes through it. During this preliminary period, as I remember it, the Fourth Battalion was under Corps command. We were put to such tasks as laying light railways and making roads. I quote from myself: 'This morning Allan, Treffry and I went up to a point from which we could see the course which was planned for our light railway. We sat behind a hedge on the crest of a ridge with before us a view some four miles deep extending into German-occupied territory. We watched the German front and support lines, their communicating trenches and their distant depots being shelled. What most struck me was the imperturbability of those two chalk lines confronting each other, some 300 yards apart, each placidly ensconced behind thick belts of dark brown wire. Not a sign of human life. Fortress-like. Now and then little spurts of flame and puffs of smoke would appear anywhere, leaving the impervious ground unmoved and indifferent. Indeed the inert but sentient earth seemed to be personalized: watchful, perhaps contemptuous, and yet fully capable of retaliation. It knew all about us. It knew exactly what we were doing, how we were scarring and defacing its surface. But for the time being it would give no sign. It was feigning sleep. I was reminded of the impression I had received from the long line of enemy breastworks seen from the front line at Laventie. But here we were looking down from above and everything was further away. Through our field glasses we could see rooks flying about the forward positions, as they will be doing after the conclusion of peace.'

During these early stages of August I got to know two of the officers who had joined the Battalion while I had been in the forest – E. Overton-Jones and A.R. Kelsey. Overton-Jones was a midlander of solid build and medium height. He had a broad forehead, short black hair, a close-cropped moustache, a quiet voice and deliberate speech, a placid expression and gentle manners. I have mentioned him before as having told me some of the peculiarities of George Edwards. It turned out that Overton-Jones was an artist who worked, as a designer of pottery, with Wedgwoods. When we moved down to the Somme he was in No.4 Company where he did not get on well with Furze. I discovered when we reached the chalk-lands that Overton-Jones (called by several people Ogger Jogger and by me O.J.) was a keen entomologist. Though Robin and I had collected butterflies when we were small boys at Cothill, I remembered little about them; but I was ready to learn. During walks I took notice of the way Overton-Jones could discern patterns which escaped me. Of these he would make neat drawings which encouraged me to see things through his eyes. At this time I knew the names of most of the common wild flowers and was mainly interested in their taxonomy. Overton-Jones caused me to see their artistic features and in so doing opened a new window. One evening we were walking along the border of a wood on the top of a chalk ridge. The wood was on our left. To our right, a stony field fell steeply into a valley. Suddenly Overton-Jones stopped and looked down at the ground at his feet. He knelt down for a closer look and called me up. He was examining an elegant little flower which I saw was a yellow and brown toadflax. Out came his pencil and note-book and in ten minutes was completed a neat drawing which, when we got back, he coloured in. His flower was the round-leaved toadflax which I had not found before but identified without doubt. What, apart from finding the flower, stuck in my memory was the expression of contemplative delight on my friend's face as he knelt and examined it. He might have smiled in that way at a responsive child who was trying to say something to him.

For some reason which then escaped me, and which I still do not entirely understand, Overton-Jones was not universally liked. He was somehow not in gear with people's ordinary moods and behaviour. I recall an incident. We were sitting after dinner round the table in a mixed mess. The talk took a bawdy turn with stories and ribald laughter. Overton-Jones sat through it unmoving and without making a sound, rather as if he were being asked to look at a picture which did not appeal to him. When the gaiety was at its height he quietly got up, left the table and sat down in a camp chair as far away as possible from the noise. His action was noticed and resented by others who wrongly sensed that he wished to show contempt. There were harsh words and angry looks. He heard some of the remarks which mystified him. He later said to me: 'I often – all too often – feel like a fish out of water. When this happens I go away. I prefer to be alone.'

His detachment could cut him off as if by a moat. Yet he was a keen and reliable officer. Without intended provocation from him, a group of officers worked up a dislike and were sometimes openly disagreeable. Overton-Jones rarely showed his feelings. He would offer no comment on these occasions. But he once told me that he had several times wondered what it was about him that people disliked. Could I tell him? I couldn't.

I now jump forward. Overton-Jones was religious along lines prepared, I think, by his mother. This lady I never met, but he showed me her photograph – a dark, rather grim face. O.J. believed, I gathered, in a personal god of righteousness. He also believed that the cause of the Allies was righteous. Hence it was for him a matter of religious faith that, in the end, we would win the war. The total deadlock puzzled him. I recall a later conversation – I think it was in the autumn of 1917 – when the war seemed to be going badly. He told me that he was mystified and depressed. He couldn't understand it. He could see no light. Outwardly, however, there was no change in him. He remained reserved and, to most people, unresponsive.

We remained close friends till the end of the war. After I had transferred to the Second Battalion we used to meet as often as we could; and on the memorable night of 11 November 1918 we stood together in silence on the outskirts of Maubeuge and looked to the east and south. Not a sound. Not a flicker. The war was over. Utterly unbelievable. Our mood at this tremendous moment was one of inexplicable sadness.

He died in 1963. In the Elysian fields in which I should like to walk with him again, there should be sunny chalk ridges, valleys, streams, beech woods and plenty of butterflies busy with the bright chalkland flowers.

I first became aware of A.R. Kelsey during a cricket match at H-Camp. He was keeping wicket and had tried to stump the batsman who had jumped out to hit a ball. Kelsey, having knocked down the wicket, looked inquiringly sideways towards the umpire at square leg, behind whom with some others I was sitting in a camp chair. He turned his face towards us as he appealed. I then recognized him as a newcomer to the Battalion and inquired who he was. A blond trimly built man of about twenty-six with a light moustache.

It turned out that he was a mathematician – a Cambridge wrangler – and something of an athlete. He played football and cricket and was a good gymnast. An unusual sort of man to find his way into the Coldstream. He had joined with a younger brother, then in the machine-gun battalion.

I discovered a good deal in common with this man. Towards the human race he felt an unsophisticated goodwill. He was without jealousy, malice or personal ambition and gave the impression of seeing life in a detached sort of way as might a mathematician. Our talks, which ranged from the war to what T. E. Huxley called 'Man's place in Nature', were often steered by him into the realms of higher mathematics where I could not follow him.

In a few weeks Kelsey and I were painfully involved in the same battle. His experiences were, I think, more severe than mine. His resulted in his leaving the Battalion not long afterwards. He went with the 14th Corps to Italy.

I revert to the autumn of 1916. At the beginning of August our company mess partly broke up. In the first week Lionel and no less than 150 men were posted to a tunnelling company. I now ask myself where the tunnelling was being done. I don't recall, but I remember thinking that it seemed a peculiar moment, with everything moving forward, to repeat the exercises in which we took part on Laventie's static front. Bingo was temporarily detached to act as Town Major. And so was Treffry who, together with Ogden his servant, temporarily left us. Treffry was an efficient administrator who rather liked the busy job. Someone who saw him sitting importantly at his desk nicknamed him 'The Duke'. Allan and I called on him one evening. We marched into his office and, with blank faces, gave him in unison a crashing salute befitting his ducal status. A few weeks later things with Bingo came to a head. We were working on the light railway above-mentioned of which the construction was nominally under Allan's direction. In a friendly way we ragged him. 'This railway should get you some substantial recognition, Woggs. Your least reward should be a DSO, etc.' Woggs quite enjoyed this badinage and was as surprised as I when, one evening at the end of dinner, Bingo suddenly turned on me angrily and told me that I should treat my seniors with more respect. (Allan was quite a lot junior to me in rank.) It was a pity, said Bingo, that, earlier in my life, I hadn't been more soundly kicked and taught my place. I sat out the tirade in silence. When it was over I turned to Allan and asked him if he thought that I had been disrespectful to him. In a conciliatory but scarcely audible voice, Allan deprecatingly assured Bingo that I had intended no disrespect. 'All that Blacker said was good-humouredly meant.' Bingo's outburst had been in the presence of a guest and was therefore singularly ill-timed. I am now fairly sure that his words were no sooner uttered than forgotten, perhaps leaving as a cloudy after-math the feeling that some compensating amiability was later called for. Anyway next morning, when I was sitting in the garden outside our billet, Bingo came up and commented on the fine weather.

But during the night just past I had come to a decision of which I now feel ashamed. In front of witnesses Bingo had broken the truce which, in H-Camp, he had promised Skeff to observe. He was to be polite provided that I also was polite. I was now free to say what I liked. I decided from thenceforth to miss no opportunity of being disagreeable. When, therefore, the morning after the outburst, Bingo commented on the fine weather, I got up and told him that I had been astonished by his gratuitous rudeness the evening before and did not intend to speak to him again unless I had to. I had earlier given an undertaking, I said, not to provoke him if he did the same by me. He had broken his side of the bargain. I then walked off. Thereafter I did not speak to him and did not answer when he spoke to me. The effect was remarkable. He became consistently amiable and, on one occasion, nearly disarmed me by asking what had recently come over me. Again I walked away without answering.

The dilemma was solved about three weeks later. I might as well describe it now, thereby closing the distressing story of Bingo. The battle of 15 September had been fought and was to be renewed. An attack was to be delivered on the 25th. Two days before – on 23 September – all the officers in No.3 Company were in various ways busy. When, in the evening, an order came in that the Company had to find a carrying party, consisting of a single platoon, Bingo was the only officer available. Pickets and wire had to be carried up at dusk and handed over to R.E.s on the far (north) side of the Ginchy-Delville Wood ridge which will enter into the story which follows. During and after the battle on 15 September this ridge had been intermittently shelled with what we thought were five-nines. They made a loud noise and much smoke. But the shells fell singly, at predictable intervals, and in much the same place on the ridge. We had all learned how to get across. You either avoided the unhealthy area which was receiving attention, or you waited till a shell came down and then moved across in double time. Almost everyone in the companies had crossed this ridge – some several times – and knew the drill. After about 18 September the barrage had not been continuous. For periods of several hours nothing would happen. But you never knew when the thing would start again.

I was later told that Bingo had not been keen to take up this carrying party of a single platoon. But he could not depute the job to anyone else. So the party loaded up and set forth. Darkness was falling when it approached the ridge with Bingo leading. Things had been quiet for an hour. Hence it came as a shock when a five-nine noisily came down about a hundred yards in front of the moving file. Bingo, I was told, halted the party and peered into the twilight not knowing what to do. After some hesitation he decided to proceed no further. Wire, pickets, etc., were deposited in an improvised dump on the near (south) side of the ridge and Bingo led the party back to their dug-outs. They were preparing for the night when Skeff received a message from the C.R.E. (The Royal Engineers' Commanding Officer) to the effect that the materials his people were expecting had not arrived. Skeff sent for Bingo and asked what had happened. Bingo told him that they could not get through the barrage on the ridge and had left their stuff in a dump on this side. Had Bingo had casualties, Skeff asked. Bingo mumbled that he hadn't. Much displeased, Skeff had then ordered Bingo to get his party out again, lead it back and carry the dumped stuff across the ridge, casualties or no casualties. The platoon did not cheer when they were roused from their first sleep and made to retrace their steps. But when they reached the spot where they had deposited their loads, the stuff could not be found. A fruitless search in the dark ensued. Finally Bingo led them back to their dug-outs. It later transpired that the wiring party of R.E.s got tired of waiting and had sent someone back to find out what had happened. They found Bingo's dump, picked up what they wanted and themselves carried them to the site where they were to be used.

The episode was not a credit to the Battalion. The result was predictable. Bingo was sent back. I will describe later the consequences for No.3 Company of his departure. He slipped away quietly.

After he had left, I felt badly about how I had behaved. My punishment came about fifteen years later. In the early thirties Bingo worked voluntarily for an ex-officers' employment organisation, which had an office in Eccleston Square. I would occasionally meet Bingo in the square. By this time I had been married several years. A battalion wedding present had been raised before the event and my shame had been great when I found that Bingo had subscribed. So that whenever I later met him in Eccleston Square, all was smiles and politeness. In due course he died and shortly afterwards I found myself in a Catholic church. From somewhere came an impulse to burn a candle in memory of Bingo. I would like to think that his spirit took the act as an expression of apology.

On Saturday 9 September we marched up to a place within three miles of the scene of the impending attack. It was a long broad valley known as Happy Valley. Why happy, we wondered when we got there. An answer of a sort may have been vouchsafed. The ground had been fought over several weeks earlier and cleaned up afterwards. As the shadows lengthened a full pearl-tinted moon rose into an indigo sky. No houses, huts, trees or vegetation in sight. Round smoking camp-fires troops were bivouacked in this smooth and featureless valley. As the sun sank and the twilight deepened the flames spurted up here and there, and the columns of vertically rising wood-smoke became more noticeable. Our own men were distributed along the northern ridge. It was only when darkness fell and the stars came out that we realized how full of men the area was. The slope opposite was covered with men. So was the valley floor below us. The calm of the evening communicated itself to the troops who were lying on waterproof sheets or sitting round fires. As the stars came out they began to sing. At first there was a medley of voices but they fell into choruses and finally into unison so that the wide valley resounded with song, rising and falling as if in response to the baton of an invisible conductor. The tempo was slow, the prevailing mood of nostalgic melancholy. Gunfire was scarcely audible. Yes, for the moment Happy Valley was living up to its name. Indeed the place itself became vocal, treating us to a lullaby of its own inspiration.

Thoughts intruded: How many of these men whose voices are now synchronized will be alive this time next week? I am surely not alone in having this thought. Perhaps the numen of the place was trying to convey through the medium of our own voices the comforting thought that, in some invisible sense, it didn't really matter.

By the second week in September it was obvious that 'the day' was near. We moved up into trenches in the area of Montauban. The village had been totally demolished but on its east side four roads converged at a point where it was inadvisable to loiter. From this place distances were short to Bernafay and Trônes Woods which were little more than a mile from enemy-held positions. These two woods, where it was said, there had been severe hand-to-hand fighting, were still uncleared and, in warm weather, reeked of gas. In the next few days they were to enter much into our lives. My spirits rose. Soon, I hoped, I would have something really useful to do. I recall how, one hot and dry morning, I was leading a section along a sunken road bordering one of these woods. The road had earlier been defensively held by a party of Germans which had been obliterated by shell-fire. Several corpses had been pushed to the side, under a chalk bank. I noticed that, as we passed these dead bodies, intermittent buzzing noises came out of them. I looked closer. It was so. When a dead man is exposed long enough to the weather, his mouth opens and his lips shrink back. Flies enter the cavity and lay their eggs. The buzzing was caused by flies escaping from the open mouths. 'A good thing that the poor devils are well and truly dead and cannot see themselves.'

One of our difficulties during this tense period was to know how much attention to pay to gas. We had been told that the Germans used some stuff called phosgene which had a sweetish somewhat repellent smell and a delayed action on the heart. Bernafay and Trônes Woods emitted a variety of odours some of which, like tear gas, were pungent and made your eyes run, while others were in various ways disgusting but did not interfere with your vision or movements. These woods were full of wire and debris, including the branches and prostrate trunks of trees, so that the wearing of a gas mask interfered with both vision and movement. One did not lightly put on one's gas mask, or give the order that others should do so. The danger, however, of postponing the order too long was brought home by the sight in a forward dressing station of three blue-faced gasping men leaning forward and retching. These, I was told, had had 'a touch of phosgene'.

Late in the evening of 14 September an order came through for an officer to go up to Bernafay Wood with a platoon from each company. Each platoon was to put into the best order it could, for later occupation that night by the company to which it belonged, a section of what had been a continuous trench. The assignment fell to me. It was not a long march but we carried heavy gear. The light was fading. I was in a state of suppressed elation.

I led the party to the rendezvous in Bernafay Wood where, after sunset, I was met by Overton-Jones and Joe Forrester. In the darkness these two guided my party through many obstacles to the trench we had to clear and smarten up. Stretches were allocated to the platoons of each company and the work was well forward by the time the companies themselves arrived.

I vaguely recall a cold night with tension rising as the hands of my frequently-consulted wrist watch moved round towards six o'clock. By 6.20 the sky was lightening in the east, promising cloudless sunrise and a fine day. Suddenly earth and sky were rent. Out of the comparative calm of the autumn morning the deafening barrage crashed forth. The air went taut in a tidal wave of sound which pressed on your ear drums and made you reel and feel dizzy. To your blunted senses it seemed that everything round you was spouting noise – the blasted trees, the iron pickets, the barbed wire, the very earth. The air seemed to go solid with it, stiffening and rounding your back. Your senses were pressed down into a lower plane of consciousness. Standing like mutes, we communicated by sign-language and gesture.

A disgression about the plan and outcome of the attack which were not the same. At a higher level things had so worked out that the first three Coldstream Battalions went over in line – a unique event in Regimental history. (A fine stone memorial to the Guards Division stands on the Ginchy-Les Boeufs road). Each of the three battalions went over in two waves in which two companies were supported by the other two. I attach a diagram which is based on map 18 of Sir John Ross-of-Bladensburgh's regimental history of the war.

It will be seen that the attack began at the demolished village of Ginchy, which was partly in our hands, and that the area to be taken stretched in a belt about a thousand yards wide which extended in a north-easterly direction. The objective, some 2½ miles ahead, was the likewise demolished village of Les Boeufs, or rather to be precise, a red line beyond it on its north-east side. The area forms a belt which curves to the right (north-east). Running like a spine down the middle of this belt, which dips into a shallow valley between starting-point and objective, is a road connecting the two villages of Ginchy and Les Boeufs. On paper the plan of attack looked feasible. Villages (reduced to rubble, but marked by partly-destroyed church spires) formed the starting-point and the objective; and down the centre of the belt ran a road which should have been recognizable as such during the course of the battle.

The phases of the attack, which were geared to a timetable, were planned to correspond with four lines, easy to draw on paper and thought to be identifiable on the ground by already prepared and duly photographed German trenches. These were called Green, Brown, Blue, and Red lines. The day, moreover, was a highlight in the history of modern war in that tanks were then used for the first time. These monstrous vehicles had been kept a top secret and it was hoped that the shock of their appearance and the discovery of their invulnerability would cause panic. No one knew what their effect would be, and high hopes were entertained. If they fully succeeded, something like a

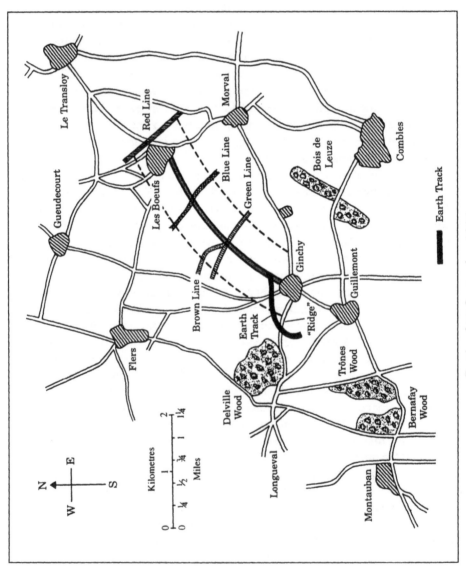

Battle of 15 September 1916

Earth Track

N
W — E
S

Kilometres
0   ¼   ½   ¾   1   2
0   ½   1   1¼
Miles

Le Transloy
Red Line
Morval
Gueudecourt
Blue Line
Green Line
Bois de Leuze
Combles
Les Boeufs
Brown Line
Ginchy
Earth Track
Guillemont
"Ridge"
Flers
Delville Wood
Trônes Wood
Bernafay Wood
Longueval
Montauban

breakthrough might be possible. Hence the battle was planned with optimism.

Ginchy had been vigorously defended. There ran into the place, from both east and west, roads which contained strongpoints still in German hands. By these strongpoints both our flanks would be threatened at the outset. Hence it had been planned that the infantry attack should be preceded by the appearance of a tank on each side of Ginchy which would secure the flanks.

In the event the plans did not work out. There were three main causes. The first was that the two expected tanks did not turn up, so that severe casualties were sustained at the start from flanking fire. The second was that new German trenches had recently been dug which did not show in the aerial photographs and of which no account had been taken in the demarcations of the four coloured lines. In the event the positions on the ground which, during the battle, were thought to have been reached were less far advanced than those which, on paper, should have been reached. The third cause was that from the low ground which lay between the Green and Blue lines the spire of Les Boeufs' church could not be seen. The change of direction – a half-wheel to the right – was a difficult exercise at the best of times. Without visible landmarks and with heavy fire from both flanks, the attack slipped to the left. The objectives planned for capture on 15 September were not taken till ten days later.

Of these events we, in the 4th Battalion, awaiting orders in Bernafay Wood, knew little. Conflicting rumours percolated, mostly brought back by walking wounded. At one moment we were told that the attack was going splendidly; at the next that there was a complete hold-up.

At last – it must have been soon after 7 a.m. – a message came through for an officer to report at once at Battalion Headquarters for a particular assignment. My state of elation persisted. I pushed myself and got the job. I vaguely remember receiving orders and explanations from Clive Piggott who was cheerful and clear in his instructions. The job I had to do was what I had half-expected. A consolidated track or earth-road had to be made through the crater-field in the wake of the advance which could be temporarily used by horse-drawn vehicles. But it was not known how far the attack had penetrated. I was told to cross the Ginchy-Longueval road east of Delville Wood, which runs along a ridge, and reconnoitre the area towards Les Boeufs. I should decide where the road should run, mark it with pickets, and send back messages on how many troops to send up. Best call them up in small groups – platoons or sections – distribute them at wide intervals and shift them about, always maintaining wide intervals. The work was urgent, but – 'We don't want to have casualties quite out of proportion to the amount of work we get done'.

The attack had taken off from positions on each side of Ginchy. On the left of Ginchy the starting position roughly corresponded with a third-class road which ran east-west along the 'ridge' between Ginchy on the right (east) and Longueval to the west. As it approached Longueval from Ginchy, this road skirted the south side of Delville Wood, by then a blasted wilderness, like Bernafay and Trônes Woods. As seen from the ridge, Les Boeufs and Morval (to the right) were pinpointed by what remained upright of their church steeples. When I received my orders, the position at Ginchy was uncertain; but it might be clarified at any moment. Our earth track would skirt Ginchy on its north-west and north sides in a wide half-circle as shown in the diagram; and in so doing would cross at right angles the road which connected Ginchy with Flers. When projected further, our course would take us up to the Ginchy – Les Boeufs road, the 'spine' of the attack. The orders were perfectly clear. I knew exactly what I had to do when I left Clive.

My first task was to reconnoitre the ground immediately north of the 'ridge'. I set out with Sergeant Davidson, a solid sort of N.C.O. with a loud bark, and two men in No. 10 platoon who could take back reports.

The weather continued to be cool and the sky cloudless when my small party set out for 'the ridge'. The battle had begun at 6.30 a.m. This ridge had since been continuously shelled by the Germans. But an hour or two later it looked as if this danger could be circumvented. And so it proved. By the time we got there the explosions were of large, noisy and smoky shells which we took to be five-nines. They came down with a forewarning crescendo of noise at regular intervals on much the same point of the 'ridge'. You waited in a shell-hole on the hither side till there was a crash. You then doubled across in your quickest time. This our small party did. We spread out till we were well separated, and ran across. We reassembled in two large shell-holes on the ridge's north side and recovered our breath. From this safe vantage-point we leisurely surveyed the recently contested battlefield stretched out below us. It was a fine broad view. But it did not correspond with maps or diagrams, and what we saw was not encouraging.

*   *   *   *

At this point I again digress. I have twice revisited this area – in 1936 and 1952. On both occasions I was forcibly struck by the same thing: how much flatter everything looked and how much shorter the distances seemed. The above-mentioned ridge on which we stood seemed scarcely raised above the surrounding cornfields which had been planted after 1918; and from the ridge the reconstructed steeples of the churches of Flers, Les Boeufs and Morval looked astonishingly tall and near. The rebuilt villages and the presence of a few outhouses and barns seemed to have contracted the landscape. This effect may have been reinforced by the standing corn. I could hardly believe that the basic distances and contours were the same. The area was, in fact, scarcely recognizable.

*   *   *   *

To return to Sergeant Davidson and myself sitting in our shell-hole on the north side of the ridge. I repeat that what we saw and heard was scarcely encouraging. The prodigious cannonade of the early morning had quietened down. It was replaced by desultory and separately identifiable noises. The first thing to strike us was the presence in the sky to our front of a large and insolently conspicuous German observation balloon. This vile object seemed to be anchored to the ground just north of Les Boeufs. Other such balloons were strung out into the distance to the north and west. It certainly did not look as if Les Boeufs had been taken or that the enemy there were seriously incommoded. The next thing to strike us was how little movement was to be seen. A pitted and smoky but dry expanse; no waterlogged shell-holes; no boggy ground. With our field glasses we searched for some sign of troops of either side. None visible. If any were about they were concealed in the hazy landscape. We looked for tanks. None to be seen. Shells, mostly of small calibre, were occasionally exploding anywhere. Nothing like a concerted bombardment. Fairly frequent bursts of machine-gun fire, but you couldn't see where they were coming from. Occasional rifle shots. Now and then the twang of an exploding Mills bomb.

We tried to pick out the Ginchy-Flers road which our track was to cross at right-angles. I thought I saw something which might be the road, but I was not certain. I would have preferred to see more movement. It looked as if the attack had been held up so that our gunners did not know where to shoot. The conclusion emerged: if we brought our platoons up and distributed them along the line of our projected road, they would at once be seen by the fellow looking down on us. His attention would be little diverted by other events in his field of vision. The quiescence was discouraging.

I decided to take a look at the area between our ridge and the Ginchy – Flers road. In what sort of state was the road? My small party set out, keeping several yards apart. As soon as we began to move we saw that we were not alone. There were wounded men in shell-holes. The first man I saw pointed to a smashed and bleeding leg which he held up for me to see. His face was contorted with pain. He besought me for God's sake to do something for him. I could do nothing beyond giving him some water and assuring him that help would soon come. Approaching us in singles, couples or threes were walking wounded, dodging from hole to hole. One was being helped along by a wounded German. There passed us a knot of white-faced, broken-spirited prisoners shuffling along unescorted. Suddenly we found what we were looking for – road metal. It was the Ginchy-Flers road. This, if built up, would provide something more solid underfoot than our earth track. Davidson and I reconnoitred it in opposite directions – Davidson towards Ginchy, I towards Flers. I soon came to what had been a German strongpoint. Several dead Germans lay over each other. In a steep-sided crater was a wounded Scots Guards officer and two quaking, pale-faced unwounded Germans, their nerves shattered by the bombardment. They had done what they could for the officer. My orderly and I gave them some ration biscuits which they ate like starving animals, having had (they said) practically no food for forty-eight hours. We did what we could for the officer who wanted a drink of water more than anything else. The further I moved towards Flers, the less broken the road became. Then Smack! A near rifle bullet. I was within sniping range. I turned and zig-zagged back. A few minutes later I rejoined Davidson who reported that the nearer he approached Ginchy the worse the road became. Between us we fixed the course of our projected earth track.

But the main trouble continued to loom above. What, I wondered, was preventing our airmen (or gunners) from shooting down these balloons? If that vigilant eye overhead could be removed from the sky we would have no doubt about what we should do about our road. Ought we to be deterred by the risk? I decided not. So I sent back a message that work could start forthwith, but that we would be in danger from the balloon. Could anything be done about having it brought down?

Off went an orderly with my written message while I waited in the shell-hole on the north of the ridge. I was in a state of mounting tension as to what would happen when the first platoon came up, and of dubious hope that, before it arrived, the balloon would no longer be there.

I forget how long I sat there watching the skyline. It might have been half an hour. Suddenly appeared a party of men doubling in open order across the ridge. It was No.12 platoon among whom Treffry was identifiable by his tall figure, riding boots and large moustache. They all got safely across in a well-timed move, and took cover in shell-holes. I found Treffry in one of these holes where we were joined by Sergeant Sheridan, his platoon sergeant. I showed them the direction of the picketed track on which they could get to work at once. The platoon had come up with shovels and earth rammers which looked like large pestles.

I drew attention to the balloon overhead. Vital to keep No.12 well separated along the track. No bunching. 'The fellow up there has field-glasses and if he thinks you a worthwhile target, it won't be long before you know about it.' The platoon was soon strung out along the projected 'road' and getting on nicely. I took the half-stretch towards Ginchy, Treffry took the other. For about twenty minutes all went well. A passable track was coming into existence which I hoped would not be noticed from above. Desultory small arms fire from right and left of which we took no notice. From our side intermittent shelling. Things seemed to be quiet enough to push ahead with the road. I decided to call up another platoon and sent back a message.

It was at this stage that a scattered party came up from the valley, scrambling past us. It was a platoon of No.4 Company. I recognized Kelsey quite close. He stopped and we had a word. I noticed that he looked hot and shaken and that his uniform was soiled with earth. No wonder. The attack below had

128

been halted and a call sent back for Mills bombs. These Kelsey had most bravely delivered despite heavy small arms fire at close range. He had lost several men.

For the next ten minutes nothing particular occurred. I was beginning to feel more relaxed when two things befell simultaneously. First, without the slightest warning, a salvo of whizzbangs came down about a hundred yards on the balloon side of our 'road' – short from the German gunners' standpoint. (Hell! Have we been seen? Are we being bracketed?) Second, a party of men appeared doubling across the ridge as No.12 had done. They were No.10, with Woggs Allan. I sent a verbal message to Woggs to get his party across, take cover, and wait. Not long to wait. The second salvo shrieked over our heads and burst about thirty yards above our track. No doubt now that we were being bracketed. These salvos could not have been accidental. 'Carry on, but keep as low as you can,' I passed down.

The third salvo burst in our midst. Treffry was standing about twenty yards to my left, and as I threw myself down I had a glimpse of a whizzbang bursting under his feet, throwing him forward so that he somersaulted like a shot rabbit. I saw his booted legs circling in the air as if he were doing a cart-wheel. The thought: 'What am I going to see in the next ten seconds,' was like a weight in the midriff as I raced towards him. Treffry was lying on his back. One leg had almost been blown off with the jagged end of a femur sticking out. An artery was spurting. The other leg had been twisted back to front. His uniform had been ripped open and his abdomen gaped with his bowels extruding. His face and moustache were a parched yellow. Stertorous sounds and blood were coming from his mouth. His sightless eyes were turned up. No first aid was possible. Through the horror two thoughts penetrated. 'Get him across the ridge; and send back No.10'. Then another dreadful thought came: 'Put him out of his misery with your Colt automatic'. Sergeant Sheridan was somewhere near me. 'Get your platoon back. Wait the other side. Tell Mr Allan to do the same with No.10.' No.12 had brought a stretcher. As we tried to lift the mortally wounded man he regained consciousness. He wanted to say something. I leant over him. In an almost inaudible voice he croaked: 'Get them out of it. Get out of it yourself. Leave me here.' Another salvo came down around us, temporarily deafening me. The trajectory was nearly horizontal. One shell passed not more than four feet over the heads of two of us who were kneeling beside the prostrate man. Corporal Fuller of No.12 platoon later said to me: 'If you had been standing up instead of kneeling down, it would have taken your head off.' Several men were lying around wounded, one severely in the thigh. Somehow Corporal Fuller and I lifted Treffry on to the stretcher and we carried him over the ridge. I took the head end so that I could not see the sight behind me. The slow barrage on the ridge had totally vanished from my mind until we were in the act of crossing. Then a five-nine came down. We heard it coming in a crescendo. The shell hit the ground about eight yards to the left of our party. It dived deep into the churned-up soil before exploding, and shot up a vertical column of earth high into the air. Some came down on our heads and on the prone man we were carrying. We lowered him for a few seconds. I hoped that he was unconscious by then. But no. As the last of the earth was coming down he shifted his head and I heard him mutter something.

When we had re-crossed the ridge I saw for the first time the red cross of a first-aid post in the dip below us, close to Guillemont. There a young R.A.M.C. officer came up and took a look. 'Hopeless,' he said. 'Nothing to do but put him to sleep'. I thanked God that those were his views and begged him to pump in all the morphia he could spare. This he did, injecting some into Treffry's arm and the rest into a collapsed vein. But Treffry had a tough constitution and did not die till nightfall.

There was nothing more I could do at the aid post. I had an impulse to get away and a half-hope that I would myself be killed. Some of those men who were wounded in the last salvo were still lying out. As I was re-crossing the ridge the thought penetrated that there was something I had not done. I had not sent back a report. There and then, on the top of the ridge, I sat down in a shell-hole and composed a message. I said that it was impossible to work in daylight on the proposed road as long as those balloons were overhead. But the complete job could be done that night by as many men as could be spared.

As I was composing this message another five-nine came down. How near it was I don't know, but the earth it threw up made such a mess of my field note-book that I had to start another message. As I was doing so I realized two things: first that a few moments before, I had not heard the five-nine coming down, and second that I was a fool to be writing the message in that place. But I had no inclination to move. On the contrary, I found myself wishing that the next one would come down on me so that I too could take my leave and join forces with Treffry.

The forgotten duty completed, I moved on to see about those other wounded men. I cannot remember how many times I went to and fro: twice I think. I recall finding the man who had been wounded in the thigh and, with someone else, carrying him back on a stretcher. I have an uncertain memory of going back for a man with a smashed foot who could hobble with help. Not long after I reported personally to George Edwards. He at once saw that we couldn't do what was expected in that area by day with the balloon overhead. We exchanged speech about observation balloons. Why had they been allowed to stay up there? Before the attack an infinity of trouble had been taken about creeping barrages and counter-battery work. Had someone forgotten about observation balloons?

Later in the day I did two more jobs. In the afternoon I went up with a couple of men carrying spools of tape. The view from the ridge was much the same. The sounds of battle were more subdued. Unwinding our spools as we covered the ground, we marked the track up to and beyond the Ginchy-Flers road where we had found the Scots Guards officer and the two German prisoners, and up to the Ginchy-Les Boeufs road. Then, about two hours later, at dusk, I led a large part of the Battalion across the now familiar ridge, where all by then was peace and quiet, and distributed the companies along the taped course. The ground on each side had by then been cleared of wounded. It seemed wonderful how quiet everything had become. A blessed calm. After the large party had got down to work, I was sent back and told to get some sleep.

The battalion did the job completely and thoroughly to the satisfaction of everyone. We were commended by the C.R.E. and thanked by later users. I don't think we had a single casualty.

That night I shared a dug-out with Overton-Jones. I was tired but could not sleep. I kept having nightmares about Treffry. I could not banish the persistent images. There he was after his first night out with the company in the Salient, jubilant about having had his 'baptism of fire'. There he was appearing with No. 12 on the sky-line, standing without knowing it on the edge of an abyss. There he was, shattered and disembowelled, his face a yellow mask. There he was on a stretcher with earth falling on his exposed mutilations. These and other images would appear, permutate and disappear, as if thrown up from a seething cauldron. This went on for two or three nights and then quietened. But Treffry persisted. After about a week he was still appearing, but against happier backgrounds. It was as if I were looking at photographs taken in earlier months. He began to show himself as cheerful and smart as when he joined us. As time passed these dream-appearances began to bring feelings of reassurance. 'So he's alive and his old self again!' Or even: 'So he's never been killed after all. Balloons, whizzbangs, the ridge were just nightmares.' These nocturnal reassurances intermittently persisted. By mid-October I was still dreaming of Treffry, but the dreams had become disconnected and repeated themselves less. But I recall two which recurred. In the first he was dancing his *pas seul* like an Indian brave, as I had seen him do at H-camp; in the second I dreamt of him fishing. Later, for several nights I dreamt of a small boy who puzzled me. He wore a white shirt with pink markings. This boy was not a central feature of the dreams, but nevertheless conveyed as if by a signal: 'See! I'm here. Don't overlook me'. After about the third of these appearances it came into my head that this was the boy who had sat by Treffry when he was fishing. Rowan trees, I realized, also came in: clean, colourful trees of modest size, with a numinous quality. The small boy never obtruded himself, but he continued to appear. He was associated with fishing; and at last something became obvious which had escaped me: that he was connected with Treffry. Some weeks later the thought came: perhaps the boy *is* Treffry who is trying to convey a message not by words or writing but through a symbol. He may be wanting to say: 'Stop fretting about me. The ordeal is over and I am through it. You can think, if you like, that I've been reborn.'

This peculiar line of thought may have come from my having at that time read a book about Wagner's operas which gave the story of Amfortas, the incurably wounded fisher-king. The fish was a symbol of regeneration, and in the last act Amfortas was healed by the miraculous spear which had pierced the side of Christ. But Treffry was scarcely an operatic figure. Had he, however, the makings of a mythical figure? He may have become so for the small boys who watched him with his rod fifty-three years ago as I write this narrative.

A week or two after Treffry's death I was talking about him to Sergeant Sheridan who said something surprising. He had noticed that, as the time for us to move out of the Salient approached, Treffry began to lose his sparkle; he had become silent and had moods of depression. 'He knew his number was up,' said Sheridan. 'He used to talk to me during route marches.' Sheridan then said: 'When we were marching up from Bernafay on that last day he was certain that he was going to be killed. He knew it, and he told me so.'

In the light of what I have since learned about what has variously been called shell-shock, battle-fatigue, combat-stress etc., I count myself fortunate that I came through the events of 15 September 1916 without suffering after-effects of any sort.

7

BITTER WINTER 1916–17

During the rest of September and during October 1916 the Battle of the Somme drew to a close. The Guards Division did a second and more successful attack on 25 September in the course of which Les Boeufs was taken, together with quite a lot of ground to the north-east of the village. Morval and Combles were at the same time captured by the French on our right. The British army eventually reached and took Sailly-Saillisel on the Bapaume-Peronne road.

During the years of static warfare, one tended to develop a frontier mentality. On the other side of the line, it seemed, you would find yourself in another planet; and one was unrealistically curious about what the people and the country would be like. In imagination the difference between the two sides of the frontier were magnified. During the 1916–17 winter the 'frontier' on our sector was the Bapaume-Péronne road, whereon Sailly-Saillisel formed a protuberance into alien territory. Sailly-Saillisel was an auspicious sort of name which did not suggest war. It suggested, rather, summer flowers – ox-eye daisies in a meadow. I used to play with the idea that, unhealthy as it was for us during those months, after the war Sailly-Saillisel should be commemorated by some sort of floral emblem of peace. The prototype of those feelings was, I believe, a story (now forgotten) which had been read to me in childhood about a frontier or border on each side of which lived two peoples who, for some transgression, had been punished by a compulsion to treat each other as enemies, though each side secretly wanted to treat the other as friendly. Publicly they abused each other. Yet both sides prayed that sometime a chthonic figure (something like Erda in *Siegfried*) would emerge from the ground, ban the feud, and bring reconciliation.

It was with feelings of joyful relief that, at the beginning of October, we moved back to a place called Quesnoy about 15 miles west of Amiens. I have fragmentary memories. The first stage of the move was a rather long march. In the dark hours of the night of (I think) 1 October, orders came that we should be ready to move at 5.30 a.m., which gave us short notice. Our kit was packed and the camp tidied. There followed an eleven-mile march which for me was tough because Temple, who was not well at the time, packed all my revolver ammunition into my haversack. I was unnecessarily loaded. By mid-morning we arrived at a railhead whence we were to be taken on by train. Rain fell as we were waiting for the train so that we became cold and wet. But the boredom was relieved by the presence nearby of a working party of recently-captured German prisoners who were unloading trucks of flints. One of these men could speak French and with this man, during a work-interval, I got into conversation. We were joined by Quincey Greene and Thompson, both of whom had a smattering of German. We encouraged these prisoners to air their views. The British, they told us, intended to keep Belgium after the war. The Germans, on the other had, were willing to evacuate France and Belgium, having no designs whatever on Antwerp. All they wanted was a peace which would guarantee the country's security. These men professed detestation of their own socialist leaders, including Liebknecht and Maximilian Harden. The Kaiser, they said, was a man of peace – in which respect he was unlike his son the Crown Prince, whom they blamed for their heaviest losses at Verdun. From their angle, Verdun had been a failure; but then we could scarcely claim either Verdun or the Somme as triumphs. The Germans, they said, were in possession of 2,800 villages; at enormous cost we had succeeded in taking back 43. They praised the fighting qualities of the French. These qualities they esteemed more highly than those of the Russians who were unwilling soldiers and badly led. These opinions doubtless reflected the propaganda which at that stage of the war was being put out on the other side.

They asked us what we thought. I replied that we esteemed highly the fighting qualities of the Germans; but their allies fell short of their standards and would be their undoing in the end. We were sick of the war, I said, but would continue to attack them until either they voluntarily withdrew from all invaded territories (where they had no business to be) or until they were defeated.

During this exchange, which ended with expressions of hope that we and they should personally survive the war, the rain began to come down, so that we were glad when our train steamed in. It consisted not of coaches but of open-doored vans. Sitting by the open doors we passed through the congestions of Amiens, and our spirits rose when, the rain having stopped, we were transported into the unspoiled countryside of the west. I recall how the train halted for ten minutes opposite some reed-bordered ponds surrounded by poplars where it was cheering to hear through the open door the tin-trumpet-like calls of coots and the melancholy calls of wood-pigeons. A pleasant change from gunfire. Quesnoy welcomed us in the person of an old and deaf but hospitable lady who, for our supper, prepared a delectable omelette. The day ended in luxury – between sheets on a bed.

On the morning of Tuesday 3 October, Dickinson received an order that he and I should report at once at C.O.'s orders. We were both mildly apprehensive. But there were no grounds for misgivings. I recall that, when approaching the improvised orderly room, we saw George Edwards, Piggott and Kelsey standing outside and grinning broadly. We were then told that Kelsey and I had been awarded Military Crosses. I was delighted about Kelsey who most thoroughly deserved his award. As for myself, I knew that Military Crosses did not materialize out of the ether and that someone or other must have written out and forwarded a story. Skeff, Clive or George had obviously taken an initiative, and after handshakings and congratulations, I wanted to thank them for taking so much trouble over so unworthy a cause. But I felt self-conscious and foolish. The occasion was one of general mirth in which Dickinson joined. I recall his face wrinkled in an amused smile as he patted me on the back.

That night Kelsey and I dined at headquarters. Skeff sat at the head of the narrow table, Kelsey and I on each side of him opposite each other. Also present were Edwards and Piggott, Sharpley, Raffle and Joe Forrester. The fact that both Kelsey and I were total abstainers from alcohol did not make for festiveness. I recorded the conversation as singularly flat. We must have struck the others as a dreary couple. These two Military Crosses were the first awarded to the Battalion. Everyone was most amiable. I recall kind words from Joe Forrester, who was amused that the first recipients were teetotallers, from Overton-Jones and from Lionel who laughingly said he was exceedingly jealous – a frame of mind which was well and truly belied by his obvious pleasure. (I was not given an opportunity to reciprocate his pleasurable feelings till August of the following year when he thoroughly earned a Military Cross for splendid work in bridging a canal during the Battle of Passchendaele.) So far as I was concerned, I had mixed feelings. On one side I was aware of embarrassment and doubt as to how far a decoration of this sort had been genuinely earned; while on the other, I must admit to a gain in self-assurance. My position in the Battalion would now be more solid. But in volatile moments I must be on my guard against hubris. Perhaps a good thing, I thought, that I don't drink alcohol. Another good thing: my parents would be pleased, but I must see that they did not get the affair out of focus.

Behind these self-centred feelings were thoughts of poor old Treffry whose last words, heard only by myself, earned him the highest merit in the halls of Valhalla, or their Christian equivalents. These and similar thoughts caused me to reflect, not for the first or last time, on how often, with the best intentions of everyone concerned, the awards bestowed by human beings on each other fail to accord with genuine deserts, on how rarely genuine merit is justly reflected by the insight of merit which they centre on each other.

The prospects of at least three weeks of peace and quiet in rural surroundings seemed good not only to myself and No.3 Company. They would also bring a temporary relief to my parents. It can be seen from their September letters what anxieties the recent battles caused. The stress had perhaps been aggravated by contrast with the peace of mind they had enjoyed during the earlier spring months when I had been safe in the forest.

But our complacent expectations were shattered on the evening of 5 October. We were sitting at dinner when in walked the tall, erect, and sphinx-like Clive Piggott who in his unperturbed voice delivered himself of the following five words: 'We return to Montauban tomorrow'. Acute despondency accompanied by loud groans. Dickinson, about whom a word below, commiserated with Clive over having to act as the bearer of woeful tidings, and added: 'It's really worse for the men than for us'. The comment was characteristic of how Dickie's mind worked. He suggested that it would be well if the platoon officers broke the bad news to their platoons. This initiative, whatever its effect on the platoons, was good for us. It prevented us from being unduly sorry for ourselves.

We did the return journey by lorry. I quote from a letter I wrote home: 'I shan't describe my feelings as we passed from the peaceful countryside with its serene agricultural pursuits and autumn tints, through the disturbed atmosphere of Amiens and into the fevered troop-ridden area of desolation where no green thing can be seen and no building stands intact, and where there stretched before us an undulating expanse of mud teeming with men horses and guns.' My words were sententious but the prospect was indeed bleak. When, however, we reached our destination and fitted ourselves in, things did not turn out as badly as we had expected.

In the mess life was transformed by the replacement of Bingo by Alan Dickinson, known to everyone as Dickie. It took a few weeks for the implications of this change to sink in and to bring home what an important factor it was in the life of a junior officer to be able to feel complete loyalty to his company commander. Dickie was a truly admirable man. As I understood him his three salient qualities were modesty, gentleness and a sense of duty. At Eton, I was told, he had had quite a distinguished career. He left in 1890, the same year as Skeff, so that he was about 44 when he came to No.3 Company. Though not soldier-like by temperament, as he frequently said of himself, he had taken part in the South African campaigns and wore the same medal ribbons as Skeff and Bingo. Unlike several people I could mention, he never talked about himself or his past life, so that I never learned much about his personal background. When the war broke out in 1914 he joined the Royal Fusiliers as a private; he transferred to the Coldstreams in July 1915. He wore a small moustache, had a small head, thin neck and lined face which readily broke into a most charming smile. He was of medium height and slender build, with a slight stoop which became more pronounced when he was tired or worried. But he was tough and could march fully laden as well as anyone in the company. In manner he was invariably gentle, considerate and courteous. He was completely devoid of snobbery and treated all ranks alike. In some respects he resembled Clive Piggott, though outwardly they were wholly different. The two men had the same feelings about Company Orders. Both much disliked dealing out punishments, but they equally understood how necessary it was to back up one's N.C.O.s. I recall Dickie once telling me how difficult it sometimes was for him to be a good disciplinarian. For some reason he had postponed marriage till late in life, and shortly before (or perhaps during) his period with No.3 he became engaged. His fiancée was a physical invalid and could scarcely walk: he used to carry her about the house. It was characteristic of Dickie that his main reason for wanting the war to end was that he would then be able to devote to her in full the time and attention she needed. He had a poor word of command and did not cut much of a figure on parades. But this shortcoming was as nothing when compared with his golden qualities. When under fire or otherwise in danger, he was splendid. But, perhaps more than most of us, he hated seeing men wounded.

After the war, he lived at Crowhurst in Sussex, and such time as could be spared from his home duties he devoted to Dr Barnardo's homes. About these he would talk freely. After his death Joe Forrester happened to see in *The Times* a notice of his will. Rather to our surprise (for no one could have lived more modestly) he turned out to be a rich man.

My letters remind me that, during this period, we occupied two tented camps at Montauban, one closer to the remains of the village than the other. But I only remember one of these camps which we thought was disquietingly near the crossroads. These crossroads were much used by military traffic, and this the Germans well knew, for they paid the place quite a lot of highly unwelcome attention. This took the form of intermittent shelling by a single long-range high-velocity gun of substantial calibre which we called Quick Dick. The shells came over singly, never in salvos. This gun, we inferred, was used on set targets well behind our lines. Carnoys, a village three miles southwest of Montauban and also a busy traffic centre, likewise received regular attention.

I connect this high-velocity German gun with the most acute spasm of physical fear which I experienced during the war – or indeed during my life. The intensity of sudden fear is determined not only by the external event which frightens you. It is also affected by your inner mental state at the moment. Primitive people work themselves up before a battle with war dances and war cries, thereby producing a sort of immunity from fear. But if the external event is wholly unexpected you are caught unawares. Your resistance is at its lowest.

This was my condition when I was occupying a tent in our camp near Montauban crossroads. I was fast asleep in my flea-bag which was laid out on a trestle about six inches above the ground. At about 2 a.m. a high-velocity shell, doubtless intended for the crossroads about 150 yards away, overshot its mark, skimmed our tent-tops and exploded about twenty yards from my tent and about eight yards from the outermost row of tents in the camp's perimeter. Three things happened in the same fraction of a second: during the last few yards of its trajectory the massive projectile rent the sky with a shriek of unparalleled fiendishness; it smote the unoffending earth like a thunderbolt of unsurpassable malignancy; and it exploded, hurling into the air a waggon-load of earth, stones and debris which showered down on the canvases over our heads. Our tent-poles rocked; I was thrown off the trestles on to the ground encased in my flea-bag; and for a moment I could not move. Momentarily I thought that my heart had stopped. The shells seemed to have fallen on the next door tent. But there was no ensuing hubbub. No cries of wounded. Instead – silence. I picked myself up, pulled myself together, grabbed my electric torch and ran out of the tent barefooted. Other officers did the same. I retain an indelible mental picture of four or five of us, with British warms over our pyjamas standing in darkness round a smoking pit six feet across into which we shone our Oriluxes. There followed some forced jocularity, some disjointed remarks about luck, and some words about what now ought to be done. Someone suggested that the best thing we could do was to get down on to our knees and give thanks. Subdued talk began in the tents. It was finally decided to do nothing and hope for the best. Some slit trenches could be dug the next day. After some shouts addressed to those who could hear us in the nearby tents of 'Go to sleep and have happy dreams', we returned to our blankets and flea-bags, some having resorted to their hip-flasks for warmth and confidence. Nothing more came over that night, nor, on the following nights, did anything again come so near.

The following day I happened to meet an officer of the Pioneer Battalion of the division which had taken over on our left after 25 September. This man gave me a graphic account of how a tank had led the infantry in the attack on Gueudecourt. The tank had reached the village, closely followed by remnants of the first wave. But the tank had been put out of action and the position could not be held. The only road back had become impossible because of shelling and rain. It took relays of men several hours to carry a single stretcher case to the nearest ambulance. For two or three days after the attack many wounded men, including some Germans, were lying out in shell-holes. The German wounded, this officer told me, knew that they would not be carried back until all the British had been dealt with, and several had begged to be put out of their misery. All available morphia and first aid supplies had been used up. The prospect was so hopeless that, during the night, some of the officers in his division had mercifully shot a few of these unsaveable men through the head, but not before an unsuccessful effort had been made to make a temporary truce with the Germans in front of the divisional position. It had been hoped that they would be able to save some of their own men, their communications in rear being in better shape than ours. It was a terrible story which my informant, who struck me as truthful, told me with reluctance. It made me feel that, though our attack on Les Boeufs had been bad enough, we had been spared some grim experiences afterwards.

By the time we were back at Montauban, the rains of the last fortnight had upset communications and the Battalion was put on to road work. We made what was called a 'corduroy road', which in part of its course passed through both Bernafay and Trônes woods – by then relatively safe areas. The work put me in mind of Clairmarais. We made what use we could of fallen trees and debris. Obstructive roots were dug out of craters which were then filled with lop debris and brushwood (to assist drainage), and a thin layer of earth was rammed down on the top, thus producing a level surface some twenty feet wide. Upon this surface logs, brought up on trucks, measuring nine feet, were laid one behind the other and side by side. The resulting eighteen foot road was rough, but it was better than nothing and we were told that it might be topped by road metal later. This work called for the use of axes and it pleased me to see how quickly, with the minimum of instruction, No.3 became competent in their use. It was pleasant to hear again in fine weather the cheerful clicking of axe strokes round about. I felled my first sweet chestnut. Stick bombs, grenades and Mills bombs were locally plentiful and we had to be careful how we used our picks. Little danger in day-time, but dangerous at night when you couldn't see what you might be hitting. A faint smell of gas still pervaded these woods, but it was nowhere discomfiting or even disagreeable.

At this period the Battalion suffered losses from departures. Seven officers left us. Jimmy Coats, to whose company I had been attached during some of the Laventie period, was a widely-felt loss. He took on the adjutancy of the Second Battalion, to which, later in the war, he helped me to transfer. Quincey Greene, Brierly, Thompson, Hanbury and Porter (who had lived most of his life in South America and whose voice had faint Spanish inflections) also left for other Battalions. The seventh departure was Kelsey. On 7 October he went to Divisional Headquarters as machine-gun officer. I was indeed sorry to say goodbye to him.

Such slender hopes as may have been entertained of the war ending soon were dispelled by the short but sharp Romanian campaign. The Romanians thought that the heavy pressures sustained by the Central Powers during the year 1916 made the moment auspicious for them to come in on our side; but they took a long time in bargaining with us about terms. They started their war at the beginning of September in the hope that the Germans would not be able to spare the necessary divisions from the Western Front to put up a fight. But the Germans had taken due account of this possible intervention, and when the time came two separate German armies were ready. Bucharest fell in early December and the local war was over the following January. General Falkenhayn, on whose initiative the Germans had decided to attack Verdun, was put in command of the German ninth army which descended on

Romania from the north-west through passes in the Carpathian mountains, and General Mackensen moved into the coastal area of the Dobruja from the south-west.

The swift outcome of this campaign on which hopes had been built, shook those who had convinced themselves that Germany was on her last legs. My own mood was reflected by a postscript to a letter I wrote home on 9 October: 'This war is *not* going to end this year. It will go on after Christmas; and next spring or summer we will have more big offensives and more colossal losses. It is useless to hope. One must be fatalistic and resigned'. I went on to extol these passive virtues, declaring that they could be cultivated if one really tried. Easier for me than for them, but the only thing they could do.

*   *   *   *

The last ten days of October 1916 CPB spent on leave in Paris.

*   *   *   *

When my leave was over, the Fourth Battalion, which had continued in use as Corps troops and was therefore still detached from the resting division, was not easy to find. At Amiens, to which I returned on 1 November, no one seemed to know where it was. Eventually I discovered by accident that the Battalion was still in the same area. It turned out that No.3 Company was on its own at a place called Méaulte, about a mile south of Albert, where there were facilities for baths. Thither I made my way by road-lifts. It was while at Méaulte that I learned of poor Temple's death in a hospital at Rouen. (Temple was my servant.) From what he had died I never discovered. He had been married in July 1915, and in March of 1916 his wife bore him a daughter whom Temple had never seen. My mother and I wrote condoling letters to Mrs Temple for whom I felt much sympathy.

I also learned at Méaulte that I had been promoted from the rank of Ensign to that of Subaltern (two stars instead of one), with seniority back to October 1915 – over a year before. There would be an accumulation of pay. This promotion, to my distress, made me senior to Lionel with whom, in the later months, I played leap-frog in the matter of seniority. Seniority meant nothing to me, but it meant something to Lionel who was a regular soldier. I tried to arrange things in such a way that he and not I should command the company when Dickie went on leave, which he did later in November. But Lionel would not hear of it. He could not have been nicer. The matter was happily righted a few weeks later when Lionel was made a Captain and took over No.2 Company – of which perhaps more below.

The Division's rest period was due to continue until the middle of November and on the seventh of that month the Battalion was moved back for a week into the divisional area from which we had been withdrawn at the beginning of October. This time we marched the eight miles to Amiens (I marched in rear of the Battalion, being what is known as 'whipper-in') where we were packed into trucks and conveyed to Airaines, a village about three miles west of Quesnoy – the place we had so regretfully left a month earlier. (We had not forgotten Clive Piggott's five laconic words.) The railway followed the picturesque valley of the Somme for the first fifteen miles and then, at Longpres, turned south-west, away from the river, through Bittencourt, to Airaines. There we detrained: alas, the season had advanced by a month since we had left. George Edwards requisitioned me as interpreter to find the way by road to our destination – the village of St. Maulvis, some eight miles south-west of Airaines. Our packs were carried by three lorries – an arrangement for which we were grateful to George – so that, the night being fine and the road good, the march was pleasant. But on arrival billeting proved to be difficult: the barns were small and the farms scattered. We got in after 11 p.m. No.3 had to be fitted into no less than thirteen different billets, the owners of which had all gone to bed.In the lovely surroundings of this pleasant village, we stayed a week.

Peace and quiet were made abundantly available by the woods and fields round St. Maulvis which I explored alone and with Overton-Jones. During one of our walks I found what I took to be a fragment of a hornet's nest which had somehow been prised out of its proper site and was lying on the ground. I opened some still-closed cells and pulled out four live young hornets one of which I took back to the mess where it became the object of quite a lot of interest. The young insect certainly looked formidable. We speculated about the aggressor: a tree rat or a squirrel? Just possibly a honey-buzzard, but rather late in the year. Almost certainly not a pine-marten. To our regret, the week came rather quickly to an end.

We did the return journey on 13 November by lorry. It took six hours with stops every two hours when we got out and stretched our legs. In the early evening we reached our destination (name of village not recorded or remembered) where, to my pleasure, we were greeted by Lionel who unexpectedly materialized out of the dusk. It got dark during the ensuing march which was long, muddy and cold. The bitter winter of 1916–17 came on us early. Severe frosts began during mid-November nights and sometimes persisted through the day; but there were remissions till mid-December when the frost became continuous and exceptionally severe. For an oppressively long period in 1917 there was no let up.

That night I shared a tent with a newly-arrived officer called Colin Bain Marais. This man was a South African aged about 25, of fine physique and conspicuous good looks of which he was not unaware. He had the nickname of Strong Man. Gold and diamonds, I understood, had formed his family background, and he spent money freely. He carried fastidiousness to the length of never wearing a set of underclothes more than once and never sending anything to the wash. He wore a pair of pants or a shirt once and then gave it away. His servant did well. So did his platoon[1].

Our kit had not arrived and we spent the night shivering on sheets of corrugated iron. Next day we marched past our old camp in Montauban, through Guillemont, to a nearby place called Waterlot Farm, close to the first-aid post where, on 15 September, I had seen Treffry for the last time.

Our duties as Divisional (instead of Corps) troops began in mid-November. A new trench was required in a much-shelled area which Lionel and I jointly reconnoitred in the morning. We profitably spent the half-day marking out the traverses and bays with tapes. That night Lionel and I, in a biting frost, took up a working party. After numerous and frustrating halts due to congestion (a relief was going on), we got down to the job which began well. Suddenly shelling started round us. The party took what cover it could in the shallow trench which by then had been excavated with picks rather than shovels. During the shelling the crouching men looked from above like praying Muslims, several kneeling with their foreheads on the ground and their hind-quarters raised. I was walking with Lionel along the top when down came a shell on our left, about thirty yards away. Almost simultaneously Lionel uttered an expletive and fell flat on his face. He got up at once feeling the back of his neck and said it was nothing. But it turned out that a piece of shell had struck the back of his turned-up coat collar through which it had made a hole. The 'piece' had smashed his back collar stud just breaking the skin on his neck and causing a visible contusion. In a couple of days he would have a large bruise. If he had been hit a couple of inches higher in the mid-line, the effect would have been that of a formidable rabbit punch from which he might not have recovered so quickly. He had been distinctly lucky. During the last half of our stint, which Lionel insisted on completing, the moon got up. The shelling of our area lifted and I walked him up and down the parapet which rose quickly once the diggers were through the frozen crust and could use their shovels. We talked, among other things, about the religious faiths of India; I had just read a book about them. Thus did we keep our minds off the shelling, which continued indiscriminately round and about, till we completed our task and marched back to Waterlot Farm. This trench, on which we continued to work

---

[1] Editor's note: Colin Bain Marais, though of Scottish parentage, had a Boer step-father. I am told by his daughter (whom I met by chance in 1999) that his mother was ostracized by many persons in the Boer community in South Africa (among whom anti-British feelings still ran strongly) because her son had fought for the British. He was awarded the Croix de Guerre and was twice mentioned in despatches. His fastidiousness as regards the shirts and pants may possibly be explained as a safeguard against lice; washing the shirts did not always succeed in getting rid of the eggs, which would hatch in the warmth of the wearer's body when the garment was next worn.

for the next few days, ran (as far as I recall) south-east from the Ginchy-Norval road. I don't clearly remember the locality, though I retain a picture of the ground falling away on our right. But I most vividly retain the episode of Lionel's busted collar-stud which, for all I know, he may have kept as a memento. By 21 November, about 200 yards of trench remained to be completed. We then handed over to Australians who, at this period, took over part of our line.

At the beginning of December the Division, and with it the Fourth Battalion, side-slipped to the right. We took over Combles which, during the September battles, had been captured by the French.

As said above, it was a severe, prolonged and dreary winter of which the most vividly remembered features were the intense cold, the rock-hard ground, and the absence of nearby amenities. Skies were mostly dull – like pewter. I recall few sunny periods or cheerful scenes. The front occupied by the Division was so deep in the area captured during the earlier battles that there lay behind us a wide belt of desolation with here and there patches of rubble which had been villages. Though the valley in whose chalky side we lived was some two miles behind the front-line posts, there was nowhere you could go for a change of scenery. I recall a longing for spring and for colour, which intensified as the monotonous weeks slowly passed. But the longing was qualified. In spring the offensive would be resumed. There would be plenty of battles.

The overall plan for the year 1917 was that, as soon as possible, the offensive would be resumed. Light railways, roads, depots, dumps and much else had to be prepared. But in the event, all our local preparations were frustrated by the opposition. From their scattered forward posts on our fronts the Germans surreptitiously withdrew according to plan to prepared positions in their rear – to what later became known as the Hindenburg line. It was a sly move which compelled us to mount our offensives elsewhere.

The small town of Combles, largely demolished but not reduced to rubble as had the villages in our rear, was the most central place in the new area. It contained deep cellars which had been used by the Germans and later by the French. Our companies were scattered. Nos. 2 and 3, together with Battalion headquarters, lived on the side of a rather steep chalk-sided valley which ran south-west from Combles towards Maurepas. Into this valley-side the French (and perhaps the Germans before them, for Combles had not been taken by the French till 26 September) had excavated numerous shelters and dugouts. The side of the valley had been covered by well-grown trees until the gunners of both sides had wrought destruction. The remains of these trees formed an elongated belt above the valley. We called the place Savernake Wood.

The most cursory glance at our future domicile made two facts obvious. While the French knew how to keep themselves warm, they did not share our ideas of cleanliness. They had no proper latrines, having relieved their needs anywhere on the hillside. Nor did they systematically dispose of rubbish or refuse. Empty tins, old straw, uneaten meat, vegetables etc. were thrown on to the roofs of their shelters, as if to help in making them shell-proof. The rats profited. When it rained an obnoxious fluid trickled through many of the roofs. But at the same time every little shelter had a neat stove and chimney of a kind unfamiliar to us. These shelters and short tunnels varied in size. They accommodated from two to ten men. A few of these places were approached through covered entries or porches where, protected from the worst of the weather, the French sometimes sat and smoked.

Our first reactions were of shock and distaste. But misgivings faded when it was realized how quickly the place could be cleaned up and how comfortable it could be made. 'Wonders,' I wrote, 'have already been done in the last two days. Nearly all the rubbish has been buried, paths have been cleared, and wooden treads laid down so that one can get about without being lost in mud. The advantage of our being on the side of a hill is that the place can be drained. When you hear the rain pelting down on the roof, it is good to know that it will flow to another part of the world and not turn your immediate surroundings into swamp.'

No.3's officers' mess could have been worse. It was a hut of elephant iron and semi-circular shape, partly let into the chalky side of the hill. It had two respectable windows of translucent oilskin, a hinged door and a primitive but effective stove. The latter, when stoked with the timber which abounded, warmed the hut without smoking us out.

On this hill-side and in these quarters we spent the worst of the winter months of 1916/17. We were bored and cramped. But we were nevertheless thankful that things were not worse The two most trying features for me were the long marches to and from our places of work, and the remoteness of unspoiled country – too far to reach on a casual walk. From such desirable country we were separated by the fought-over battlefield behind us – a belt one to two miles deep of desolation. I recall a trivial incident which showed how cheering it was during that winter to see occasional civilians. When marching out of this area some two months later we passed on the road our first civilian. She was an old Frenchwoman dressed in peasant's black with a black bonnet, pushing a wheelbarrow. As the column marched by she was mystified but by no means displeased by the effect she produced. She was subjected to a running barrage of greetings in pidgin French and Tyneside dialect. 'Ullo Grandma: Good to see you Grandma: Three cheers for Grandma,' etc. She dropped the handles of her wheelbarrow and stood smiling and waving at the passing column. Now and then there were rambling cheers and racy jocularities.

Our work during the early weeks of December was taxing and did notably little to shorten the war. It consisted of digging an inordinately long communicating trench across open country to the grounds of what had once been a château at Sailly-Saillisel. The trench began at a point we called the 'Terminus'. This place became a central feature of marches up to Sailly. There ran for a short distance north-eastward from Combles a third-class road, doubtless used before the war as a farm track. This half-sunken road ran along the side of a slope which fell away to one's left and formed a bank on one's right. Into this bank shelters had been dug like the ones in Savernake Wood. These were continuously occupied by changing bodies of troops. When you were marching south along this road, where vehicles could discreetly move, you could not be seen by the Germans over the ridge to your left. But when you reached the Terminus – the point where this road melted away into open country – you came under observation. It was here that our communicating trench was planned to begin. Its projected destination was the château of Sailly, which, from our terminus, looked rather remote on your right front, on the far side of a shallow valley.

I was not cheered when I first took a look at the area beyond the Terminus. If you wanted to get from Combles to Sailly, why, we naively asked ourselves shouldn't you use the already existing road which, passing through Frégicourt, conveniently connects the two places? The answer was that this road, though close at hand, was not in our sector. Horrific muddles with the Division on our right would follow if we used it. The communicating trench which we were expected to make would, I saw, be immoderately long and difficult to keep in repair. Shelling and bad weather would quickly put it out of use. Reliefs and carrying parties would then prefer to walk along the top.

And so it proved. After several days' work we were switched from digging to laying a duckboard track along the surface. What manner of man, we wondered, was the remotely situated planner who, sitting at his desk, thought of a communicating trench of that length in that place? Not, we thought, our C.R.E., Colonel Brough, who would know better.

In this connection, I recall the following minor incident. Shortly after we had begun the early digging programme I was in charge of a party of two platoons of No.3 when I beheld approaching from the direction of Sailly a small party of officers of which the central figure was revealed as Brigadier-General E. Seymour, a ginger-haired Grenadier known to the world as Copper (perhaps because of his ginger hair). As I saluted him he eyed me critically. He asked what we were doing and planned to do. I explained. He then pointed to a feature well ahead of where we were standing and told me that my party would not knock off till the trench had been taken up to that feature. The task was impossible. It would require another day's work by a party of our size. I said that I would bear his order in mind and that we would do our best. This did not satisfy him. He repeated the order. We would not knock off till that point had been reached. Did I understand? I replied that I fully understood and repeated that we would do our best, adding 'as this company always does'. We parted without cordiality, after which my two platoons completed their pre-arranged task. On my return to Savernake Wood, I reported the exchange to Dickie and then to Skeff. Both supported me. No more was heard of the incident, the issue of which bore out a precept which someone – it may have been Quincey Greene – had once recommended: never let yourself be intimidated by people of high rank, least of all by generals.

To return to December 1916, I recall discussing with Dickie at this time the effect it had on the morale of the officers and men to feel that the work they were doing was useful. I had formed an impression that there was a vague association between the uselessness of the work assigned to us and its unpleasantness. I thought of those torrential nights when, at Laventie, we tried to improve the morass-like condition of Rotten Row. Our work could scarcely have been more unpleasant – or, as it turned out, more useless. By contrast, all the occasions when No.3 had done good work had been stimulating to everyone concerned. Dickie and I agreed that there was an association, especially when the difficulties were caused by bad weather; but the association was not close. Now and then (but not often), your job might be repulsive but useful.

My own day-to-day morale was certainly affected by how useful I felt No.3's work was and by how helpful it was acknowledged to be by other units. If I now look back on the 2½ years I spent with the Battalion, I think that my morale was highest during the early months of 1918 when No.3 was at Blangy east of Arras. While there we prepared a defensive position on high ground. The work was enjoyable, worthwhile and good. The number of casualties made little difference to your morale. Casualties disturbed and shook you at the time. But if despite them the job was well done, they could enhance your feelings of satisfaction, especially if wounds rather than deaths had been caused. On that ridge east of Arras we dug and revetted some splendid and durable trenches which after-events proved to have been of substantial value. During April 1918 the German advance in that sector was stopped by troops holding the line we had prepared.

I have mentioned the severity of the cold during this winter. But I find on re-reading my old letters and diaries that during the first half of December the cold was more intermittent that I remember. For example I noted on 11 December that a drizzling rain had not ceased for four days. I described our feelings on coming to a part of the communicating trench we had dug the day before and left in passable condition. We found that it had mostly fallen in and had become unusable. The frost had let up. We had heard of men in the Ypres salient so engulfed in Belgian mud that they could not be got out. The same thing could happen on the Somme but was rare. Early one morning, at a point not far from the beginning of our communicating trench, we came across an

Irish Guardsman who before daybreak had somehow got lost and had sunk in mud to the waist. He was completely stuck. The unfortunate man was worn out with his struggles. We pulled him clear. In his exhaustion he was pitiably grateful. 'God bless you, God bless you all,' he kept repeating, 'without your help I'd have surely died.' Outside the trench the conditions became almost as bad as they were inside. In continuously wet weather the ground underfoot depended on how many men were passing over. After a relief the track along the top was deep in mud. We reported these conditions so that Skeff and Edwards came up and took a look. Revetments, they decided, were what was needed. But the idea was sensibly abandoned since by then the risk had become less of using a duckboard track along the top. The job of making such a track was finally assigned to us.

But when the severe and continuous cold set in the position was drastically changed. At first a frozen crust was formed which mysteriously varied in thickness. In one place the crust would be firm. You walked forward confidently. Then through would go your boot. You were then liable to sink in up to your calves or knees; and you counted yourself lucky if your other foot did not also go through. But after the severe frost had persisted by night and day for long enough, the whole top stratum of mud, however deep, froze to the consistency of rock. To be shelled on the Somme was then as dangerous as to be shelled in the Alps. The missile exploded on contact, often making a hole no deeper than a saucer. The fragments tended to blow out laterally endangering people quite far away. Wounds in the legs became commoner than in normal weather.

The 'news' I used to give in letters and put into my diary fell into two categories: the war and No.3's mess. The war included some unpleasant experiences in the Sailly château area which became about the unhealthiest of the circumscribed places on our front. I recall a salvo coming down when a carrying party from No.3, laden with duckboards, was passing through. We heard it coming, but the heavily laden men were so concentrated on picking their way over the pitted ground that not a man abandoned the erect position. I later heard that this performance had been observed by a senior officer of another unit who had been impressed by the party's nonchalance. The ground was soft that morning and no one was hurt. No.3 was luckier than other companies in the château area. I recall how, on another morning, a German aeroplane swooped down on a working party of which Lionel was in charge and gave them a burst of machine-gun fire. I recall in particular how, during the evening of 8 December 1916, Savernake Wood was shelled during my twenty-first birthday dinner party. The incident was humorous though we didn't think so at the time. I had been sent a bottle of green chartreuse. Of the contents of this bottle, urged by Lionel, I was partaking at the end of a convivial meal when three shells in sequence, and equidistantly from each other, exploded in our valley. The first fell some 250 yards away, towards Combles.

The explosion, which was unfamiliar in that area, took us by surprise. The conversation abruptly stopped and there was a mystified pause. 'What was that?' Indubitably a German shell, we decided, perhaps a four-point-two. A ragged conversation followed as we wondered if more were coming. Doubts were settled about two minutes later when a second shell exploded appreciably nearer and seemingly on our hill-side, but short (from the German gunners' standpoint) of No.3's area. Amour-propre enjoined that we should sit tight and hope for the best, which we did. At that moment I felt the need for a gramophone. It would have been a relief to bestir oneself purposefully and put on something loud. After another two minutes or so, we heard a third one approaching. It came down with a gut-constricting crescendo a few yards on the Combles side of our mess. The burst was followed by a cascade of debris on our tin roof. It was at this moment that Espin's servant, a sheep-faced man with reddish hair, burst in and said in a high-pitched voice: 'We are being shelled, Sir. That was one from Fritz.' It was amusing how this fool's panic infuriated us. It was because of Dickie's silent influence that no one cursed him and told him to get out. Either Espin or Dickie merely thanked him for the information adding that we fully understood what was happening and told him to go back to his shelter. We thereupon abandoned the festive board to investigate. During our meanderings about the hillside we quickly found a smallish smoking hole in the chalk. Nobody had been hurt and nothing damaged except the bole of an already disfigured tree. Wondering when the next one would come, we prolonged our survey of the hill-side, exchanging pleasantries with men in shelters and dug-outs. The longer the delay the more we were reassured, so that when we finally returned to finish the chartreuse, some cheerfulness had returned. 'Thanks, Fritz, for your three birthday presents, and thanks for not sending a fourth,' remarked someone on my behalf as the last of the syrupy liquid disappeared.

Forewarned by the events of the previous Christmas, the Higher Command had peremptorily forbidden all fraternization. We were told (though I think the story was baseless) that on Christmas Eve someone in a forward post had tied a white handkerchief to a stick and had walked across to the German post in front. There, it was said, he had shouted from outside their wire that we had orders to shoot anyone who showed himself next day. The gunners were busy most of Christmas and there was enough small-arms fire to prevent any outbreak of Peace and Goodwill.

But when the weather later hardened, some conventions developed on both sides. The forward posts on both sides gave only partial cover, and to deepen them was like excavating rock. A tacit understanding had grown up that you did not shoot provided that the other fellow did not show more than his head and shoulders.

No.3 saw less of the front posts at Sailly than it had done in Laventie. The Germans were living in the same conditions as ourselves except that they had

1. C. P. Blacker, Summer, 1915.

2. CPB's parents, Carlos and
Caroline Blacker.

3. CPB's brother Robin.

4. Sister Cora Mayne (see p.21).

CPB's companions in the wood-cutting detachment in the Clairmarais Forest: Kirk (left) and Chard (see p. 91 *et seq*).

Clive Piggott "of whom in the ensuing three years I became an ardent admirer" (p. 36).

7. Lionel Bootle-Wilbraham, later Lord Skelmersdale.

8. Officers and NCOs of No. 3 Company, 4th Battalion, Coldstream Guards. Front row, left to right: W. Bruorton, D.S. Lumsden,

Monday. 20th October 1915.
10 ADELPHI TERRACE. W.C.

My letter of yesterday needs a postscript. This evening Carlos took me into the study; produced the letter which Robbie had sealed up; and asked me to read it. He was tortured with the idea that there was something horrible about Robin having crawled into the thicket and died a lingering death there. To my great relief, I found that the letter was not only quite perfect in its tone, but that the little sketch map which the writer (Lloyd) had carefully made, showed clearly that Robin had dropped just as he had charged out of the wood, and gave not the slightest reason to feel that he had moved. I urged Carlos to read the letter, which gave me a very favorable opinion of the good sense and genuine consideration of the writer. He just gave the necessary information carefully and exactly and finished with a grave gesture of sympathy: nothing could have been better done. Carlos was enormously lightened by my assurance, though he still could not face the letter.

I spent nearly two hours with him this morning, just listening whilst he let himself up. He worked off a tremendous head of steam, and I think it did him good. Ross & Payne shared guard at times, when I left him. He presented me with two pairs of braces!

Your mother was much happier this afternoon. She talked a great deal about you & Robin, and showed me your earliest effort in picture. I took their farewell quite reassured as to the worst being well though Carlos kissed Charlotte & broke down a little at parting. G.B.S.

9. Bernard Shaw's postcard to CBP (See Appendix 2).

10. Clairmarais Forest: "Towards its centre the forest rose to an eminence crowned with splendid beech trees".

11. The Somme: Treffry's grave in the war cemetery near Guillemont.

12. Corbie: The Towpath.

13. Corbie: The Wood.

14 & 15. Canal du Nord. Top: Iron girder bridge where Mouse Post had been.

Bottom: View looking south from near the bridge; Carey Trench must have been close to the clump of trees on the left.

unspoiled country behind them. In both winters the main enemy was the weather.

Some changes occurred in our mess. Dickie's advent had removed the background of tension, but we suffered a loss. For a reason which I have forgotten, Mike Peto left No.2, the command of which fell vacant. Lionel, raised in status by a third star, took his place. Thenceforth we saw less of each other. This promotion righted the priorities between us and was in accord with his ambitions as a regular soldier. Though sorry to lose him from the mess, I was delighted for his sake. His second-in-command was an amiable man, a mining engineer in civilian life, by the name of G.A. Grayston, known to the world as Graybags. He was short in stature, wore a fairly fixed wide smile and an untidy moustache, was flat-footed and had prominent ears. He was no Adonis, but he was good-tempered, reliable and wholly loyal to Lionel. No.2 was no less happy a company under its new commander than it had always been.

To No.3 were later posted two South African officers – C.E. Espin and D.S. Lumsden. Espin, who came from Grahamstown, was an exceptionally tall man who moved somewhat clumsily but was even-tempered and had nice manners. Espin's speech, unlike Lumsden's, showed no trace of South African inflections. I never got to know Espin well, though I liked and respected him. Later he transferred to the Second Battalion, was wounded, decorated and survived the war. Lumsden felt at first somewhat lost. The best cure for this condition is to have a nickname, so I asked him if he would mind if we called him D.S., his initials. Espin thought this a fine idea and so did Dickie, so that Lumsden, whose inner qualities contrasted favourably with his exterior façade, settled down. His platoon was puzzled at first, but took to him when they saw that he comported himself well under fire. Later in 1917 we were joined by two other men called Boycott and Bruorton, both South Africans in early middle age. These newcomers showed me a consideration for which I was grateful. I was younger than any of them and must have seemed silly and tiresome. At this time I immersed myself in the two large volumes of William James's *Principles of Psychology* which they thought drivel. Indeed, they doubtless reckoned that I must be a bit mad to take such stuff so seriously when light literature and light gramophone music were the order of the day. Another sign of mild dottiness was that I did not smoke or drink alcohol. Bruorton, a red-faced rather choleric man, once commented on the undrinkability of two bottles of red wine which, then being mess president, I had supplied the mess. There were further friendly complaints over a bottle of champagne which I later bought in a small town with no hotel. The obvious solution was that Bruorton should take charge of the drinks which he duly did. There were fewer complaints but larger mess bills. A good deal of whisky went into hip flasks, the free use of which was prompted by the cold weather and the shelling when we were out at night. Dickie, though not a teetotaller, discouraged lavish resort to hip flasks. Since the men haven't got them, he said, the officers should use restraint. Serious conversation could now and then be held with both Dickie and Espin, who occasionally showed tactful interest in William James, etc., etc. But harmony was best maintained by the preservation of a low level of conversation.

*   *   *   *

In the winter of 1916–17 CPB's parents decided that they did not wish to return to Torquay while the war lasted, and they settled in Dinard in Britanny.

*   *   *   *

Savernake Wood, into which we moved on 10 January, consisted of a thin belt of well-grown but war-scarred trees on the eastern side of a steep slope. The wood overlooked a valley at the north end of which (on your right as you looked across) lay the ruins of Combles. Over the skyline of the ridge opposite could just be seen the tops of a few trees which must have fringed Leuze wood, the scene of fierce fighting. Our spirits did not exactly soar when, on our first glimpse of the place, we beheld, on the floor of the valley and tucked well into our side just below our belt of trees, a battery of well-camouflaged eight-inch howitzers. Their short barrels were raised and pointed over our wooded belt. So closely (we later discovered) did their shells skim the crest above us that the gunners had lopped the tops of a few ash trees silhouetted on what was their skyline. The crowns of these trees could have caused premature bursts.

So close to the steep hillside had these eight guns been emplaced that they were in no danger from counter-shelling from the direction in which they fired. They could only be reached by flanking fire coming down the valley from the general direction of Combles.

This battery, we quickly learned, was more active by night than by day. I recall our first experience. We were about to sit down to a late tea in our elephant-iron hut when there was a blinding flash and a stunning concussion. The door burst open and a hanging window was blown inwards knocking over everything on the table below it. Dazed consternation. I got up to shut the window and was knocked off my feet by a second detonation. Among the effects was that of a hard punch in the face, a feeling that your facial bones had been crunched and you noticed an acrid smell at the back of the nose; also dizziness, deafness and a wild singing in your ears. The other guns then fired simultaneously. After we had come to our senses and could hear each other speak, our first thought was of ear-plugs. A roll of cotton wool was supplied by Raffle which we divided and distributed in wads to our platoons. Would there, we asked ourselves, be retaliation? The question was quickly answered. A German shell came sailing down the valley making a peculiar chanting noise. Three more followed. They did no damage to the gunners below or to ourselves. But the Battalion had some luck. One shell landed four feet from the

Orderly Room. It stowed in a sandbag wall and bent the elephant iron; but it did not explode. Two N.C.O.s were sitting inside and shot out as if catapulted. Later, at about 9 p.m., a similar missile landed a few yards from No.3's servants' dug-out and was also a dud. That two such well-placed projectiles should have been duds despite the chalky and frozen ground seemed so extraordinary as to border on the miraculous. Skeff, who had a superstitious streak, had said a few weeks earlier that the Battalion was protected by a Guardian Angel. Various parties had recently had lucky escapes and there had been some near misses of billets like the one described above close to Montauban. These two duds on our first night at Savernake Wood confirmed Skeff in his re-assuring belief. The next day he paid a visit to No.3. It was while he sat at our improvised table with a glass of whisky and soda in his hand that he told us about the Guardian Angel. Dickie, I remember, proposed that we should drink not exactly to the health of this being (because angels enjoy perfect health) but to a continuation of its friendly patronage. Someone discordantly suggested that we might be tempting providence, especially if the angel was a teetotaller. Skeff sharply dissented. Celestial Beings, he said, were not narrow-minded.

Later that night and during the next few days we took a drab view of our future in Savernake Wood; we did not relish the prospect of regular nightly firing exercises or of the ensuing retaliation. But things turned out better than we expected. The battery rarely fired more than once a night and little in the way of reprisal came down the valley. I don't recall No.3 Company having casualties in the 'wood' and nothing was mentioned in my letters. But I may have said nothing by design.

This battery of large squat guns, whose shells skimmed the hillside slope a few feet over our heads, taught me a useful lesson about the effects of noise on sleep. In a manner which our first experience led us to think would be quite impossible, we became accustomed to these nightly cataclysms. We soon learned that there was a prelude of signals. Before the guns were fired, distant voices could be heard in the valley shouting orders; there was blowing of whistles, and moving lights flickered in the darkness below. If you were asleep when these signals were given, you roused yourself, plugged your ears and curled up like a wintering hedgehog with your head inside your flea-bag and your hands tightly pressed over your ears. The shattering concussion of the salvo, which shook the hillside and rocked the wire frames on which you slept, would seem to heave you into the air. The shock, which momentarily stupified you like a concussion, would make you shake your head like a dog with water in its ears. Then back you would sink into a semi-conscious doze in which you waited for the next salvo. So it went on while the programme lasted; and when you woke up next morning, little sleep had been lost. So accustomed did we become to these volcanic experiences during the dark hours that we finally came to expect them and take them for granted. Indeed someone

(I can't remember who) declared that he would sooner put up with these nocturnal earthquakes which, when the last salvo was fired, were well and truly over, than have to endure unceasing attentions from the whining mosquitoes which pestered us during the short summer nights in the Salient.

I recall that after the second night on which the battery fired I had a talk in the valley below with one of the battery officers. I knew that gunners, particularly naval gunnery officers, were liable to go deaf and took regular precautions. I asked for advice. He said that, in our hillside dugouts with the shells passing close overhead at short range, we were subjected to a type of noise and shock which was unusual. It was different to stand, as the gunner officers did, behind or beside the gun, than to be placed so that, when it fired, you were almost looking down its barrel. This man gave useful advice about barricading the dug-out entrances and about getting under cover before the first salvo. 'You will be all right,' he said, 'if you are in some sort of shelter. Don't if you can help it, get caught walking about on the hillside. You might get a busted ear-drum.' I recall an arrangement that, when the shooting was finished, a prolonged blast on a whistle would be sounded. So effectively did we close our ears and minds to explosive noises that I was surprised to learn one morning in early March that, during the night, our valley had been shelled. Neither Dickie nor I had woken up.

The news of the Russian revolution, which began on 12 March by a mutiny in a Petrograd garrison, had a mixed reception. It signalled an important change in the configuration of the war; yet it was not entirely unexpected. I think that my mother's hopeful reaction was widely shared, despite its complete lack of realism. The Empress of Russia was believed to be surrounded by a pro-German clique which was poisoning the country's moral well-springs at their source. The revolution, some declared, had been provoked as a reaction to this malign influence. To my mother it seemed that it could only lead to good. My father was less hopeful. Food shortages, heavy casualties and ever-multiplying restrictions, he thought, had produced the revolutionary impetus rather than court intrigues. The causes were doubtless complex and were rooted in the country's recent history which included a defeat in distant parts of the world by the Japanese and serious riots in big cities in early 1914. The news was exciting. The revolution might possibly bring nearer some sort of negotiated peace; but it could scarcely expedite the decisive military victory which most people held to be necessary. I thought of Salomon Reinach's opinions of a year or two before: he believed that the Russian steamroller would remorselessly flatten our enemies: he had discounted the possibility that something might go wrong inside the steamroller.

Our eight months amid the chalklands of the Somme had a configuration. This consisted, first, of the afflictions of a relentless, sustained and inconclusive battle lasting four months; this ordeal was followed by a savage and paralysing winter lasting another four months: and finally the total period ended in a double *détente* which brought a transitory sense of relief and release: the iron winter yielded to springtime which came in manifold glory; and the war slowed down when the Germans withdrew. The relinquished hills, valleys and woods and the scarred earth then relapsed into a silent and empty void, decked by crosses and peopled by ghosts. A waste land at first, but soon to be blazing with poppies. Little did we then suspect that, within a year, the tide of war would again sweep over these hills and valleys.

8

SPRING 1917: CORBIE –
THE WOOD AND THE TOW-PATH

During April and May we passed out of a ferocious winter into a balmy spring. Tremendous events were being enacted in the outside world. But for our small component of the British army these were months of respite. We were withdrawn to a back area where reorganization and training were begun for a new offensive operation on the same huge scale as that just concluded on the Somme. We did not know it at the time, but Belgium was to be the scene. The same major expectations were built up: a break-through and a knock-out blow which would end the war.

The three major events of April – a red-letter month for the Allies – were enacted within a few days of each other. They were the entry of America into the war on 6 April; the battle of Vimy which began in a snowstorm on the 9 April; and the offensive delivered by General Nivelle in the Aisne region which was launched a week later on 16 April. Earlier in the year the Russian revolution had begun with a mutiny in the Russian capital. Disorganization had spread with astonishing speed and on 15 March the Czar abdicated. Of all these events we were inactive and somewhat dazed spectators. The sudden transformation into belligerency of the United States was especially difficult to get into focus. Wildly irresponsible and contradictory opinions were ventilated. A minority declared that it would make little difference. The Americans, a few people said, had been too proud to fight and could not be counted on to do much. The war, however, might be shortened if the blockade were tightened. Such troops as might come from overseas would take a long time to arrive, and by then the war would be over.

But most people took a more favourable view. They echoed the newspapers which welcomed our new ally. There was, however, no exultation, no cheering or rejoicing. I recall a conversation in our mess about how crass the Germans had been to bring in the Americans against them. Both sets of belligerents, it seemed, pinned their faith on blockades. We, on our side, thought that our fleet would starve the central powers into surrender; they, on their side, thought that their submarines would bring us to our knees. Round the mess-table we irresponsibly speculated about probable clashes between different strategical schools in Germany. The higher command of the navy (dominated by the semi-comic von Tirpitz who wore a forked beard) was probably confident that, by livening up the submarine offensive, they could force a quick finish. German advocates of drastic action must have weighed the anticipated advantages against the obvious risks of further antagonizing world opinion and of bringing in the Americans against them; and they must have decided that the gamble was worth while. They may even have concluded that the Americans would never come in; too isolationist or, with their vocal German minority, too divided.

Could there, we wondered, have been a conflict in the enemy camp between naval and military advisers? What, for example, would old Hindenburg think of a naval policy which would bring an American army into the land war? He was level-headed and influenced by tradition. By temperament he may have provided a corrective to the vain, volatile and impulsive Kaiser, who, despite the old Field-Marshal's sobering influence, may have been talked into favouring unrestricted aggression and a policy of frightfulness. Submarines were expendable and, if sunk, incurred no risk to the Kaiser's most treasured asset – his resplendent but inactive High Seas Fleet.

These were the issues on which we speculated in our Nissen hut where much nonsense was talked. Our only undisputed conclusion about the American entry was that it reduced to near-nil the possibility of our definitely losing the war. There was some excitement about Nivelle's offensive on the Aisne. But early optimism faded when we heard rumours of the tremendous casualties; and we were not surprised when, in the middle of May, this handsome and persuasive officer was replaced by General Pétain whom all held in affectionate respect as the saviour of Verdun. I have a clear memory of the morning of 9 April – the first day of the Canadian offensive which, after the explosion of an enormous mine, ended in the capture of Vimy Ridge. My memory is of an untimely snowstorm. I remember leading a couple of platoons through a crater-field in a blizzard and wondering about the drum fire in the north. With heads bent down we laboured forward, fronting with our tin hats horizontal gusts of sleet which blew straight into our faces and retarded our progress. No joke for the attackers. When news of the successful outcome of the battle reached us we wondered if the main object was to help the French by diverting enemy reinforcements or to capture high ground from which we (the British) might be threatened in later battles to be staged in Belgium. The Somme having been neutralized by the enemy withdrawals, eyes were beginning to turn north.

From mid-April to mid-May we made what in retrospect seems a pleasant contact with the River Somme which had a nasty reputation in the British army. In two days, during which I saw my first swallow of the season, we marched from the deserted battlefields of 1916 to a small township called Corbie about 15 kilometres east of Amiens. I have no note or recollection of the march. Close to Corbie the River Ancre, flowing south-west from Albert, joins the Somme which, in loops and bends, winds almost due west from Péronne. The Somme skirts the south-east side of Corbie, flows (through Amiens) about sixteen kilometres to the west, and meanders on through Abbeville till it debouches into a bay with St. Valery on its south side.

At Corbie we spent a rather tense four weeks, warm, summery and almost rainless, from mid-April to mid-May. Dickie had gone on leave at the beginning of the month so that I was in command of the company. I was involved in a good deal of correspondence with headquarters at this time which detracted somewhat from my *joie de vivre*, since there was no one in the company with the administrative experience which I then lacked. Two new officers – H.C. Boycott (who died of wounds received on 21 March in the following year) and W. Bruorton whom I have mentioned before – figured more prominently in the mess. The Battalion was put through a revised training programme which seemed to envisage a period of active trench warfare, with patrols and raids, no less than a breakthrough offensive. I used to box every other evening. Indeed, I did something to turn the massive and good-natured Sergeant Sharp into a focus of boxing activities. In his bouts with me and others he used to stand motionless on the defensive, his left arm extended and a complacent smile on his heavily moustached face; in this posture he would invite his lighter opponents to attack him. The more vigorous your attack the more broadly he smiled; and if you succeeded in landing on him, he would definitely grin. I would either feint at him to draw out his left, duck underneath and hit him in the midriff, or try to get him to lead at me. One evening he produced from his company (No.4) a middle-weight N.C.O., Corporal Deane. This young man was experienced and clever, and we (he and I) were well-matched in build. Sharp, who had trained police in Australia, would stand by in a sweater and make running comments to each contestant and, in the intervals, would sponge our faces acting as second to both. One afternoon an officer in No.4 called J.L. Stops, a dark, genial, overweight man and something of a humorist, came and watched us in our work-out. He was amused by Sharp's bulk and afterwards remarked that he would sooner take on a tank.

We also exercised ourselves by bathing. Skirting Corbie was a poplar-bordered canal with a tow-path on one side. This canal, I suspected at the time and have since confirmed was the authentic River Somme, here confined between banks. At one point there was a pleasant grassy verge from which you could dive into deep water which was about as clean as the water at Parson's

Pleasure in North Oxford. I was not the only person to enjoy this amenity. I bathed most evenings either with Clive Piggott, Lumsden, or Philimore, the padre. The latter was a well-covered, smooth-faced high churchman who preached in a highly-pitched sing-song voice with ecclesiastical inflections, almost as if he were chanting. He preached with upturned eyes, not looking at us but at the sky.

At another point further upstream, a proper bathing place had been dug before the war. I have a clear recollection of how an inter-company swimming and diving competition was held there one afternoon. I had to judge the diving, the results of which do not settle themselves as do those of a swimming competition. I remember not enjoying the exercise; but whether this was due to the difficulty of judging the somewhat mediocre diving or to illogical feelings about the River Somme, I do not recall.

Towards the end of March there was posted to the Battalion an instructor in bayonet fighting. I quote from a letter: 'Bayonet fighting, as taught today, is not a clean or gentlemanly exercise. The fact was impressed on us that there were no Queensberry Rules. Apart from the primary objective of getting the bayonet into your adversary, you should use your rifle-butt either in his face or ribs and your knee or boot in his crutch. You are adjured to kick, stamp, claw, gouge, and if you can, bite.'

I asked our instructor, a smallish man, if he had ever himself taken part in a bayonet charge. He evaded the question. Later in the year I met a middle-aged officer who had been connected with the school which turned out bayonet-fighting instructors. He seemed a quiet sort of man. I asked him how many of the qualified instructors had actually bayoneted anyone. 'Very few,' he said, 'but we don't insist on their telling the strict truth when asked that question.' The important thing, he said, was that they should be able to raise the aggressive spirit and put it across to their audiences.

In a revised training programme introduced at this period, different roles were assigned to the four platoons of each company – as bombers, rifle-bombers, Lewis gunners and riflemen or snipers. The results, it was thought, were good. Each man could regard himself as something of a specialist in a particular weapon.

While we were at Corbie, Battalion sports and concerts were organized. A good deal of trouble was taken by the organizers of the sports – Lionel and Furze. But the result did not quite come up to expectations in that, on the pre-arranged afternoon, only about half the Battalion turned up to watch. I went in for a 120 yards officers' race. I was doing nicely and at about 100 yards had a short lead. I then tripped and fell flat on my face.

But the foregoing activities, though remembered, are not vivid. In contrast are two events, one connected with a wood, the other with a walk along a canal by moonlight.

The day after our arrival I had noticed from our parade ground a wood

crowning a nearby hill. A good place to explore. I walked up in the early afternoon of the next day in bright April sunlight. One reached the place by a narrow
path which bordered a ploughed field. The chalky path led upwards to a barbed
wire fence which enclosed the wood on that side. I had made the ascent un-
observantly, my eyes on the rough path, till I reached the barbed wire. I then
looked into the wood and stood still in astonished delight. The floor was ablaze
with white, yellow and blue flowers. The luxuriance was so unexpected as to
make me feel that, as in a fairy story, I had inadvertently broken into some
secret and privileged place where I had no business to be. The white flowers,
pinkily nodding in the sunlight, as if in timid recognition, were of course wood
anemones; the yellow flowers were lesser celandines and primroses. The blue
flowers, hanging in graceful racemes, defeated me. Nor was I any wiser after I
had climbed over the wire and examined them closely. Later I learned – how
I have forgotten – that they were chionodoxas, glory of the snow. What a place,
I thought in astonishment, to stumble upon on a sunny April afternoon! What
a revelation! What a recompense for the icy winter! As I picked my way through
the trees I came to a concealed clearing thick with wild daffodils, mostly in bud
but a few in flower.

On later days I took several people to see this small wood. Philimore, the
padre, was amazed; he had never seen such a sight, and talked about a
theophany. Nor had Overton-Jones or, later, Dickinson who came back from
leave on 10 May. By then the wood was full of birds. Dickie had a good close-
range view of a singing nightingale, and he heard for the first time in his life
the liquid call of the golden oriole. I spotted the male with my field glasses, but
to his disappointment Dickie did not manage to get the restless bird in focus.

Two or three days before we left the area I visited this wood for the last time.
There were changes. The blue chionodoxas had been replaced by bluebells;
the yellow primroses by yellow archangel and buttercups, the white wood
anemones by stitchwort and wild strawberry. And new flowers had appeared.
In a light wind the wood-floor seemed to undulate under the drooping leaves
of Solomon's seal, among which grew the queer quadrangular Herb Paris. The
change in the pageantry was impressive but sad. How short was the heyday of
the first and most welcome of the year's flowers! It was goodbye to anemones
and primroses for many long months – goodbye till next spring which not all
of us would see.

During this final visit, I contrasted the small hilltop wood with Clairmarais
Forest. This diminutive place had a particular brightness, perhaps due to the
chalk in the soil and to its elevation above the surrounding fields. But it was
small and detached. The year before, the men in our wood-cutting detachment
had felt that they belonged to the wide and welcoming forest where, supervised
by the green-coated *Gardes Forestiers* who were themselves part of the place,
we had placidly worked for several months on end. But here we were no more
than visitors in transit – interlopers – by then due to leave within a week.

I have also mentioned a walk along a canal by moonlight. But I find the experience difficult to describe. Indeed, I hesitate to try. But the little story might interest A.C. Hardy[1] to whom, sometime, it will be shown. I hope that he won't think it egotistical.

While spending an afternoon hour alone in my hilltop wood, a mood of depression had come down. We were due to move in a few days. The background of winter ought to have made easy an unvarying response to this ideal place. But that afternoon the responsiveness had been lacking. After supper in the mess I felt restless. I wondered if the full moon shining down from a cloudless sky had anything to do with my mood. A walk by the canal might make it easier to sleep.

I walked eastward for about two miles along the tow-path and then turned about. The nearer I drew to the village, the more alive my surroundings seemed to become. It was as if something which had been dormant when I was in the wood was coming to life. I must have drifted into an exalted state. The moon, when I looked up at it, seemed to have become personalized and observant, as if it was aware of my presence on the tow-path. A sweet scent pervaded the air. Early shoots were breaking from the sticky buds of the balsam poplars which bordered the canal: their pleasant resinous odour conveyed goodwill. The slowly moving waters of the canal, which was winding its unhurried way from the battlefields to the sea, acquired a numen which endorsed the intimations of the burgeoning trees. The river conveyed that it had seen me before in other places and knew something about me. It was now concerned with my return to the village. But I couldn't decide whether my movement along the tow-path was being encouraged or hindered. A feeling that I was being absorbed into the living surroundings gained in intensity and was working up to a climax. Something was going to happen.

Then it happened. The experience lasted, I should say, about thirty seconds and seemed to come out of the sky in which were seemingly resounding majestic harmonies. The thought: 'That is the music of the spheres' was immediately followed by a glimpse of luminous bodies – meteors or stars – circulating in predestined courses emitting both light and music. I stood still on the tow-path and wondered if I was going to fall down. I dropped onto one knee and thought: How wonderful to die at this moment. I put a hand over my forehead as if to contain the tumult and fend off something. Wonder, awe and gratitude mounted to a climax and remained poised for a few seconds like a German star shell. Then began the foreknown descent. The revolving flares in

[1] A.C. [later Sir Alister] Hardy was one of CPB's fellow students of zoology at Oxford after the war, and who later started The Religious Experience Research Unit at Oxford. Some of the account which follows was published in his book *The Spiritual Nature of Man*, Oxford 1979.

the sky were extinguished; the orchestration faded into silence; the river and its guarding poplars lost their magic. And the moon, which was still shining in exactly the same place overhead, regained its impersonal detachment. I got on to my feet and the thought came: Get back to your room and get into bed. You can think about all this tomorrow.

In a dazed state I found my way to my billet. The mess was empty, the others having dispersed. When I looked at my wrist-watch I saw that the hour was late. It was after two.

I kept the story to myself and have never mentioned it to anyone. My only allusion to it was a sentence in a letter to my parents in which I said that I no longer worried about the war or its outcome. I didn't care what happened.

When I woke next morning I did not remember at first the event of the night before. But everything came back as I got up and dressed. At breakfast someone remarked on how late I had come in. What had I been up to? Ha Ha!

This experience was the first of its sort I had had in my life and it has been the last. I called it, in a sort of private vocabulary, my tow-path revelation. I did not quite know how to take it. The year before, I had read William James's *Varieties of Religious Experience*. The actual volume is on a shelf in front of me as I sit at midnight on 7 December 1969 and scribble these notes. I used to have the habit of dating in pencil when and where I began and finished a book. I find that I began this one on 4 September 1916 at Morlancourt and finished it on 8 October at Montauban. Between these dates I had some severe experiences and it was at this time that I read about the illuminations and other religious intimations which had sometimes changed people's lives. Later I came to associate my tow-path experience with Trônes Wood. In that insalubrious place, where we had spent short periods before the battle of 15 September, the sustained din of our own artillery, the fairly regular German shelling, the pervasive malodours of gas and putrefaction formed a background to anticipations of what lay ahead. How welcome before the impending ordeal, I had thought, would be an experience of the kind described by William James. A gift of grace which would immunize against fear and failure of nerve.

Our period by the canal was an *entr'act* between two such ordeals. I had come through the first in better shape than I could have expected. But clearly another was drawing near. The unescapable prospect, perhaps abetted by the full moon and other circumstances, may have made me restless that evening and may have prompted my night walk.

The next day I tried to put my tow-path experience into focus by asking myself how different people I knew would react to the story. Some would say I had been moonstruck: a short interlude of lunacy. Others might think I had had an attack of minor epilepsy with hallucinations of hearing and vision. Others that I had worked myself into a state of hysteria. But others, perhaps including William James, might think that the experience had not been pathological. I had picked up enough in those days from sketchy reading to recognize such possible interpretations.

The answer, I decided, must be waited for. It will depend, I said to myself, on what later happens. How will the experience work out? What will be the sequel? If similar episodes occur, if they get out of hand and result in breakdown, then you will have one sort of answer. If, on the other hand, the occasion remains unique, or is rarely repeated and then with stabilizing rather than disruptive effects, the answer will be different. Wait and see, I said to myself. If you are not killed, time will give your answer. What you must in no circumstances do is to flatter or plume yourself, or think you are in some special way favoured.

After the war had ended, I occasionally thought of my tow-path experience which I connected with the River Somme. When I thought of the one, the other usually came to mind. I did not think of committing the story to writing till I heard that my old friend A.C. Hardy had become interested in experiences of this sort. He now plans, as one of the activities of a projected institute, the collection of accounts of personal experiences which could be broadly described as religious in the sense used by William James in the title of the above-mentioned book.

When, therefore, I came to write the story, I asked myself how it compared with the generally similar experiences of other people. St.Paul's account came to mind. It prompted the following line of thought. By their fruits you shall know them. This had early been borne home on me. But what determined the nature of the fruits? At least three things, among which the following stood out: first, how far you were prepared to receive the experience before it occurred; second, the intensity of the experience itself; and third, what your attitude was to it afterwards.

First, you could be in various degrees prepared for a particular experience. Your state of mind could vary between, at one extreme, a complete lack of preparedness, a total absence of premonition or anticipation; and at the other a tense expectancy (which might come to you alone or in the company of others similarly keyed up) of a theophany or miracle. Second, the intensity of the experience itself: this could be placed anywhere on a spectrum with, at one end, an agreeable feeling of elevation such as might be induced by a small dose of a drug-producing euphoria; and at the other, an annihilating transformation of your earlier self – something felt as an essential rebirth. 'I have never been the same; I will never be the same again.' The conviction could be so profound as to resist all later doubts or erosions. It could be 'marmorized'. And third, you could afterwards adopt towards your experience an attitude varying from contemptuous scepticism to enthusiastic acceptance and gratitude. To return to St. Paul's experience on the road: he had been prepared for it by tormenting doubts and misgivings about how he had treated Christians; it came as a blinding revelation which swept his mind clean; and he afterwards thankfully accepted the revelation which re-cast the pattern of his life.

My own experience had, by comparison, been feeble. It had come un-expectedly. My only preparation had been an oppressive awareness of an impending and testing ordeal; a sense of the nearness of my dead brother – a sense which fluctuated but which was still sometimes intense; a mood of depression in the afternoon; and the reading of certain books which had suggested that your preparedness for any ordeal could be influenced by forces beyond yourself.

These preparatory influences had not been remarkable: they could have been shared by tens of thousands of soldiers who had lost relatives in the war and who were about to take part in the battles which lay ahead. My actual tow-path experience had been vivid and memorable, though it had involved no personal message such as had been conveyed to Paul by a vision and a voice. But no inner change had been wrought: I was the same man after as before: my behaviour, purposes and conduct were the same; no one saw, or knew of, any difference. As for the sequel, it had depended on personal choices and decisions. It had depended on my interpretation of the tow-path experience, on the value I was prepared to place on it, on what I did with it, on how I allowed (or encouraged) it to guide my conduct.

I now ask myself: what has in fact been the influence of this experience on my conduct during later years? I cannot, I find, answer this question. But of this I am certain: that it has not had the effect it might have had if I had made more of it. Scepticism may have reduced the potential fertility of the soil. But I cannot at the same time say that it had no effect. Some of the seeds may have germinated over the ensuing years without my knowledge. Others, it now occurs to me, may yet germinate, half a century later. Yet others may never germinate. The remarkable thing, as I now see, about such seeds – stored as bare memories of past experiences which, in the past, have fallen on unrecep-tive ground – is their capacity to remain dormant for long periods, perhaps waiting inertly for an auspicious change in the soil which contains them.

I would like to think that my old friend A.C. Hardy, who has unwittingly prompted me to include my neglected tow-path experience in a biographical sketch of the first war, may have been responsible for a (perhaps belated) improvement in the receptivity of an area of ground wherein there has been insufficient change for too long.

My fraternization by moonlight with the River Somme set going some irresponsible thoughts. Again I hesitate to record them.

If you look at a map of the 1916 battlefields you will see that the Somme flows northwards till it reaches Péronne. This small town lies south of the main battle area. At Péronne the river takes a sharp turn to the left and proceeds to meander leisurely westward in wide bends through Corbie to Amiens. At Corbie the Somme receives as a tributary the Ancre, which comes down from the areas comprising Miraumont, Thiepval and Albert. Hereabouts, at every village, there had been terrible battles. The British army's main fighting had therefore been north of the Somme and on each side of the Ancre whose waters mingled with those of the Somme at Corbie.

The Somme was so peaceful in these lower reaches that (the agreeable thought occurred to me) it might be inhabited by a Naiad. What would such a river-goddess, dwelling in these placid waters, think of the events enacted in her territory upstream? Outrage that she had been so savagely desecrated might perhaps be softened by other feelings. Was it within the character of Naiads (mostly, one gathered, locally residential and parochial entities) to temper resentful indignation with less self-centred emotions? We, a battalion of British troops like many others she had seen, were about to leave her without regrets. She likewise would have no regrets at seeing us go. But would she, if articulate, be capable of assuring an interested stranger, of whom she was about to see the last, that she had had nothing to do with the hideous deeds perpetrated in her catchment area? For these dire events alien and uninvited men, converging on her territories from remote countries beyond the sea and the Rhine – people like ourselves, in fact – were responsible. But could the nymph rise to the perception that, though we were agents of destructions, we had not *wanted* to ravish her territories – to ravage her woods and valleys and pollute her waters? 'You may be glad to leave me,' she may have said, 'but do not blame me. Blame yourselves. You may soon find yourselves in worse places and wish that you were back.'

These fantasies were not recorded in my letters; but they are clearly remembered through the decades. They are connected with deeply ambivalent feelings about the area of the Somme. They are revived whenever I look at a large-scale map. The place names then become alive and possess you – those of the Somme more compellingly than others. The manifold horrors successively enacted in each village and wood are fused into something whose main attribute is awesomeness. Week after week holocausts followed one another in a remorseless tide slowly creeping eastward. The deeds done in tornadoes of fire and turmoil merge; they seem to become physically perceptible as a subsonic monotone, a chthonic stirring of voiceless ghosts. The monotone is a wordless chorus of lament for past deeds and sufferings. Memory invests the place names with an aura of muted tragedy which silences speech and makes the present seem unreal. Something of the numen of these villages and woods overflowed into the River Somme, which it was easy to personalize.

A recent memory comes to mind. In April 1960 Max Nicholson and I paid a five-day visit to an area of lakes south of Chatillon. On the return journey we parted at Beauvais and I motored alone to Boulogne. While driving along the road from Poix to Abbeville, my mind being on other things, there came over me as a kind of oppression the awareness that, out of sight on my right, lay the battlefields of 1916. It seemed as if a dark cloud were hanging over the distant countryside. Yet the cloud was rimmed and shot through with light. This impression, which arose spontaneously from the past, was vivid and conveyed well the ambivalence of those charged memories. The cloud came from infernal regions; the illumination, which came from elsewhere, honoured the multitudes of dead.

9

SUMMER AND AUTUMN 1917 –
BEHIND THE LINES AT PASSCHENDAELE

Uppermost in our feelings in June 1917 was relief that we were moving away from the area. Yet below the surface some of us (I was certainly one) had misgivings that, ere long, our mood would change.

The chalky and well-wooded downs were firm underfoot and bright to the eye compared with the dark and watery lowlands to the north: there a minor impairment of age-old ditches and canals, laboriously dug along faintly perceptible gradients, quickly produced a stagnant morass. If one stripped from the undulating country we were leaving the features imported by war and the unusual weather – the remorseless slaughters and the exceptional severity of the recent winter – the area had something to commend it. If heavy rains were to fall on the lowlands into which we were moving (as, in the event, they did), we might find ourselves wishing that we were back amid the hills and valleys of chalk. For these had the outstanding merit that they could be drained. I well realized that I had not seen the Salient at its worst. It had provided me with no horrific experiences to offset the happy memories of early 1915. But nevertheless I knew well enough what the Salient could be like and what we were to expect.

It was a hot afternoon when we marched, heavily loaded, to a siding about three miles away where a train was patiently waiting. It consisted of the usual vans with sliding doors and coaches with here and there a dilapidated first-class compartment. I would personally have preferred to travel in a van on the floor of which you could lie down and, with your unrolled valise, make yourself quite comfortable.

No.3, with Dickie leading, was the first to arrive at the siding where a R.T.O. (Railway Transport Officer) was waiting. No.3 was entrained, mostly in vans. To the officers was assigned a dingy first-class compartment where we unloaded and spread ourselves.

No.4, commanded by Furze, then arrived. Furze, whose temper and manners had not been improved by the heat, came along the siding. He declared with animus that he was the senior company commander and that therefore he and not we should be occupying that particular first-class compartment. Dickie, who understood Furze better than most and who hated rows, did not resist. In some ill-humour No.3's officers then assembled their scattered belongings and moved out.

Despite the heat of the afternoon the night was cold and uncomfortable. We relieved the monotony of the early hours by a peculiar impromptu meal of bread and butter and bananas. We de-trained at Bailleul (the station being some way out of the town) and spent an hour and a half in a pleasant field of which I have no mental picture. We then took to the road. Our destination was the picturesque Belgian village of Locre, about five miles from Bailleul and three miles across the frontier. Our route took us along an elm-bordered pavé road through country which differed increasingly from what we were leaving behind. The fresh impression bore home that the Flemish lived less gregariously than the French. They preferred secluded farms, partially hidden by well-grown trees, to scattered villages. The country was less open than in France. Heavy hedges of blackthorn and may form the boundaries between fields along which trees give shade to grazing cattle; and on the roadsides elms tended to replace poplars. The countryside seemed friendly and familiar. I found myself welcoming the miniature forests of hop poles, the Belgian estaminets (called *'herbergs'* and *'winkels'*), the squat churches and the lush meadows. It was good to see again the red-collared Belgian policemen and the roof-gables, graduated like steps.

Our destination was the above-mentioned village of Locre, about three miles across the frontier. Peculiar elevations appear on each side of this stretch of border. Locre lies at the foot of one of a complex of separate hillocks from the tops of which you can overlook the low-lying ground to the north and east which includes the ill-famed Ypres Salient. This high ground does not sweep and undulate as do the chalklands of the Somme. It consists of a pattern of rounded protuberances, like warts or boils, suggestive of localized volcanic activity in the remote past. Other place names in this complex are Dranoutre, Westoutre, Mont Rouge (rising above Locre) and Mont Kemmel. These high places extend into France. Indeed Cassel may be the most western outrider.

The rainfall hereabouts seemed plentiful and there coursed downhill, through soft ground, small rivulets. Lower down these formed streams or *'beeks'* (many of the local place names ended in 'beck' of 'beek') most of which flowed north-east, finding their way to the Lys.

On arrival at this destination we saw that our camp consisted of a few huts and boardless tents intended for officers, and bivouacs for the men. These were placed on a sloping grassy meadow, lavish in cuckoo-flowers. Indeed, Locre is indissolubly connected in my memory with cuckoo-flowers. A canvas marquee provided an officers' mess which No.3 shared with Nos.1 and 4, No.2 being on some sort of detachment. Apart from mosquitoes, it seemed, the place should be near-perfect in fine weather. Not so in rain and cold. No visible signs of war. Trees and hutments intact. Locre undamaged. But with the war so near the peace and quiet and the cuckoo-flowers might be deceptive.

After we had settled in we had time to relax. The thought occurred that in our mode of saying 'Goodbye' to the Somme and 'Good Morning' to the Lys, we had something to be grateful for. Corbie had eased us out gently from the hills and valleys of chalk: Locre seemed to be easing us equally gently into the black lowlands and the enigmatic future. The epilogue of a closing chapter had been harmoniously geared to the prologue of the next chapter. Perhaps an act of consideration by Skeff's guardian angel?

That evening, when the midsummer light was failing, I walked half way up Mont Rouge and took a look at the horizon. The front was quiet. Distant mutterings, intermittent, sounded almost devotional as if uttered by a kneeling circle of priests reciting prayers and responses, absorbed in another world. Desultory singing floated up from the bivouacs below. The scene reminded me of Dante.

Our movement north to Belgium was in advance of that of the Division. We were attached to a corps but I have no record of what corps it was. In general our job was to make preparations in what was then an entirely peaceful area for the big operations which were planned for the months ahead. At first the area was ignored by the Germans, but during the period of our stay, which extended from 16 May to 6 June, things became increasingly lively. The enemy had obviously tumbled to the fact that a build-up was under way.

My letters and scattered memories recall that we worked on variable shifts, some close up to, and others well behind, the line. One of the safe daylight jobs consisted of making a dam in a stream for ponding water to be used by horses; others were the loading of sleepers and flints on trucks. The forward work was by night. I have notes of periods at Wulverghem and Kemmel.

During these three weeks the war was visibly hotting up. We had some casualties during the night work, among them Woggs Allan. On 29 May he was artistically wounded in the leg: a perfect flesh wound touching no vital place and causing little pain or loss of blood, but guaranteeing perhaps six months away from the war. That night we drank to his health and leisurely recovery. Someone who went to see him in hospital found him lying comfortably in bed, radiant.

The small village of Locre contained a convent. The nuns could supply you with quite good tea of which Espin and I partook twice; and they also ran a workroom where lace was made. After our second visit, we were taken up to the first floor where, in an apartment not unlike a large schoolroom, about a dozen Flemish girls, mostly fat and square-faced, were sitting at desk-like tables industriously engaged in manipulating bobbins. There resulted ribbons of lace of varying width and complexity. The work was done under the super-vision of nuns who spoke English with outlandish Flemish accents. I wanted to buy some of this lace to send to my mother, but the nuns regretfully refused to sell; they had too many orders. Neither the nuns nor the lace-workers took any interest in the nearby troops. I was struck by the calm with which these busy women sustained such dull work for long hours amid increasing concentrations of troops, with war creeping up. When, that evening, Espin and I returned to our camp, we found that six cows were grazing in our meadow. The cows paid no more attention to the troops around them than did the lace-workers. But the pleasant atmosphere of rusticity they imported proved transitory; for that same night both Dranoutre and Locre were for the first time shelled. Happily no damage was done in Locre. At this time I used to sleep in the open under a tall elm through which the stars were visible. I was rudely awakened at about one o'clock by the detonations. It may have been the proximity of high ground, or perhaps the stillness of the night, but the explosions of the shells from this long-range German gun were followed by prolonged reverberations, like long-sustained bursts of thunder. These struck the would-be sleepers as ominous, as if the skies were participating in the disturbances. We learned next day that Locre had been more fortunate than Dranoutre where buildings had been hit and casualties inflicted. We called on the nuns the next morning. They were calm and composed having decided to get ready to move at short notice but not to do so unless things got worse. Their attitude was fatalistic. We were all in the hands of the *Bon Dieu,* who, they thought, would take special care of their convent.

I well remember the next night. I had been out with a party somewhere between Kemmel and Wulverghem where we were shelled for half an hour. It was a brilliant summer night with a moon. Furze, who had been occupied nearby with a party of No.4, had things worse than I did. He told me next day that his life had been saved by a ditch; and he discoursed amusingly on how intensely grateful one could feel to a ditch. On the way back we were conveyed by lorry through Dranoutre which had again been shelled – this time more heavily. I saw for the first time a sight which had provided a theme for many war pictures. We overtook on the road between the two villages little parties of hurrying women, some half-dressed and wearing shawls, dragging along their sleepy children, having abandoned all their possessions in their flight. I was sitting in front next to the driver. There were four or five of these scurrying groups. As we approached them from behind with our headlights dimmed, the women would look backwards and up at us, their faces scared and pale in the moonlight. No men. I wondered why. One woman beckoned to us to stop. I jumped off. She wanted to know if she should go on to Locre. She had it in mind to go to the convent. Was it safe? I could only tell her that Locre had been undamaged when we had left seven hours before. I asked about her menfolk. 'Ah! They are all old and cannot walk far.' They had stayed behind to prevent the pillage of their homes.

I was glad for their sakes that the night was fine and warm. This picture of scattered parties of women and children scurrying by night along a road and looking back and up at the lights of the looming lorries slowly overtaking them, is my clearest memory of our three-week stay at Locre. It came back to me painfully a few days later, as I will describe.

On 4 June was celebrated an Old Etonian dinner at St. Omer. On a warm and cloudless evening, Skeff, Dickie, R.J. Paterson and I were driven in a comfortable and fast private car to St. Omer. The roads were good, broad and empty. The slanting light threw long shadows. The drive was the best part of this dreary occasion. When we arrived the meal had begun. Three long tables, parallel with each other, occupied the floor of a large hall. A select group of senior officers was sitting on a stage at one end. From chandeliers suspended over the middle table hung down long ribbons of light Eton blue. A band was playing. About 300 people were present, seated according to their approximate ages when they left school. Skeff was placed at the top table. With some difficulty, places were found for Dickinson, Paterson and myself at the ends of the three long tables, furthest from the stage and nearest the entrance. We had no choice as to whom we sat next to. The people nearest to me were mostly my juniors who had boarded at Hare's. I sat next to a man called Vaughan-Morgan whom I remembered as an accomplished boy singer at school concerts. He was two years younger than myself. To open the conversation I remarked on how much I had enjoyed his singing in the past. To my astonishment he took the gambit badly, as if he were now ashamed of his musical talent. The first part of the evening was moderately enjoyable. But champagne, which I did not drink, flowed in copious streams, and it was not long before the din (augmented by the band) was such that one could not hear oneself speak. By the savoury stage there was general chaos and uproar. People were shouting and throwing things at each other. The playing of *God Save the King* momentarily stilled the clamour. But it intensified when school songs were played. By the third verse of *Sonent Voce Omnium* many officers were standing, bleary-eyed and gesticulating on their chairs. This was the moment when a speech was attempted by Lord Cavan. Not a sound reached us. I did not hear a word. Then came the *Eton Boating Song* and the *Vale*. By this time some people had climbed onto the central table and three or four, forming a ram as in Eton football, began to sway it from side to side. The table then collapsed. Deafening cheers. The ram was thrown to the floor. Someone then got hold of the blue ribbon hanging from the central chandelier, and others formed a queue behind him holding the ribbon. To the raucous bellowings of the Boating Song, the chandelier was pulled rhythmically to and fro in a widening arc until it crashed to the ground. Tempests of laughter and applause. Then, during the ensuing half-hour, everything breakable in and around the room – tables, chairs, bottles, glasses, windows – was systematically smashed. It occurred to me that if a message had been sent down earlier, before pandemonium had set in, from the high table that the Corps Commander did not want French property damaged, a brake might have been applied. But nothing came down from Lord Cavan or anyone else. Was this, I wondered, an example of moral timidity or of worldly wisdom in high places? Was it a question of 'Bad behaviour in a foreign country by British officers who consider themselves an élite, but we mustn't interfere,' or of 'Why shouldn't these young men, most of whom have had hell in the last twelve months, enjoy themselves for once?'

While the central chandelier was being pulled down I caught a glimpse of two Frenchmen in black suits with pomaded hair, standing together at the side of the hall looking on. The expressions on their faces interested me. With raised eyebrows and half-open mouths they were gaping and half-smiling as if they had never beheld such a spectacle before. No sign of disapproval or distress. They might have been officials or middle-men responsible for the dining arrangements; and they might have been smiling over the bill for damages they would put in. Who, I wondered, would in fact pay? There ensued a general mêlée in which several drunken officers tried to fight each other. Someone knocked off my glasses so that I saw little of what was happening by the time our party of four left. Nor did I see much during the car-ride back to Locre.

My disgust with the performance made me feel out of gear with my old school. Such conduct might be expected from occupying Germans to whom it might seem masculine; but I would scarcely have expected it from Etonian officers. My feelings were obviously connected with the fact that I had drunk no alcohol. Could they also be a matter of temperament?

'*In vino veritas*,' I said to myself sententiously. In some people the *veritas* might be a liking for violence; in others a dislike of violence. Was it perhaps compatible with some military tradition, of which I knew nothing, that officers, whatever their backgrounds, when drunk at a stag party, should behave like destructive savages? Dickinson and Paterson, both entirely sober, on the whole deplored the performance but seemed to regard it as condonable. Skeff had dined well; but during the return journey in the car he was not loquacious. In fact, he was sleepy. He said, however, that it had been a grand party. I rather hoped that the grandness resided less in the behaviour of the diners than in the fact that Skeff had sat amid military luminaries at the high table.

During this same return journey by road, I remember hoping that I would never see troops run riot – looting, raping, and burning and killing – in a captured city. And I also thought of those refugees whom we had overtaken on the road from Dranoutre two nights before. There was no logical connection between the plight of these fugitives and the behaviour of Etonian officers at St. Omer. But the two were juxtaposed in my mind and have remained so since. Several times has this Fourth of June performance in France in 1917, by people who ought to have known better, come back to me.

It was while we were at Locre that it was announced that Skeff had been awarded a D.S.O. The general reaction was of pleasure qualified by amusement. Nobody supposed that Skeff had earned the decoration by any particular act of gallantry or initiative. His merits as a commanding officer had been passive rather than active – but none the less valuable for that. He was a good judge of character and shrewd. While not indifferent to his own comfort and safety, he used his officers well and did not show favouritism. He was on nickname terms with several major- and lieutenant-generals with whom he had been at school, at Sandhurst or in the South African war. His was a status rather than a merit award, and also, doubtless, a token of the recognition by higher command of what the Battalion had done in the last two years. I recall Skeff appearing informally dressed, bare-headed and beltless, in No.3's area during the morning of the day after the award was announced. He spent some time wandering about the camp alone. We took turns to congratulate him, as he seemed to expect us to do. He looked complacent and slightly amused. He received our congratulations impassively, with little nods. He did not convey to our group of three (though he may have done so to others) that, in respect of the award, he felt that he owed anything to the Battalion. He may have thought that if a debt existed it was the other way round: that the army and its ways being what they are, the Battalion might count itself quite lucky to have had him as its commanding officer.

On 6 June 1917 we left Locre. Our departure reminded me somewhat of my 21st birthday party when, in December of the previous year, during supper in our elephant-iron hut in Savernake Wood, the last of three shells (which were coming nearer as the German gunner enfilading the valley north of Combles, lengthened his sights) burst on the door-step of No.3's mess.

Locre itself had been occasionally shelled, though not much damaged, during our stay. The other side of the village – the Dranoutre side – had received most of the attention. The nearest burst to us was about 400 yards away.

During the early hours of the day we were due to leave, shells had been falling on the far side of the village. We paid little attention. But in the middle of the morning, an extraordinary thing happened. The Company was formed up on parade, dressed and standing at ease, ready to march off. We could scarcely believe our ears when we heard the crescendo of an approaching shell: then – Crash! A shower of debris fell onto the tin hats of the standing men. Blank astonishment! Thereafter our departure was in no sense delayed or in any way prolonged. Rarely can the command 'By the Left Quick March' have fallen on more welcoming ears. Truly remarkable, we thought with tense mirth as we stepped out, that the Germans, who had left us alone for three weeks, should have postponed to the very last moment the presentation of this bouquet. Was the timing of the crash, perhaps, a final act of grace by Skeff's guardian angel?

There was a tragi-comedy in our departure. The comedy lay in our intact state as we marched off, in our self-congratulation over having thus escaped the devil's last throw; the tragedy in the foreseeable doom of this hospitable village, with its placid cows browsing round our camp, with its convent of pious nuns and its courageous inhabitants. These could not move out as we were doing. They had to stay and endure the intensifying war which was creeping up. 'Goodbye Locre, Dranoutre, Mont Rouge, Mont Kemmel,' I inwardly said as we marched off; 'Goodbye and God bless you'. To which valediction a sepulchral reply might have been heard by a prophetic ear: 'Satanic forces will swallow us up before God will again bless us.' During the rest of the year and in the following year, that corner of Belgium passed under the harrow.

The ensuing march to Bailleul, where we were to entrain for a short journey, was hot and dusty. The railway siding was about a mile south of the small town. While waiting for the trucks to arrive, Paterson told me about a rough night he had had shortly after the dinner above-described. While marching in the dark with a party of No.1 along a road packed with transport, he was suddenly heavily shelled. One of his party was killed and two wounded. The first shell hit the road almost under the belly of a mule. In the flash of the explosion he saw, as in a snap-shot, the unfortunate animal hurled into the air, as if it had been a kitten.

I remember nothing of the transit by rail to St. Omer where we detrained and again took to the road. But I recall the march to Arques, the village which was our destination. I was keen to get a glimpse of the beloved Clairmarais Forest nearby, about which I had almost proprietory feelings. There is a substantial road from St. Omer to Arques. But to reach the road we would have to traverse the town. Instead we marched along a broad and solid track which bordered a canal there called the Canal Neuf-Fosse; it formed part of a ramifying system of waterways which connected the Lys with such places to the north and west as Bergues and Gravelines. The south-western margin of the forest should have been visible from this canal road, but little could be seen. The railway and some buildings on the outskirts of Arques obstructed the view.

Arques lies to the south-west of the forest. We slept in tents on the outskirts and messed in a building connected with the village school. The schoolmistress was amiable and hospitable.

The week which followed ought to have been exhilarating and memorable, for it was spent within sight of the forest for which I had the sort of affection one feels for home. I had left the area almost exactly a year before – on 30 June 1916, the day before the battle of the Somme opened – a hot day like this but with the air vibrating to the distant drum fire. As we marched towards Arques along the canal, I recalled that earlier day of the year before, and thought to myself that it might then have been comforting to know that I would be so near twelve months later. But the week did not fulfil these vague hopes – for reasons which are given below.

*   *   *   *

During the week spent at Arques, CPB revisited the Clairmarais Forest, which he found in a depressingly neglected state; he was given a typhoid inoculation, to which he had a severe reaction; and there was a divisional boxing competition which was held in the nearby village of Renescure.

★   ★   ★   ★

This divisional boxing competition brings something else to mind, namely a speech delivered by Lord Cavan, the Corps Commander, from inside the ring before the boxing began. It was about the essential importance of the bayonet. This heavily decorated officer told with relish some bouncing stories about how various units had used the bayonet during the recent battles at Vimy. Every man in this ringside gathering, he told us, was equal to bayoneting at least two Germans, and he had no doubt we would do so when we had the chance, which might be soon. 'The real business of this war,' he said, 'is done with the bayonet. The rest is mere by-play.' The speech was vigorously delivered with semi-jocular conviction and went down well. But the spirit of the bayonet did not accord with the spirit of Clairmarais Forest (as that spirit had been conveyed to me) which was visible as a dark belt of impassive trees in the background.

When I look back on the four war years, I realize that my private morale sank to its lowest during the autumn of 1917. The decline had begun imperceptibly when it became impossible to doubt that, during the second half of that year, a major offensive operation on the scale of that of the previous year on the Somme – an operation designed to bring about a total defeat of the Germans and an end of the war – was to be staged in Belgium. But we had heard such talk before, and seeds of scepticism had been sown. During the preparations, material and moral, for the offensive on the Somme, conclusive victory had likewise been predicted. The enemy were to be driven back on a wide front, their line was to be broken at several points, and our cavalry would have their long-awaited opportunity. The German positions would be turned and their army would fold up. The civilian population in Britain and most of the expeditionary force, which included Kitchener's divisions of ardent young men, shared this glowing expectation. But after 1 July 1916, when it was gradually realized that our immense losses bore no relation to the exiguous strips of territory gained in each successive attack, hopes slowly faded. As the prospects of a victorious battle of movement dimmed, we had begun to hear more of an ultimate victory by attrition. Dreary thought and dreary talk which neither kindled hopes nor raised morale!

Why should we expect anything better from this second grand offensive? In 1914 and 1915 the army had had a taste of what the Salient could be like. Unless the Germans could, at the start, be driven right back and the advance carried into virgin territory, shellfire would turn the Belgian lowlands into a morass; no joke for the infantry or the gunners and impossible for cavalry or tanks. By the autumn of 1917 the units of Kitchener's army had lost the fire which had carried them forward on the Somme: and Kitchener himself – a background father-figure – had been dead for over a year – sunk in a ship carrying him to Russia. The unwisdom of selecting Flanders for a decisive operation aiming at the fragmentation of enemy forces was not only apparent to anyone who had served in the Salient; it was also seemingly dawning on politicians at home who had not questioned the strategies adopted the year before. Rumours came through of tensions between political leaders and the military command. It was, of course, splendid that our forceful Corps Commander should tell us that the real business of war was done with the bayonet and that the rest was mere by-play. But bayonets would not stop the autumn rains or dry up the waterlogged crater-fields.

As we walked away from the ringside near Renescure, these thoughts occupied my mind more than did the pleasure caused by the good showing put up by the Battalion in the boxing competition. I wondered what were the Corps Commander's inner thoughts. He might have whole-heartedly believed that the bayonet actually was the key weapon in modern war; or he may have thought of the bayonet as a symbol of the infantryman's combative spirit – something which, even if never used, should always be carried and kept in mind; or he may have decided that if the troops in our division were to be given the opportunity of taking a look at their Corps Commander – of seeing him and hearing him – the bayonet provided as good a theme for a short address as anything else. The first supposition seemed the most probable.

To our Corps Commander's exordium on the bayonet on that June afternoon, I later traced the beginnings of my own loss of morale. Something of the sort slowly spread through the army and persisted till the Battle of Passchendaele was abandoned. And something of the sort happened in the French army where there were mutinies in 1917. A new estrangement began in the following months between, on the one hand, the rank and file floundering in the mud and, on the other, the higher command and their sleek staff officers who ate and slept many miles back. The Commander-in-Chief, Sir Douglas Haig, was an admired soldier, a man of faith, character and determination, an impeccably dressed man of fine appearance. But was he perhaps lacking in imagination and flexibility? Did he really know what the conditions in the line were like?

We also wondered how far a major offensive by the British was called for by the predicaments of our allies, for example the Italians. We also vaguely asked ourselves where else on the Western Front such an operation could have been staged. We had no clear ideas. We were told that the Germans had naval bases in Belgian ports and that these ports had to be captured in order to defeat the submarine blockade which was becoming increasingly serious.

Our week at Arques was by way of being a rest period. It came to an end on Thursday 12 June. These mid-June days were oppressively hot. We returned to Belgium on foot, and marched seventeen miles on the first day. I had not properly recovered from my inoculation and did not carry a pack. Nevertheless I was exhausted when we got in. I recall a most devouring thirst. A long march in great heat produces a quite different effect on one's terminal state of mind from a similar march in extreme cold. The heat generates acute irritability. Overton-Jones had been sent ahead to do the billeting and I was surprised when Dickie, who was of light physical build and may have suffered much from the temperature, unexpectedly lost his temper over a triviality. He pitched into Jones, who, I thought, had distributed the company in the best way possible. Later I gently remonstrated in defence of Jones and Dickie at once sought him out and apologized. The minor breach was at once healed without loss of friendliness. No.3's mess had been located in a farmhouse and we bivouacked in a nearby field. On the evening of our arrival the heat suddenly broke in a thunderstorm. Rain sluiced down. The farmer who had gracious manners and a distinguished appearance – a distant resemblance to General Smuts – insisted on our taking refuge in his parlour. I recall that he had a strapping, good-looking daughter who, on some pretext, came in to take a look at us. I enjoyed a ten minutes' conversation in French.

The next day I was sent forward to do the billeting. Despite the thunderstorm of the evening before, this was about the sultriest day of the early summer. I made the billeting arrangements in my shirtsleeves and by the time everything was fixed I felt as exhausted as on the day before. I remember an exchange with Joe Forrester's RQMS Fricker whose temper at that time resembled that of the goddess Fricka at the moment when, in the second act of the *Walkyrie*, riding on a goat, she caught up with Wotan in a ravine, sitting disconsolately on a rock. I remember thinking at the time that RQMS Fricker looked more like the goat than the goddess. I discussed with this authoritarian character what we could do for the company to ease them in when they arrived. We decided to lead them straight into the shade of some elms about a hundred yards from the site of the camp where they would have an opportunity to cool down and recover. At about 2 p.m. Fricker and I, both of us sweating profusely, felt as if we had ourselves done the march fully loaded.

I had never seen the Company so beaten as when they staggered in at about three. Most of the men subsided in the shade without taking off their equipment and lay there gasping. Many had fallen out on the march and came in later. Dickie was in a bad way. Possibilities of heat stroke crossed my mind. Skeff, who had done the journey by car, was shocked. He had come round wanting us to do some nearby job. But nothing, he said, should be attempted till they had rested. He said he had not seen men so knocked by heat since the South African War.

Our destination was an unimposing wood of scrub oak not far from H-Camp – the place on which the Battalion had been based in 1916. To this place, Beta

Wood, we moved the next day. The first thing I noticed was how emerald moths were swarming in the crowns of the trees. I don't know the precise location on the map of either H-Camp or our 1917 destination. But our emerald-moth wood was near Proven and by that name the camp was known. Spring had given place to summer. July flowers, I noted in my diary, were coming out: meadow-sweet, bindweed, milfoil and, in the ditches, purple loosestrife, cat's valerian and knotted figwort. We slept out of doors in dry weather and, as before, were heavily attacked by mosquitoes. On our first night I was quite severely bitten under my right eye which, the next day, swelled to an absurd size. Mosquito netting and insect-repellent lotions were in demand. Reports on the forward areas were not discouraging. They suggested that, at first at least, our work would be clean and useful.

But these reports were belied by events on the Company's first night out. As if angered by our arrival, the gods were in an earth-punishing mood. It began in the late evening as the party was setting out. What seemed to be a stray shell crashed down into Beta Wood. Nobody hurt, but the send-off did not augur well. Dickie was in charge, supported by Boycott and Lumsden. (Dickie and I took turns.) As darkness fell the noise and general tumult increased. Crashes, flashes and smoke all over the place. I dossed down in my uniform and spent a restless night in foreboding. The sun was rising when the company filed back. I could see that there had been trouble. It was led by Dickie who looked about a hundred – a worn-out old man, tottering unsteadily and using his stick. The company had lost five men killed and seven wounded of whom one later died. My platoon (No.11) had suffered most with four men killed and two wounded.

One of the killed was an excellent young NCO, Corporal Neasham, of No.11 platoon. He had been physically struck by a shell which had literally blown him to pieces so that it had been difficult to collect the remains. Neasham had a close friend in the company's post-corporal, named Beck, a universally popular figure since he was the bearer of welcome mails from home. Beck, who had not been out that night, did not hear of the other's death till the company got back. I recall his reaction. Though shaken, he remarked philosophically that Neasham's death was worse for the survivors on the spot and at home than for the victim, for no death could have been more instantaneous. He obviously counted himself among the afflicted survivors.

Dickie had supervised and helped the stretcher-bearers throughout the sustained shelling and machine-gunning. As I have said, Dickie disliked more than most the sight of wounded men in pain. The lobe of one of his ears had been cut by a small fragment and his shoulder bruised so that he could scarcely move one arm. Lumsden came back shaken and trembling; for twenty-four hours I was in doubt as to whether he would have to be sent back as a casualty. But Wilfred Raffle plugged both Dickie and Lumsden with sedative and made them bed down for twelve hours.

The Company's hot reception on its first night matched the heat of the weather during the days we moved into Belgium. The preoccupying question that day was whether such liveliness was usual or exceptional in this sector. The uncertainty was largely settled on the following night when I took the company up to finish the uncompleted digging and wiring. I recall the hot, steamy, windless and short hours of darkness. We duly did the job and repaired the damage amid little disturbance. The nearest shell fell about fifty yards away. But the area was much machine-gunned. One man was non-lethally wounded. But two nights later, my diary tells me, I had another rough time with two men wounded and one shell-shocked. Part of the rather long journey to and fro was by then being done by truck so that we had to work at top speed during the short hours of late-June darkness. The work was close to the front line at a place which was under enemy observation. There was more long-range shelling of the back areas than there had been in 1916. Our oak wood with its emerald moths received attention. The sultry, sticky heat, the insecurity and the unpleasing prospect of what lay ahead in this sector, caused us to compare Beta Wood unfavourably with H-Camp the year before.

*   *   *   *

At the end of June he had a period of leave, which was spent at Dinard, where his parents had taken a small house.

*   *   *   *

On getting back to the Battalion I found that there had been no move from the wood with its emerald moths, few of which were by then visible. During my absence, the company had had some rough nights with casualties. In the middle of July there befell an event which, in the ensuing weeks, lowered my morale. Of all the four companies No.3 had had the foulest time since moving into Belgium. Under trying conditions we had lost about a third of our working strength. The stresses and strains imposed by losses largely depend on how they are incurred.

In an attack, when your energies and attention are wholly focused on getting as quickly as you can to an objective, you may know little about casualties till the attack is over. In the excitement you don't notice what is happening round you. When you re-form and count yourselves, you may find that a third, half, or two-thirds are not with you. But when you are in charge of a party on night work, you hear every shell coming and every machine-gun bullet as it cracks past. And if anyone is hit, everyone knows it. The call for stretcher-bearers as it is passed down is rarely missed. It was in such conditions that No.3 had its losses, with the result that this good Company became jumpy.

At this period the Battalion had to find a detachment to work for an unknown period under the Corps. No.3 was selected by Skeff who, in deciding which company to choose, may have thought of Dickinson. The work under the Corps turned out to be dull and safe. It was not the sort of work we wanted when the Division's time was partitioned between delivering difficult attacks and holding an awkward line in bad weather. Hence there grew on several of us, not least myself, a dispiriting sense of isolation and of waning zest. Indeed, these are the feelings which now mainly colour my memories of the early autumn of 1917. I look back on it as an inglorious period. As Corps troops we took no active part in the two big attacks of 31 July and 9 October and we had minimal casualties on those two important days. Indeed, the attacks took place humiliatingly far from where we happened to be located: we were out of range of machine-gun and rifle fire, and the only trouble we had was from occasional long-range gunfire.

During most of this period of detachment we were out of touch with the rest of the Battalion. When news reached us that the other companies were busy in the forward areas, then dejection would be acute. My own morale fell to its nadir on the day of the main divisional attack, 31 July. I cannot recall ever having felt more suicidal. During a day of inactivity I tried to console myself by reading. Because I felt that, during our detachment, life was too safe and too easy, I used to set myself difficult tasks. This was a stupid thing to do. If I failed to understand the tough books I had sent out from England, I would get irritated both with the books and with myself, thus unnecessarily adding to my ill-humour.

With intermissions we were away from the Battalion from 28 July to 22 September. During most of August we were attached to a Pioneer Battalion of the York and Lancs Light Infantry. Thereafter No.3 was somehow linked under a Corps command with a South African Railway Operating Company whose ideas of discipline differed much from ours. At first we continued to be based on Beta Wood (of the emerald moths) from which area the rest of the Battalion had departed. But on about 4 August we were moved to a peculiar site between a road and a railway on the outskirts of what remained of the Belgian village of Elverdinghe about 3 miles north-west of Ypres. In this accessible but increasingly unsafe and noisy place we stayed until 22 September.

During August I had two quite lucky escapes. The field (between a road and a light railway near Elverdinghe) in which we were camped had at first been empty. But as the weeks passed it filled up with troops from several units and received increasing attention from enemy gunners and airmen. Our officers' tents were sited in a single short row about four yards apart. When, after a long night out, I got back in the early morning, I was astonished and shaken to find a medium-size shell crater perfectly placed in the space between my tent and the one next to it. The crater could not have been better sited. Exact equidistance; exactly similar dislocation of the two sets of tent pegs. If I had been asleep in my tent, the rim of the crater would have been about a foot from my head. Not for the first time, I 'thanked my stars' with an understanding of the astrologer's as well as the astronomer's idea of stars; and I thought of Skeff's guardian angel.

The other occasion, which occurred a week later, was somewhat as follows. To No.12 platoon had been assigned the job of keeping in repair a Deccaville railway on which, through the swampy lowland, depended supplies for the forward areas. This railway, the object of which was well understood by the Germans, was regularly shelled both by day and by night. The railway connected two dumps, one far back, the other (kept well camouflaged) near the support line.

No.12's party, when inactive, spent the time in a dugout opening into a short trench at right angles to the railway. A camouflaged truck loaded with the necessaries for repair was kept in a nearby siding. Throughout the night the line was patrolled by pairs of men from our party, who reported damage. The officer in charge of these repair parties had sometimes to use his judgment. The track was repeatedly smashed in definite places on which the Germans had guns trained; so that if you were working at a break, you never knew when the next salvo would come down. All you knew was that you were on a dangerous spot. So you kept your ears trained for the first sound of an approaching salvo. You usually had a second or two to get your party into the nearest shell-hole. I found it mildly exhilarating to be responsible for these repair jobs.

My second escape occurred in this way. In the half-light of the early hours of an August morning I was supervising a repair some two hundred yards east of our track-side dugout. When we were half-way through the repair it was passed to me that I was wanted in the dugout. A message had been received. I therefore left the party under an NCO, and went back to the dugout. I there dealt with whatever it was that needed attention and was returning to the repair party, which still had about half an hour's work to complete, when I heard a shout behind me. Sergeant Sheridan had come out of the dugout and was beckoning to me to come back. Another message had been received. I turned about and was moving along the track towards the dugout when – swoosh and crash – down came a salvo behind me. The bursts were on, and each side of, the track between myself and the working party. When, a few moments later, I was examining the new damage with Sergeant Sheridan, he remarked that it was a good thing that he had shouted to me to come back when he did. The salvo had come down on just about the point I would have reached if he had not shouted to me to come back. He said: 'I reckon I saved your life, Sir.' If I had been superstitious I would have regarded these two incidents – the shell coming down so near my tent when I happened not to be there and my being called back at just the right moment on the railway track – as providential. If, as the old Romans believed, there was a goddess of luck, I had been favoured by her. Anyhow, looking back a few months later on this period, I realized that my morale had taken a turn for the better after this perfectly timed call-back on the Deccaville railway.

I now clearly remember how variable was the damage to this miniature railway caused by the directed fire. For the most part the shells were not large. But one day, when fortunately no one was about, a single large shell – we surmised an eight-inch – came down in the very middle of the track. The rails on the hither side were blown upwards in a huge arc which towered backwards high over our heads like a steel rainbow or, as someone said, like a scenic railway at a fair.

It was impossible to camouflage the track along its full course. The German airmen and gunners between them had it well taped and, it seemed to us, paid it increasing attention as the weeks passed.

I quote from my letters.

'The night of 10–11 September was lively in a novel way. Just after 2 a.m., in almost pitch dark, gas shells began to rain down on the railway. These shells descend to earth from a high trajectory, having been fired a long way behind the German line. The sound of their descent is quite different from that of high explosive. For nearly two hours these gas shells, which were of small calibre, streamed and swished down lazily, with little terminal acceleration, and hit the ground with a soft 'phutt'. No bang or crash or flying bits of metal and no earth thrown up. They are un-vicious, unalarming, almost soothing. Feeling sluggish and constricted in our gas masks, we sat in our rail-side dugout in darkness. The wearing of a gas mask, particularly in the dark, discourages you from moving. Breathing is laboured, especially expiration through the valve-like tubing of the mouthpiece; and the celluloid eye-pieces, greased to prevent mistiness, impair the acuity, and restrict the field, of vision. In the dark you are dis-inclined to move. A gas-proof blanket draped the exit of our dugout wherein the air became heavy, so that we sat motionless and huddled in the pitch darkness. You are reluctant to move when you can see so little. Finally somnolence descends and you lazily doze. . . .

'It was at half-past five, during a lull, that I got out and took a look at the railway track. I found that a train with one of our conducting parties in front had driven straight into a shell-hole, and that the driver and party had abandoned the train and made for some trenches nearby. Gas or no gas, the hole had to be repaired and the parties sent back to their units. So we got down to the job. There was a light wind blowing but the gas clings to the loose earth of the small saucer-like craters and continues to exude from them, especially in early morning mist and sunshine. The air was full of it. An unpleasant sweet smell that irritates the membranes of one's nose and throat, causing one to spit and cough. However, we mended the break quite quickly and got 'home' by 7.30. Though not feeling at our best, we were in better shape than I expected when we were getting strong doses. The next day we were little the worse. . . .

'Yesterday evening I went for what has become my usual walk alone: a beautiful September evening with cottony clouds lit by a clear pink sunset. A few desultory wild flowers – purple loosestrife, chamomile and meadow-sweet. In a line of poplars bordering a stream and bent over by the prevailing S.W. wind was a vast congregation of starlings which could be heard half a mile away. . . . Last night the Padre came to dinner and afterwards we had a lively exchange about war aims which broadened into issues of religion, destiny etc. A likeable and tolerant man. . . . Yesterday George Lane came to lunch. Someone remarked 'The Bosch has control of the air on this front anyhow'. No sooner were the words spoken than loud noises of anti-aircraft fire burst out around us. Overton-Jones looked out of the shelter and ejaculated: 'By Gad, there are about 20 Huns almost over our heads!' We streamed out and there, sure enough, flying low were eight German aeroplanes shining silver against the sky. Suddenly over the road a column of smoke shot up and there was a cracking report. Three further reports followed from nearby. We took to our funk holes with ostentatious leisureliness while, on all sides, there was a hasty scattering. Then the Bosches disappeared in a cloud. Bruorton took a look round through his glasses and saw the unpleasant sight of men stooping and picking up things and putting them on stretchers and then under sheets. We later learned that the casualties had been quite heavy, taking into account the wide area covered by the raid.' (13 September 1917).

An interim word about gas-shelling. I have often been grateful that a bombardment was by gas shells and not high explosive. The use of gas might be held to be an atrocity. But our experience was that gas shells were in all respects preferable to other kinds of shell. They were less alarming in their descent; they did less damage when they hit the ground; and such injuries to lungs, heart and skin which they caused were less often lethal than those inflicted by high explosive. I have rarely met anyone who took a contrary view.

*   *   *   *

Between 3 and 6 October CPB was unexpectedly given four days Paris leave. In the course of this leave he bought a green parrot at a pet-shop on a riverside Quai. It became a company pet and was nicknamed Skeff after the Battalion's commanding officer.

*   *   *   *

On 17 October Skeff (the Colonel) left us. In a short speech he said that this command was the greatest honour he had ever received in his life, that the Battalion could never have gained its fine name if every man had not given of his best, and that he himself felt personally grateful to every one of us. Before leaving he shook me by the hand and told me that I had 'served him grand'. An affection which had been incubating for two years sprang to life so that I spoke from the heart when I told him that none of us, who had served under him, would forget him. I am sure none of us has.

George Edwards took over as the Commanding Officer of the Battalion

On 21 October a young Etonian officer, Leonard Bower, was posted to No.3. For some forgotten reason we nicknamed him Bolo. A contrast to the South Africans, Bower was a blond, long-haired, rather feminine-looking youth who, at first sight, made me think of Greek mythology in which he might have figured as cup-bearer to the gods. He dressed expensively and was musical. Bolo introduced us to Strauss's *Rosenkavalier* of which the waltz was later much played on the mess's gramophone.

In October No.3 was again detached for a short time from the Battalion and again worked on the same light railway. The conditions of work had deteriorated while we had been away, and it was obvious that the maintenance of the railway was becoming an increasingly important factor in the local conduct of the war. By then there extended on each side of the Deccaville track an expanse of shell-craters full of water. Over much of the ground, especially in certain much-shelled areas round the track, the craters were rim to rim and overflowing; so that, if you stood on the track and looked from side to side, you saw more water than earth; and what earth you saw had the consistency of porridge. Efforts had been made to lay duckboard tracks which wound their way through the morass, skirting the worst parts. But the duckboards swivelled, tilted and slowly sank so that, with each new spell of rain, they became increasingly unusable.

There was an order that troops should not use the Deccaville for carrying-parties, reliefs etc. But the order was increasingly ignored as the conditions worsened and it became difficult to enforce. One of us once remonstrated with an officer of another unit who was leading an exhausted party down from the line. They were soaked and plastered with mud. The officer said: 'Show me where else we can go. Show me your duckboard track.' By this time most of it was invisible.

The importance which the deteriorating conditions gave our railway was not lost on the Germans. The Deccaville track was increasingly shelled so that our work became heavier, more difficult, more important and more dangerous. How far this change was recognized by our own higher command we did not know. But I doubt if our 4th Battalion ever gave more useful service to the Division than during this last phase of the Battle of Passchendaele. I remember thinking what a good sight it was to see rations going up and casualties coming down on wheeled vehicles (light trucks) using the Deccaville!

I also remember some lively times during those last few nights: 'I had the second shift last night when what amounts to a miracle occurred. I had about 30 men working on a curve that had been shelled rather heavily in the morning. All of a sudden there was a hideous noise of something big coming down and an eight-inch shell burst like a volcano in the middle of the strung-out party blowing up three sets of rails. Not a man was touched. One felt like kneeling down and offering up a prayer of thanksgiving. . . .'

*   *   *   *

The above extracts from diaries and letters convey little idea of the experiences of the Division as a whole and of the other three companies of the 4th Battalion during the autumn months. The almost continuous rain made life quite diffi-cult and disagreeable enough for No.3, but we knew well that our troubles were but a pale reflection of those which afflicted the Battalions which had to attack and hold the line in that degenerating swamp. The conditions seem to have been about the worst to which the British army in France was exposed during the four years of war.

Two main causes contributed to the sagging morale. The first was the relent-lessly bad weather which steadily worsened the conditions of the soft and wet ground. The other was the gradual realization that the army was failing to make good its strategical objective. We had been told that the overall purpose of the operation in Flanders was to clear the Germans out of the Belgian ports of Ostend and Zeebrugge which they were increasingly using in their submarine campaign. The submarine war had been undertaken, after some hesitation, by the Germans as a calculated risk. This war under the sea had brought the Americans in against them and had been ruthlessly pursued. As seen by us, sinkings of cargo ships were increasing and anxieties about our food supplies were mounting; and German hopes were correspondingly soaring. Our own Higher Command knew well enough how difficult it would be to effect a break-through in the familiar Belgian lowlands of canals and dykes. In a direct line, Ostend lay some 27 miles north-east of Ypres, our approximate starting point, and Zeebrugge some 35 miles. Our Higher Command knew that the ground, bad enough already, would get worse if the weather turned bad; and they knew that the slower our advance the more the ground would be churned up, water-logged and rendered impassable by artillery fire.

To many of us in the periphery – to Overton-Jones and myself, for example – it seemed that a big gamble on the weather was being taken by our Higher

Command. And we speculated on how far our leaders, hoping and praying for the best, had in mind the possibility of a major breakthrough which would give our cavalry and tanks a field for manoeuvre. Whether or not such sanguine hopes were entertained – and it was known that our Commander-in-Chief was a deeply religious and prayerful man – it was fairly obvious that initial successes and a rapid advance into unravaged country were essential. Time (giving to the gunners of both sides full opportunities of converting the battlefield into an impassable morass) and rain were our main enemies; and in our sometimes lively discussions in No.3's mess the hope was freely ventilated that, if the weather turned seriously against us, Haig would have the flexibility to call off the offensive in Flanders and attack elsewhere. We hoped that our strategy would have been geared to a precursory decision such as: 'If by . . . (a particular date) we had not reached . . . (a particular position) we will call it off in this area'. In the event, something of the sort happened; but the Battle of Cambrai (see below) did not begin till 20 November by which time the damage to morale had been done. The consequence was that the morale of the British army probably then sank lower than at any time during the war. Mine certainly did, though I had an easy time compared with many. Another consequence of how the Flanders battles were planned was that grave stresses developed between our leading politicians and the army's Higher Command. Confidence was being lost in high places as it was being lost in the swampy lowlands north-east of Ypres.

Instead of our attack leading to a war of movement, the opposite happened. Sir John Ross-of-Bladensburg, the regiment's historian of the war, tells us[1] that by September 1917 the Germans had changed their system of defence. They were holding their forward positions lightly, keeping troops in close reserve, and delivering counter-attacks before we could consolidate. 'To meet these tactics,' we are blandly told, 'some modifications were introduced in our own dispositions. Our objectives were not to be so far forward as they were before, the assaulting troops were to have a less distance to go, and our artillery were to be prepared to disperse at once the hostile counter-attacks directly they developed.' What in fact we did was to shorten the range of our attacks, thereby diminishing the chances of penetration and slowing our rate of advance. Hopes of manoeuvre were gradually abandoned. The Flanders offensive had become a senseless slogging match in swamp, inflicting unprecedented hardship on both sides. This had not been the original intention. Hopes of victory evaporated, and with them was dispersed some of the rank and file's confidence in the leadership. The French army had had mutinies in early 1917. It is perhaps to our credit that nothing of the sort happened in the British army later in the same year.

---

[1] *The Coldstream Guards 1914–1918*, 1928. Vol.2, p.101.

For our particular Division there may have been something dispiriting about the area captured between 31 July and 12 October 1917. The total operation came to be known as the Battle of Passchendaele. In fact the village of Passchendaele, which I beheld for the first time when I motored through it in mid-1958, was well outside our divisional zone. It lies about four miles east and somewhat south of the area captured by the 3rd Guards Brigade in the course of the last divisional attack on 12 October. The zone of divisional activities was an elongated strip some five or six miles long and three-quarters of a mile across. Its narrowness conferred importance on our Deccaville railway as a means of supply. The strip extended from Boesinghe towards a small place called Staden: it pointed north-eastwards in the general direction of Ostend and Zeebrugge. Two swollen streams flowing through the strip at right-angles to its long axis had to be negotiated: the Steenbeck (reached on 31 July on the first advance) and the Broenbeck (crossed on 9 October, the day of the Division's second main advance). Landmarks which might have helped the advancing troops were mostly farms with English, French or Flemish names (such as Signal Farm, Montmirail Farm, Gruibezule Farm) which, by the time they were captured, had been reduced to various stages of demolition. It was during this period that we first took notice of 'pill-boxes', or heavily protected strong points. Some of these were located in farms, where they were well camouflaged and inconspicuous; others were placed in the open when they struck the eye as menacing square structures of concrete, with good fields of fire.

Though the Division was successful in its two main battles, the Flanders campaign as a whole failed in the sense that it did not get near either Ostend or Zeebrugge. That it was going to fail became fairly obvious by the end of September. At this time gruesome stories began to circulate. I was told of how a party arrived in rain to find two sections they were expecting to relieve so stuck in the deepening mud that they could not get out. And we heard rumours of individual men and small parties being totally engulfed, like cattle sunk in a bog. Many unfortunate horses thus perished.

The realization that the Flanders campaign had essentially failed reinforced the relentless weather in reducing the morale of the army to its lowest ebb. Though I myself had to endure little compared with the officers of other Battalions, my own ups and downs of morale followed the track of theirs. I found myself wondering which was worse – to share or not to share the hardships which others like oneself had to endure. One alternated between thanking God and floundering in discontent and self-disparagement; so that the better one's reasons for thanking God, the deeper became one's dejection.

Another consequence of this phase of the war was an estrangement of the rank and file from the staffs whose members wore red tabs or red cap-bands. After most engagements the Higher Command circulated to the rank and file expressions of praise. The troops were told that their fortitude and endurance

had upheld the highest traditions of their formations and were much appreciated by the various commanders on the ladder of authority. But the worse
the conditions and the more taxing the moves up to the line through the
mud, the less (perforce) was seen in the forward areas of these colourful figures,
of whom it was increasingly felt that there would have been less need for their
eulogies if their strategies and battle-plans had been more imaginative. One
inconspicuously-placed officer, whom I later got to know well in the Second
Battalion, developed for the staff a mounting dislike, which as the war drew to
its conclusion, turned into an obsessional hatred.

10

NOVEMBER-DECEMBER 1917:
BATTLE OF CAMBRAI

As I mentioned in the last chapter, I spent quite a time during October and November 1917 away from the Battalion. I had a short period of Paris leave during the first week of October and then, three weeks later, my turn for the usual fortnightly leave came round. This I spent in Dinard. I had left the Battalion near Elverdinghe. No.3 had moved out of tents and I recall our mess being located in a semi-demolished house. The upper storey no longer existed, but, by someone's ingenuity, the ceiling of the ground floor had been made rainproof. It was in this place that Bolo had joined us.

By then it was obvious that the Flanders campaign had been a strategical failure. But we had no idea what was to come next. There was a widely felt hope, amounting to an expectation, that we were going to be moved out of the Ypres Salient.

When, on 28 October, I left the company on my fortnight's leave, I had no idea where I would find it on my return. The short-term prospect of the war was not encouraging. It was becoming increasingly plain that little more could be expected of the Russians and, on 24 October, the Italians had sustained a defeat about the dimension of which there had been various conjectures. But it was obvious that the position in Italy was serious: serious enough for troops to be sent there from the Western Front. We were to lose our popular Corps Commander, Lord Cavan, whose staff would include my old friend A.R. Kelsey. Some of us talked about Italy being a possible destination for ourselves and we thought about Christmas in Venice or perhaps in the upper reaches of one of those Italian rivers with euphonious names such as the Piave, the Isonzo or the Tagliamento.

I have no records of my leave in Dinard; nor have I any but the scantiest recollections. The Flanders offensive, which impended during my earlier period in June, was over. The beautiful long days of high summer had given place to the fading tints and gales of late autumn. The tension had relaxed. No major ordeal now impended – or so it most definitely seemed. But the future contained nothing to encourage hope. Indeed the prospect was dreary: more sinkings at sea, further shortages of fuel, stricter rations, and another grim winter.

My clearest memory of my leave is of a walk with my mother through fields. The fieldside hedges of Brittany yield a generous crop of blackberries and my mother knew of some good places. On an afternoon which I clearly remember, a gusty but purposeful wind was streaking the autumn sky overhead with wisps and tufts of cloud. The baskets which we carried were half full of blackberries. We had picked as many as we wanted. So we sat with our backs to a hedge behind which, in a pink and unsettled sky, the sun was stormily setting. In silence we watched the tumbling procession of dead leaves as they raced overhead from behind us – singly, in twos and threes, and in scattered parties. They wildly plunged and somersaulted over our heads and hurried away into the distance, to be replaced by continuous reinforcements which, in their turn, disappeared in the waning light.

My mother fell into a melancholy, a thing she never allowed herself to do in my father's presence. I knew how her mind was working. 'You are thinking,' I said, 'that the sunset is the coming winter of war; the wind is time; the leaves are the future's casualties.' Yes, she said. What saddened her were the leaves, because she did not believe that death was like that. When we die, she said, we don't dry up and fade like those leaves; we are not blown away into nothingness. My mother fervently believed in a life after death: heaven was a place of brightness where you rejoiced to see again the people you had loved during your life. A terrible thought, she said, which loomed in the background and slipped past her defences in weak moments when faith ebbed, was that those wind-tossed leaves were telling the truth. They were showing you what really happened after death. She had to fight back that thought.

It was quite a short exchange. Robin was not mentioned, but I knew well enough that he was in my mother's mind. As it was getting cold, we got up, shook ourselves and, with our baskets, walked home where a warm fire cheered us. During those moments under the hedge, I renewed the contact with my mother which I had first made two years before during our walk round the lake in Paris's Bois de Boulogne.

I left Dinard on Saturday 12 November. There followed a tortuous return to the Battalion the whereabouts of which were not exactly known to the people from whom I made enquiries. I was sent on from place to place: from Calais to Boulogne, from Boulogne to Etaples where I spent the night in a luxurious officers' hostel; and from Etaples to St. Pol. There I learned that the Battalion was on the move. It was then heading for a place called Diéval on the St. Pol-Bruay road – about 18 miles due west of Lens (of sinister memory).

I arrived at Diéval as the Battalion was marching in and I was at once plunged into the arduous but not difficult duties of finding billets. It was good to be back with No. 3. Dickie, I learned with chagrin but not surprise, had been struck off our strength. A final severance regretted by all. His wife had come through her crisis successfully. But two hours after its birth the child had died. (An aspect of death to which we were unaccustomed.) Overton-Jones had commanded the Company well and everyone seemed happy. No one knew where we were heading for; but the general movement was obviously south-east.

The next day (Friday 16 November) we left Diéval. I went ahead by bicycle to a village called Moncheaux. There and in two adjacent villages called Monts-en-Ternois and Buneville, all due south of St. Pol, I fitted the Battalion in. Rather to my surprise, I found the civilian population of these three places less co-operative than usual. I recall the following scene: I spent the night of 16 November in the kitchen of a farm with an old farmer and his aged and stooping wife. The latter sat on one side of the stove, bent over some sewing – the mending of an old coat of her husband's. A continuous muttering to herself would now and then be interrupted as she sat up, straightened her back, took a deep breath, and resignedly pronounced the two words: '*Ah! Oui.*' These words expressed a weary recognition of the afflictions brought on everyone by the war. The old man sat silently and sullenly on the other side of the stove and, at regular intervals, spat on the floor. That was his opinion of the war and of the condition of France. Both these old people lamented the shortage of labour, the absence of their sons, and the high prices. Few were the cottages of north-eastern France where this lament was not heard.

The next day, after saying goodbye to the farmer and his wife and wishing them and their absent sons well, I pushed on some 25 miles south-east to a village called Bailleulmont (later to become quite familiar) which lies a mile south of the Arras-Doullens road. There again the Battalion was later fitted in. By then something had become noticeable; most of the Battalion's movement was being done by night. It began to look as if we were heading towards a 'push' somewhere near. But what sort of push at that time of year? We speculated. The beginning of winter was not the best time to start a major offensive. Also, there was little in the way of artillery to be seen about and no tanks. It looked more like a large-scale raid than a serious effort to break through.

Uncertainties were resolved at 6.30 a.m. on the morning of Tuesday 20 November. From one moment to the next the sky flickered and lit up. And the heavens were filled by a tremendous tumult. The curtain went up on the Battle of Cambrai.

A word about Cambrai. From what we could make out from the inhabitants of the surrounding villages, Cambrai, which we hoped soon to take, was not primarily an industrial town. But it had historical interest and, in past centuries, had produced a fine sort of linen called Cambric. It had a population of about

25,000. Cambrai was nearer to the Somme battlefields of 1916 than I realized till after the battle. Ginchy and Trônes Wood were within a day's march of Bourlon Wood – roughly twenty miles – so that when, a year before, one had looked east from the Bapaume-Péronne road into German-occupied territory, Cambrai would have been ensconced in the filmy distance. Yet the immediate landscape was different. The area south of Cambrai undulated in hills and valleys, like that round Combles; but it was more irregular. It was intersected by two canals and gashed by several ravines in which troops could assemble unobserved before an attack. I don't recall that round Cambrai the ground was chalky; but my memory may be misleading.

At this point in my story I find myself in a difficulty which has not occurred in quite this way before. The longer you stay at a place the more firmly it is stamped on your memory; and conversely, the shorter your stay the more evanescent your recollections. During the three weeks I am now trying to write about, I was busy and almost continuously on the move. My letters are short and disjointed, and likewise my diary. The latter gives little more than place-names recording our nightly moves. Memories of these numerous and often exhausting movements are scanty and unreliable. I had hoped that more would come back from my letters; but it has not done so. There have remained but two definite recollections. They are of the *Canal du Nord* and of *Havrincourt Wood*. The rest is a jumble, chiefly of shell-fire by night and day, of casualties from shell-fire (none from small-arms fire), and of struggling along muddy paths through woods in rain and pitch dark. I will begin with an outline of the course of the battle and then describe the little I definitely remember.

The battle was not prolonged. Indeed, it was short but sharp. It lasted little less than three weeks – from 20 November to 7 December 1917. On the surface, it seemed to have been a failure. But below the surface, as we came to see later, things were different.

The main object was to relieve pressure on the Italian army which, on 24 October (a little less than a month before), had sustained a severe defeat at Caporetto, a village in the extreme north-east of Italy, on the Isonzo River above Trieste. A second objective of the battle of Cambrai was to try out a new method of attack wherein (as vigorously argued by a new school of military thinking) surprise, speed and the massive use of tanks were to take the place of a prolonged artillery bombardment. No forewarning was given to the enemy of what impended. No unusual shelling or patrolling: perhaps less than usual. And all the preliminary movements had been by night. So that, before the storm burst on them, the local Germans were in a state of unsuspecting calm.

The Battle of Cambrai was a failure in several senses: the town itself was not taken as planned; after rapid advances during a wonderfully successful first three days, there was no breakthrough; and within ten days or so of the first day, two-thirds of the captured ground was lost. But the battle was a success in that it opened new long-term possibilities. It demonstrated that the tactics of surprise, speed and the massive use of tanks yielded incomparably better results in unfortified country than the prolonged artillery preparation, hitherto familiar. The encouraging possibility was disclosed that these new tactics might render obsolete the attritional methods which had turned the Somme and Passchendaele into slow soul-destroying ordeals for both sides.

The German commander on the Cambrai front was General Von der Marwitz who was a quick mover. In his counter-attack delivered on 30 November, ten days after our first onslaught, his troops also made use of surprise. In the first few hours they broke through the south-east side of the square salient we had made in their positions. The Germans advanced westwards without serious opposition till after midday on 30 November (the first day of their counter-attack) when they were stopped at the village and wood of Gouzeaucourt in a battle wherein our Second Battalion played a creditable part.

The battle can thus be divided into two phases; the first covers the period 20–30 November, before the enemy counter-attacked; the second covers the period 30 November to 7 December by when the battle was over. During the first of these periods the regiment sustained severe losses at Bourlon Wood and Fontaines, both lying west of Cambrai in the northern part of our blunt and square salient; it also lost heavily during the second period in the battle further to the south round Gouzeaucourt village and wood.

An important feature of the battle was the village of Masnières, which lies about 7 kilometres south-south-west of the town of Cambrai. This village was transected both by the Scheldt Canal and by the straight Cambrai-Péronne road. The road crossed the canal in the middle of the village. An important objective of the plan for the first day of the battle (20 November) was that the bridge over the canal at Masnières should be seized and, at the earliest possible moment, crossed by cavalry and tanks. These should then have fanned out to the east and north and enveloped Cambrai, thus opening up the battle to one of manoeuvre. Masnières seems to have been taken quickly – whether by cavalry, infantry or tanks I don't know. But by the time the village was in our hands the bridge had been blown up. Hence neither cavalry nor tanks were able to fulfil their allotted tasks. They never fanned out to the east and north in the manner planned. Who can say what would have been the outcome of the operation as a whole if we had seized the bridge at Masnières intact? If it is true that, on the morning of 20 November, the Germans were wholly unaware of the impending attack on that sector of the Western Front, they must have acted with rapid prescience in destroying this bridge when they did.

During the first stage of the battle No.3 Company was occupied in clearing wire and other obstructions from the dry bed of the *Canal du Nord*, which had formed part of the Hindenburg Line – the line fortified by the Germans when they withdrew from the positions they had held on the Somme the previous year. The canal had not been completed when the war began. One of my two visual memories of this period is standing at a point in the bed of the canal from which, if you faced north, Bourlon Wood was visible on your right. There had been severe and inconclusive fighting in Bourlon Wood which, we were told, was partly in our hands. My memory is of the vigilant appearance of this sinister wood which reminded me of Klingsor's castle, Klingsor being the evil magician in Wagner's *Parsifal.* Were we being watched from up there? If yes, our position was exposed and dangerous and we might at any moment have to move away in a hurry. The sight of this wood brought back something of the feeling I had had the year before when, from the top of a range of chalk hills on the Somme, three of us, Allan, Treffry and I had surveyed the expanse below.

The quiescent battlefield was like a monster that was pretending to be asleep. In its own time it would wake up and savagely retaliate. It understood exactly what was happening, and it had a long memory. Wariness and respect were enjoined.

I now realize that this picture of Bourlon Wood in November 1917 has been fixed in my memory by what happened in the following year. The hands of the clock of war had so turned that, in September 1918, I found myself in almost exactly the same spot, looking upwards again at the dominantly-placed Bourlon Wood. But this time the entire area was in eruption. 'A good thing,' the wood (then being pounded with heavy artillery and shrouded in smoke and mustard gas) seemed to be saying in 1918, 'that you did not see me in this mood last year.'

My other clear memory of events in late 1917 is of the second phase of the Battle of Cambrai. The German counter-attack had been delivered and, in the mid-afternoon of 30 November, No.3 Company received orders to move back to a position west of Havrincourt Wood. Nearby was the base of an observation balloon. There I fortuitously met a Flying Corps officer of the name of Griffiths of whom Robert Dell had spoken to me. A charming man, I remember, with whom conversation was pleasant and easy. We arranged to meet later in the evening. But before this was possible, a carrying party from No.3 was ordered to retrace its steps to a point well to the east of Havrincourt Wood – which was in fact big enough to qualify as a small forest. This order reached us when the Battle of Gouzeaucourt was ending to the south-east. We were told that on arrival, an urgent task would be assigned to us. I recall a stressful march in rapidly waning light to a rendezvous to the east of the wood. It was not a pleasant march. We were carrying up a supply of pickets and wire, and it was raining. In increasingly opaque darkness, the heavily loaded party floundered in single file along a boggy forest track strewn with wrecked trees and debris. In getting round these obstacles you were liable to trip, lose contact with the man in front, injure yourself and split the party. Progress was exhausting and slow but we managed to hold together somehow, with many stops. In the wood we bumped into (or rather there rose out of the darkness in front of us) a small party of exhausted British soldiers. They were demoralized and lost. We guessed that they were fugitives from the morning's battle. They told us that there were Germans in the wood. This I doubted. But if, I said to myself, there really are Germans about, they would not cause us trouble. They would be at the end of their tether and would probably be quick to surrender. But we met no Germans.

We finally reached our destination somewhere to the north of Gouzeaucourt Wood which lies to the south and east of the much larger Havrincourt Wood. The rendezvous was with a party engaged on digging a trench, which, when completed, they had orders to hold against possible German attacks. With our wire and pickets, from which we were glad to part company, we erected a belt of concertina and barbed wire within talking distance of the diggers. But the newly-made position was not attacked. A day or two later, the Germans withdrew.

I look back on that night, which remains vivid, with mixed feelings. While the exercise lasted, the scramble in darkness and rain through the battered wood, the fear of losing one's way, and the risk of the file being broken so that the party would come to pieces, were nightmarish. But the ensuing satisfaction, when the assignment was completed, of getting through intact, made the earlier stresses worthwhile. We had no casualties either from shell-fire or from accidents – which can happen easily when troops are carrying pointed metallic objects in file over bad surfaces in the dark.

When the battle was over and we were withdrawn, I again had mixed feelings. It seemed to some of us that an opportunity had been missed of using our well-proven battalion of pioneers to resist the sudden counter-attack. Unlike the pioneers of the 1939/45 war, we were fully armed and trained as combatant troops. In particular we regretted our move back to the air-force post when, instead, we might have moved forward, occupied a defensive line, and awaited events. On the other hand we had no cause to reproach ourselves. We were kept so much on the move that we suffered much from fatigue and loss of sleep; and in a confusing general situation we did exactly what we were ordered to do. And later we were able to see that what we had done was useful. Our best work was put in during and after the German counter-attack. How useful our activities in and around the Canal du Nord later proved to be, I don't know. There was heavy fighting round Bourlon and Fontaines during the initial British attack and the German counter-attack; and for several days most of Bourlon wood was in our hands. But we lost these places – or rather we were compelled to withdraw from them – in the course of the German counter-attack. I recall George Edwards thanking some of the officers of No.3 for the way that they had dealt with their various assignments, and I also recall how rock-like Clive Piggott was throughout.

During the Battle of Cambrai as a whole, the Battalion had thirty-seven casualties which included three killed. The other three Coldstream Battalions had conspicuously higher casualties, amounting to a total of 41 officers and 750

Other Ranks. Among the officers was an old friend, H.C. St. J. Thompson, with whom I had served in the autumn of 1915 in Jimmy Coats's Company at Laventie. Tommy, as we called him, was overweight for his short stature. I recall a habit which I have come across in others, but never so obtrusively as in this amiable man. He was talkative and inquisitive and would ask you questions. But he was impatient when you tried to answer. He would interrupt your reply and finish it for you. But he invariably finished it the wrong way. You would then say: 'No, Tommy; it wasn't quite like that,' and try again to convey to him what you wanted to say. But after you had said a few words, he would again wrongly forestall your reply. I recall an occasion two years before when it took three attempts to circumvent interruptions and convey correctly what happened on a given night. Thus communication was not always easy.

But the peculiar thing was that this habit, which would have been exasperating in anyone else, did not annoy you in this man. He reminded me of a French comedian who built into a comic turn the habit of asking everyone questions, interrupting them, and wrongly anticipating their answers. The end of the turn was that he was hit on the head. I got to know the good-tempered Tommy well enough to tell him about this comedian. In another Battalion he had later been awarded a D.S.O. Alas! He died of wounds.

Up to this time the four Battalions had suffered fairly equally in casualties. The fact that, for this battle, the casualties of the other three Battalions had been so much heavier than ours distressed me less than I would have expected because I felt that, in respect of its performance, the Fourth Battalion had most fully justified itself. But in the ensuing months I became over-sensitive about this issue. In general, the Battle of Cambrai raised rather than depressed my morale which never fell again to the nadir of 31 July in the Salient.

*　　*　　*　　*

I add something about my grandmother's death which occurred on Tuesday 27 November. It seems that a week before her death Granny was taken ill with abdominal pains. But the serious nature of her illness was not at first recognized. Her symptoms responded to treatment and for a few days she was better, but on Saturday 24 November her pains became severe. Various doctors were consulted. All concurred, saying: 'There is nothing to do. There is an operation, but so complicated and dangerous that it wouldn't be of any use and only make her suffer.' It seems almost certain that she had an inoperable growth.

The main responsibility seems to have been taken by a Dr Maumus who was in some way a friend of the family. From my mother's account of Granny's ecstasies over her impending death, it would appear that Maumus (quite rightly) made full use of morphia. How humane and sensible! But my father (his letter of 29 November) tells me that Granny had nothing to eat for nine days before her death (from 18 to 27 November) so that starvation may have contributed in a small way to her visions. *'Mon Dieu comme c'est beau de mourir,'* she kept repeating; *'Que tu es beau, mon Dieu'*; and in Spanish: *'Señorito Jesús que lindo eres.'*

A letter from my mother dated 1 December contained the following passage: 'I am terribly sorry for poor Aunt Carmen, so cut off from everyone, and my thoughts go out to her all the time. It will be terrible for her when she knows. I shall finish this later on as I still have something to tell you. I should like you to keep these letters as, in future years, for you and your children (D.V.), it will be interesting to hear something about her wonderful death.'

The matter about which my mother still had something to tell me was explained in a later letter of 5 December. She wrote: 'I have wanted to tell you this ever since Granny died, but put it off till I had more time and space, as it is very solemn and touching. It seems that when she heard of our beloved Robin's death, she was so horror-struck at his being taken so young and she left at her age, and her anxiety for you . . . was so great, that she made a solemn offering of her life if the younger ones were spared. For a long time she had talked as though her death were a certainty, and I repeatedly heard her say: 'I shall never see Carmen again.' When the Parishes saw her in the summer, she told them that she was going soon and they were not to be sad. She hoped, poor darling, that her sacrifice would be accepted, and was only waiting the call. As soon as this last illness began, and before it was thought at all serious, she told Dolores that it was the end and how happy she was; but she said: 'I won't tell you the reason yet. I shall wait a few days till I am quite sure.' When there was no more hope, she told Dolores about her offering and how happy and full of joy she was that it had been accepted because she took it as an assurance of your safety. You were the one she loved and worried most about. . . . I cannot help thinking, and the thought comforts me much, that God accepted the offering of the life she loved so much, and enjoyed to the utmost, and rewarded her by taking her out of this sad world and giving her such a glorious fearless and happy passage to the great unknown peace and splendour.'

★   ★   ★   ★

The Battle of Cambrai faded out on 7 December, so that there remained before us the last three weeks of 1917. This short period provided a sort of epilogue to a year during the last half of which my morale had sagged. Why had it sagged?

The answer was clear enough. The Company's role had been too easy. We had not been put through the mangle as had the other companies in the Battalion and the other Battalions in the Regiment. We had lost some of our self-respect. At least I had.

It had been dispiriting for No.3 to be attached to a battalion of another regiment, though the people in that battalion could not have been more considerate. Though we had had a fair amount of physical hardship and back-area danger, our casualties had been comparatively light. The seventeen days of the Battle of Cambrai (20 November to 7 December) had been better. We had returned to our own Battalion which had played a useful and later-recognized part in the short battle. Indeed, the Battle of Cambrai, though it had been costly in casualties and had failed in its main objective – the capture of that town – had been exhilarating. There had been some lively movement to and fro, and no quagmire. Hence our morale rose and we were prepared to enjoy the three weeks' rest which followed.

It was during these three weeks that the thought began to enter seriously into my mind that I ought to transfer to another battalion. Such a step would obviously raise the chances of my being killed. That this would happen had been an almost settled conviction in 1915 when I remember discussing it with my brother Robin who, after we first heard of Oscar Hornung's death, had taken it as settled that he and I would both be killed. But after I had been assimilated into the Fourth Battalion in 1915, the thought had faded. My being killed raised no problems for me. But it was otherwise for my parents for whom the issue of my survival had been made more acute by Robin's death.

In early December the Battalion moved to rest billets, or 'details' as they were called, in the village of Fosseux, west of Arras. CPB was sent ahead to arrange the billeting. He arrived after dark, having walked much of the way from Arras, and was directed to a mess.

Being cold and hungry after the long day, I was thankful for a large mug of hot and strong tea which comforted one's insides and took the chill out of one's bones. I remember going to sleep in a camp chair and being roused for an abundant dinner which proved convivial. One of the party was a young Grenadier, the owner of a good gramophone which was kept in the mess. Especially well do I remember what came after the meal. Records from Verdi were played. I heard for the first time *La Forza del Destino* which everything – the long hours of marching in the cold, the warm room, the good meal and the pleasant company – conspired to make enjoyable. Sitting relaxed in a canvas chair I was lifted out of myself and wafted to and fro above the earth by the rich, exquisitely modulated and perfectly blended voices of two consummate Italian singers.

'That was wonderful,' I said feelingly to the Grenadier. He was standing near the gramophone, waiting to change the record. 'Yes,' he said, 'those two are vowing eternal friendship.' 'I hope it proved durable,' I said. 'Unfortunately not,' replied the young Grenadier. 'The tenor later kills the baritone; the baritone kills his own sister who is in love with the tenor; the tenor kills the father of the baritone; and the tenor finally throws himself over a cliff. In fact the complete cast is exterminated.'

But that evening spent in the canvas chair at Fosseux, after a long day on the road in the cold, remains, as I look back, one of the superlative moments of the war.

From Fosseux the Battalion was moved to the nearby village of Barly, where they remained until Christmas. During this period CPB was promoted to the rank of captain.

11

WINTER AND SPRING 1918: THE GERMAN OFFENSIVE

The war, of course, ended in mid-November 1918. That year was sensational and astonishing in a way that distinguished it sharply from the three preceding years. The years 1915–17 were spent in monotonous and dispiriting trench warfare punctuated by terrible but unsuccessful offensives. In 1918 the quality of troops arriving on the Western Front (I speak here more of the army as a whole than of our Division) was perceptibly deteriorating. I heard comparisons between the alacrity with which the battalions of Kitchener's army would go over the top and the reluctance of some recently arrived units to attack unless the way was led by tanks. There was a background feeling of staleness and apathy which became apparent in the view that the French and British armies had done their stint and should take it easy until the war was finished in 1919 or 1920, mainly by the Americans. So taken for granted during the ensuing decades has been the sequence of events which led up to our total victory in 1918 that it is easy today to forget how dubious the future looked till just before the end, and how great was our astonishment when the end came. The year 1918 brought, as the months passed, a transformation of prospects in which stages were recognizable. These I will try to describe.

The earliest stage was one of apprehensive expectation of a German offensive which would dwarf all earlier offensives. The next stage was marked by the recognition that the tremendous effort made by the Germans in March had failed and that similar attacks made later might likewise fail. Confidence revived. There followed a lull during which it came to be expected that no great demands would be made on the British army during the rest of the year. The French and ourselves would sit tight and prepare for a culminating battle in 1919, wherein the Americans would take the leading part.

But in fact there was little lull. To the surprise of many, French, Australian and Canadian troops by then acting under the supreme command of Marshall Foch, suddenly attacked on a fifteen-mile front south of Albert. In a thick fog early in the morning of 8 August 1918, a strong squadron of tanks headed a breakthrough. A local defeat of such severity was inflicted on the Germans that General Ludendorff later wrote of August 8 as 'the black day of the German army'. This bold initiative came from Marshall Foch and the credit for turning the tide so early should go to him. A good case could be made for regarding 8 August 1918 as the turning-point of the war.

But of the importance of this unexpected attack none of us at the time had an inkling. It was believed (and the belief had some plausibility) that the Germans had prepared positions well behind, to which, if they wished, they could withdraw as they had done on the Somme in the early days of 1917. To the west of these positions, we thought we might again have to entrench ourselves and prepare for the culminating effort in the ensuing year.

The possibility that the moral and material resources of the Germans had fallen so low that the war might be won in the autumn did not seriously occur to us till later. Such hope, I should say, began to flicker towards the end of August but did not become an expectation till the end of September. As I see it, the essential story of 1918 is of how, in an initial darkness, this hope first flickered intermittently like a will o' the wisp, and then steadied – first to an uncertain glow, and then to a continuous illumination which quickly intensified and culminated in a victory so total as at first to seem unreal.

Without our clearly knowing it, the rising morale of the Allies was accompanied by a failing morale of the rank and file of the German army. Military opposition in the field patchily disintegrated; the German Government began to talk about peace; and suddenly the truth burst on us that the war was about to end. I was wounded at the end of September in a battle wherein the Hindenburg Line was penetrated. When I got back in mid-October what had been a hope of a quick finish had become a certainty that the end was a matter of days.

During the first quarter of 1918 the British and German armies in the west exchanged roles: we moved to the defensive, they to the offensive. In response to the general transformation the Fourth Battalion changed both its role and structure.

I begin my account of these events with a comment on the letters which my father wrote to me at the time. They refer to a remote event – the Treaty of Brest-Litovsk.

The year 1917 had been disastrous for Russia. The Czar and his family had been murdered[1] and the huge empire was floundering in anarchy. Organized

---

[1] On this point CPB's facts are incorrect: although they were deposed in 1917, they were not murdered until 1918 (ed.).

military opposition to the common enemy had crumbled; and it was about then that the words Bolshevik and Bolshevist made their entry into the English language. They denoted an extreme type of revolutionary who followed Karl Marx and Lenin. The Russians, now represented by Bolshevik leaders, wanted a peace based on three conditions: no annexations; no indemnities; and self-determination for all peoples. Germany and her allies declared that they would support these principles on the condition that all the belligerent powers should likewise support them. The Russians accordingly invited the Allies to send representatives to Brest-Litovsk. But the Allied Powers refused. The issues to be discussed were complicated. They were not confined to the general principles on which peace could be concluded. They further involved territorial issues including cessions by Austria and Turkey as well as by Russia. Deadlock was reached, the conference was broken off, and hostilities were resumed.

But after German troops had advanced unopposed yet further into Russia, the conference was reconvened and the Germans stepped up their demands. The Russians, knowing that their position was hopeless, signed the re-drafted treaty of Brest-Litovsk under duress on 3 March 1918, three weeks before Lundendorff's hammer fell on the west.

My father was exercised over the refusal of the Allies to attend this conference. He took the view that we could have given useful support to the Russians, who by then had lost all bargaining power; and he thought that the possibilities of a peace by negotiation, which he favoured, would have been brought to the surface and strengthened by the exchanges at Brest-Litovsk. There existed in the German Reichstag a small but expanding Social-Democratic party which had opposed the war and now favoured a settlement. There was a corresponding party in Britain. But a settlement could only be possible if the relatively small parties favouring it on the two sides recruited supporters and gained influence. It was not easy to know how strong was the desire for peace in the belligerent countries. Many people thought that the desire was widespread everywhere, but latent, and that the spark of serious discussion was all that was needed to release a demand which could not be ignored and might become effective. My father thought this. I was doubtful; and subsequent events justified doubts. It later became obvious that the governments of the Central Powers were, at that time, no keener on a settlement based on no annexations or indemnities than were the governments on our side. Nor was the principle of self-determination universally favoured. The Austrians, with their patchwork empire, did not want it. Nor did France who counted on regaining Alsace and Lorraine.

France also wanted an indemnity for the devastation of her invaded territories and may have been doubtful about how far the payment of such reparation would have been compatible with a 'no annexations and no indemnities' clause. The military party in Germany, moreover, insisted on military guarantees against further invasions, and some even talked about the annexation of Belgium and Luxembourg; and outside the military party many Germans suspected (perhaps not without reason) that the Bolsheviks were planning to carry their propaganda into the German army which would become increasingly susceptible the longer the by-now unpopular war lasted. The main hope of the German leaders, who had never lost faith in complete victory on land, was to knock out Russia so completely as to remove all anxieties about their eastern frontier and leave them free to concentrate everything in the west. To us it was obvious that, if the submarine threat could be held, time was on our side. The longer the war lasted the more massive would be the influx of fresh American troops pouring in from a virtually inexhaustible reservoir. To the Germans this menace was as obvious as to us; but what was more obvious to them than to us was how their country's food supplies were running down. Here was another reason for the elimination of Russia from the war and for her speedy reduction to helplessness. The Russians should be made to provide the food and other needed supplies for Germany's supreme effort.

Thus did events enacted at Brest-Litovsk switch the British army to the defensive. I recall attending a lecture shortly after moving up to Arras. It was delivered to the officers in our division by a trim and fluent staff officer. Aided by a large map of western Europe, this persuasive man vividly explained how the German troops in front of us were, at that very moment, being heavily reinforced by divisions from the now inactive Eastern Front. At some time in the spring a massive attack, on which the enemy were doubtless pinning high hopes, would certainly be delivered against us. In the meanwhile, our tactics of defence would be changed. No longer were packed forward trenches to be held till the last man. No longer would every square foot of French soil be regarded as sacrosanct. The defence would be elastic. The front line would consist of lightly held carefully sited posts. The further the enemy advanced, leaving his artillery behind him, the stiffer would become the opposition. Our defence would be organized in depth, the main line of resistance being some distance back, accessible to our own counter-attacking troops.

While this sensible lecture proceeded, two thoughts assailed my mind. 'Not much fun,' it first occurred to me, 'to be in a front-line post when the attack opened. If you were not prepared to surrender, death or a totally disabling wound would be your lot.' The second thought was accompanied by a mixture of gratitude and irritation. 'Thank God that, at last, the Higher Command had woken up to what, for the last two years, had been obvious to the humblest infantryman. But why have we had to wait till 1918 before G.H.Q. woke up?' The image of Sir Douglas Haig was raised. A high-minded man of integrity and faith, confident, distinguished, immaculate; but not a receptive or imaginative man. The Battle of Passchendaele represented his thought on how the war was to be won. He would have pushed on further into the morass if the winter had not stopped him. He would have done the same on the Somme in 1917 if the Germans had not retired. Who, I speculated, had changed the mould? Was it French influence – possibly Foch? Or was there at St. Omer some acute and resourceful figure of high rank, some chief of staff, who understood how attack and defence should be conducted from a starting point of static trench warfare, and who also understood the mind of the Commander-in-Chief? We speculated in vain. No rumours or myths were current in our circle about what went on at G.H.Q. This staff officer's lecture put a new slant on the war. Things were about to happen which would expedite the tempo. Good! But let us hope that we won't ourselves be holding any of those front-line posts or outposts or listening-posts at zero hour!

By this lecture the year 1918 was distinguished at its outset from the three preceding years. A tremendous ordeal impended in a few weeks. It was in the interests of the attackers to expedite the moment of crisis. Speed was enjoined on the enemy by the increasing number of American troopships and food-ships arriving at our Atlantic ports; and by the obvious fact that our earlier offensives had all started too late. Loos had begun in September; the Somme at the beginning of July; Passchendaele on 31 July. The onset of winter had cut them all short. It would be something new to start a major offensive early in the year.

I do not recall our forceful staff officer surmising that the impending attack would be the enemy's last. Nor, had he said this, would we have believed him. Up till then there had been no signs of Germany cracking. We had prolonged our attacks on the Somme and in Belgium in the belief that the Germans were on their last legs and, as in a tug-of-war, 'one more heave will do it.' But they had held on; and even at Cambrai, where they were taken by surprise, they recovered in counter-attacks most of the ground they had earlier lost. Instead of believing that the enemy's total defeat and surrender would follow this last of their attacks, we were inclined to think that the capitulation of the Russians would so add to Germany's strength that, whatever happened in the near future, the war would continue indefinitely.

Yet despite these uncertainties the early months of 1918 were not dark. There were no sinister forebodings such as had oppressed some of us at Locre in early 1917. There were no anticipatory misgivings. On the contrary, till mid-March 1918, life in our camp east of Arras was mainly bright and cheerful. For No.3 Company this lightness of spirit was largely accounted for by the conditions in which we lived and worked. Our rest billets were safe and dry, and our work provided its own reward.

The order to move on 26 December came, I think, the day before – on Christmas Day. Our destination was a camp called Rifle Camp (how or when the name originated I do not know) consisting of Nissen huts south of the destroyed village of Blangy, about a mile east of Arras. We were conveyed most of the way – some 14 miles – by truck and light railway. Keeping close to the straight Arras-Doullens road, the light railway ran east with stops about every two miles. The nearest of these stops to our village was at a place called Laherlière about three miles south of Barly.

We got up at about 5.15 in the dark. We covered the distance to Laherlière on foot and thence we were conveyed to Blangy by truck. With the slow daylight paling the eastern sky, in came penetrating cold. Packed in the small trucks we stamped our feet, clapped our hands, rubbed our ears and sat closely together. Indeed, during the few days after Christmas the weather, as I described it in my diary, was 'stingingly cold,' rivalling in severity the arctic spell in 1917. Our destination was Arras which lies north of the Somme and in a different watershed – that of the Scarpe. The Scarpe does not figure in the annals of the war as dramatically as does the Somme, but it played a definite part in our lives during the next three months. From the slightly raised ground behind our huts you could look across the shallow valley of this small waterway. My topographical curiosity was raised and soon after our arrival at Rifle Camp I tried to find out something about the Scarpe. I asked some civilians in which direction it flowed and where it debouched into the sea. I was surprised to find how confused were their answers. '*Ça se perd là bas,*' said a rustic character who waved an arm in a north-easterly direction. Our local maps were not helpful. The canal-like river, we found, had little current. It seemed to broaden to the east and lose itself, merging with the River Escaut, in a complex of canals and waterways between Douai and Tournai, well behind the German line. Thus the Scarpe flowed to the east, in an opposite direction from the Somme. Its waters would have more affinities with those which, at Laventie, we tried to coax toward the Lys, which meandered through Belgium, than with those of the Somme which flowed more purposefully westward into the English Channel.

In its eastward movement, the Scarpe skirted Arras on its north side, and east of the town it separated our village of Blangy from a somewhat larger village, also demolished, called St. Laurent Blangy. I recall the ground between these two areas of rubble as low-lying and in parts boggy; and as being some-times frequented by snipe and wild duck.

The area of Rifle Camp has remained so clearly and pleasantly memorable that I owe it the debt of an attempted description. The huts, built on a gentle slope, faced westwards and downhill. If you stood above the camp, behind the huts, and faced westwards towards Arras, the war was going on behind you. It was from that side that the noise came and it was on that side that, at night, the sky was intermittently lit up by gun flashes and Very lights. On your right ran the valley of the Scarpe, and between you and the river ran a road which led eastward out of Arras into German-held Douai.

At Rifle Camp No.3 spent two of its best months of the war. The place had every merit. It was safe; we were scarcely ever shelled and I recall no casualties in the camp. The huts were warm, dry and rainproof. The slightly raised and sloping ground on which the camp was pitched had not been fouled by the war. The work, to which we marched (it varied from three to five miles away), was clean and in a high degree rewarding, the earth being fresh, stony and workable. There was an overall and broadly conceived programme involving the construction of a defensive system of trenches which we sited and marked out ourselves. For this system, as it took shape under our spades and picks, we developed a strongly proprietary feeling. We knew beforehand what had to be done each day and by whom; and in the eye of the mind we could visualize what the finished product would look like. Drains running westward downhill were cut at intervals, for though the ground was nowhere waterlogged, the winter rains were to be expected. As far as I can remember that was the only task performed by the Company during the war which evoked from higher authority a later expression of appreciation and congratulations. And for a good reason.

These trenches remained dry through the February rains and stood up to the weather during the following eighteen months – till well after the war was over. In June 1919 I visited this low ridge with Leonard Bower with whom I bicycled from Arras to Douai. We left our bicycles by the roadside and walked along the partly demolished firebays and traverses abandoned for over a year. We found some Mills bombs on a firestep. These we unpinned and bowled overarm into the semi-demolished belt of barbed wire which lay in front. There they all exploded with the familiar twanging noise, as if they had been carried up the night before.

It was by this defensive system, I later learned, that the Germans were stopped when, in early April 1918, they attacked Arras. It was shortly after this successful defence that the Battalion received the compliments and thanks of higher authority.

A valued amenity which was available to everyone in Rifle Camp was that the township of Arras was but some 25 minutes walk away. Civilians in small numbers had returned. Though considerably demolished at various times during the previous three years, the houses had been well shored up and the streets cleared of rubble, so that when you walked through the town it struck you as bright and clean, with occasional shops and accessible canteens. There was one functioning hotel – the Hotel de l'Univers. Until 21 March, Arras was rarely shelled or, as far as I remember, bombed. Various entertainments – theatrical and sporting events (for example a boxing competition) – were held there. Unlike Ypres, Laventie and Poperinghe, I recall Arras as welcoming and friendly – rather like Dunkirk had been in early 1915.

The weeks at Rifle Camp were also pleasant in the mess. We had a good portable gramophone and a varied collection of records including the since-popular waltz introduced to me by Bolo from Strauss's *Rosenkavalier*. Skeff, the green parrot, became a show figure whom people used to come to see. He reacted to music and to certain tunes; he would sway from side to side, turning his head towards the ceiling on each swing. He liked to sit on our shoulders, holding on by our shoulder-straps. He would climb up your back, hauling himself up by the strap of your Sam Browne belt which passed over your right shoulder. When he became excited and affectionate, which he sometimes did under the influence of music or if you scratched his neck, he would move his head up and down in regurgitating movements and, if he was standing on your shoulder, would deposit a pellet in your ear. He would relieve himself to order, and it was wise to give this order before you allowed him to perch on your shoulder; otherwise he would streak the back of your tunic with bird-lime.

In the mess we entertained quite a lot and were visited by various people in and outside the Battalion. George Edwards developed the habit of dropping in during the long dark evenings. He seemed to enjoy both the gramophone and the parrot. We bought some rolls of coloured wall-paper with which, in place of sacking, we covered the elephant-iron of our Nissen hut, thereby decorating and insulating it.

In effect the 2½ months spent at Rifle Camp were the most agreeable of the war. From the standpoint of work, they were profitable and rewarding; and they were also socially convivial. We commented, now and then, on how good it was that Arras and our camp were not shelled. We wondered why. It did not escape us that the Germans would not want to stir us up and get us on our toes just before they loosed a major offensive. We did not forget how, the previous November, we had let everything quieten down at Cambrai before we delivered our attack. But I do not recall that we felt the calm on our front to be particularly ominous. Our cheerfulness during this period was less impaired by forebodings than it had been at Corbie and Locre, before we were committed to the offensive battle of Passchendaele.

I saw quite a lot during January of E.W. Hornung, Oscar's father. He had reacted in rather a peculiar way to Oscar's death. He had felt a strong desire to have personal experience of the sort of life Oscar had led in France before he was killed. The best approach, he had concluded after inquiries, would be through the YMCA which provided canteens behind the line. How these forwardly placed canteens came to be located I never found out. It appeared that much was left to the enterprise and initiative of the people who were put in charge. These made what arrangements they thought best, subject to appropriate permissions being obtained from the formations and units in their areas.

This is what E.W. (as we called him) had done. He based himself on Arras. But instead of establishing his canteen in as safe and comfortable a place as he could find, as most people in his position did, he fixed himself up in a sunken road close to the front line. Here he dispensed mugs of hot tea and biscuits for which troops of all the local units were grateful, especially during cold spells such as we were having during the first weeks of 1918. E.W. was not in his first youth and he had put on a good deal of weight. He was also subject to asthma so that, during spells in his sunken road, he had to put up with a good deal of hardship. But this he actively enjoyed. The worse the hardship, the more he was pleased; the nearer he felt to Oscar, whose experience he was sharing. There was little shelling at the time; but an occasional rifle shot or burst of machine-gun fire would greatly cheer him. I looked him up several times in his YMCA centres in Arras and once took a mug of tea with him in his 'tea-totallers' bar' which was no more than an excavation, with corrugated-iron sides and roof, in the chalk side of the sunken road. Being a civilian dressed in nondescript khaki, he brought a touch of home to his 'customers' (as he liked to call them). Everyone admired him and was grateful for the strong sweet tea which he dispensed. He would encourage his 'customers' to talk about their homes which they were glad enough to do. It got around that he was a distinguished writer. His Raffles books were popular. He made friends with some officers who passed up and down and with some gunners who were located nearby. He had offers of help and by no means suffered from loneliness.

E.W. felt strongly about the war. His views accorded with my mother's. Peace was unthinkable until the enemy had been thoroughly defeated and sued for it. I learned that among his co-workers in the YMCA was a man who was 'unsound about the war: little better than a pacifist.' I avoided arguments about the war. He liked me to talk to him about Oscar and about Bartle Frere who had been killed in November 1916. In mid-January E.W. spent a night with us in Rifle Camp. I fixed him up on Lumsden's trestle (Lumsden being on leave) which was in the same half-hut as mine. Before going to sleep we talked about Oscar. Any new thing I could tell him, he said, was like a priceless jewel. We talked about what we would do after the war if we survived it. He supposed, he said, that he would go on writing, but I could see that he had misgivings. He had lost zest and seemed to have little to live for.

I remember clearly that when dining in our mess he was alarmed (though much amused) by Skeff who tried to climb on to his shoulder. George Edwards, Wilbraham and Forrester came in after the meal when a lively conversation was enjoyed by him and us. George, tall, handsome and immaculate, was both cordial and gracious. I remember feeling grateful to him and also proud of him.

I also recall a warm feeling compounded of affection, esteem and pity for our brave but physically handicapped guest, outwardly so unheroic yet so heroic in essential purpose. The hardship to which he was subjecting himself during the long hours in his sunken road derived from his bereavement. He was honouring the memory of his son by giving the humblest service to those whose experiences came closest to Oscar's. There was both pathos and, for those with eyes to see, honour in the homely implements of his service – in the steaming kettle – the chief emblem and token of his ministry – which he watched, tended and served; in his half-dozen enamel mugs; in the tins of sugar and condensed milk; in the dry biscuits and spoons which could disappear so easily. The cold, the wet, the exposure, the total lack of amenities were endured in a spirit of commemorative self-dedication where courage, kindness and a deep humility born of affliction were combined.

⋆   ⋆   ⋆   ⋆

I quote from a letter I wrote on 2 January: 'The other day a Bosch plane flew over our lines and dropped a message saying: 'We want the war to end and we want Peace; the French want the war to end and want peace; the Russians want the war to end and want peace; the English are the ones that want the war to continue; if England refuses to attend the Russian Conference and to discuss Peace, her blood will be upon her own head.''

I remember discussing this communication with Joe Forrester. The meaning of messages about peace from Germany, he sensibly said, depended on who sent them. If they were to come from the Social Democratic Party, which had wanted peace all along, they might mean something. But messages from that source would not be dropped from aeroplanes on our front line. Thus delivered, the intimation could only come from military leaders who, we knew, were planning a mammoth attack. Their object was probably to soften us up before the 'day.' Could the message have anything to do with what was going on in Brest-Litovsk, we wondered. Difficult to see how it could, but just possible that it might.

*   *   *   *

During the next few weeks my connection with No.3 Company was not continuous. My account of what happened is narrowly personal and can be of no interest to anyone but myself. I was shifted about. I was twice given command of No.4 Company, the first time temporarily, the second time till the company was unexpectedly disbanded. I was next given command of No.1, and shortly afterwards went on leave.

*   *   *   *

I have mentioned that in 1915 the decision to add a pioneer battalion to each division had resulted from the way the battles of 1914 and early 1915 had resolved themselves. The war of movement had ended in the stagnation of trench warfare for which no one had been properly prepared. Conditions were bad everywhere, but worst in the Salient. To the twelve battalions of every infantry division a thirteenth pioneer battalion was added to deal with the conditions resulting from the effects of wintry rains on trench warfare. These conditions altered little during the years 1916 and 1917. But at the beginning of 1918 a definite change was planned. The huge offensive which the enemy were preparing would not be met by troops densely packed into front and support lines. The defence would be in depth and would come from carefully sited posts and machine-gun nests from which cross-fire and enfilade fire could be directed on an enemy seeking to infiltrate our positions in small units. There was less need than in earlier years for pioneers in forward positions; and in a definitely mobile battle there might be little need for pioneers at all.

If a defensive battle was in question pioneers would be mainly used in preparing positions well in rear; if an offensive battle was to be undertaken they would be used in repairing and maintaining communications behind the advancing formations. In either situation pioneers would be less exposed than in conditions of static warfare. These considerations doubtless influenced the decision to cut down pioneer battalions from four to three companies.

This change in the role of our own pioneer battalion was recognized by those responsible for the posting of officers. It had become noticeable that, in the course of the last year, we had on the whole (there were several exceptions) been receiving older officers than the other three battalions. I had been conscious of this trend and had become unduly touchy when people in other battalions alluded to it either openly or by hints. The issue (in so far as it affected myself) was settled by the arrival of Mark Dorman about whom more below.

*   *   *   *

On my return from leave on 16 March, I found a change in the air. Before I had left, the big attack was in everybody's minds. But no immediate date was envisaged. We did not constantly look at our calendars to see how many days were left. But on my return I learned that there had been a few days of what was then called 'acute wind-up.' From 4–8 March the attack was momentarily expected. During the following week, however, the agitation quietened somewhat, but by 16 March recent and definite information, gleaned by our intelligence, had again raised the wind. Defence stations in nearby trenches had been allocated to all troops; and these were being exercised in getting into and out of them with maximum speed.

I spent the next three days studying and practising these movements so that we knew to within a minute or two how long after receiving an order in Rifle Camp it would take us to be at the ready in our stations. One of the four platoons would be separated from the other three, which would be in the same small area.

At 4.30 a.m. on Thursday 21 March the hammer fell. 'Exactly as a pianist runs his hands across the keyboard from treble to bass, there rose in less than one minute the most tremendous cannonade I shall ever hear.' That is how Winston Churchill, who was on the spot, put it in a later year.

'For about two hours,' wrote General Ludendorff, 'the whole of our artillery engaged the enemy's batteries: then most of it was switched on to trench bombardment in which the trench mortars also took part. A little before 9 a.m. most of our fire – only a portion being left on hostile batteries and special points – was concentrated to form a barrage. Our infantry advanced to the assault.' The German plan therefore was to knock out as many as possible of our guns before the infantry moved into the open.

The eruption which almost threw us out of our trestle beds seemed to belong to the sky rather than to the earth. The shattering pandemonium transported me into an unfamiliar dimension where normal speech was impossible. You could not hear what was said or make yourself heard. You dressed in haste but mechanically, as if responding to some external directive.

The eastern sky from far south to way north was aflame. I could tell the time by my wrist watch. It was about five. Impossible to see, against the wall of fire and thickening smoke to the east, whether dawn was breaking.

With my gas helmet at the alert I stood in battledress on the duckboards outside my hut. The light mist which enveloped Rifle Camp was turning bronze as the flames on the eastern horizon were shrouded in smoke. I was quickly joined by others. Their unshaved faces were clearly visible in the artificial light, tense and wide-eyed in excited cheerfulness. You could not hear what they said, but their expressions conveyed: 'Safe for the time being, thank God. But how long will it stay like this? What next?' Two thoughts occupied my mind: gas and action stations.

The Germans, we knew, would probably smother in gas certain areas in their line of advance. These they would ignore when moving forward as if they were lakes or impassable swamps. If Arras were one of these areas, we should soon know it. But there was no smell of gas. We half expected to move at once into the trenches on either side of the Scarpe. These were our action stations – in the speedy occupation of which we were well trained. But no order came. No one at this stage knew where on the Western Front the main onslaught would come. Until this was known we would doubtless be kept central and mobile.

The order was: pack up everything; get ready to move at a moment's notice. Tea appeared in a dixie and was distributed. As we sipped at our steaming enamel mugs, still stamping on the duckboards, speculations were renewed. What would be the attack's main objective? Ludendorff might have his eye on the channel ports in which case he would move north-west through Belgium and against the British. Or he might aim at Paris which he nearly captured in 1914. The main attack would then come in the south – perhaps in the French sector – perhaps along the Oise or Marne. The Germans liked to attack the junctures of armies, preferably armies of different nationalities. Arras was in the northern sector of the Third Army which linked with the First Army some five miles to our north. 'Old Luders' (as General Ludendorff was disrespectfully called) in whose shoes we had speculatively placed ourselves and whom we regarded as the opposition's planner-in-chief, probably had several plans up his sleeve. He might open proceedings with one or more diversionary attacks in the hope of our committing our reserves before the main event.

Now that the crisis was upon us, these and other previously discussed possibilities came to mind. A cold dawn began to lighten the sky at half-past six. Still no smell of gas. No shelling of Rifle Camp and no order to move into the Scarpe valley. Slowly the main fury of the shelling concentrated in the south. It looked as if the old 1915 battlefields of the Somme and the areas to the east which the Germans had evacuated of their own accord in early 1917 were receiving the main attention. Suddenly our ears were assailed by a new sky-rending sound overhead, cutting through the main din. It was followed by a definitely audible crash from the new direction of Arras. Not long after, the same sound and crash recurred, and it was obvious that Arras was being shelled by a long-range gun of substantial calibre.

★   ★   ★   ★

Henceforward my record becomes sketchy and my memory hazy. During the ensuing days the company was much moved about and I had no time to myself. My letters are irregular and short and the entries in my surviving diary are difficult to follow. My own story might be simplified and rendered more intelligible if I digress by relating it to the main strategical events, dramatic but complicated which, during March – June 1918, were enacted first to the south of us, then to the north, and then again to the south. During March, April and most of May, Ludendorff directed his main attacks against the British army in the north. At the end of May he turned his attention to the French in the south. The tide turned (in the sense that the Allies took the offensive) at the beginning of August in which month, four years before, the war had begun. Six main battles were fought from March to July 1918, the first three in the northern part of the Western Front, the next three in the southern part mainly occupied by the French. These six battles were as follows:

21 March 1918: Battle of St. Quentin. Better known by its date – 21st March 1917. It lasted a week (till 28 March) when Ludendorff called it off. Deep penetration as far as Montdidier, captured on 27 March. Striking tactical successes gained by Germans in first few days. But the battle was an over-all strategical failure. Ludendorff's hope of a massive breakthrough to the coast was disappointed.

28 March 1918: Second Battle of Arras. The German attack began within a week of the start of Battle of St. Quentin. It lasted eight days. The Germans were stopped on the line east of Arras earlier prepared by our Battalion. Germans everywhere repulsed. Neither then nor later did Arras fall.

9 April 1918: Battle of the Lys. Lasted eleven days (9 – 20 April). Ludendorff's expectations here were temporarily exceeded. The Germans broke through a sector held by Portuguese and in two days (by 11 April) familiar places in north-east France near the Belgian frontier had fallen – Armentières, Estaires, Merville and Laventie. This was probably the most critical moment of the second half of the war. On 11 April (two days after the Battle of the Lys began) Haig sent out his 'Backs to the Wall' summons. German captures included, in the south-west extremity of Belgium, such war-famed places as Messines, Ploegsteert and Wytschaete. Ludendorff unexpectedly desisted when, on 17 April, after little more than a week, eight German divisions failed to take Mont Kemmel.

The upshot of these three battles was that the enemy had carved two large bulges in our positions. The first (the outcome of the battle of St. Quentin) intruded like a gigantic nose pointing south-west towards Beauvais and threatening the area north of Paris. At the western tip of this bulge, Montdidier had fallen into German hands. The second bulge (the product of the battle of the Lys) involved both Belgian and French territory (mostly French) and pointed westwards towards Hazebrouck, Cassel and the Channel ports. (The second German attack aimed at Arras had not penetrated and there was no bulge.)

The scene now moves southward to a part of the line mainly occupied by the French. There was a pause for over a month.

27 May 1918: Battle of Chemin des Dames. Lasted seven days till about 2 June. Something of a French disaster. Till 26 May, the day before it was delivered, the French did not know that an attack was impending. The Germans advanced southward on a front extending about fifty miles from Noyon in the west to Rheims in the east. On the third day of their advance they captured Soissons (29 May) and on the sixth day they reached as far south as Château-Thierry on the Marne, some sixty miles from Noyon from which the attacks had started. Château-Thierry is little more than fifty miles from Paris. In early June therefore the position looked ugly.

9 June 1918: Battle of Noyon. Lasted for three days, till 11 June. It can be seen from a map that Montdidier, Noyon, and the Chemin des Dames are in an approximately straight line with Montdidier (captured by the Germans at the end of the battle of St. Quentin) to the west, the Chemin des Dames to the east, and Noyon between the two. As said, during the Battle of the Chemin des Dames, the Germans had advanced far to the south of Noyon to Château-Thierry. There thus remained a French bulge into the German line between these two areas of German advance – Montdidier and Château-Thierry. The object of the Germans in the Battle of Noyon was to drive the French out of this bulge. In the course of the battle, the enemy advanced some ten miles southward to the area north of Compiègne at the confluence of two important tributaries of the Seine – the Aisne and the Oise. But French counter-attacks slowed down the rate of advance and Ludendorff broke off the attack 'to avoid casualties.'

15 – 18 July: Battle of Rheims. During these four days there took place three locally distinct battles, the first two initiated by the Germans, the last by the French (General Mangin). On 15 July the Germans attacked the French on both sides of Rheims which lies some 15 miles north of the Marne. South-west of Rheims the Germans, moving southward, crossed the Marne between Château-Thierry to the west and Epernay to the east, and established themselves on the south side of the river. East of Rheims and well to the north of the Marne the Germans made another attack and were stopped by the army of General Gouraud. Three days later (on 18 July) the Germans were taken by surprise on their right (west) flank and defeated by the army of General Mangin which, previously concealed in the forest of Villers Cotterêts, was led by a fleet of 330 small Renault tanks into an attack which grievously hit the Germans in their right (west) flank. Thus, the Battle of Rheims, opened by the Germans, began as a qualified victory for them insofar as they crossed the Marne east of Château-Thierry on a four mile front; but it ended in a defeat of which one result was the cancellation by the Germans of a second and massively planned offensive in Flanders (the Lys again) in a final bid for the channel ports.

These six German attacks show that Ludendorff favoured sudden and massive but short and sharp assaults. When the rate of advance slowed down, or when the gains of ground, prisoners, and guns ceased to justify the cost in casualties, Ludendorff would call a halt and deliver an attack elsewhere. He favoured sudden powerful strokes (lightning strokes or blitz-strokes) planned well ahead; and he was prepared to switch from one such stroke to another. In this strategy Ludendorff differed from Sir Douglas Haig insofar as the attritional and costly battles of the Somme and Passchendaele reflected the latter's offensive strategy. In these prolonged offensive operations there was little concern for secrecy or surprise. You merely pushed ahead regardless of weather and losses in the continually sustained belief that the enemy had reached the end of his tether and was about to crack. It was because of its break with this unimaginative tradition that many people were cheered by the Battle of Cambrai, despite the fact that at the time it could scarcely be called a final victory.

*   *   *   *

I return to the morning of 21 March at Rifle Camp. Contrary to expectations, we did not move that day. The noise to the east diminished somewhat in the afternoon, but it did not abate to the south. Rumours poured in, among others that the Germans had taken Bullecourt. At the time, this was difficult to believe; but it turned out to be a fact for, on the first day of the attack, they took Croisilles which is west of Bullecourt. Though we did not then know it, the area around Arras was well to the north of the developing Battle of St. Quentin as it had been planned by the Germans. None of the Coldstream Battalions was engaged on that first day of fighting. But some units withdrew to Arras and to villages (such as Mercatel) south of Arras.

The tense hours of Thursday 21 March passed slowly. We chafed at the inactivity. We would have been happier in our action stations on the Scarpe expecting an attack. I noted in my diary that, on the afternoon of that day, Clive Piggot, Charles Pittar and I worked up some excitement chasing a stoat. Meanwhile the bombardment of Arras continued and, in the late afternoon, the news reached us that our old friend H.C. Boycott (who had served with No.3 at Savernake during the severe winter of 1916/17) had been mortally wounded. With two other officers he had been standing in the street outside his billet when down on the group came a shell from a long-range gun. Boycott was a good-looking and most likeable South African. He died in the evening of 21 March. Memories of Boycott, particularly of nice things about him, kept returning during the ensuing forty-eight hours. Boycott was a trim and reticent man of medium height, neat and good-looking, with a light moustache and a friendly expression. What has stuck in my memory about him is his good appearance and his good temper. His death forcefully impressed on us how bad luck played a part in violent deaths and how good luck could play a converse part. Some confident and cheerful people, especially if they had had a few narrow escapes, came to believe that, like Achilles (who as an infant was ducked in the Styx by his mother), they were invulnerable or (for the duration of the war) immortal. Minor superstitions about talismans, amulets, and phylacteries were widespread. Most Catholic women commended their relative to certain saints and said prayers or burned candles for them. My mother had Catholic relatives in America who sent her luck-bringing objects or small scrolls for me to wear. Some of these I carried about to please my mother. Those I did not use I passed on to Catholics who were grateful for them. I recall a discussion in No.1's mess between two officers of whom one was the talkative Canada Cartwright. Could a patron saint invoked by Boycott's wife the other end of the world have caused the German gunner who laid the gun to alter the sighting by a minute fraction of a degree so that the shell would not have landed in that exact place? Or the sighting might have been influenced by some unsuspected kind of telepathy without the German gunner or anyone else knowing. The discussion showed how some people liked to think that protective influences existed and could be directed, while others preferred to take a deterministic view: if your name is written on a bullet or a shell that settles it for you: everything is fated. Anyhow, poor old Boycott had not had much luck.

It was not till next day that we were moved from Rifle Camp. We had been told that we would spend a single night in Arras and then move south or south-west in conformity with a general shift of the Division. In the meanwhile, a German attack on Arras was (rightly as it turned out) expected in the near future. Work still remained to be done on defensive positions which would be sorely needed when the time came.

There was a lovely dawn next day – Friday 22 March. With an orderly I walked up to the positions east of Gavrelle and handed over the unfinished trenches to an officer of the West Yorks who belonged to the Pioneer Battalion of the incoming Division. A lot of noise, and Gavrelle was being intermittently shelled; now quite an unhealthy place. While I was showing this officer what needed to be done that night, my own Battalion marched out of Rifle Camp into Arras. Since the roads east of the town were receiving considerable but capricious attention from German gunners, my orderly and I made our way back across country, leaving Rifle Camp on our left. In thought I said goodbye to the place and offered thanks for the happy weeks we had spent there.

On reaching Arras, I found No.1 installed in quite good billets in the Rue Jérusalem. My thoughts turned to E.W. Hornung, and I thought of trying to find him. But we had received orders not to move about the town. I was told that the YMCA had moved back. The bombardment continued during the night, but nothing came near. Being tired after a long day on my feet, I slept well. But reveille was early – at 3.30 a.m. in the dark. The shelling of the town had increased during the night so that, when No.1 marched off without mishap at 6.00 a.m., we considered ourselves lucky.

We set out for an area to the south-west of the town. We would be told the precise destination later. We marched through Achicourt, a sort of suburb, to a place called Wailly. Our road followed the north bank of a small tributary of the Scarpe called the Crinchon. This uninspiring waterway runs parallel with the Arras-Doullens road and the light railway by which, shortly before Christmas, we had been conveyed from Barly to Rifle Camp. Wailly was mostly rubble, so we bivouacked in an open field. No hardship whatsoever, the weather being fine.

To the south of our bivouac the battle was rapidly developing. New defence positions were urgently required. In the afternoon George Edwards and the C.R.E. (Chief Royal Engineer) took me with them by car to a village called Boiry St. Rictrude which lies on a fairly substantial road leading south of Arras towards Albert. Livelier shelling here and nearer to the main battle south of Wailly. Further south of Boiry St. Rictrude the road takes you through Ayette and Bucquoy, of which places more below. I have a vivid but perhaps untrustworthy memory of our party of three. George Edwards and the C.R.E. were on good terms. A new line of defence was needed to meet a probable attack from the east or south-east. This new position was to be known as the Purple Line, with which we (the Fourth Battalion) were to be much concerned in the next few weeks. The C.R.E. was mainly responsible for the siting. I recall with pleasure thinking to myself that this exercise with two such senior officers was real pioneering, and in exalted company. The course of the Purple Line was provisionally settled.

A cheerful supper awaited me on returning to Wailly with four of No.1's officers (Cartwright, Dumaresq, Cordingly and Corbould) under a waggon sheet to the accompaniment of heavy shelling to the south (seemingly from the direction of Boiry St. Rictrude) and of occasional shelling nearer to our field than we liked. Wild rumours continued to fly about. It was said that Monchy le Preux which was about a mile and a half south of Fampoux – quite near – had been evacuated and that the Fifth Army had cracked in a big way.

I wish that I could recall better what happened during the ensuing fortnight. The agitation contrasted with the static dullness of other periods. I have confused memories of mixed weather – of hot spring days alternating with downpours of soaking rain when we had no shelter and of nights which, whether wet or dry, were uncomfortably cold; of confusion as to what was happening round us; of extraordinary rumours; of frequently changing work, mostly on the Purple Line; of makeshift billets under waggon sheets or sheets of corrugated iron or in long-abandoned dug-outs and dirty cellars; of being shelled at unexpected times both by day and night. I was cheered by the fact that at no stage of the war had my physical health been better. Or my morale. I found that I was less affected by the shelling and small-arms fire than during the preceding years.

My scanty letters and scrappy diary compel me to rely on my memory. Several scenes have come back. I recall our feelings about the breakthrough and also some trivial events which, perhaps because they provide a contrast to the continuous tension, have remained. It seems that dangers, and episodes involving danger and fear (provided that one's feelings do not rise above a certain threshold of acuteness), are the first to be forgotten. Pleasant memories of those tense weeks have stuck best.

I remember a talk on 26 March with Overton-Jones about the breakthrough. Though we were then in different companies we met when we could. I had not seen him in the last three days. It was late in the afternoon about sunset. First we walked up and down the parapet of a long-abandoned trench and then sat down. The din to the south, though no longer deafening, forced us to raise our voices.

Feelings about the breakthrough were contradictory. Prominent was the thought of how bitter was the loss of places which, scarcely two years before, had been fought for at such cost. When the villages and the woods of the Somme had been serially destroyed and laboriously captured, these events had been hailed as victories, though the separate captures one by one had had no effect on the course of the war. By March of 1918, two years after these battles, the terrible but sanctified names of these places, with their overtones of heroism, tragedy, horror and triumph, had acquired auras. Hence it was bitter that, during the last week of that month, in a mammoth engagement which dwarfed in scope, though not in savagery or tragedy, the many creeping battles of 1916, the dearly-won gains of two years before had been lost in a single week – as if by a single scythe stroke.

Feelings of dismay formed one side of the dialectical turmoil. The other was a sense of re-assurance which welled up at intervals like a spring of hope: 'All this is terrible, certainly; and things may get worse before they begin to get

215

better. But there is an exit to the tunnel and, if you look for it, you can already see a glimmer at the far end.' What, after all, had been the main change in the war between 1916 and 1918? No doubt about the answer. The Russians had moved out and the Americans had moved in. At that moment we were suffering from the disastrous consequences of the first event before we had begun to reap the slow benefits of the second. The discomfitures and perils of the moment should not blind us to the fact that a crumbling edifice was being replaced by another which could prove indestructible.

The gravity of the position in early April was acknowledged by no less a person than Sir Douglas Haig in his message to the army: 'With our backs to the wall and believing in the justice of our cause. . . . each one of us must fight on to the end.'

As any map of the Arras area will show, a main road runs south from Arras to Bapaume and another west towards Doullens. These roads form two sides of a broadly-based triangle with Arras at its northern apex. It was in this area (mainly south of the Arras-Doullens road) that we were to spend most of the next three months. The names of villages such as Ransart, Berles-sur-Bois, Hendecourt, Adinfer, Pommier, Bienvillers-au-Bois and Ayette began to be familiar.

By mid-April we had moved from Wailly to La Cauchée and thence to Ransart. Afterwards came trenches near Hendecourt and then trenches near Ransart. During this period we worked hard on the Purple Line where we were sometimes shelled. We had some casualties which I do not remember. We used to return to our home-trenches in the evenings exhausted. One of my few clear memories is of a cellar near Gastineau. We were to sleep in the cellar that night. We took a short look at it on our way to the Purple Line. My spirits sank. The proposed company headquarters and officers' billet was malodorous, dank and dungeon-like, strewn with litter and decomposing straw. In one of the walls was a blocked fireplace. A fine home for rats and fine breeding-place for lice.

But when in the early hours we got back to this unalluring place we had a memorably pleasant surprise. Two of our servants had cleared away the litter and filth and had disinfected the floor and walls with carbolic. They had unblocked the fireplace in which a bright fire was briskly crackling away, drying the place out and giving a cheerful light. A transformation indeed! We were tired and cold. A mug of hot tea and an improvised meal mostly of bread and jam shared with Dumaresq and Cordingly have never been forgotten. Nor the night's undisturbed sleep which followed.

On the afternoon of 27 March there was a lull in the sounds of battle which we thought might be sinister. Then early the next morning the noise started again in a big way. But much of it was coming from an unfamiliar quarter – the north-east. The second battle of Arras had began.

On 28 March (my father's birthday) the Germans attacked westwards along both banks of the Scarpe. But, as said above, they were decisively repulsed everywhere. Among the places where they were stopped (or did not reach) was the Ayette-Bucquoy road which was being held by troops belonging to various units including our Third Battalion. There it was that my old friend Quincey Greene (in 1915 the Fourth Battalion's bombing officer) was killed. I did not hear of the death of this cheerful and likeable American till some days later, after our Third Battalion had been engaged in heavy fighting near Nieppe Forest to the north, during the Battle of the Lys.

We spent one or two nights at the end of March in the Purple Line where there was no shelter. Company headquarters was fixed in an old emplacement a few yards away from the newly dug line where we warmed ourselves by a fire made with match-boarding purloined from semi-destroyed huts at Hendecourt. My clearest memory is of how the Germans had brought forward observation balloons. These, poised in the sky to the east, revived memories of 15 September 1916 and induced a mild anxiety state sometimes known as scoptophobia (a dislike of being looked at). A low ridge east of the Purple Line was occasionally shelled causing casualties. The Purple Line itself was also shelled. Some near misses but no one seriously hurt in the Company's sector.

The Battalion remained in the area of the villages of Adinfer, Ransart, Hendecourt and Blairville for the next fortnight – till, in fact, 14 April when it moved back for a needed rest to the gratefully remembered village of Barly. By then the battle of Arras had ended and the battle of the Lys, well to the north had begun. Before being moved back to Barly, the Company fell into something of a routine. We were kept busy with long hours and heavy but important work, reinforcing scantily prepared positions in the Purple Line. Four officers other than myself worked in shifts of three or four days. Cartwright (talkative as ever) and Corbould would take turns with Dumaresq and Cordingley. I stayed up continuously which caused no strain seeing how near our home-trenches were to the Purple Line. For some three days there was some grousing about the rations, which was unusual. A new Company Sergeant-Major – CSM Richards – was posted to No.1: it was not long before he was respected and liked. But one thing happened during this fortnight which was unimportant but tragic. Skeff, the green parrot which had remained with No.3 after I had left, died.

The onset of spring was less noticed than in 1916 at Clairmarais Forest or than in 1917 at Corbie. The best places were Hendecourt Château Wood and Adinfer Wood. The Château wood was situated on the south-west side of the small village of Hendecourt, near its church. Here I heard my first chiffchaff of the year. Cowslips grew in profusion and with them we decorated our dugouts. Adinfer Wood was quite large and shaped like a cradle. A thickly wooded valley ran down the middle. Later the Germans unaccountably took to shelling it at night, sometimes with gas shells. It was a good place for nightingales and at least three pairs had established territories in it. I remember how, later in the year, on a moonlit night, Overton-Jones and I sat above the wood watching the unseemly performance. A pearly mist hung round the boles of the trees, and at infrequent intervals smallish shells came leisurely down and burst in the wooded valley. The crashes were not particularly loud, but they solemnly reverberated into the distance for several seconds. It was unforgettable how the dying echoes merged into an indignant chorus of nightingale song in which birds in several territories joined. They seemed to be defiantly saying: 'You cannot frighten us with your war. Here we stay.' When the echoes subsided, the placid moon overhead seemed to endorse the angry protest. It said Bravo to the nightingales. And so did we.

It was while we were at Barly that I first learned of the posting to the Battalion of Mark Dorman which was to have an effect on my future. His story was peculiar. We were told that he had joined the Regiment early as a guardsman and was soon made a lance-corporal. It was then discovered that his educational and social background fitted him for a commission, which was duly bestowed. As an officer in our Third Battalion, he had served in France early. In 1914 and the first half of 1915 he had been through heavy fighting at Givenchy and Festubert, and also, in the autumn of 1915, at Loos. In 1916 he had his full share of the Somme and, in 1917, of Passchendaele. As I mentioned when writing home, the bare recital of these names gives a feeble impression to people who are ignorant of what they imply. Suffice it that by October 1917 he felt that his nerve had suffered and he applied for six months' leave. As this period drew to its close, he came to feel that he might not be equal to further service in a fighting battalion, but that he might be able to keep his end up in the Fourth Battalion whose role in the war, for the reasons I have given above, promised to be less exacting than during the earlier years. Dorman had a 1914 medal (known as a 'Mons Star') and a Military Cross. He was a substantive captain and was therefore much senior to me (my rank being that of an acting or temporary captain, I forget which) and he came with a glowing reputation from the Third Battalion. I was asked if I would mind serving in No.1 as Dorman's second-in-command, retaining the rank of captain. Not in the least, I replied, and things were thus fixed.

Mark Dorman was a lightly built man of average height and gentle somewhat diffident manners. He could not have been more considerate to me and I was as happy to serve under him as I had been to serve under Dickinson and Piggott. We got on well and I grew to respect and like him, as did everyone else.

But the reasons he gave for wanting to be posted to the Fourth Battalion confirmed a feeling which had been developing while we were at Rifle Camp – that I ought to apply for a transfer to one of the other battalions. There recurred to me at this time a remark which L.C. Leggatt made before he left No.3 when the Company was at Savernake Wood – that he regarded himself as a worthy piece of cannon-fodder, or, as he put it, 'kanonenfutter.' (This, alas, he duly became on 31 July 1917 at Passchendaele). I have a hazy recollection of telling Mark Dorman about how I felt and of his trying to persuade me to stay where I was, saying that I had served long enough with the Battalion not to have qualms of conscience about its recent change of function.

My last days with the Fourth Battalion covered the six weeks from 26 April to 11 June, during which time No.1 was mainly based on the sunny village of Bienvillers au Bois (called by the troops Beanvillers or Beanyvillers). A few days were also spent at Pommier and Warluzel.

An agreeable feature of the Division's tactical retirement to the south-west was that we found ourselves in almost virgin country. The little-damaged villages were thinly inhabited by an aged population. I recall no children or young people. But my diary and letters, now re-read, have shown that my memory of these weeks was misleading. I thought that Bienvillers had been almost wholly ignored by German gunners. But I learn that that was not so. The Germans had brought up at least one high-velocity gun of medium calibre and long range. With this piece they provided for the villages behind the line fairly regular reminders that there was a war on. I had almost forgotten how a civilian – an aged Frenchman – was killed in the garden of our billet.

Though the shrill arrival of high-velocity projectiles was unusual, it was always unexpected. German gunners often performed according to a time-table, so that you learned what places to avoid and when. Not so during this period. There resulted a faintly perceptible anxiety-state, but it was never oppressive. On most of us its effect was to enhance our appreciation of the predominantly idyllic conditions in which we were living, and of fending off somnolence and boredom.

These last weeks were coloured by my impending departure from the Battalion to which I had then become much attached. But they were good weeks and this I realized at the time. Indeed, if, in late December, our first spell at Barly had constituted for the Fourth Battalion a bright epilogue to the year 1917, our six weeks at Bienvillers provided for me personally an even brighter epilogue to my three years in that Battalion.

That No.1 was to be located in Bienvillers away from the rest of the Battalion was decided in a late change of plan. Dorman and I went on ahead.

For some reason now forgotten there existed in Bienvillers several deep cellars which were in good condition. They could almost be called catacombs. Into these subterranean chambers No.1 moved when, later in the day (26 April), they arrived in the village. Here they were better off than were Headquarters and the other two companies further forward at Adinfer. Our officers were fixed up in two rooms of an unoccupied and entirely bare house with whitewashed walls. The house gave on to a yard on the far side of which was a divisional canteen. This was not much frequented and did not trouble us. The damaged Church was nearby. I clearly remember the two rooms with the whitewashed walls. The first opened into the yard (no midden this time) and also into the second room which had but this one door. We messed in the first room and Dorman and I slept there on trestle beds. The company and the other officers (Richards, Dumaresq, Corbould and Bushby) arrived in the evening. Disconcertingly, the village was shelled three times the day we moved in. The last and noisiest instalment came down as the company was settling into its 'catacombs.' That such attentions could scarcely be frequent was a comforting inference from our partly intact window panes. That time there were no civilian or military casualties and little harm was done because, by great luck, all the shells landed in gardens or orchards. This was on a Friday. No further shelling till the following Wednesday.

At this time movement in the Divisional area was mostly by emergency cross-country tracks. There had been a fair amount of rain during the last half of April and in places these tracks were quickly deteriorating. No.1 spent the next few days repairing these tracks and also in making what were called 'artillery bridges' which were crossings over trenches and other obstacles which could impede the movement of artillery.

Some trivial things about our arrival at Bienvillers have stuck in my memory. I heard my first nightingale in Adinfer Wood on 28 April and saw my first swallows two days later. It had been raining so that the swallows looked be-draggled and tired. They were flitting weakly a foot or two off the ground where insects were scanty. But conditions improved during the ensuing week. On 2 May, a beautiful spring day, the swallows, by then plentiful and flying high, were joined in their cheerful aerobatics by several house-martins.

It may be remembered that the Battle of the Lys began on 9 April. The dire news that heavy fighting was taking place round Locre did not reach us till 30 April. Back came memories of pastoral scenes – the placid cows, cuckoo flowers, lush water meadows and the whortleberries which skirted the track to the summit of Mont Rouge where, of an evening, one could sit and admire the rising mists and sunset tints of the country below. We did not forget Locre's well-ordered convent with its pious lace-making nuns trustingly resigned to the harsh fate which, in mid-May 1917, was creeping nearer every day. Little that was pastoral or pious could now be left. I recall at this time reading Tolstoy's *Resurrection* which, in an obscure way, was comforting because the book's title and message were applicable to what the future might hold for Locre and its convent.

*   *   *   *

My narrative now becomes introverted. It is concerned with my decision to transfer to another battalion and my difficulties in reaching this decision. It was in the inner of our two whitewashed rooms, by lamplight sitting at the table which had just been cleared after the evening meal, that the issue came to a head and I decided that I must move. I was being pulled strongly in opposite directions. Three considerations impelled me to stay where I was. The first was my devotion to the Fourth Battalion, including my feelings for such people as George Edwards, Clive Piggott and others. By then I was well-established in the Battalion. I had served in its three companies and knew by name most of its men. It was probably true that, by mid-1918, I could be more of an asset to the battalion than ever before. The second consideration was the fact that I had developed fluctuatingly pacifist inclinations. It would sometimes come over me that there was something crass about how most people could be turned into enthusiastic advocates of homicide by a declaration. The person who declared war might be a monarch, a prime minister or other ministerial personage. He solemnly declares that your country is at war with another country. You immediately believe that it is both necessary and meritorious to kill certain people of that country who have done you no injury, who have committed no crime, who have no responsibility for bringing about the provocative situation and who are behaving exactly as you would behave if you had been born a citizen of that country instead of your own. Those, moreover, whom you were urged to kill have close relatives who would grieve over their deaths exactly as you had grieved over the deaths of your own relatives and as the latter would grieve over your death. Such thoughts would sometimes sweep over me with great force, particularly at night. To my semi-secret pacifist side it had been a relief to serve in a primarily non-combatant unit; to use the in-offensive spade and pick instead of the bomb and Lewis gun. I did not, moreover, hate the Germans.

But these were relatively minor reasons. The third and strongest considera-tion was the thought of my parents. For them Robin's death had been a shattering blow which had magnified for them the importance of my own survival. It can be seen from their letters how continually I was in their thoughts. One of their reasons for leaving England and settling in France was that they both would be at hand if I was dangerously wounded. They followed my move-ments (insofar as the censor permitted them to know) from place to place, breathing relief when I was safe and harassed by anxiety when I was in danger. They had seized the opportunity presented by my having been sent to Clairmarais Forest to go to Rome for three months. The letters they wrote in 1916 from Italy showed what this respite had meant. They had sometimes mentioned how grateful they were that, in the Fourth Battalion, I was relatively-speaking safer than Robin had been in the First Battalion. After landing in France, Robin had been killed almost immediately. By 1918 my parents felt that they had cause to be grateful that I had survived for nearly three years. My mother, who had prayed much for us both, had, since September 1915 (when Robin was killed), given thanks that my posting was less hazardous than his. My mother had from the first known that I understood her feelings about all this. Yet she had characteristically urged me never to allow thoughts of my father and herself to influence me in dangerous situations.

It used to strike me that, in their emotional reactions, my parents were not typically British. They did not try to assume the Anglo-Saxon's undemonstrative and phlegmatic façade behind which feelings were concealed. My mother's reactions were probably more American than British, and my father's more Latin. Things would have been easier for them if they had had sons and daughters of differing ages instead of two sons of perfect military age. It would certainly have been easier for E.W. Hornung if Oscar had not been his only child. That my father had no professional occupation may also have made things more difficult; also, perhaps, that he and my mother had strong literary tastes. Such people live more in their imaginations than do people with exclusively vocational interests or those for whom books are no more than oblong objects you see on shelves.

On the other side of the balance sheet, the reasons given by Mark Dorman for asking to be sent to the Fourth Battalion, the discernible fact that in recent months most of the officers posted to us were no longer in the first flush of youth, and the surmise that, as a result of the changes occurring in 1918 from static to mobile warfare, the Battalion would be decreasingly occupied in the forward area. These considerations cumulatively gained weight as the summer months advanced.

Thus began an inner debate which was intensified when we moved out of the area of the Purple Line into the security of Barly where the arrival of Mark Dorman brought it to a head. During our last three days at Barly, I told myself that, as soon as possible after we moved forward, I must definitely make up my mind one way or another.

I come back to myself sitting at that table by lamplight. A decision was slow in coming. I asked myself whose advice in this predicament I would most value. A clear answer came at once: my dead brother Robin's. Better than anyone else he would understand the dilemma, particularly my feelings about my parents and theirs about me. In imagination I put the issue to him. What should I do? An answer came with perfect clarity: 'Apply to move.' There and then I so decided.

A sense of relief and release followed. But how should I set about this transfer? It would not be easy to tell my parents; and George Edwards might not approve. No hurry, I told myself, about deciding in what order to make the moves. I would wait a couple of days before doing anything more.

In the course of the next forty-eight hours, I decided to postpone saying anything to my parents until the matter had been definitely settled and approved at my end. They must in no circumstances be *consulted*. The drill, I thought, should be first to decide what battalion I wanted to go to; then to communicate privately with someone in it who could put the matter to the battalion's commanding officer; then if the latter would have me, approach George Edwards; and if he consented and when everything was settled, inform my parents. I saw no difficulties and, in the event, none materialized.

My choice was the Second Battalion of which the adjutant was Jimmy Coats.

In the meantime I would tell Overton-Jones but no one else. Let the others find out in due course of their own accord. On Saturday 4 May I wrote as planned to Jimmie Coats. On Tuesday 7 May I had to pay a visit to the Second Battalion about some drums. I met Tom Barnard who gave me a note from Coats saying that Edwin Brassey (the Battalion's Commanding Officer) would take me. But I would at first have to drop my third star – that is to say revert from the rank of captain to that of lieutenant. This I was happy enough to do. Next came the approach to George Edwards. I raised the matter with him that same evening. I remember the scene with pictorial vividness. I had dined with Battalion head-quarters, by then situated at the nearby village of Pommier, named after its flourishing orchards. I was uncertain how George would react. I must catch him alone. The moment did not come till after dinner, when George, who retired early, got up to go to bed. It was a fine moonlight night. I followed him into the deserted village street and asked if I could speak to him about a private matter. He said yes, and I told him the story which ended by my saying that Edwin Brassey would have me if he (Edwards) would let me go. George stood, tall and motionless, listening till I had finished. In the bright moonlight, his face was in shadow. I ended by telling him with what reluctance I would leave the Battalion (if he allowed me to do so) and that my reasons for regret were many. Prominent among them were my personal feelings of gratitude and loyalty to him. I stumbled a bit at the end of this declaration. When I had finished, George said that he would not oppose my transfer. He added some kind words which still further strained my composure. When we parted in the bright moonlight of that village street, I was nearly overcome by feelings which have since coloured my sentiments for the Fourth Battalion.

About a fortnight later I received the following letter:

25.5.18

My dear Blacker,

Just a line to congratulate you on getting a mention (in despatches) for your good work between September and March last.

It is little enough reward for all that you have done. There is no one who has served this Battalion more loyally and unselfishly than you have. I wish that they had done more for you. Please accept my congratulations and grateful thanks for all that you have done.

Yours ever,

G. Edwards

His remark about 'little enough reward,' I learned later, refers to the fact that he had put me in for a bar to my Military Cross. 'They' were the divisional authorities. I had no knowledge of this recommendation which I was glad did not materialize, for I had done nothing during the six months in question to deserve this award.

Here is another letter which reached me about the same time from Clive Piggott. By the end of May it had got around the Battalion that I was shortly leaving. Clive was then on leave. I felt that I had become so indebted to him in the last two and a half years, and was by then so close to him, that I should myself tell him about my impending departure rather than that he should hear about it in some roundabout way. I have some hesitation in quoting this letter:

From Clive Piggott   25. 5. 18

> . . . I am so sorry I missed you. So far from thinking you a 'fool' I admire the action you have taken. . . . I know that you have done it solely . . . because you think it is your duty. As I have done in the past, so in the future I shall always respect your actions because I know they are the outcome of careful thought and consideration. I shall miss you more than you will ever know. We have had so many happy times together, haven't we! Let's hope for more after the war.
>
> You know, old chap, that my very best and sincerest wishes for your happiness and good luck in your new Battalion go with you.

> Yours ever,

> J.C.P.

It remains for me to mention my parents' reactions. George Edwards had given his green light on 7 May. I did not definitely tell my parents till five days later. I wrote on 12 May enclosing the letters from Edwards and Piggott, which I have quoted, asking that they be kept.[2] My transfer was thus put to them as a *fait accompli*. There was nothing they could say or do. My father refers to the matter in his letter of Whit Sunday (19 May) and my mother in her letter of the same date. My mother wrote: 'You have balanced the question into exchanging into another Bn. in your mind and decided that you will do so. . . . It is not our part to dissuade you, or try to do so, from following your conscience.' On 2 June, my father wrote: 'I was much moved by the letters which you enclosed with your letter. I will not dwell upon all this because I am sure that you realize that my words cannot express what I feel. May all good be with you.'

These letters came as a relief to me. They had both accepted my decision in just the way I had hoped, and I was grateful to both. My father's few words, I was sure, had not been hurriedly composed. Much was left unsaid.

---

[2] Since both the letters were written on 25 May, CPB could not have enclosed them with his letter of 12 May. In fact he sent them with a letter also dated 25 May.

That I should move was settled on 7 May. But the exercise had to be approved by higher authority who, in due course, would make it the subject of an order. This order was not issued for a month. It reached the two Battalions on 10 June and I did not physically transfer myself till the next day. I therefore spent a further four weeks in the Fourth Battalion where I had told nobody except Overton-Jones that my days in the Battalion were numbered. It became a matter of curiosity how long it would take for the news to spread and how it would come round to me. I suspect that the secret came out on 25 May when George wrote the letter I have quoted. On that day he had sent for me to ask if I had reconsidered my application. George, I think, wanted to be certain where he stood before making consequential changes in the distribution of officers. The next day Jock Boyson was permanently posted to No.1, and when I left a few days later he took over the Company. George probably explained the move to Jock and others so that the impending changes became quickly known. Before Jock arrived one of No.1's officers (E.G.C. Richards) had hesitatingly asked me in the mess if it was true that I was leaving.

In the meanwhile, to my regret, Mark Dorman had been posted to the Division. Why, I never properly knew. It may have been because his tough experiences and fine record were deemed to equip him better for a role on the staff than as a peripheral company commander. He therefore commanded No.1 for a little less than a month – from 28 April to 23 May. When he left I again took over the command of No.1 which I continued to hold till my departure.

Before this narrative says goodbye to the Fourth Battalion, I will mention some casual events of the month of May spent at Bienvillers. My main feeling when I look back is of peace and quiet – somewhat inappropriate in view of the big battle still continuing in the west. I have mentioned that, on 27 May, Ludendorff attacked on the Chemin des Dames – a month after he had broken off the Battle of the Lys (on 19 April). Up till the day when the southern battle began, we momentarily expected the next blow to fall on us. Though we did not know it at the time Ludendorff was throughout the summer and early autumn preparing another attack on the Lys. Troops were being quietly moved into the northern sector for that battle. But the reverses later suffered by the Germans in the Battle of Rheims (15–18 July: mentioned above) and in the ensuing Battle of Amiens (started by us on 8 August: see below) caused Ludendorff to divert southwards as re-enforcements, the troops which were being concentrated for this second offensive on the Lys. These moves so depleted the German reserves in the north that this offensive was finally called off. After the Battle of Amiens the tide of war turned in our favour.

To return to Bienvillers during May: in the course of the month we daily expected a resumption of German attacks – perhaps on the Somme, perhaps at Arras, perhaps in Belgium. It was not till the end of May, when news reached us of the Battle of the Chemin des Dames, that we could breathe more easily.

Thereafter the prospects of an attack on our front temporarily receded.

I have mentioned that Bienvillers was shelled three times on the day we arrived, but not often afterwards. I quote from a letter dated 4 June. 'Our life continues here uneventfully. The other evening when I was dozing in bed the Germans started to put gas shells into the village. They were neither yellow nor green cross, but acrid and sulphurous. They burned one's throat and nostrils but did not trouble one for long. We got down into a cellar. I feel deeply sorry for the scanty civilian population here. . . . Recently an old woman told me that refugees get such little sympathy in the towns of the back areas that they prefer to come back to villages like this where the food they get only just keeps them from starving, and where they can sell their little wares and products to the troops. Most of them have small gardens which they cultivate and a few keep cows. When we get back at two or three in the morning, we sometimes see these old souls moving about with buckets of milk which they sell to the men when they are thirsty and tired.

'There are no young people. Those one sees are old, mostly decrepit and very poor. Soon after we came here one of these old men was hoeing his garden when a shell burst four yards away from him and hit him in the back, arm and leg. Though he was within calling distance of our anti-aircraft guard with their machine gun, he never called for help. He crawled under the shelter of a wall where, without making a sound, he just quietly died. He was found by some men in No.3 platoon who went into his garden to look at the hole.'

I end my account of this period with a tribute to Bienvillers. As I have said, this village and nearby Pommier were ensconced in fruit trees. Behind our billet extended a luxuriant orchard surrounded by elms. Between the boles you could see the damaged village church which had a gaping hole in the roof and a partially demolished spire. This orchard proved to be a perfect place to sit.

If one was not otherwise occupied in the afternoons, one carried out one's canvas chair and, in hot weather, relaxed under a flowering tree. I particularly recall one such afternoon when the iterated call of the cuckoo was resounding and a cool breeze was sending down a shower of petals. The cuckoo was telling you that this was paradise, and the intimation was confirmed by the appearance in purposive flight, as if from another world, of the first swallow-tail butterfly I had ever seen. The ground below the trees was decked with flowers. On a tall ox-eye daisy the beautiful insect settled, opening and closing its wings. The unexpected descent was like a theophany; it evoked from the beholders exclamations of delight and wonder.

In the week which followed, more swallow-tails appeared, and yet more until, for a short time, they were as common as cabbage whites. Paradise was also suggested by another feature of this orchard – the almost complete absence of mosquitos and midges. The contrast in this respect with the marshy lowlands of the salient where, during the long summer evenings and at night, biting insects were a torment, was striking. The incisive calls of blackcaps and the melodious flutings of a restless golden oriole further combined in this flowering orchard to evoke an elusive intimation of musical harmony. I could not at once place the music. It came to me the next day. It was the Good Friday music from *Parsifal*. When the travel-worn knight pauses by a river and rejoices in the beauty of the riverside meadow ('*Wie dünkt mich noch die Aue heut so Schön!*') Gurnemantz tells him that the flowering meadow is responding to the magic of Good Friday. The association of ideas brought pleasure. It enriched the scene and enhanced the place. For a day or two an intimation of magic enveloped the village and even extended to my last days with the Battalion. Every time that I have since heard the Good Friday music, I have thought gratefully of swallow-tail butterflies and this French village.

12

THE SECOND BATTALION

My last days with the 4th Battalion were spent in 'resting' in an unspoiled village called Warluzel which lies about two miles from Barly, in which place we had spent two earlier recuperative periods. Both these villages lay north of the main Arras-Doullens road and were more remote than the Bienvillers, Pommier, Berles and Adinfer areas where the war by now obtruded in uncomfortable ways. By the time of our move, a six-inch naval gun had been emplaced near Bienvillers; and when this piece of artillery was suddenly shelled while we were in the act of marching out of the village, we were reminded of how a farewell salvo had expedited our departure from Locre the previous year. No damage was done, but our regrets over saying goodbye to this hospitable area were lightened.

Our start had been at 7.15 and we marched lightly, minus our packs, in rather hot weather, arriving at one o'clock at Warluzel, an attractive village recently evacuated by Americans whose conduct had been exemplary. I shared a room over the mess with Jock Boyson. On the far side of the yard beyond the usual midden, was a barn of which the roof was covered with bright yellow stonecrop. During the first twenty-four hours I enjoyed the feeling of freedom and lightness which follows withdrawal to an entirely safe zone. We did not have to carry gas helmets.

Inter-company cricket was played in sunny weather and pleasant walks were to be had. South-west of Warluzel was the well-grown Forest of Lucheux with, at its southern end, a château and a running stream. The ground falls steeply on its western side which was clothed in splendid beeches breaking into early leaf. Below these majestic trees the shaded ground was studded with the demure pink flowers and aromatic leaves of the crane's-bill geranium.

In the company of Overton-Jones, to whom the award of the Military Cross had just been announced (an event which gave me keen pleasure), I enjoyed a few happy midsummer evenings in this handsome and unspoiled forest. Beech forests are usually silent, but I recall how this place resounded to the soothing call of wood-pigeons.

In the course of a company parade on the morning of Tuesday 11 June, Bertie Whalley, our smart and heavily moustached second-in-command, appeared to tell me that my transfer had come through in that morning's orders. I had better move, he said, that afternoon. After the midday meal I did a round of the companies, saying goodbye to as many officers and NCOs as I could find and wishing them luck, I removed the third stars from my shoulder-straps; and accompanied by Lionel (who was most kind on this rather stressful occasion) set out on horseback to the nearby village of Saulty where the Second Battalion was billeted. Tate, my servant, followed with my kit. (I had earlier told him about my move and asked if he would like to come with me. It pleased me when he unhesitatingly said he would.) On arriving at Saulty, I reported to Lt.-Col. E.P. Brassey, the commanding officer. He received me quietly but kindly. A word about this man.

Colonel Edwin, as he was affectionately known by everyone, had a slight stoop, as if he had indulged in studious or scholarly activities (which he had not). He did not cut a conspicuously soldierly figure. I had the impression that he was somewhat shy. He had a diffident but winning smile and a quiet voice which could not have resounded on the parade ground. Earlier he had served in the Hussars and had been twice wounded. He was not a man with whom conversation was easy, and I never heard him talk about himself. He was a keen rider to hounds and an expert judge of horses. We would, I think, have got on more briskly if I had been a keener and more experienced horseman. He survived both wars and lived to be over eighty. He never married. He had a young nephew in the Battalion, Gerard Brassey, who contrasted with his uncle in being ebullient, cheerful, talkative and amusing. The nephew had the knack of making people laugh. A most likeable boy who had left Eton in 1917. Though quite unlike, and geared to different tempos, both uncle and nephew were intelligent and perceptive. I digress to say that when, later, the Battalion was in occupation of Cologne, Colonel Edwin appointed me the Battalion's demobilization officer. Demobilization had become by then a burning issue over which there was much discontent (more in some units than in others: happily little in ours). I had an office in Cologne and sat at a tall desk. Correctly regarding this issue as having a high claim on his time, Colonel Edwin would visit me nearly every morning, sit down in my chair and light his pipe. There, emitting a cloud of smoke, he would silently study the orders, memoranda and other often numerous papers which had come in. There he would sit, gazing at the documents, hunched up and scarcely moving but sucking away at his pipe, for as much as a quarter of an hour without saying a word. He would then point with the mouthpiece of his pipe at a sentence or paragraph and make a brief comment which went straight to the point. My respect for his intelligence, already high, was jacked up a degree on each of these mornings. He acquired from the first a complete grasp of the required procedure of demobilization which involved complex and sometimes controversial priorities. His terse and sensible decisions undoubtedly contributed to the Battalion's almost complete freedom from demobilization troubles. Colonel Edwin (or Uncle Edwin, as his nephew's friends called him) was universally liked. I never heard a critical word.

I come back to the afternoon of 11 June. Colonel Edwin, whom I had not met before, posted me to No.1 Company then commanded by E.J. Watson-Smyth, whom likewise I had never met. The company mess was located in a Nissen hut whither I was led. A sort of trellised arbour had been erected outside the entrance, giving shade from the midday sun. Here some officers were sitting in shirtsleeves. Among them was Tom Barnard who introduced me to the others. I will say something about these officers.

'Teddy' Watson-Smyth, as he was universally called, was a young-looking and intensely sociable man of middle height some two or three years older than myself. He was well off to the point of opulence and had extravagant tastes in food and dress. Parcels of many weights and shapes would arrive for him by most posts. Those containing such luxuries as hams, tongues and foie gras, cakes and biscuits, assorted chocolates and other delicacies would be thrown into the mess and eaten by everyone in quantities limited mainly by the consumer's manners and appetite. Clothes and underclothes likewise arrived in supplies which expanded to its maximum capacity T.W-S's officer's valise. There was much entertainment of people serving in other companies, battalions and regiments. On most evenings people came to dinner. To this meal we usually sat down late and from it we rose late – sometimes not till after eleven. Watson-Smyth had an active and genial but trivial mind. He especially liked gossip. There would be effusive anecdotes about fashionable people – about their witticisms, parties, indiscretions and affairs with one another. Christian and nicknames were mainly used, so that, if you did not move in the relevant circle, you did not know who was being talked about.

The officer most in gear with Watson-Smyth was Tom Barnard. Down the middle of the Nissen hut in which we messed ran a long table at the 'upper' end of which sat Watson-Smyth. Barnard sat next to him, the side (right and left) depending on whether guests were present. At the upper end gaiety and loud voices prevailed. At the 'lower' end (nearest the entrance of the hut) sat the South African and other officers. These conversed little and in subdued voices. Tom Barnard was definitely an ornament. Watson-Smyth was a little puzzled to know how to place me. I had certain educational qualifications admittedly. But I was not socially inclined and had little connection with the circles of people in whom he was most interested. He probably thought that I was too serious-minded and could be a bore, but that if taken lightly I was tolerable. The approach, he seemed to decide, was to treat me humorously as a well-meaning eccentric. He was always considerate and amiable so that this line suited me. I responded with special politeness and an occasional touch of deference.

At the same time I had much sympathy with the people who sat at the other end of the table and talked in lowered voices. I took to placing myself in the middle segment where I could join in the conversation on either side. I became, so to speak, a medium of communication between the people on each flank and in this role I may possibly have done some good.

Tom Barnard I have known for so long that the memory of my first contacts is blurred. He was two-sided. On one side he was offhand, arrogant and conceited; on the other amusing and engaging. We came together at Oxford after the war where we took degrees in zoology. In 1920 we were at Plymouth, with John Baker and Alister Hardy, immersed in the study of marine zoology. These and other contacts brought me nearer to him, as also did his special interest in birds. In later years he married and had children. For a time he was a professor of anthropology in South Africa and, in a different direction, has become distinguished in horticulture. He is an authority on the irises. I now feel for him nothing but goodwill. He left the Battalion in early September, as told below. His self-confidence may not have been so unassailable as, in those days, he wanted the world to believe. Artifice may have been needed (as it is needed by most of us) to conceal misgivings at the core.

G.C.L. Atkinson was a young man who had come from the Bedfordshire Yeomanry and had been awarded a Military Cross for leading a successful French raid during a recent tour of the line. He was known to the world as 'Atters' and showed an interest in boxing. Later we held boxing sessions. A sturdy and dependable officer.

W.R. Scott was a middle-aged man of heavy build who had settled in South Africa and wore a South African War medal ribbon. Teddy W-S. showed friendliness to Scott, whom he used to call 'Scoot,' and would gently pull his leg, which the older man, who was good-tempered, rather liked. Scott was slow in thought, and in speech somewhat hesitating. When in doubt as to what he should say, or uncertain as to whether he should say anything at all, his rugged face would suddenly light with a diffident and attractive smile, and it is this smile which appears when I think back over the years.

Two other officers were F.D.Bisseker who had come into the regiment at the end of October 1917 and W.Jackson. Before the war Bisseker had held a responsible post in the Imperial Tobacco Company and had lived in China. I recall him as a quiet retiring man and a friend of W.H. Corbould who has come into this story. Jackson was a nice-looking young man without inhibitions. He was anxious – perhaps over-anxious – to be friendly with everyone and he made the mistake of calling everyone by their Christian names too soon. T.W.-S. did not regard him as an asset to the mess where he was treated somewhat coldly. I felt rather sorry for him.

All these officers were second lieutenants (ensigns) who wore one star. I was the only full lieutenant. Into this easy-going and sociable life I fitted quite pleasantly. I was asked to meals with other companies where everyone was hospitable. Life was easy. In the mornings there were parades and drills: company drill, musketry, bayonet fighting, Lewis gun drills and gymnastic exercises. We had the afternoons to ourselves. My chief weakness, I felt, was in the sphere of the Lewis gun which, in open warfare, would be more used than Mills bombs or bayonets. I took all opportunities of learning about the Lewis gun. Physical exercises figured more in the daily routine than in the Fourth Battalion. They were quite enjoyed by everyone. I recall that Jackson gave lively demonstrations; I congratulated him on his agility.

Saulty, where I found myself, was within easy walking distance of Warluzel where the Fourth Battalion had remained. On 25 June I was asked to referee a boxing competition at Warluzel, which Overton-Jones had got up as part of a company sports programme. There were five fights of which one presented me with a problem. Two close friends by the name of Roach and Greenwood met in the finals of the middleweights. These two had often sparred together and it was immediately obvious that they had arranged beforehand not to hit each other. They did no more than touch each other affectionately with the tips of their gloves, exchanging knowing looks. I stopped the round and told them that if they did not box properly I would disqualify both. My caution had no effect. The pantomime continued. So I sent them to their corners and cancelled the fight.

At the time the Second Battalion contained a full complement of officers, and short leaves were started. On 26 June, just over a fortnight after I had joined the battalion, a young officer of the name of G.R.M. Caldwell and I were surprisingly told that we could have 72 hours' leave at the small coastal resort of Le Tréport – a place that I was to see again ere long. 'Scotty' Caldwell, as he was known to the world, was a tall thin ex-Cliftonian in his twenty-first year. He told me that at school he had led a withdrawn life and had never properly asserted himself. He had come from the Argyll and Sutherland Highlanders. For a short leave he was a pleasant but not stimulating companion.

We made our way by road from Saulty to Arras where we reported to the Railway Transport Officer (RTO). Our train was an hour late. I was sitting on a platform reading Bertrand Russell's *Mysticism and Logic* when I felt a hand on my shoulder. I looked up and beheld a powerfully built, Scottish-looking man, the RTO, who wore a blue cap at a jaunty angle and talked with a faintly French accent. Declaring that it was unusual to find people sitting on his platform reading books on abstruse subjects, this forthcoming man asked me some personal questions. It turned out that he was Romaine Patterson, a distinguished linguist and scholar. He travelled with Caldwell and myself to Le Tréport and lunched with us on the train. He had brought with him the proofs of a book by Israel Zangwill. An animated conversation was sustained at high pressure for over an hour. We ended on easy terms. He pulled my leg by calling me a metaphysician, which shocked me. This train journey was quite out of the ordinary and has remained vividly memorable, but it led to nothing. I never saw Patterson again. At Le Tréport Caldwell and I made for the Grand Hotel de la Plage where we shared quite a pleasant room on the third floor over-looking the sea. The resort was not beautiful. The beach and the tidal movements were rather like those later familiar at Dieppe. Tall chalk cliffs flanked the little estuarine township. At the top of the cliffs vegetation was scanty, the country being windswept and treeless. The upper and steeply sloping part of the beach consisted of rounded grey stones; the lower part was a flat expanse of sand exposed at low water. The tide was low when, next morning, I bathed before breakfast. I had to walk over some sixty yards of sand before reaching the water's edge and another forty before reaching the depth of a yard. But the chalky shallow sea was invigorating.

Later in the morning, while lying on the beach, I made friends with a small boy of eight called Émile who had lost his right arm. When I inquired, he told me the following story. He and his family were at St. Pol.

> *'J'étais au lit avec Cathérine, ma petite soeur qui a deux ans. Tout a coup il y a un grand bruit et la maison s'écroule sur nous. Maman me dit: 'Donnes-moi ta main droite'; je répond: 'Je ne l'ai plus'.'*

The child told the story casually as he threw rounded pebbles down the sloping beach towards the sea. He had good manners. When we said goodbye he fetched my tunic which I had taken off.

That afternoon Caldwell and I were again sitting on the shingle where we were joined by three little girls called Angèle, Marie and Jeanne. They were unrelated but friends and played together. Their familiarity with each other banished shyness: they talked and asked questions freely. It was unusual, said the eldest, to find an English soldier who could speak French. After I had asked them about their families they inquired about ours. Where did we live? Had we children? How long had we been soldiers? Had we seen many French soldiers? Or German soldiers? What was the war like? They listened with the utmost attentiveness. They lay below us on the shingle, their faces propped between their hands. All three looked fixedly at us without interrupting or moving. Peculiarly perfect, I thought at the time, was the communication which established itself spontaneously between us two and these three little girls of early school age. That we were foreign solders who were talking to them as one of themselves may have made us interesting. I felt at the time and later that communication had been astonishingly easy. In talking about the war I sensed that I had been perfectly understood. The motionless and silent recep-tiveness of those three up-turned faces has remained a happy association with Le Tréport and its pebble beach.

On our second afternoon Scottie Caldwell and I trammed out to a village inland of Le Tréport which had the peculiar name of Eu. The auspicious Greek meaning of this monosyllable disposed us favourably to the place. From the modest village we walked inland up a stream. On our right an imposing beech forest, draped in fresh June greenery, rose steeply before us. A pity we would not have time to explore the upper margin of this noble forest.

As I look back, it seems curious that, for half a century, I have retained such vivid memories of these three days of the first war – days which had to do not with the war but with its absence and remoteness. What have come back, as if they occurred yesterday, have been my contact in Arras station with Patterson and our lunch on the train, the polite small boy's story of how he lost his hand, the three little girls on the shingle, and the steep forest close to the happily named village of Eu.

At the expiry of the seventy-two hours, we returned to Saulty where the same routine of life was resumed. Two clear memories have survived – the first having to do with Battalion Sports and the second with Alex Wilkinson.

The sports, in which I did not participate, included some short races, among them one over a hundred yards. There appeared in early afternoon to see the sports the officer commanding the first Guards Brigade which included our Battalion. This senior officer, a Grenadier, was the much respected Brigadier-General C.R. Champion de Crespigny. His Christian name was Crawley, and as such he was spoken of by his subordinates. Before the war this man had been a formidable amateur boxer. It was, I think, in the finals of the Army officers' competition in about 1913 that he met General Q. Le Martel, best known because of his influence on tank warfare, but also a redoubtable boxer. Both men were aggressive fighters with rather similar reputations for being unstoppable. It was agreed by everyone who saw the fight between these two that it was one of the most memorable encounters between amateurs ever seen. Crawley was a powerful man of stocky cruiserweight build, handsome in a snub-nosed way, and conveying an impression of fearlessness, masterfulness and pugnacity. A man of few words.

When at our Battalion sports the competitors for the hundred yards were being formed up behind the starting line, I was standing at the other end of the track by the finishing tape. I noticed Crawley walking alone towards the starting end where, without saying a word to anyone, he took his shoes off and pulled his socks over the lower ends of his trousers. When the competitors were being lined up for the start, Crawley, again without speaking to anyone, took his place on the extreme right. The starting pistol was fired and the all-out sprint began. After about five seconds Crawley was in the lead which increased till, charging down like a steam-engine without any movement of his arms, he breasted the finishing tape several yards in front of everyone else. I noticed his face as he passed me. It was entirely expressionless without trace of the rictus which often accompanies intense physical effort. Again without addressing a word to anyone, Crawley walked back to the starting point, readjusted his socks, put his shoes on, and shortly afterwards drove away. The most impressive feature of the performance was how everything was done without a word being said beforehand or afterwards to anyone. Those who knew him said that this performance was entirely in character.

It was a day or two later, I think, that I first met Alex Wilkinson. I had heard him talked about before as a fine officer, a first class cricketer, and a man who did not mince his words. If he liked you, you knew it. If he did not like you, you knew it no less clearly. He spoke his mind freely. He had been nastily wounded in the right hand by a bullet at the beginning of the attack on 15 September 1915 on the Somme. But this has interfered little with his cricket.

Late one evening some of us, including Atkinson, were sparring outside the mess in our shirt-sleeves. I was practising them in straight left leads and left stops. During a lull someone came up with an athletic-looking officer with dark eyes and a dark moustache to whom I was introduced. It was Alex. I told him that I had heard much about him and was glad to meet him, which was true. Alex had commanded No.1 before Watson-Smyth took it over, and was regarded as an exceptionally capable company commander – confident, energetic, resourceful and brave. The light was failing. I had left off my glasses for the boxing but in the dusk I could see him looking straight at me in a relaxed and friendly way, sizing me up. I found myself liking him: a good man to follow in a battle. He again commanded No.1 after the battle of the Canal du Nord on 27 September when I was wounded. He will come into this story later. A man with splendid qualities among which may be counted an unfailing loyalty to his friends and to the troops who served under him.

Nothing noteworthy happened between my return to Saulty on 30 June and my first tour in the line from 6 to 9 July. I was lucky to have an easy period – warfare against the Germans that imposed no stresses. What taxed me most was the heat and the scarcity of sleep. I was glad to take part for the first time in the routine of trench warfare. By this stage of the war three officers in each Company went up at each tour. In earlier years it would have taken more, perhaps as many as six – the company commander, the second-in-command and the four platoon commanders.

Barnard went ahead with a sergeant (Dunn) and four corporals to take over. Watson-Smyth and I followed later in the evening. We were conveyed by bus to Blairville where tea and rum were issued. We marched in the dusk through the village of Hendecourt (in the château grounds of which our guide lost his way) and through Boiry St. Martin which is almost adjacent to Boiry St. Rictrude (through which I had driven with George Edwards shortly after the Germans first attacked in March). After picking up water and Lewis guns we were guided for the rest of the way by an NCO of the Dorsets whom we were relieving. Darkness fell as we marched up. I will say something about the dispositions, the routine and my impressions.

First the dispositions. You have to distinguish between *Systems* and *Lines*. The terminology arises from the adoption of defence in depth. The front-line system comprised a front line and, close behind, a support line, both consisting of lightly held posts. About half a mile further back the support system is similarly divided into two lines, and yet further back there might be a generally similar reserve system. The separate posts might be connected laterally by shallow trenches or slits, and the front and support lines of each system might be connected by a communicating trench. The confrontation with the enemy in the forward positions was, in mid-1918, looser than in earlier years. By this stage of the war, when major offensives were the order of the day and when the forward areas were lightly held, trench warfare had acquired something of the character of an interim operation. There was little of the feeling that we were grappling in a deadlock. Though the Germans made occasional use of trench mortars ('minnies' or minenwerfer), less attention than I expected was paid by artillery to the forward systems, and such shelling as came our way was not perceptibly regular. At night there was less illumination by Very lights.

During intervals of varying length, the remoteness in the sky of distant gun-flashes – so remote that no sound reached you – and the long periods of silence between occasional rifle shots, could make you briefly feel that by design the war was being suspended. I have a recollection which probably belongs to this time of someone remarking that the angel of peace could, in July 1918, spread his wings and hover over stretches of front for longer periods than had been possible since the war began. I recall how sometimes these periods on night duty would monotonously drag so that one was more receptive to external impressions than during the corresponding stints of night-digging in the Fourth Battalion when one was supervising strenuous activities.

The periods of silence could become eloquent and, in a peculiar way, undergo a sort of inverted crescendo. You would stop and listen – with increasing intentness. Nothing whatever to be heard. The silence, you would feel, cannot last much longer. The break must come soon. The longer the silence lasted, the more the tension rose until an inner climax was reached whereafter abruptly the tension dissolved. These moments never occurred when one was sleepy. On the contrary, wakefulness and alertness were at their height. Someone – I thought perhaps my friend Drury, who was a clergyman – might suggest that those moments of rising tension before the bubble burst, were messages from the same angel of peace who, unknown to us, was exercising his wings over our heads. I clearly remember one occasion when such a 'crescendo of silence' was terminated by a nearby rifle shot. When the bubble was reaching its largest size, a German gunner or sniper could do you a service by busting it for you. A comparable, though wholly opposite, relief was provided by a sudden noise when you were in danger of dropping off to sleep. In combatting the craving for sleep, the officer had an advantage over the men doing sentry-duty. The officer could move about. He could walk up and down the trench, and the movement provided an attenuated stimulus. The static sentry had to stay in one place.

The routine in the line depended on the season of the year to which the hours of stand-to and stand-down were adjusted. I will describe the sequence during our tour at the beginning of July when the long hours of midsummer daylight were just beginning to shorten.

All three officers were on duty during stand-to and stand-down – from 3.15 to 4.15 a.m. in the early morning and from 9.30 to 10.30 in the late evening. These periods of standing-to were dictated by the questionable belief that the enemy were most likely to attack at dawn or dusk. A more cogent reason was that, attack or no attack, troops should be thoroughly alerted and put on their toes at daybreak and nightfall. During stand-to everyone stands in the fire-bays, alert and at the ready with bayonets fixed.

In addition to these two periods of standing-to, each officer in turn did a long watch and a short watch during every twenty-four hours. The three long watches of about four hours ran from morning stand-down at 4.30 a.m. to 8.30 a.m.; from 8.30 a.m. to 12.15 p.m.; and from 12.30 to 5.30 p.m. The short watches were mounted during the evening period from 5.30 p.m. to stand-to at 9.30 p.m. This evening period of four hours was divided into three short watches of about an hour and a half for each officer, thus making an evening meal, taken in turn, possible.

On the different days of the tour, I did long and short watches at different times. Each watch had its special features. The best of the long watches was the first of the day, after the early morning stand-down. In fine weather it was good to see the sun rising and enjoy the cool air. The second (midday) and third (evening) watch could be unpleasantly hot. My two were stifling and there was little shade. The night watches, though then not longer than an hour and a half, could be tribulating because of the longing for sleep. For the sentry to fall asleep on duty was regarded as a serious crime. For an officer to be found asleep on duty was *a fortiori* about the last word. I had not properly known till this tour how intense could be the craving for sleep. It could seem almost irresistible. If you leaned against the side of the trench for more than a short moment, your consciousness would insidiously and insensibly dissolve. Your brain seemed to melt and you slid down into the region of unstable mists. When you felt yourself to be in danger of slithering into this state, you welcomed a noise of war – a shell or a rifle bullet which roused you.

The Very lights not only illuminated no-man's-land, they also alerted dozy sentries. I sometimes asked the latter if they had private means, other than the traditional expedient of pinching oneself, of keeping awake. I encouraged them to think up methods, practise them on themselves and report to me any that were effective. One resourceful man, I remember, practised deep breathing exercises. In retrospect, I have wondered why we did not treat ourselves with small doses of caffeine.

During the middle and afternoon watches, the heat was oppressive. The parching sides of the trench flaked so that the trench boards were sometimes covered by a layer of friable earth. In one's movements up and down one could be followed by a swarm of insects – mostly noisy bluebottles. The sides of the trenches which were not exposed to the sun would be cheerful with wild flowers – fumitory, bindweed, mustard and clover. A yellow hawkweed was prevalent, much of it covered with aphids. The fields on the top, mainly seen over the parados, were brilliant with poppies, cornflowers, camomile and mustard, all of which pleased the eye after the bleak wastes of winter.

During one fine sunrise I was able to notice and enjoy how colour returned to these cheerful flowers. At one place where the parados was low you had a passing glimpse of the rough field behind. At stand-to and during the first watch I took pleasure in noticing, each time I passed this place, how, in the gaining light, the wild flowers brightened into their normal colours. I recalled from school how rosy-fingered dawn would cheer Homer's warriors and seafarers. I could not remember if it was counted among the goddess's bene-factions to restore to their full glories the colours which the night had extinguished. Was it possible that the early-morning somnolence of poets had dulled their perception of how the dawn-goddess restored at first light the bril-liance of spring and summer scenery? It seemed impossible. Among the poets of India and Greece there must have been some early risers. But perhaps the goddess had been insufficiently thanked for this aspect of her goodwill towards mankind. The scarlet poppies, shining buttercups and blue cornflowers of the fields near Ayette, lit up by the rising sun and seen though gaps in the parados, evoked the grateful thanks of at least one commonplace and temporary soldier.

The company headquarters which we took over was a tunnel excavated in the embankment of a light railway which, if working, would have taken you towards Hamelincourt and (further south) towards Bapaume. This railway transected at approximately right-angles our front and support systems. What I remember best about this tunnel was its dark coolness, which was welcome after the ferocious midday heat outside. The heat, which was trapped by the parched trench, made you sweat, raised a fierce thirst, and abolished your appetite. But after an hour in the tunnel, you began to feel hungry. It was then important not to eat too much. If you did you would pay for it when, later, you went out again into the heat.

I recall how, in the early mornings, you could catch sight far off of small parties of Germans moving about. There was a sniper's post which I succeeded in spotting with field glasses. Though well camouflaged it showed as a whitish patch against a darker background. This sniper turned his attention on me when I was crossing a sunken road by a shallow trench which did not afford head cover. I was bent well forward, when, crack, a rifle bullet momentarily deafened my right ear. When across the road, I found a place where, un-observed, I could see through glasses what looked like an isolated post. I saw a German clearly whom I took to be the sniper. He conformed with our idea of a typical 'Gerry' or 'Hun'. He had a close-cropped head and wore, to my surprise, not a tin hat but a peakless forage cap. I moved a Lewis gun from its post some yards up our front line in order not to draw fire on its proper position. I laid the gun on the post, gave my field glasses to No.2 of the Lewis gun team who had good eyesight with instructions when the sniper showed himself, to tip off the Corporal with the gun who would fire a burst. I then returned to the sunken road from which I fired a rifle grenade which burst two hundred yards from the post. The noise induced two Germans to lift their heads and bodies inquisitively above their parapet. The Lewis gun corporal then let them have fifteen rounds. The man with the glasses said that he was certain that one of the Germans had been hit in the forearm. More likely, however, that the wish was father to the thought. But the sniper kept quiet for the rest of the day.

During these tours in the line certain rules called for observance. Perhaps the first was punctuality. Never be late in turning up at the appointed place to relieve the officer who had completed the earlier watch. If you plan to have a sleep before beginning your tour, arrange to be woken up. Never rely solely on yourself to rise on time. Always put on a cheerful face however upside down you may be feeling inside. Don't forget how lack of sleep (of which you certainly will not have enough during your tour) can impair your memory both for long-passed and for recent events. At the end of a long bout of sleepless-ness you can all too easily forget what happened a few hours or even minutes before. If a message or order comes in, you will be liable to open it, read it, put it in your pocket and then completely forget that it was ever delivered. Your faculties are impaired and your power of recall blunted or even abolished. (What prolonged sleeplessness can do has been demonstrated in later decades by the practice of brain-washing wherein the victim is kept forcibly awake for long periods. Some falconers tame their birds by such treatment.)

During this tour I wanted to lead a patrol in no-man's-land. I mentioned the matter to Watson-Smyth who noted my request but postponed the exercise to our next tour. These exploits call for a minimum of preparation, without which you can easily get yourself shot by your own side. Whether or not you consulted headquarters or obtained their leave depended on the scale of what you were proposing to attempt.

The company front was thinly held. We had two platoons in the front line and two in support, about 300 yards behind. At approximately the mid-point of the company's front, both lines were transected at right-angles by the railway embankment in which was our company headquarters. Of the two front line platoons, No.2 (under Sergeant Chamberlayne) extended to the left from the railway and was under enemy observation. On the left of the railway you had to be careful how you moved about. On the right you were not visible and could move in the open. I remember no observation balloons in this sector.

During the daylight watches I spent some time in posts and short trenches on the railway's left. Here it was that I had been shot at by the German sniper whom we had tried to outwit. From one of these posts, the ground fell away to your left so that, with the exercise of appropriate caution, you could get a view of the Cojeul Valley and, beyond the valley, of Hamelincourt. You could also see, in the mid-distance, a line of poplars near which a trench-mortar emplacement was suspected. I spent some time watching this area in the hope of spotting some movement, but I saw nothing other than the static poplars for which I developed quite a friendly feeling. I recall that there were visible about seven of these trees, one or two quite straight, the others in various degrees bent over by the prevailing wind. As you looked at them through your field glasses they became invested with certain attributes. At one moment they were sentries posted by the Cojeul River; at another they became mourning women lamenting the sufferings which foolish men were inflicting on each other; at another they became sybilline and were weeping over the future. Since the days of Clairmarais I had liked poplars and had listened to how their tough long-stalked leaves whispered in the lightest breeze. I tried in vain to detect some cheerfulness in this line of poplars. But they remained self-absorbed and un-responsive, perhaps communing with the Cojeul River in its slow flow towards the Sensée and the Lys.

Movement between the front and support lines was awkward. Hence it was decided (I forget by whom) to dig a communicating trench between the two, close to the railway. The job was done by stages at night. The Germans took cognizance, and on the second night we were shelled on the job. The diggers were, I think, two platoons who, during the day, occupied the support system; or they may have come up from the reserve. Once on the job, these men did not need to be told that the quicker they could dig down the better protection they would make for themselves. As diggers they were not quite up to the standard of the Fourth Battalion; nevertheless it gave me pleasure to walk up and down the rising parapet of excavated earth and to look down on the strenuous activities below: the bent backs followed by the straightening and heaving movements when the shovelfuls of earth were cast upwards and outwards into the open. The metallic scraping of the shovels on the stony bottom and sides of the deepening trench was accompanied by the whispering sound of the earth sliding down outside of the parapet and by the deep breathing of the fully exerted men. On fine nights when the earth was friable and dry I had many times been stimulated in the Fourth Battalion by the combination of these sounds which raised your morale and made you conscious of teamwork at its best. It cheered me to supervise this work in the Second Battalion. I was later told that this trench proved more useful to the troops which took over our sector than we thought likely while we were digging it.

No.1 Company was relieved on 9 July by No.4 which was brought up by an officer of the name of F.W.P. Fletcher, known to the world as Boggles. The company moved back to Boiry St. Martin and thence to Bailleulmont in which village I had billeted the Fourth Battalion in November of the year before. I was reminded of the old French man who, sitting by his fireside, had repeatedly spat on the floor in disgust over the war.

It was in this month of July that, further south, the Battle of Rheims began. Here the Germans made initial advances. But they were then taken unawares by a sudden and successful attack on their right flank by General Mangin who burst on them out of the Forest of Villers-Cotterêts in an onslaught of numerous fast and small Renault tanks. The effect on us of this major battle in the south was to reduce still further the expectation of a German attack on the Arras front and to strengthen the by then burgeoning hope that the war might end sooner than everyone expected.

I have mentioned that, in No.1's mess, the South African officers did not mix as freely as might have been wished with some of the others. I have also mentioned that I would have liked to know more about the mechanics and tactics of the Lewis gun. I was able to remedy part at least of this shortcoming while at Bailleumont. There had recently been posted to the Battalion a rather remarkable and unusual character called G.F.B.Handley. This man took Lewis-gun classes on most mornings and from these I profited much. I quote from a letter I wrote in mid-July. 'Handley is a subaltern of the age of 36 who has had a wide experience of most aspects of soldiering. He also has a double Military Cross and has been twice mentioned in despatches. He was at Woolwich in 1898; thereafter, disappointed at not being allowed to take part in the South African war, he ran away and enlisted in the marines and partici-pated in the storming of Alexandria. He has lived much of his life in the colonies where he partly depended on his rifle and big game for food. He has commanded a battalion of the KOYLIs (Kings Own Yorkshire Light Infantry) and has taken part in two South African campaigns. After being wounded last October he came to England and, in consequence of a disagreement with his commanding officer, transferred to this regiment. He is a smallish, wiry, dark-haired man with a curious trudging walk and a very deep voice.' I found him an excellent Lewis-gun instructor and came to admire him.

Consequently it distressed me to find that he was actively disliked by Teddy Watson-Smyth, Boggles Fletcher and several of the young Etonians in the Battalion. I did not think that resentment of his record or jealousy of his in-trusion into the queue for promotion could be held accountable, and the ill-will shown towards this (to me) admirable man remained both mysterious and disturbing. Indeed, my esteem for Handley became a cause of minor distress to me when, on 17 July, I was restored to the rank of captain over Handley's head. I told Handley how badly I felt about this, but he would not listen to me. I also mentioned it to Jimmy Coats (the Adjutant), but he was not sympathetic.

I did not discuss this issue with Watson-Smyth or any of the younger officers except one – Frederick Chitty whom I have not mentioned before. He had been at Eton and was a couple of years younger than I. From our first contact I liked him. I discovered that he reacted exactly as I did to the factionalism within the Battalion between the younger officers (mostly Etonians) and the older South Africans. His sympathies inclined towards the South Africans. Chitty did not enjoy robust health; but he survived the war and settled in the USA.

The Battalion continued to hold the Hamelincourt – Ayette – Ransart – Bailleulmont area from the second half of July till the last week in August. Then movements began. During these six weeks, the company stayed nowhere long. Company movements were numerous and local – from one position in the front, support and reserve systems to another. These moves involving short periods in one place were badly documented in my diary and perforce were referred to vaguely in my letters.

During the last ten days of July we were closely geared to an American infantry company which had mainly been recruited in the Middle West. The left half of our front line was held by one of our platoons; the right half by an American formation of similar strength. The British platoon had behind it in the support line an American platoon, and the Americans in front were similarly supported by a British platoon. Maximum opportunity was thus given for the newcomers to learn the subtleties of trench warfare.

Towards the end of the afternoon watch on Sunday 28 July, the Germans mortared the front line at about the junction of the British and American sections. Two of our men (Corporal May and Guardsman Becker) were killed and another (Guardsman Barber) was wounded. By the same salvo an American sergeant was wounded in the leg, but not badly enough to impair his mobility. Company headquarters was placed in the railway embankment earlier mentioned. I was sitting there when the earth was shaken by the rending crashes of mortar shells. As I was hurrying down the trench towards the crater, I made way for a tall American sergeant with a white handkerchief loosely tied round a bleeding calf. He was making at full speed to the point close to the railway where our communicating trench opened into the front line. This man, who was moving at top speed, would not stop to tell me what had happened or to let me improve on his handkerchief which was not containing the bleeding. 'I'm getting to hell out of here,' he said as he raced round a traverse. On arrival at the point where the Minnies had landed, I found our party, including the wounded man, commendably calm, and likewise the Americans who had reacted with more composure than their sergeant. (This man, I was told, had been knocked down and buried as well as wounded.) The trench had been blown in. I sent back our wounded man who could get along with help. The other two were beyond salvation; one had been killed instantaneously, the other was alive, but did not recover consciousness. They were carried back at dusk which was beginning to fall. The Americans were friendly saying that they reckoned that they had had better luck than we had. Both parties joined in mending the damage to the trench. A lot of the ice thawed and inter-allied good-feeling warmed. It was not long before our gunners put over some retaliation.

The Americans showed their rank-consciousness differently from us. 'Yes, Capt'n,' 'No Lewtenant,' etc. with a sometimes odd mixture of formality and racy friendliness. I recall how one man who had brought up his section's rations in a sack disposed of the contents. Instead of handing the rations over to a NCO to distribute, he emptied the contents of the sack on the trench-boards, and delivered himself of the monosyllable: 'Scram'. Momentary pandemonium. I was later told that this man, who had recently joined, was doing a fatigue and was sick of carrying so much weight. The Americans normally distributed their rations as carefully as we did.

During the watch I chatted with several Americans who were friendly and willing to talk. I began by asking them about their relatives. Several produced snapshots as had the Germans with whom fraternization had taken place at Laventie during Christmas 1915. Several seemed to come from German farming families. They asked sensible questions about the war. I had earlier seen a nominal roll and had been struck by how many men had German names. One of these German-Americans told me that, when the Americans came into the war, he had felt a pull between his family loyalty to Germany, where he had several close relatives, and his more recent loyalty to America. The present German government, this man said, did not reflect the true Germany. It would not be long, he confidently predicted, before the Allies won the war. Then the ruling military caste would be ousted and replaced by a democratic regime. It would be uphill work, he reckoned, to re-establish friendly relations, but he was confident that it could be done within two or three years after the fighting had stopped.

These men seemed to feel little bitterness against the Germans. They talked less bloodthirstily than the Australians and Canadians that I had come across. They contrasted with the American women whom I had met in Paris of whom I heard several shrilly agree that they would never again speak to or shake hands with a German. Our Americans were mostly big men of the same build as Coldstreamers. This contact with our Allies brought home what an enormous accession of power the American army was going to bring to our side during the coming months; and it perceptibly strengthened the still faint hope that the war might end sooner than was expected.

The officers with whom we shared some meals were easy to talk to. Few were in the first flush of youth. No recent school-leavers. Most were in their early or middle thirties. Their conversation turned much on financial and business matters. I made the following note on an evening's exchange: 'Much dollar talk'.

The failure of the Germans to win the war by a decisive victory on the Western Front – a failure which was confirmed by the defeat which they had sustained in the last phase of the battle of Rheims – seems to have opened the flexible mind of General Foch (later called the Generalissimo) to the possibility that the war might be won sooner than he had hitherto thought possible. Perhaps, he may have sensed, the enemy had spent themselves in their recent desperate onslaughts; perhaps, he may further have sensed that the allied armies, (fortified by the influx of Americans and by the manufacture on an increasing scale of tanks, which initiative the Germans but feebly emulated), were beginning to feel that the tide was turning, that our side was gaining an ascendancy in numbers, equipment and morale, and that the balance of military power in France and Belgium was changing in our favour.

That this change of balance could bring about a quick and dramatic end to the war may not at first have occurred to Foch as more than a bright possibility, not to be loudly talked about (Nivelle-fashion) but to be cautiously explored. The highest credit was due to this Frenchman of genius for his combination of far-sightedness and caution – caution both in deed and word. The Allies were indeed fortunate in their new Commander-in-Chief.

Whatever thoughts about the future may have occurred to the Generalissimo after July, he kept them to himself. When his views were asked, we have been later told, he would answer cautiously that the end could not be expected before the spring or autumn 1919. In the meanwhile, he decided that the Allies might take certain precautionary measures to improve their positions.

At this stage of my account, I find myself increasingly departing from personal narrative to describe the events enacted at higher levels. (Of these we, at the periphery, knew little at the time.) This I do because nothing was of keener interest to everyone during the last half of 1918 than the possibility of a quick end to the war. In the three last months the views of my father and myself changed drastically from total scepticism about an early finish to its opposite of certainty that the end was at hand.

In today's retrospect the steps of this change played an increasing part in our lives during the last half of 1918. This change from one pole of expectation to the opposite pole affected one's feelings about survival. I had earlier made up my mind that I would not survive the war. But the shorter the war's duration, the better became the chances of being alive when it ended. Thus were the tensions of the last months linked with the course and tempo of wider events.

That the precarious position of Amiens seriously threatened British railway communications was, by mid-July, clear both to Foch and Haig. Indeed, in that month, Haig had assigned to Sir Henry Rawlinson (commanding the Fourth Army) the task of preparing an offensive against the large German salient which threatened the city. With Montdidier in the position of its left nostril, this salient projected like the profile of a protuberant nose into the allied positions east of Amiens. The enemy were too near the important city and railhead. They must be pushed back. The essence of Rawlinson's plan was a surprise tank battle. Six hundred tanks were available of which over half were of the new mark 5 pattern – fast, manoeuvrable, and each weighing over thirty tons.

In the early morning of Thursday 8 August, the Fourth Army, aided by natural and artificial fog, attacked without a preliminary bombardment on a front extending from Moreuil to the Ancre. Australians, Canadians, Cavalry and (further to the right) French troops participated. The remarkable course of events has been lucidly described by Winston Churchill[1]: 'In less than two hours, 16,000 prisoners and more than 200 guns were taken by the British, and by noon tanks and armoured motor cars, followed by cavalry were scouring the country 14 kilometres behind the German front'. A long-awaited consummation of a battle by cavalry!

The Battle of Amiens, as this battle was later called, was the first in the series of allied operations which won the war. How far the credit for this particular success should be partitioned between Foch, Haig and Rawlinson I do not know. No more eloquent testimony to the importance of the Battle of Amiens could be found than the much quoted words of General Ludendorff, recorded in his hurriedly composed *War Memories*[2]: 'August 8th was the black day of the German army. . . . The 8th August opened the eyes of the staff on both sides. . . . The entente began the great offensive, the final Battle of the world war, and carried it through with increasing vigour as our decline became more apparent.' The German commander also throws light on what was going on in the Kaiser's mind after the Battle of Rheims in July: 'The Emperor told me later that, after the failure of the July offensive and after August 8th, he knew that the war could no longer be won.'

I was among those in whom, during early August, hopes, previously nonexistent, began to flicker. But I dismissed them as chimerical – as wishful thinking. Had we not learned during the Battles of the Somme and Passchendaele how optimism about impending collapse of German resistance could be misplaced? We should not deceive ourselves again.

I say something here about Ian Bullough, who was our second-in-command. He was a tall, good-looking, smart man with a peculiar kind of vulnerability. This condition arose from his having married a beautiful and celebrated actress who was a popular idol. Her stage name was Lily Elsie. Before I had met Ian I had seen his wife in musical pieces. She was tall, distinguished and poised.

Ian, who was an uncomplicated sort of man, adored this woman with an abandon which, at that time, was unique in my experience. Ian liked to talk about her and did not conceal his feelings. She was, he told me, never out of his mind. Wherever he was, whatever he was doing, his thoughts were with her. It would be untrue to say that he was jealous of her, for it would not enter his mind that so perfect a being could give cause for jealousy. For him the central

[1] *The World Crisis*, 1931, p.796.
[2] Vol. II, p.679.

event of each passing day was the arrival of a letter from her. She had a bold handwriting so that her letters were easily recognizable from the envelopes. Their arrival was a delight to Ian and a relief to the rest of us who entered more than he knew into his feelings. In situations of danger it was not of himself that he thought: it was of the effect on his wife of a disfiguring or maiming wound or of his sudden death. There was, I thought, an almost religious element in his devotion and in his concern for her happiness: a sort of reverence. Indeed, it occurred to me at the time that Ian would have been happier and less vulnerable if he had been a Catholic and had dedicated himself to a particular saint.

Ian duly survived the war and I later met him once or twice at regimental dinners. I last came across him in the cloakroom of the hotel we were leaving after one of these dinners. He took me by the arm and led me outside. He then began to tell me on a note of despair that it had not been his fault. He swore by God and by everything he held sacred that it had not been his fault and I must believe him. I inferred that his marriage had broken.

It came back to me that, during 1918, I had thought that there might be something excessive about Ian's total absorption in this woman. There is no shield that can protect one so vulnerable. Further misery had seemed so predestined that a German missile during the war might have provided the most humane long-term solution. I knew nothing about Lily Elsie beyond what Ian had told me. But it struck me that, however fine a woman she might have been, it would be difficult to live up to the ideal in which he had framed her.

The Battalion was occupying trenches in the reserve system near Ransart. Nights were spent in shelters – mostly dugouts in the parados, roofed with corrugated iron battened down by sandbags. Days and nights were undisturbed except by an occasional leisurely shell that meandered down from high up and exploded with little commotion.

At about midnight I was roused from half-sleep by one of these things coming down about 150 yards away. I drowsily noticed how little noise it made on hitting the ground and wondered if it was a gas shell. I had begun to doze off again when I heard a scuffling outside, the gas-blanket over the entrance was lifted and a voice breathlessly told me that the last shell had come down in an occupied shelter. I arrived on the scene of the stricken shelter in a half-dressed state. Acrid smoke was emerging from the entrance. About half a dozen men were coughing in the trench outside the shelter. When the hanging blanket impregnated against gas was removed and the smoke had thinned I ducked my way in. I could see with my electric torch. A truly extraordinary thing had happened. A small shell had crashed through the roof and gone off inside the shelter without fragmenting. The empty steel casing and the heavy fuse were lying on the floor almost on top of a dead man who had been instantly killed by one or other of these objects. There was little blood. The man's chest had been staved in and his recumbent form was blackened by the powder which had burned without exploding. None of the men outside could remember hearing the shell coming down. All that they could tell me was that they had been woken up by a tremendous crash to find the shelter full of smoke. Apparently without panic, they got out as quickly as possible in the dark. While I was wrapping the corpse in a blanket and tidying the murky cavity which was littered with items of kit and equipment, a head was poked through the entrance and a voice asked if I was all right. It was Ian Bullough who had someone else with him – a warrant officer carrying a hurricane lamp. I suggested that some hot tea would do no harm to the men outside, especially if a little rum could be spirited in. When I came to give an account of what had befallen it became clear how astonishingly bad and good luck had been combined. It was a piece of extraordinarily bad luck that this stray and some-what feeble projectile, which had a large expanse to come down in, should have selected the minute area of this shelter. But it was also a piece of most remark-able good luck that, having come through the roof of a dugout containing a lot of men, it did not explode and play havoc with everyone. Which, I later asked myself, was more remarkable, the bad or the good luck? The question now comes back over fifty years later; and I do not know the answer.

After Ian had left, I was alone in the dugout with the dead man. His face was blackened but his eyes were open showing the whites so that he bore a macabre resemblance to a nigger minstrel. I was struck by the serenity of his expression. If, I said to myself, the soul of a dead man ever hangs about the lifeless body, what would this man's soul want to say to me at this moment? His placid expression caused me to think that he was reposeful. Why should he be reposeful? I asked myself. 'Because,' his expression seemed to say, 'my death could not have been more merciful and not a single other man in the section was touched.' It was not long before the others came back from the cooker fortified with mugs of tea. They provisionally restored the roof and tidied up the dugout so that, apart from a residual smell of powder, one would not have known that a mishap had occurred.

I sat with them for a few minutes and we talked about the dead man. I told them how well I thought they had behaved. One of them remarked that it was a miracle that any of them were alive, to which the general response was 'Amen'. I did not know, I said before leaving, if any of them were prayerful men. If yes, the padre would have them offer a private prayer as they went to sleep for the dead man. I bade them goodnight for the short remainder of the night: and never has a conventionally-expressed wish been more heartfelt.

I was told that my name had gone in for attendance at a Lewis Gun course at Le Touquet organized not by the Corps but apparently by the Army. Its address was G.H.Q. Lewis Gun school, B.E.P. There I spent the week 18–27 August. About mid-August Jimmy Coats had made it known that when, at a later date, the Battalion took part in an attack, three officers only would go in with each company; and each company would be led either by its company commander or its second-in-command. No. 1 would be led by me. This pleased me. But I said nothing about it when writing home.

By this time the Battle of Amiens was over; and an expectancy was growing that other attacks might soon begin. I did not want to be away from the Battalion in its next attack, and said so to Jimmy. Had I perhaps better not absent myself for this Lewis gun course? 'Don't worry,' said Jimmy. He had no reason for thinking that the Division was likely to be involved so soon. I could go away without misgiving. The people who would be likely to know best, I said to myself, were the gunners. So I paid a visit to the nearby 205th Siege Battery. There I was emphatically assured that a general offensive involving our Division was in the highest degree unlikely to take place so soon.

So on Sunday 18 August I lightheartedly set out for Le Touquet, where the course in Lewis gunnery was strenuous and well-organized.

I enjoyed the course, from which I felt I was profiting, until the evening of 22 August, when on a notice-board of the officer's common room, which I glanced at in passing, I read a brief statement which came like a blow in the solar plexus. It merely said: 'Guards Division attacked this morning.' That day I asked the commandant of the school if he would allow me to return at once to my unit. I forget what he replied beyond that he produced a strong argument that I should see out the course for the next three days and, in effect, refused me permission to leave. I did not at the time know whether the Second Guards Brigade which contained my Battalion had taken part in the attack. It had, in fact, not taken part. But I was not to know this till later.

I had luck on the return journey. After several fortunate road lifts (one from a Brigadier) I reached the Battalion's rest billets, by then at Berles-au-Bois, in the early afternoon. Then it was that I learned the shattering news. The Battalion had attacked that morning (27 August). Watson-Smyth and Gerard Brassey had been killed. Handley had been mortally wounded and by then was probably dead. Jackson had been severely wounded in a hand which had been amputated. Eccles, Espin, Atkinson, Barlow, Lutyens and Graham had been wounded. Tom Barnard (the third officer in No. 1) had come through. Watson-Smyth's death was specially terrible because I should have been in his place.

It was a sunny afternoon when I got back to Berles. The sunlit world suddenly turned to bitter ashes. If it were not for my parents, I thought, how much better now to be dead. The ensuing night, when sleep evaded me, was a haunting torment. With the possible exception of the night of the third of September 1939, the first day of the Second World War, this was the most miserable night I have spent in my life. I will not say more.

The night after the battle had been spent by most of the Battalion in trenches near Hamelincourt; and the next day (28 August) it marched back to Berles-au-Bois where I was waiting. I was struck by how smart and fit the company looked. In the lead was Tom Barnard of whom I remarked in my diary that he was 'positively dapper.' I wondered how he would appear. He had seemingly been attached to Watson-Smyth; and he might have been subjected to grievous experiences. After an exchange of conventional greetings he said in his off-hand way: 'The Huns in front of us were charming.' This peculiar remark was clarified later, as I will mention.

I was busy during the next three days with such activities as writing letters to the next of kin of casualties, dealing with losses of kit and its replacement, and attending conferences. Some facilities for baths had been set up in Adinfer where I took the company on Friday 30 August – an oppressively hot day.

The company's battle on 27 August formed part of a comprehensive battle which later came to be called the Battle of Bapaume which, from our standpoint, was not felicitously named, for our battle took place some five miles north of that demolished town upon which we did not then set eyes. Yet the engagement as a whole was well-named. It lasted for about a fortnight – from 21 August to 3 September; it extended over a front of some 50 miles (from the River Scarpe to Péronne); and Bapaume was captured (by New Zealanders) on 29 August.

Our battle was fought at a village called St. Léger. This place lies east of Hamelincourt which was mentioned above as lying to the east of the Arras-Amiens railway in the embankment of which we had lived in early July.

Though I took no part in it, I should say something about this battle on 27 August. The Battalion attacked in three waves. The people from whom we took over on the night before (I do not remember who they were) had assured us that the area of no-man's-land in front had been well patrolled and that no Germans were concealed there. No posts, trenches or machine-gun nests. The relief was not concluded till late and the hours of darkness were still short, so that there was no time for us to confirm this report by patrols of our own.

When, however, our attack went in at Zero, it was met by a heavy and unexpected machine-gun fire from close in front. The first wave was held up; the second wave came up in support of the first and was likewise stopped with heavy loss. No.1 Company, in the third wave, was likewise stopped. It turned out that a short trench or strong-point had been overlooked confronting the centre of our line of attack where the Battalion was held up and heavy casualties suffered. (Oh for a single one of the six hundred tanks used by General Rawlinson on 8 August in the Battle of Amiens!)

But on the flanks progress was made. Some sections had advanced far enough to be cut off. Enfilading fire from the strong-point and activities further out on each flank, however, made these advanced positions untenable. So that by the end of the day the decimated battalion was back at the starting point with all four companies mixed up. During the ensuing night the Germans of their own accord withdrew to prepared positions further east. Hence, on the following morning (28 August) British troops advanced unopposed over the previous day's battleground. Here were picked up those of our wounded who had lain out during the night.

It then turned out that German stretcher-bearers had been active during the hours of darkness. They had carried back as many of their own wounded as they could shift in the time before they themselves withdrew; and to our wounded they had given what first aid they could (the primary need being water), assuring them that they would be picked up next morning by their own side who would be advancing unopposed.

This was what Tom Barnard had meant when he told me that 'the Huns in front of us were charming.' I did not myself make contact with any of our casualties; these had almost all been evacuated by the time the Battalion got back to Berles and Adinfer. But I spoke to two of No.1's stretcher-bearers who had picked up wounded men next morning. One of these had told the stretcher-bearers that when, during the night, he became aware of a German coming near, he expected to be bayonetted. Instead he was bandaged and given a needed drink. This was one of the few occasions during the war that I learned first-hand how German troops had behaved.

13

CANAL DU NORD

The battle fought by the Battalion at St. Léger on 27 August (part of the more comprehensive Battle of Bapaume) was followed exactly a month later by another more important battle – that of the *Canal du Nord*. This canal, which was still under construction and contained no water, had, in November of the year before, played a part in the Battle of Cambrai about which I have said something.

During the month which intervened between the Battles of St. Léger and of Canal du Nord, the British army moved forward unopposed. The Germans had withdrawn to the heavily fortified position named after the German Field Marshal, a figure whose imperturbability and solidity, had, for Germans, become legendary. From the standpoint of German morale, the Hindenburg line was well-named.

The depression which had afflicted me after the Battle of St. Léger fluctuated and, in about a week, lifted. It was a busy period during which I felt unsociable. I kept as clear as I could of the mess and became absorbed in Hardy's *Tess*. I went for walks in Adinfer Wood where, earlier in the year, the nightingales had so indignantly protested when, at night, their territories had been shelled. In the thicker parts of the coppice there still lingered the smell of mustard gas; and tanks, concealed with branches and leaves, were concentrated in dry places.

Two new officers joined us. Geoffrey Howard, whom I had known two years earlier in the Fourth Battalion, was one. The other was W.G.Bulteel, a Cornishman and contemporary at Windsor.

On Monday 2 September, at short notice, we began the expected move to the south-east. Our first destination, which did not involve a long march, was Hamelincourt which had fallen into British hands in an early phase of the Battle of St.Léger. I tried unsuccessfully to catch a glimpse of the poplars bordering the Cojeul River which I hoped had come intact through the shelling. The next day (3 September) we resumed our march in the same general direction, our destination being the ruined village of Lagnicourt. As we were starting, Bisseker turned up. By then he had become a definite asset to the company and was welcome. At the same time another good man joined us – J.C.Hayes. Hayes was a competent, cheerful and companionable South African who sometimes wore a monocle and whom Bisseker therefore called Monocled Moses, though there was nothing in the slightest biblical or hebraic about him.

Grim scenes of battle surrounded us as we marched steadily in hot weather through St. Léger, Ecoust-St-Mein, Longette and Noreuil. Corpses disfigured parts of the roadside and the smell of high explosive still pervaded the week-old shell craters. Several dead horses, also lying at the sides of the road, buzzed with flies, like the human corpses, as they awaited burial. Some men seemed to feel more indignant about the dead horses than the dead men; horses and men were co-victims of the war; but men knew what they were doing while horses did not. The horses were more passive sufferers. Their bulk and strength, of which men made use, was commensurate with their incomprehension of what was happening around them; and this added to their pathos. These faithful beasts, it could seem, were being wantonly sacrificed by men.

The early part of the march took us through the battlefield of 27 August and someone pointed out to me the approximate place where the brave Watson-Smyth had been buried. As we approached Lagnicourt, a wood-topped hill became visible in the far distance ahead. It was Bourlon Wood. Memories flooded back of this sinister eminence vigilantly frowning down on us as we worked in the dry bed of the canal below. Bourlon Wood had then reminded me of Wagner – of the castle of the demonic sorcerer Klingsor in *Parsifal*. Now it looked harmless enough in the distance. Indeed, it seemed almost benign, particularly when some of the men in No.1 raised a cheer when told the name of this distant feature. But these were not the men with whom I made my first contact with the wood. The latter has been the members of No.3 Company of the Fourth Battalion. It seemed a happy coincidence that while this thought was in my mind we walked through a party of Fourth Battalion men working on the repair of the road. A happy recognition scene was enacted when several cheerfully called out as I passed, and greetings were exchanged.

That night was spent in shaft dugouts on the Noreuil-Lagnicourt road. After half an hour's rest and some refreshment in the form of mugs of tea, Jimmie Coats gave us a half-expected job. A party of fifty men was wanted to bury thirty-six dead horses. We dug pits for twenty-two and a party of Irish Guards disposed of the remaining fourteen.

While we were living in shaft dugouts during our transit, Wilbraham and Bower paid us a welcome visit – the Fourth Battalion having moved forward ahead of the Second. Also Oliver Baldwin who, at school, had been a close friend of Oscar Hornung. Oliver was in the Irish Guards where he was having trouble with his commanding officer about whom he spoke with feeling. We also enjoyed convivial periods with my old friend W.H.Corbould and with E.G.C.Richards who was best known to most people as 'Bon' (pronounced like the German town on the Rhine). He had acquired the nickname because of the frequency with which he used this monosyllable to express his reaction to all forms of news, whether good or bad. We talked about the swallow-tail butterflies at Bienvillers-au-Bois.

The early days of September were not cool and autumnal. They were immoderately hot. On 5 September I ended a letter saying: 'We have been lying on the grass with handkerchiefs over our faces. There is no shade, both buildings and trees in this area having been destroyed. Our activities mainly consist in doing physical exercises during the cool hours and in burying dead horses.' Rumours were floating about, but they were mostly cheering and did not, like most rumours, seem unrealistic or absurd. It was for example going round that our impending attack was to form part of a tremendous assault on many fronts in which troops of several nationalities would take part – not only French, Americans and ourselves but also Belgians, Portuguese and Italians. These rumours were cheering. The break-up of the central powers might be nearer than we realized.

In comparative comfort we remained in the above-mentioned dugouts in the Lagnicourt-Noreuil road for four days – from 4 to 7 September. By then the evenings were perceptibly shortening. We then moved further east to the destroyed village and wood of Louverval. These lie half a mile west of Boursies of which the ruins bestride the straight and tree-bordered main road connecting Bapaume and Cambrai. Boursies appears on the left side of the diagram which is included below. Our dugouts opened into a sunken road of which the surroundings, until we cleared and disinfected them, were almost unbelievably filthy. If, as seemed probable, German troops had been in recent occupation, it was obvious that, at this stage of the war, they bothered little about sanitation.

Louverval was about half a mile behind our defence system of which the front and support lines were connected by a short communication trench named Fish Avenue. My memories of these days are jumbled but I have notes in the diary I then kept. On 8 September I wrote that 'the advance is held up on the canal in front, but is going well further south.' During the first night at Louverval there was some nearby shelling which woke me several times. And on the night of 11 September an attack was delivered (not by our Division) on some positions in the Hindenburg support system for which we had to form a defensive flank in the communicating trench above mentioned – Fish Avenue. 'A wall of smoke rose into the air parallel with the canal and there was a tremendous noise. But nothing came near us.' I have no recollection of this exercise, but I remember how our nearness to the line agreeably raised the tension and abolished such depression as lingered after the Battle of St. Léger.

On Friday 12 September we moved back to Lagnicourt where we stayed for just short of a week. Tom Barnard had gone on leave and there had been reposted to No.1 a splendid officer – G.C.Firbank – who had been wounded no less than three times. The last of these wounds had been severe. He had lost an eye and his eye-socket was damaged so that he was compelled to wear a black eye-cap. His three wounds had in no way impaired his zeal to get back to the war. 'Firks' (as his friends called him) was the gentlest, most modest and unpretentious of men. He would speak apologetically of his own capacities as if he felt that allowances had to be made for damage to his brain. Happily he survived the war. We were also joined by another officer, John Beck, who likewise survived the war and came up to Oxford. He later became widely known as a top-ranking exponent of golf.

On 18 September some of us were moved right back to the familiar village of Berles-au-Bois which, despite the Division's moves forward, continued to accommodate the battalion's 'Details.' I clearly recall two events relating to this stay at Berles: – one musical, the other medical. The first was in all respects pleasant; the second was exasperating, tribulating and humiliating.

When I arrived at Berles I found that this simple place had been toned up by the arrival of a selection from the regimental band over which presided the Director of Music, Major J.Mackensie-Rogan. Upon this distinguished and impressive man, who might have been in his middle fifties, several foreign decorations had been bestowed. His resounding name was matched by his fine appearance, especially when he was in full uniform. He and his team brought to the unpretentious complex of small villages south-west of Arras something of the panache of peacetime soldiering. Mackensie-Rogan, a modest and friendly figure, had the appearance and something of the manner of an ambassador or a high-ranking diplomat. He was a powerfully built man whose fine carriage and presence were supplemented by a sweeping grey moustache; also by the dignified composure with which he wielded the baton, thereby raising the morale of all who thronged his open-air performances.

The regimental band had played to us in France before, for example in the township of Estaires during the gloomy winter of 1915/1916. But I do not recall being cheered – perhaps because of the impending operations on the Somme about which it was difficult to feel sanguine. But by the autumn of 1918 the course of events had so changed that martial music could produce the right effects. The hopes raised by recent successes were primed by colourful displays reminiscent of Whitehall and Windsor which were now being enacted close to battle zones where events had moved so well. This time our spirits were raised and some of us were made to feel quite proud of ourselves. The possible end of the war and ensuing return to England were brought nearer.

Mackensie-Rogan became a member of the officers' mess at Berles which also included Scottie Caldwell with whom I had spent a short leave at Le Tréport. Rogan had his meals with us. He was scrupulously polite and considerate to everyone irrespective of rank, but did not join in the light talk which went on round him. He was, however, a good listener and his face would some-times light up with a smile. We felt that he must have a copious store of reminiscences and anecdotes with which, if he wished, he could regale us, but we did not succeed in drawing him out. I tried to do this by asking questions about which composers appealed to him most as a conductor and about his experiences in the countries in which honours had been conferred on him, but none of us could persuade him to speak about himself. We did not penetrate his modest reserve.

The medical event to which I have referred was an attack of acute synovitis in both knees which assailed me at the worst possible moment – the moment which would produce the intensest possible shame and humiliation. The afflic-tion was excruciating and peculiar.

In later years, during the inter-war year period and the Second World War, I did a good deal of running which I had come to regard as providing the simplest and best method of keeping fit. But during the 1914–18 war I did little cross-country running before the last months. It was while I was at Berles-aux-Bois in September that the idea occurred that some runs would get me into good shape if heavy physical effort proved to be necessary in the near future. Two officers felt as I did: M.W.J.Biddulph and G.W.J.Farquhar, both Etonians younger than myself. I now remember little about Biddulph beyond that he was a pleasant companion for this sort of exercise. Farquhar was a somewhat peculiar young man whom I came to like. He had a habit of glower-ing when he unsmilingly talked to you. But it soon became obvious that his forbidding demeanour implied not hostility so much as mystification arising from a possible failure to follow what was being said to him. The more he glowered, the greater the interest he was actually feeling in what you were trying to say to him.

Characteristically and stupidly I overdid the running. On Saturday 21 September I ran round Adinfer Wood with Biddulph. The next day, in heavy rain, we ran a circuit round De Cauchie, Pommier, and Bienvillers-aux-Bois. The next day after a run of about the same length, I found that my left knee was stiff and painful. But by next morning the pain had gone. Cheered by the fact that my wind was improving nicely, I repeated the exercise; but the pain in my left knee came back and then my right knee began to hurt. Nothing in the way of redness or swelling was visible in either knee, but the joints were tender round the articulations. I paid no attention, and the next afternoon I set out with Biddulph on another ambitious round. But we had not gone far before the pain became so severe that I had to stop. I apologized and limped back to Berles. Subsequent events were briefly recorded in my diary.

On Tuesday 24 September we were moved up again by lorry from Berles to Lagnicourt which was now becoming familiar. On arrival we learned for the first time of the event which was to be enacted three days later. My diary has the entry: 'A colossal show is to come off on the 27th. My knees are still sore.' On 26 September, the day before the 'colossal show', I recorded that my right knee was beginning to give as much trouble as my left. Movement of all kinds was becoming increasingly painful. I now clearly remember how on the day before the attack, misgivings about my fitness to lead the company began to assail me. My spirits declined, but I decided to keep my troubles to myself. It had by then been decided that Bisseker and Beck would be with me, making up the prescribed three officers. On no account must I say or do anything which would impair their confidence. As the day wore on – Thursday 26 September – both knees became more painful and signs of fluid appeared in my left knee. There was no redness or inflammation, but fine crepitations could be felt when I flexed the joints. I had no salycilates or other analgesic drugs and decided not to send for any lest misgivings or suspicions be aroused. Only one course was possible: to say nothing to anyone and carry on as best I could with the ridiculous and untimely affliction. My chief trouble was that there was so little to show for so much pain and disablement.

I was tormented by the possibility that, in the attack, I would fall short in such a way as to cause casualties or let the company down. Anything, including death, would be preferable to having it thought that, after missing the Battle of St. Léger, when someone else had been killed in my place, I was trying avoid the next battle.

The Battle of the Canal du Nord was fought on 27 and 28 September 1918. We had about three hours sleep the night before (the 26th). Those restless hours were spent on a wire bed in an old German dugout somewhere on the east side of Lagnicourt. Here I was alone. I slept little, not being able to find a position in which my knees did not ache. I remember those three hours. My thoughts rotated round four topics: Was there anything I had left undone or forgotten? Was tomorrow going to bring a trouble which would balance the luck I had had in the last three years? What a crass fatality if my accursed knees, which had handicapped me so much in earlier years, were to let me down on the day when, above all other days, I needed them to be strong and reliable! And lastly what a blessing that the two at Dinard did not know how I was placed! The prospect of getting on to my feet to start the day was forbidding; but I was restless and wanted to get on with whatever lay ahead.

We got up just after midnight – at 12.15 a.m. It was pitch dark and raining. Bisseker, Beck and I foregathered and ate a meal of bacon, tomatoes and hot tea. We paraded at ten past one. Owing to the rain the company took longer than they should to get formed up, so that we were five minutes late in reaching the starting-point. But since Brigade Headquarters were a quarter of an hour late, our five minutes did not matter. We then had a march which, with various stops, took about two hours. Brigade Headquarters were leading, followed by our own Headquarters, followed by No.1. I hobbled along, aided by a stout stick, first along a muddy and pitted road; then across country – also pitted and wire-strewn. It was not long before we had something to be grateful for. The rain diminished, a moon got up, and quiet reigned.

But the further we went the more I cursed my joints. The next half hour was something of an ordeal. We traversed a battery zone where stillness and expectancy contributed to the tension of those early hours. Shadowy figures of gunners could be seen standing by their places. I was stupidly reminded of shepherds standing by their flocks.

We finally reached our assembly positions – a trench called Sturgeon Avenue, east of Boursies. There I sat down on the firestep and enjoyed a welcome rest. I felt better. It was good to have Ian Bullough ahead. There we stayed for an hour or more. I dozed fitfully. The rain, which had been inter-mittent, stopped. The clouds thinned so that the moon and stars shone down. The stars seemed intelligent, as if they knew what they were looking down at and were interested in what was about to happen, though they knew the outcome. The pervading silence continued.

Zero was at 5.30. At 5.10 Ian Bullough passed down the trench followed by Headquarters. 'Follow with No.1,' he said as he passed me. I mobilized myself. In the mounting tension I found that, for short moments, I was forgetting about my knees, though my movements were retarded. The rear file of Headquarters passed and scurried fitfully ahead so that, with my slow progress, I was apt to lose touch. I detailed two men as connecting files, one of whom I kept by me.

A road formed the right boundary of our assembly positions and, on to this road, Headquarters (ahead of us) debouched from Sturgeon Avenue. By the time I reached the road, I could no longer see the rear file of Headquarters which had turned to the right. But I could see the connecting file. The man was gesticulating to us to follow him. In the first light of dawn I glanced at my wrist-watch. Nearly half-past-five. Sergeant Peck (acting Sergeant Major) who was with me said: 'A very few seconds now, Sir.' His words seemed to produce the expected result: the sky to the north turned electric blue. And then, over our heads and in every direction round us, everything erupted. It was as bright as daylight.

One artillery bombardment is much like another, especially when you try to describe them. But this one was made special by the remarkable brightness which lasted for several minutes until we were enveloped by the inexorable shroud of smoke. The turmoil of sound which assaulted the ears was like a sort of deafness – a deaf man's nightmare. We communicated by signals.

The Company hurried after Headquarters along the road, which was banked up on our left. From under the bank three batteries of field guns sprang into feverish life: the salvoes struck us like blows on the side of the head. We reached the ruins of Demicourt, which had been a small strung-out village, and we swung to our left along another sunken road. Along this road we scurried for what seemed to be about a quarter of an hour, through a zone of machine guns which were simultaneously engaged in high-angled overhead fire. Here we

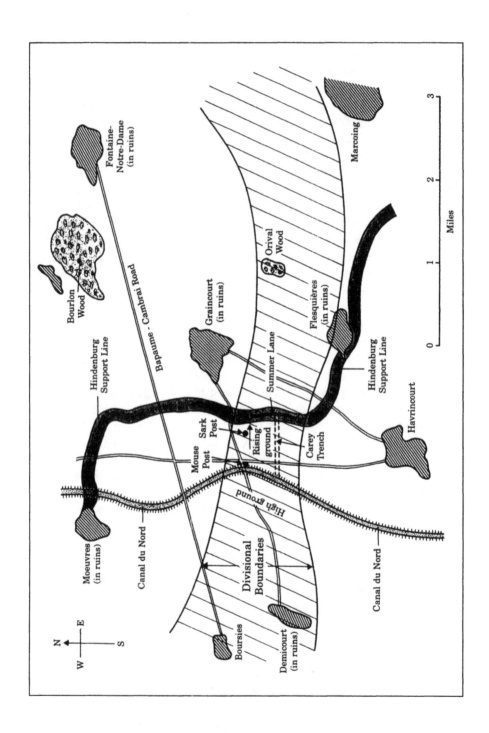

258

caught up Headquarters who had halted and were squatting in various excavations at the side of the road. I went on to report to Ian Bullough who told us to stay where we were. While I was with him, German gunners, who had withdrawn in the night, started on our road. It was now getting light. They shelled towards us with what sounded like five-nines, starting about where we had debouched from Sturgeon Avenue. Luckily for us, their fire was a bit off target. It came down west of the road and I don't think anyone was hurt.

After about a quarter of an hour we moved off our road, bearing south-eastward (to the right) towards the canal which we could not see. By this time the Germans were plastering the crest of the ridge which, ahead of us, bounded the canal on its west side. (The canal here ran north-south.) Our direction was across this ridge which was thick with broken belts of tangled wire; and, to our left the ridge was heaving with exploding shells. The explosions of these enemy shells were peculiar because the encompassing din prevented you hearing the sound of their approach and descent. They exploded without audible forewarning as if they were mines detonated from a distance. You heard a savage rending thump followed by 'bits' whizzing.

I was following close behind Headquarters, in front of No.1, when a shell burst a few yards ahead of the leading file of Headquarters. Ian Bullough (leading Headquarters) bore to his left and then down came another shell behind Ian in the middle of Headquarters. A snapshot vision of reeling men and bits of earth flying. The smoke cleared disclosing prostrate forms. Those who could do so had made for a shallow trench leading tangentially half-right. So did No.1 behind me which was following close behind Headquarters. At the side of the smoking crater I found Symon (Assistant Adjutant) and Stubley (Intelligence Officer), in contorted postures, both with broken legs but conscious. Philip Wells (Medical Officer), an unusually cool and brave man, was applying first aid to another prostrate figure. Shouting at him, I mouthed a question as to whether Ian Bullough was all right. By a nod Wells conveyed that he thought so and pointed to the trench on our right.

Ian was lying against the side of the trench, pale, relaxed and composed. I was much relieved for, if he and the adjutant had been knocked out, responsibility for direction might have fallen on the senior officer of the company which was following Headquarters. My knowledge of the direction was not exact. Ian had been knocked down, shaken and deafened by the explosion behind him but was unwounded. He led the Battalion splendidly for the rest of that day and, I was later told, did the same on the ensuing days. Philip Wells also did splendidly. Later on 27 September he had another escape which was close enough to seem miraculous. Having had others of the same kind before, he said that he no longer believed in luck: 'I prefer to believe in the Bon Dieu.'

We (that is Headquarters and No.1) waited in nearby trenches for about twenty minutes during which time the barrage mostly moved further to the left. The Third Grenadiers had to pass through us. It was not long before they appeared. I retain a clear mental picture of a moustached, middle-aged and well-scarfed Grenadier officer, nonchalantly smoking a pipe, picking his way with careful deliberation through the wire over the crest at the head of the column. He moved without looking to his right or left as if he were solely interested in his pipe and in where he placed his feet. I never learned the name of this imperturbable pipe-smoker.

Headquarters (Bullough leading) followed the Grenadiers, and I followed Headquarters. After the shaking they had received, No.1 clambered briskly out of the trench and in a thin column followed me, threading their way down the steepening embankment through the continuing barrage. By this time the sun was peeping over a murky horizon. Suddenly below me was a chasm which, momentarily forgetting where I was, I mistook in the smoke for a deeply sunken road. It was the Canal du Nord.

During our downhill move, through what was probably the enemy's main defence barrage, we had luck. As far as I knew we were caught but once. I retain the memory of a haunting glimpse. I was struggling to get through some strands of wire when the shell came down without warning a few yards behind me and about two yards in front of two men who were walking next to each other. One was a middle-aged man whose name I forget; the other was a young newcomer called Gratridge who wore spectacles, looked studious, and resembled President Woodrow Wilson. The older man was literally dismembered in a way I had not seen before. The other had his face blown off, the soft parts being detached from the front of his skull from below upwards. As the smoke cleared he subsided slowly to his knees, making ineffectual groping movements with his hands, pawing forwards like a blind man. He came to rest like a praying Moslem, with his head down and what had been his face a bleeding mask. The image of this groping sightless figure, kneeling and pawing the air, has often come back to me since.

The Canal du Nord was a familiar place in which, the year before, No.3 Company of the Fourth Battalion had spent some hours. Our task had been to clear the bottom and turn it into a passage-way for vehicles. The bed of the canal was still dry. Wooden ramps had been let into, and scaling ladders had been lowered against, the steep sides, making a climbing angle of about one in two. At this point the canal, which varied in depth, was about twenty feet deep. I let myself down a ladder cautiously, the easiest way for my knees. At a point about a hundred yards to the north, the canal was being heavily bombarded. The explosions reverberated between the steep sides, visibility being obscured by volumes of blue smoke.

I later learned that this activity may have centred on Mouse Post (see diagram) where the Demicourt-Graincourt road crossed the canal. Here it was that C.H.Frisby (our First Battalion) earned a Victoria Cross. The First Battalion (in which Robin had been killed three years before almost to a day) had been held up in the canal by German machine guns concealed under the girders of an iron bridge which had carried the above-mentioned road over the canal. The Division's advance over this area of the canal was seriously held up by intense enfilading fire. Calling for volunteers to follow him, Frisby ran forward and 'with three other ranks climbed down into the canal under point-blank machine-gun fire and succeeded in capturing the post with two machine guns and twelve men' (the citation).

When, with No.1, I reached the canal, a German field gun was firing at us from the left front, seemingly along open sights; it was mostly hitting a bank at a point close on our right, which stood up above the brick sides of the canal's western side. No.1 followed me down.

From the bottom, I saw Ian Bullough standing on top of the eastern embankment. He had fully recovered. He told me to lead No.1 into a trench, shown in my diagram, as *Carey Trench*. I could see its opening into the east wall of the canal a few yards to the north.

I thought that I had better reconnoitre this trench before taking the company into it. I had with me an orderly, a composed, bronzed middle-aged man with a decoration called Carnham. As I was climbing out of the canal up a ladder into Carey Trench, the German field gun fired again; the shell came from half-left skimming the parapets of Carey Trench, which had been captured soon after Frisby's exploit at Mouse Post just to the north. The trench was well revetted and fairly deep, with side-trenches saps and cavities in the sides. In brightening but murky daylight I hobbled up the trench. Into most of the recesses at the side severely wounded men had crawled or been carried. Some of these shouted or gestured for first aid, pointing to their wounds.

I had moved about fifty yards down this trench when – crash! – concussion and darkness. The light went out. Full stop. Blankness. I came to myself half-buried in earth. Carnham was bending over me. He lifted me to the side of the trench and sat me up. The left side of my head was numb and my left ear was singing. I could hear nothing. There was an acrid smell of powder. My head was bleeding. I was irritated by a bright orange thread which kept dangling in front of my left eye and which persisted in spite of efforts to brush it aside. In my dazed condition some seconds passed before I realized that this waving orange thread was a fine jet of arterial blood which was spurting out of my left temple.

Carnham's first thought was to get out of the line of fire of that German field gun. With his assistance I hoisted myself on to my feet where I discovered, first, that my knees were hurting me more than my head, and second, that I could see perfectly well out of my right eye.

I have several vivid memories of the rest of that day. Carnham tied my head up as tightly as he could with a field dressing, but I went on bleeding. The left side of my battledress became soaked, and stiffened as the blood clotted. I was carrying maps in the flap of my box respirator which was tied on my chest in the alert position. My maps became soaked. My precious Lens Eleven retains brown smudges; and another, a Cambrai Sheet 57 B, is a discoloured souvenir. Later Philip Wells who, with Headquarters, had followed No.1 up Carey Trench, took a look at me. He said that my left temporal artery had been cut. A ligature would stop the bleeding better than a field dressing. I had been lucky not to lose my left eye. With a curved needle he scooped a ligature under the artery through the muscle. This had the desired result. For the next few days I had some head pains but they troubled me less than my knee-joints. This well-timed and well-placed wound at once lifted a heavy weight. If my knees were to let me down, the wound and the loss of blood would provide an excuse.

Bisseker, Wells and I sat together for some time in a traverse close to where Carey Trench was crossed by a girder bridge. Here it was that I learned that Henry Dundas (Scots Guards: friend at school of Cecil Sprigge and Robin) had been killed. The Scottish stretcher-bearer who told me the news added a story which I was later told was untrue; but it is worth mentioning because it shows how quickly myths can arise when people are excited. The story was that when Dundas died, one of his sergeants was with him and took his papers. On his way back to the canal this sergeant saw a party of German prisoners making their way along the top of the canal. His feelings were such that he turned a machine-gun on the prisoners. From what I knew of Dundas, this is about the last thing he would have wanted.

Ian Bullough had gone on ahead with some of Headquarters. A message came down for No.1 to follow along Carey Trench. The inactivity had stiffened my joints and the pace I set was slow. Side-trenches and saps still contained wounded men; and deep shaft dugouts were emitting smoke from bombs which had been thrown down. Between the Canal du Nord and the Hindenburg Support Line, Carey Trench sloped uphill. At the same time the ground fell away to the left so that, at certain points where the tall parapet had been demolished, one got good views to the left. Then it was that, for the first time on that day, I had a glimpse of Bourlon Wood. It was an unforgettable sight. The place, which was strongly held by the enemy, had been bombarded from zero hour by guns of every calibre. The shelling was being continued. The crowns of the trees only could be seen; the boles were hidden by a mist of yellow smoke which filled the coppice and was drifting slowly away to the east. Towering columns of smoke were shooting upwards, overtopping the trees. Parts of the wood were on fire; and, from a few yards above, the tree-tops were being spat upon by bursts of shrapnel. It was believed that mustard gas manufactured by us was here being used for the first time.

In moving up Carey Trench I recall coming to a spot where the parapet on the left had been blown down: dead and wounded men were lying about. As Bisseker and I came up a wounded man lying on our side of the gap raised his arm in a stopping signal. 'For God's sake take care,' he said. 'There's a sniper over there.' He pointed out to the left. 'He has done all this.' I have a recollection of slowly poking forward a tin hat on the end of a stick. Crack came the bullet, missing the tin hat. Two of us scampered over, and the gap on the left was filled up from both sides; so that, by ducking low, you could get by at the double. The trouble had begun a few minutes before. The parapet had been intact when Ian Bullough had passed along earlier.

I remember how a party of about thirty Germans passed us doubling down-hill on the right. They were physically small men who were chattering like monkeys. They looked like green gnomes, their uniforms surprisingly clean. I was standing with Bisseker at a point in Carey Trench from which a side-trench opened when this party came by us on the top. Suddenly they threw themselves on the ground, and I beckoned to one of them to come down. This man understood neither English nor French. I said something about their clean battledress and there followed a spate of words in a dialect from which I gathered that his party had only put on these uniforms the day before. They had been rushed straight into the line, arriving a few hours before zero. My German was fragmentary but I asked him: '*Haben Sie unser Angriff erwarten heute morgen?*' He seemed to reply that an attack was certainly expected but not then. By this time the other Germans, realizing that they were not going to be shot, were gaining confidence. They began to filter down into Carey Trench. Then a rather amusing incident occurred. Higher up the hill to our left appeared a diminutive German advancing hesitatingly towards us with a comic bobbing step. His tin hat was several sizes too big. He was solemnly carrying on a stick a large triangular white flag with a red cross painted in the centre. This flag he was energetically waving from side to side, holding it as high as possible. Shouts of laughter went up. The party of Germans pointed at him and held their sides. One rotated his arms as if he were unwinding a coil of wool and guffawed. They seemed to think that the flag was his private property which he carried in his kit intending to surrender at the first opportunity. This party scarcely formed part of the élite of the German army.

In due course Bullough, who had been ahead, moved us up out of Carey Trench. We strung ourselves out under a bank which may have formed part of the western slope of the Hindenburg support line. We occupied a trench which, I later learned, was known as Summer Lane. On our left were Nos.3 and 4 Companies, and yet further to the left were trenches held by Germans. I tentatively reconnoitred the area to the east of our part of Summer Lane, over the ridge. No sooner did I show myself than a machine gun opened, kicking up the earth round my feet. The fire seemed to come from the ruins of Graincourt, half-left in front. A young corporal who was with me suddenly stumbled and began to limp, saying that he had been hit in the foot. In a shell-hole he took off his boot. He was right. A bullet had shot off the distal phalanx of a middle toe. It was the sort of wound that a suspicious officer or NCO could think had been self-inflicted. I wrote out a note certifying that the wound had not been self-inflicted and sent him back. The hours passed. We spent them under the western embankment of Summer Lane. Towards sunset we could see, about half a mile below us on the left, a battery of German field guns which had been shooting continuous salvos. (I wondered whether it had been by one of these that I had earlier been caught.) When by evening the German gunners realized how insecure their position was becoming, and that No.4 was bombing along a trench which would bring them close, they decided to withdraw. This they did efficiently and with maximum speed, moving east towards Cambrai along the straight Bapaume-Cambrai road. Here they presented targets to Nos.3 and 4 Companies and also to us. By this time No.1 had swung forward about six sections into a position which overlooked the valley to the north with the road down the middle. No.4, on our left, distinguished themselves by improvising local bombing attacks. Geoffrey Howard led the way round a strongpoint called Sark Post, near the north end of Summer Lane, took it, and captured some sixty men and five machine guns.

Having passed through a course in a Lewis-gun school, I was glad of the opportunity of using this weapon otherwise than in the formal schemes and practices. Bisseker and Beck had planted our Lewis guns in good positions and we three took turns on each gun. When the evening came on, the Germans to the north of us (half left) began to move out. As the light failed the targets they presented improved. I spent some time directing other people's fire through my field glasses. Whether we hit any Germans I do not know. Since the range was long and the visibility deteriorating, I am doubtful.

In view of the hammering Headquarters had taken early in the day, when the Adjutant and Intelligence Officer had been severely wounded, Ian Bullough had led us splendidly. I was not alone in admiring the way he handled all four companies. Shortly after 6 p.m. he came round to tell No.1 that we would probably spend the night where we were. He also gave me a personal order. 'You will go down and get your head seen to.' I remained long enough to fix the Company's positions for the night, and then, accompanied by Tate, and in a mood wherein relief and reluctance were combined, I retraced my steps along Carey Trench to the Canal du Nord.

I have no memory of the walk back to the Canal, but I remember climbing down its east wall and up its west wall. There, standing on a parapet, I looked back over the ground we had covered and over the unforgettable day which was ending. At about an hour before sunset there had been a lull in the shelling. But now the guns on both sides were opening up again. The noise was rising as shells of many calibres were streaming in ever thicker droves and coveys over our heads. At first the din brought on a mood of exultation; not because the renewed bombardment would kill or maim Germans, but because it would bring the end of the war nearer. But I was lightheaded and the mood suddenly changed. I found myself thinking of the procession of dead leaves which, the autumn before at Dinard, my mother and I had watched whirling and somersaulting overhead as we sat under a hedge at sunset. This procession of dead leaves had reminded her of another sort of procession – of the souls of the men who had been killed in the war. The exaltation of the moment suddenly changed into melancholy. Now things were the other way round. The procession of vicious shells, streaming and screaming into the horizon, leaving snake-trails of vanishing sound in their wakes, had replaced that earlier procession of leaves, dead, but behaving as if not quite dead, as they were carried into oblivion.

I was suddenly aware of a hand on my arm. It was Oliver Baldwin who, in the failing light, looked handsome and rather formidable. I was surprised when he later told me that, while I was admiring the artillery display, I was uttering a soliloquy of praise and exhortation. 'Fine. Go on. Drive them out. Give it to them in the pants till they reach the Fatherland,' etc. I wondered if Oliver were attributing to me his own sentiments, for by the time he had joined me, that mood had passed. I recall a sense of kinship with Oliver, and of gratitude that we had been thrown together at that dramatic moment. As we parted he said he was glad to have personally discovered that my bloody state did not imply that my wound was mortal.

Tate helped me to a dressing station which had been improvised a few hours before in a large excavation of the canal-side at a point where the construction of a lock was planned. The sides of the canal were high, perpendicular, and made of concrete. Here my head was dressed with a generous application of iodine by a cheerful Scots Guards orderly. The field dressing was replaced by a bandage. Another Scottish orderly then led me in the direction of an advanced field dressing station. Thitherward I laboriously hobbled, aided by my stick, feeling like a cripple. On the way I met Wilfred Raffle, the medical officer of the Fourth Battalion, whose good wishes cheered me. He told me that my old battalion was camped in nearby trenches and was in good shape. I was conducted to a point in an open field where a horse-ambulance picked up stretcher cases. Such an ambulance was waiting for cargo, and I was about to climb in next to the driver when two small shells slothfully meandered down from the clouds and burst with much noise about thiry yards away. Their performance was rather like that of the stray shell which came down in the occupied dugout near Hendecourt. The ambulance driver did not know how long he would be waiting for his full complement and suggested that I should push ahead on foot. The organization seemed to be so haphazard that I decided to take his advice.

There followed a further laborious walk which ended at a main dressing station further back. There I parted from Tate. We wished each other good luck and I told him that I would be back soon. The main dressing station was at Demicourt – a large elephant-iron hut in the side of a sunken road. This place had well-organized medical services. While waiting there I was glad to meet two people I knew – Jolland, a Wesleyan padre who was interested in botany with whom I had had pleasant contacts, and a doctor called Drew who had once taken Raffle's place in the Fourth Battalion. Jolland supplied me with a mug of hot tea and some biscuits which were welcome. This main dressing station was in the zone of heavy batteries where there was loud continuous noise but no counter-shelling. At this stage I was having short spells of faintness.

There followed a short drive by ambulance, of which I have no recollection, to a place called Beaumetz-les-Cambrai which is about half a mile south of the Bapaume-Cambrai road, and about seventeen miles west of Cambrai. The further back one was conveyed, the more highly organized the services. Here was a field hospital of some capacity. As I stumbled into the dressing room of a large marquee, a wounded man lying prone on a table called out: 'Hullo Mr Blacker!' It was Ogden, who had been Treffry's and then Quincey Greene's servant in the Fourth Battalion – a likeable and intelligent man. He had wounds in a thigh (fractured femur) and in a knee, sustained when our First Battalion had stormed the canal at zero that morning. Having had an injection of morphia, his pain was bearable, and we had a chat about some of the people we had known in earlier days.

I was then steered out of the dressing room into what was called the waiting room, in which a friendly young padre gave me more tea and some bread and butter. I have retained through the decades a vivid – almost a haunting – memory of that waiting room at Beaumetz-les-Cambrai. We sat round a stove and the floor round us was tightly packed with stretcher-cases. At this stage of the day, and at this distance from the front, the noise was more intermittent than at the main dressing station which I had left an hour before. The assault on one's ears fluctuated in intensity depending on the proximity and the calibre of the batteries. My loss of blood caused a procession of inappropriate images. There was a background din of salvoes being fired and of the searing of shells diminishing in intensity as they rose in their trajectories and sped into the distance where their sound faded into inaudibility. They seemed to be saying goodbye to us. They reminded me of the salvoes of rockets which on the Fourth of June at Eton were admired by gaping riverside crowds as the rockets hissed their way upwards. These fireworks were beautiful and hurt no one, but the salvoes which were coursing over our heads and away from us into the eastern sky would maim and kill. They would do to other human beings what had been done to the figures packed on to the stretchers on all sides. I did not at first notice how, around us, the sounds expressive of physical suffering rose and fell. But soon the dimly lit marquee began to remind me of a torture chamber in which spasms of pain were being inflicted by invisible tormentors at fixed times, so that the cries of the victims were synchronized. I had not noticed at first how these choruses occurred rhythmically. This recognition came when I was falling into a fitful sleep. Some of these sounds were imitative. A man would emit a sigh or a howl of pain as he tried to move a limb or to invoke help. Another man would take it up and then another until it seemed that all the prostrate men on the packed stretchers were wailing in unison. A chorus would soar upwards into the ceiling of the marquee, revolve there, and then subside. I had never heard wolves howling at the moon by night; but the comparison came to mind. The sound would rise in a crescendo to a climax and then die down. I then noticed that these choruses would be started up by one of our salvoes, so that the crashes of the explosion, instantly followed by the diminuendo of shells speeding into the distance, would in its turn be followed by an agonized wailing as if in lament for what such salvoes had done to the sufferers on the stretchers and would do to others for whom they were destined. I wanted to doze off and lose consciousness, more especially as my head had begun to hurt. But I could not sleep. Instead I became agitated, depressed and restless.

I had noticed that the noisiest of the wounded men near me was a German of peculiar appearance. He was no more than a boy who had been severely wounded in the arm, chest and stomach. He was very thin with a greenish complexion and cup-like depressions, like yellow half-moons, under his eyes. His forehead tapered towards the crown and his lips were square with pain. His eyes and hair were pitch black so that he looked like a Red Indian. He kept up a continuous gasping moan punctuated by shrill noises. I made my way to him and asked if I could do anything. He looked at me fixedly and did not answer. He went on groaning. He was obviously delirious.

I asked a sister what my next move would be. I was told that it was not known for certain, but as many as possible of the stretcher cases and walking wounded were to be conveyed, probably by ambulance, to a railhead.

An ambulance duly arrived and I was put into it with four stretcher cases of whom one was the wounded German. I sat on a box with my back to a partition which separated me from the driver and an orderly, so that I faced backwards. After I had got in, the four stretcher cases were lifted into place with their heads at the partition end. The German was in the upper tier on my right. As soon as the ambulance began to move, his moaning turned to sharp cries. I tried to soothe him but could not. Two of the others, who were in pain but not delirious, began to curse the German, telling him to shut up: he was not the only one who was having hell.

We travelled in this way for about half an hour during which I got very cold. I dozed fitfully with pains in my head and knees. The German had periods of silence when he seemed to have lost consciousness. But then he would burst out: '*O Gott, O Gott, O Gott,*' repeated many times. Sometimes he seemed to be invoking his mother. Sometimes he sobbed: '*Nein, nein, O nein*' as if he was talking to his pain, saying he could not stand it. After what seemed a long drive the car stopped and remained still. I was woken up by a noise in the road outside the car; or was the noise coming from something inside the ambulance? I switched on the Orilux torch on my belt and was horrified by what at first I took to be a hallucination.

Standing facing me, brightly illuminated against the lowered curtain at the back of the ambulance, was the figure of a man, stark naked, with a bleeding gash in his chest and side. The German had climbed down from his stretcher in the upper tier on my right, had torn off his dressings and was supporting himself by his splinted arms outstretched over the two top stretchers on each side. His head was drooping on to his chest, and blood was running out of his side and mouth. In the flash of my electric torch, I momentarily thought that I was seeing the crucified Christ – or a parody of that figure, for his contorted face was more reptilian than human.

The orderly sitting next to the driver had got down and was unfixing the curtain at the back of the ambulance. But before he could do so, and before I could move, the figure in front of me staggered. His knees gave, he extended his arms, and then – horror unbelievable – fell backwards out of the ambulance so that his naked body crashed on the wet and flinty road. I had an impression that some people in uniform ran out and helped to carry the limp and stark figure indoors.

I was myself helped down to the road where, in another flash of my Orilux, I had a final glimpse of my travelling companion. As I left the scene I hoped – indeed I prayed – that he had been killed by the fall and would suffer no more.

In later years this nightmarish scene has several times come back. A cruci-fied figure with a reptilian face and a bleeding wound in the side looks down on me but does not see me. The figure staggers and is about to fall. I try to move forward to hold him up. But I have a handicap and I am too slow. On each side of me are prostrate men, suffering and inert, with bleeding wounds.

I was piloted into another large marquee which, I later learned, formed part of a casualty clearing station at Beaulencourt, south of Bapaume. Here rows of men – walking wounded – were sitting on benches. Some were having wounds dressed. Others, including myself, were given massive injections in the left triceps of tetanus anti-toxin. My knee joints had stiffened in the cold and hurt ferociously when I tried to walk. But I did not mind. Indeed the pain was comforting. Its effects mattered to nobody but myself. How different from my predicament in the early morning when I had to lead a company!

From my bench I was helped into a ward where a kind-looking sister was sitting behind a screen, her face lit by a green-shaded paraffin lamp. She allotted me a bed and gave me some pyjamas. I undressed and wrapped myself in the blankets which were folded on the bed. Then another cup of tea and biscuits. Though I had eaten nothing for more than twenty-four hours, the events in the ambulance had so cut my appetite as to put me off solid food. Cold afflicted me more than my wound or my joints. A nice-mannered orderly brought me an extra blanket and a hot water bottle which, when hugged and applied to front and back, radiated comfort like a new vital centre.

I dozed uneasily till about five when I was roused from bad dreams and told that I was to be moved as a stretcher case. Still wrapped up in pyjamas, I was carried on a stretcher to a siding where a Red Cross train was waiting. My uniform and such belongings as I had taken into the battle, including revolver, compass and maps, were packed into a sort of haversack from which I did not thereafter part.

I seem to remember that a RAMC officer came round the train and asked me if I was in pain. My answer, whatever it was, caused him to give me an injection as a result of which I dozed off into semi-oblivion. Quickly things took a turn for the better; everything became basically all right. The wounded German who had fallen out of the ambulance came to mind. He was now physically restored and serene in a happier world. I caught a glimpse of his face on which was the ghost of a smile. The guardsman who had reminded me of President Wilson and whose face had been blown off, had also been made whole and had begun a new life somewhere. No.1 Company had had a quiet night under a bank parallel with the Hindenburg Support Line and the next morning had advanced with minimum casualties towards Orival Wood. Bisseker, Beck, Tate, Carnham and Sergeant Peck were safe. The war was going splendidly and would soon be over. What a relief for my parents to know that I was not in worse shape. My knee-joints were hurting less. I was basking in a drug-induced euphoria.

Such were my thoughts and mood. I roused myself twice for light meals which I ate without repulsion. Indeed the second was almost delectable. At about two o'clock the drowsiness began to lift and I began a long letter on which I have drawn for much of this account.

When I was writing in the date (28 September) it came to me as something of a shock tempered by surprise that it was on that exact date three years ago that Robin had been killed. No one could doubt that I had had more luck in the Canal du Nord than he had had amid the chalk-pits of Loos. The thought of guardian angels (in which my old Irish nurse firmly believed) came to mind. Why, I asked, had mine protected me so much better than his had protected him? This thought led to another: perhaps Robin had functioned as my guardian angel the day before; or he might indeed have taken on part of the job for the last three years without my knowing or noticing it. I was disquieted by this thought. He had been far worthier of preservation than I. Our roles in September 1915 should have been reversed. He got out to France before I did. He was quickly killed whereas I had survived for three years. But he need not have been so pressed to get killed; and I need not have been kept dallying so long. In yesterday's battle I should have been looking after him, not he me.

But what is all this, I next asked myself? Is it anaemia or morphia which now makes me feel so convinced that his world and mine interpenetrate? And is it my self-centred obtuseness which has prevented me from realizing this all the time? Probably anaemia and morphia at the same time. But in any case I should be thankful – though I did not know for certain to whom. Meanwhile the Red Cross train was slowly meandering through an autumnal countryside; and I had not even begun my long letter! The writing of the date had distracted me.

By about four in the afternoon my knee-joints had begun to hurt again and I found that I was tired of lying on my right side – the left side of my head being painful to pressure. And in a small way my anxieties began again about No.1 Company.

I have conflicting memories of when it was that I learned that our destination was the friendly little town of Le Tréport where, in June, I had spent a happy three days with Scottie Caldwell. I may have been told by someone on the train. Or I may not have known until we got there, which we did at five in the evening after a slow transit. In failing light I was conveyed by ambulance up a steep hill to Lady Murray's hospital which I had not heard of before.

The hospital was pleasantly situated with a good view on the top of a chalk cliff behind the town. I was carried up to a well-appointed room on the third floor. A large window gave on to an ample lawn with, in the middle, a trim tennis court. The lawn was surrounded by beech trees which were beginning to assume autumnal tints. The room contained two beds other than mine. One was occupied by an American officer who left the next day.

While having supper in bed I was visited by Lady Murray. I noted that she was an ample woman with a gentle voice and gracious manners; and that in her presence I felt something of a brigand not having shaved for three days.

The next morning a breezy doctor (Captain Newman) examined my wound in the surgery. After probing, he pulled out a piece of metal the size of a bean and removed a large blood clot. No inflammation or sepsis. A strip of gauze was inserted. Soon after I was X-rayed. No more metal was discovered.

14

THE END OF THE WAR

When I parted from Tate on the evening of 27 September, I told him I would do my best to get back soon. In the sequel, I did not get back for over three weeks. I rejoined the Battalion on Tuesday, 22 October at a place called Carnières, about as far east of Cambrai as the ruins of Bourlon Wood were west of it.

Carnières, we found, was located about five miles from the middle of Cambrai along the road to Le Cateau. This last place name came as something of a shock. It prised one violently back to what most of us felt was the 'prehistoric' period of September 1914.[1] I remember reacting strongly to a signpost pointing to *Le Cateau* and *Landrécies*, both powerfully evocative names. They told us that we were about to enter a new phase of the war which would revive and perhaps rectify the past. Then we had been falling back to the south and west; now we were advancing to the east and north.

Carnières was in a better condition than I expected. It seemed that the Germans had withdrawn or been hustled out without serious fighting. Battalion headquarters occupied a well-appointed mess with papered walls and intact doors. It contained a mirrored cupboard, two upholstered armchairs and – an unfamiliar object – a harmonium.

The avidly sought news was both good and bad: the good more important than the bad, but the bad such as to depress and annoy. First it was good to learn that in the course of its advance from the Canal du Nord, whence I had made my exit, the Battalion had had light casualties. But there had been one dire loss. On 9 October Scottie Caldwell had been killed. I thought of our pleasant three days in Le Tréport in June when we had sat on the beach and he had diffidently told me about his school life.

---

[1] A fierce battle had been fought at Le Cateau in August 1914 when the Allies were retreating (ed.).

Then I discovered that all the letters which had been posted to me at Dinard, whence my mother had written every day, had been thrown back into the Army Post office franked 'Address Unknown.' This event was of no real importance; yet it was acutely irritating. It was some weeks later that I first heard of Robbie Ross's death on 1 October.

Then, lastly, in the absence of Jimmy Coats, I was made adjutant of the Battalion. My dismay, which was excessive, had many causes, among which was a vivid awareness of how little I knew about Army Regulations. What, I asked myself, *did* I know? When I searched my memory I drew a discouraging blank. So much had I to learn that I could make a dire fool of myself several times over before the lacunae were filled. A splendid opportunity if I hoped to become a regular soldier. As things were, an unwelcome and forbidding prospect. But in the event my troubles did not last long and they might have been worse.

I had joined the Battalion at Carnières on 22 October. There we stayed till Thursday 31 October on which day we moved to a village called St. Hilaire, a mile to the north-east. On the afternoon of the following day (1 November) we marched to a place called Vertain, north-east of Solesnes and east of the Valenciennes – Le Cateau road. I retain scrappy and colourless memories of these nine days. The best experience was meeting and making friends with A.D. Cross, known to most people as 'Ex,' or 'old Ex,' or 'Archie.' This peculiar man remained a close friend for about seventeen years. He was about four years older than myself and had come to the Regiment from the Leicestershire Yeomanry in December 1916. He was unusual for several reasons among which was an obsessional hatred of the staff. The higher the individual's rank and the larger the unit he served, the more intense were Ex's feelings. He might tolerate a staff captain attached to a brigade, but anyone of higher status who wore red tabs or red on his hat inspired him with such venomous feelings that when such a person came near you could sense him inwardly buzzing like a wasp.

But Cross did not mind his leg being pulled, and his aversions caused amusement to his friends. If he were in the mess, you had but to ask him if he had come across any members of the staff that morning and you were kept amused for as long as you cared to listen. He had an inexhaustible repertoire of derogatory anecdotes; but he was perceptive and never bored his listeners. His was a polarized character which ran to extremes. On occasions he could be extraordinarily kind and generous, often in surreptitious ways, so that you did not hear of what he had done till long afterwards. But if someone gave him offence he could be an unforgiving enemy.

While Jimmy Coats was on leave and while I was occupying the adjutant's chair, Cross was appointed temporary assistant adjutant. In this capacity he was definitely helpful. In civilian life he was connected with a flourishing family business in Glasgow and he had had useful experience of business methods.

He used to say that he had his full share of Scottish canniness. He knew how to deal with money and I found that he could cope better than I with certain administrative problems. Our views on the war were much the same. It should, he said, be stopped as soon as possible. The Germans should, of course, pay reparations, indemnities etc.; but these were less important items on the post-war agenda than the steps which should be taken to prevent the thing happening again. He was an abstemious man who disliked politics and politicians but was keen on horses. While at Carnières we went for a few rides. He showed consideration towards all Other Ranks with whom he was popular.

At this time letters from home showed much elevation of mood. On 18 October, my mother wrote as follows: 'We woke up this morning to a wintry day. There was a cold mist and the autumnal feeling had passed out of the air.' My mother was sensitive to the seasons. 'But now,' she continued, 'the sun has come out and it is a glorious winter's day . . . the papers have just arrived with the news of the taking of Lille and Ostend . . . I simply long to see you and have you with us for a little while.' And the next day (19 October) she wrote: 'Here, in spite of a little reaction after the first *allégresse*, which was brought by the thought of peace, we have been happier than at any time during the last four years.' My father, she said, was completely changed and had 'come alive' again. She went on to say: 'It affects me curiously to see this change as it makes me realize how unhappy he has been all this time. I think that he has now perhaps swung too much to the other extreme and is too hopeful as he thinks that Germany will accept all the allied conditions without delay and that the war is virtually over. I pray that he may be right, and I cannot tell you how I long for things to get to the stage when the fighting is stopped. After that, the final negotiations can take as long as they like.' My mother also said in this letter: 'I cannot tell you how homesick I am for you these days. I want the sight of you, to get into personal touch with you and have you under the roof. After a separation has been prolonged beyond a certain point, letters get to mean little and do not fill the emptiness which forms when you are longing for someone's actual presence.'

The intense desire to have me near her came over my mother at this time because of feelings which had been evoked by the unprecedented course of the war and which were therefore new. These feelings were compounded of exultation over the allied victories, awareness that I was actively involved again after being wounded (when it had seemed that I might possibly be out for good), and fear that, after being spared for so long, I might be involved in a last-minute fatality. Fatalities are more likely to occur when things are accelerating than when they are slowing down, so that the accelerating approach of peace intensified anxieties.

During our stay at Carnières we did not know if we would be called on to do another attack. Most of us hoped that we would not, though all knew that we would soon be continuing the advance to the east which had begun at St.

Léger. In the event, we moved out of Carnières on the last day of October, and marched to the nearby village of St. Hilaire which lay to the north-east. This was the first of several short moves. I had a fixture in St. Hilaire before the Battalion: I had to attend a court-martial which did not keep me for more than ten minutes. I noted that the Battalion's brief stay in St. Hilaire was pleasant, our mess being located in a room with a piano and carpet.

The next day (Friday 1 November) it came in that we had to move again that afternoon and fight a battle on the following Monday (4 November). News of Austria's unconditional acceptance of terms had reached us the previous Tuesday so that we speculated on what the impending battle would be like seeing that the day of reckoning for the Central Powers was so near at hand. There might possibly be little resistance.

The afternoon move took us to the village of Vertain which lay to the north-east of the larger township of Solesnes which had figured in the 'prehistoric' battles of September 1914. My diary tells me that the billeting in Vertain was done by Leonard Gibbs, that we slept comfortably in tents, and that we were not shelled.

The following day (Saturday 2 November) the Battalion was moved further north-east to Ruesnes, where, arriving in the evening, we took over from a battalion of the Oxford and Bucks Light Infantry. Ruesnes (then little more than a cluster of houses round a crossroads) was again little damaged and the out-going commanding officer made an apt remark: 'One can be lured into a sense of false security by the standing houses round you.' It seemed peculiar that the front line was (or was thought to be) but a few hundred yards away.

The main object of the battle planned for 4 November was the taking of Villers Pol. Villers Pol was a small village, somewhat larger than Ruesnes, which was skirted on its west side by a stream called the Rhonelle (fordable in two places which would have to be crossed by troops advancing from the west). The village lay about 300 yards to the west of a major road which ran northwards from Le Quesnoy to Valenciennes. This road was to play a part in the day's activities. It was christened 'The Blue Line.'

The plan for the battle had been carefully though hurriedly drawn up. Boundaries between advancing units, forming-up places, pauses in the creeping barrage etc., were shown on maps circulated beforehand. All seemed nicely set when an unexpected order came in. 'Send out patrols.' The Germans were apparently retiring. They had definitely moved back on our left and were ranging with high shrapnel on Villers Pol. Did this high shrapnel imply that they had withdrawn from the village?

Ian Bullough was again commanding the Battalion. He sent orders to Wilkinson and Spencer (respectively commanding Nos.1 and 3 Companies which were to lead the attack) to probe into Villers Pol and try to establish contact with the enemy. Off went these two with their companies at 7.30 pm. Headquarters followed at 11 pm., stopping for half an hour at a place called

Mortry Farm about a mile and a half west of Villers Pol. Thence Headquarters moved forward, aiming to reach a site on the east side of the village which Ian had selected on the map.

We moved from Mortry Farm along an abominable road towards the village. As we approached we saw and heard good-sized enemy shells falling into Villers Pol which (we inferred) the Germans had evacuated. The sky cleared and the stars came out. Our approach road dipped between embankments of the stream above-mentioned – the Rhonelle. Both sides had been thickly strewn with wire and shelled with 'sneeze gas' which made your eyes and nose run. We crossed the Rhonelle at one of the two fording places and clambered past various obstacles seemingly prepared for defence and then abandoned; and Headquarters were cautiously advancing into the village when we ran into long-range machine-gun fire of sufficient liveliness to cause Ian Bullough to decide to send someone forward to take a look. Tiles were clattering down into the street. Accompanied by Sergeant Freeman, who had served in No.1 with Watson-Smyth, I cautiously crept along a street wall with my Colt automatic at the ready. A brick fell ahead of me and I saw a movement. I challenged and a familiar voice responded in English. It was Guardsman Couzens, who had been my orderly in No.1, sitting on a pile of bricks. Captain Wilkinson and some others, he said, were down there. He pointed to a door leading into a cellar, through which a chink of light could be seen. There I found Alex, Yam and Spencer in good form smoking and eating biscuits by candlelight. Greetings and mirth. A cheerful moment. Ian Bullough was quickly with us. Wilkinson and Spencer reported that their companies had found their way unopposed through the village in the dark. But, emerging on its east side, they had been met by lively machine-gun fire which seemed to come from the Blue Line – the main road west of the village running north-south which seemed to be held by Germans with plenty of machine guns. It had been felt that some preparation would do no harm in an attack on the Blue Line, so the two companies had dug in about two hundred yards on our side of it (the west side). Hereabouts were some minor roads on the outskirts of the village, and some sort of line had been established.

A lively discussion ensued in our cellar. Seeing that the Germans had definitely evacuated Villers Pol and for the moment seemed to be holding the Blue Line in strength, could the gunners' plans be changed at such short notice? Could a barrage be put down by zero hour (6 am) as far ahead as the Blue Line which would become the Battalion's first objective? How about units on each flank? I recall that Ian was understandably dubious but said that he would do his best. I also recall that Alex had expressed himself strongly: and that someone asked if zero could be postponed till later than 6 a.m. and a revised programme worked out. (If the barrage were not geared to movements of the infantry, there was a risk of our own troops being caught.)

Ian and I left as soon as we could and made for the place he had picked as our headquarters. The upshot of some quick talk with the Brigade was that there would be no change in the timing. Zero would be at 6 a.m. as arranged, but objectives were defined east of the Blue Line.

The fact of the matter was that new problems, of which the army had had but little experience, were raised when the enemy were retiring in their own time. Among the troubles which can arise is the formation of gaps between adjacent units belonging to different higher formations; and things are not made easier for gunners who have to change their targets at very short notice. Nothing is worse for morale than for men to come under shell-fire from their own side.

Revised orders were issued during the early hours of 4 November which were rushed round to the companies. But I felt some disquiet (justified as it turned out) as to whether they had been received and had had their proper effect. I knew that everyone was sleepy. Ian Bullough agreed that I had better make contact with Alex and Spencer to make sure that they knew exactly what was going to happen and that they were properly in gear at the juncture of their two companies. I would wait on the road from which they were to jump off at zero. Ian would join me there shortly after six o'clock. I first went to No.3 which was furthest from the village. To my astonishment I found Spencer, whom I reached at 5.30 a.m. (half an hour before the attack was due to start), asleep with his two junior officers in a narrow dugout. Spencer held a high rank among captains. Unlike the rest of us, he was, I think, a substantive captain. He had spent much of his time at Windsor having come to the regiment in March 1915 from the Artists Rifles. I politely but urgently alerted this somnolent trio, delivering from the Commanding Officer a message about being specially careful about keeping close contact with No.1 on their right.

I then turned back to No.1, my old company, which I found on their toes and in fine form for the impending battle. I have retained a vivid picture of Alex Wilkinson whose exuberance had not been impaired by lack of sleep. He had positioned himself at about the centre of his company extended along a minor road confronting the Blue Line which ran parallel some 200 yards away.

The weather was fine and cold, and Alex walked to and fro stamping his feet and literally champing for the battle. 'This is going to be a day to remember, No.1. . . . We are going to have a damned fine battle this morning, No.1. . . . As you move forward, keep the best line you can, keep shooting and don't bunch. . . . As soon as you see the Hun, let him have it. . . . Our direction is due east, so make for the rising sun.' Rarely in the Regiment's history can a company commander have communicated bellicosity and fighting spirit more contagiously. The men were laughing, evidently enjoying the tense moment. At six o'clock a salvo of our shrapnel came over from behind us high in the sky. The salvo burst about a quarter of a mile ahead of our road, perhaps well ahead by design in order to be well clear of our position. The barrage seemed thin to me. 'Magnificent barrage, No.1,' shouted Alex as he clambered out of the road and headed eastward. As he led the way, with platoons well strung out on each side close behind, he kept his chin down as if he were forcing his way against a strong headwind, his face protected by his tin hat. I recall one or two German red rockets bursting in the sky well ahead – a signal to their artillery. A battery of German field-guns opened, the shells coming in low – at almost head level. As one of these passed close on Alex's left, he deliberately shifted the position of his head so that, instead of facing to his front, he faced half-right for a second. After the shell had burst behind him, with equal deliberation, as if conforming with an item of drill, he then turned his head back to its original forward-facing position as if saying to the German gunner: 'You're not getting me this time.'

A steady pace forward was maintained with the platoons keeping up in a well-spaced line. Not long after Yam Eccles followed leading No.2 in artillery formation. The creeping barrage was supposed to lift a hundred yards every three minutes; but No.1 seemed to me to be moving forward faster than that. By this time the sun was peeping over the horizon. I watched Alex and No.1 merge into a misty distance, paying no attention to a continuous small-arms fire. I saw them disappear with regret wishing that I could have been with them. There for several minutes I stood in solitude, feeling lonely and disconsolate. Not long after, Philip Wells and some Headquarters staff joined me. We waited there for Ian Bullough to arrive.

A peculiar thing then happened which caused some painful stress to Ian Bullough. But luck was with him and no harm ensued. Probably through No.3's right not advancing as fast as No.1's left and perhaps through No.3 moving too much to their own right so that they were behind No.1's left, a gap formed between the two companies of which the two flanks overlapped each other above and below the gap.

How long it was after zero that Bullough and Gibbs decided that the moment had come for them to reconnoitre the position reached by the companies, I do not know. But set out together they did, after it had slipped Ian's memory that I was awaiting his arrival on the road from which the attack had started.

It was by mischance that, in moving forward, these two found their way into the gap which had formed between the two companies. Their composure was short-lived. The more ground they covered, meeting and seeing nobody and finding no casualties, the more anxious and mystified they became. Finally they found themselves in front of a wood surrounded by a thick hedge behind which they heard noises. They peeped cautiously through, and to their amazement beheld a party of over a hundred Germans sitting and standing about. Instead of acting on the unsoldierly precept about discretion being the better part of valour and tactfully withdrawing, Ian and Leonard drew their revolvers, burst through the hedge, and shouted at the party that they were prisoners. The bulk then moved off but a remainder of about thirty gave themselves up. Ian, however, was not consoled by this remarkable feat. He had lost his Battalion. God only knew what had happened. He later described himself sitting disconsolately by a roadside wishing that a German shell would come along and put an end to his troubles. But at this moment two of our Battalion runners appeared smiling and all problems were solved. Later the Brigadier appeared in excellent humour and the Battalion was leap-frogged by Grenadiers.

Not long afterwards Battalion Headquarters established itself in a cellar at a place called La Flaque farm, east of Villers Pol, where the company commanders assembled and reported. Everyone was very tired and sleepy, but Alex delivered a vivid account of No.1's battle. That evening Headquarters moved back from La Flaque farm to Villers Pol where we spent the night in relative comfort. And that night Jimmie Coats returned from leave. I spent the next morning going over papers with him.

In the afternoon (of 5 November) the Battalion moved a short distance north-east into the château of a small village called Wargnies-le-Grand. A sticky march along an execrable road. The external structure of the château, which was situated in the middle of a small wood, was almost undamaged. But inside, the destruction, chaos and dirt were almost unbelievable. All windows had been broken; and I recall how some drawers in a chest of drawers had been used as a latrine. I had the impression that, before the Germans had moved out, discipline had broken down, and that the filth they left behind was designed to make the place uninhabitable for the British army. The drawers contained presents for the incoming troops.

On the following morning (Wednesday 6 November) German gunners unexpectedly shelled the château of Wargnies-le-Grand and put a shell through the roof. Three men in No.1 company, including Corporal Doe and Guardsman Penny, were killed and others wounded. The château, we decided, was no longer habitable, so Harold Lake and I looked round for alternative accommodation. This, for Headquarters, was found in the house of two old ladies whose hospitality (I remarked in my diary) matched anything I had hitherto come across in France. We spent a pleasanter evening under their roof than in the squalor of the château.

The two old ladies were the first French civilians whose stories I had properly listened to. I described our conversation – in fact I gave their words – in a letter. One of them said: '*Vous ne pouvez pas vous rendre comte du soulagement que je ressent en vous voyant ici. Vous êtes nos amis! Et vous ne pouvez pas vous imaginer ce que ça veut dire de vivre parmis des amis après ces quatre ans de tyrannie.*' She kept repeating that she was surrounded by friends as if the fact could not be properly grasped. She had come to look on herself as shut in on all sides by enemies by whom she was mistrusted, disliked, suspected and exploited. Her life had become set in this nightmare of discord. '*Je sens qu'une lourdeur a été levée de ma poitrine. Je ne peut pas exprimer ce que j'éprouve – ce que nous éprouvons tous! Nous marchons tous dans l'air. Nous ne savons plus ou nous sommes: car vous êtes nos amis, n'est ce pas, Monsieur, nos amis.*' She wept and squeezed my arm as she repeated that we were her friends. I can still see her ecstatic face looking up at me. When, before we left, I tried to induce her to accept some francs to cover what she had spent on us, such a look of pain came over her face, such a note of distress entered her voice, that it would have been the acme of boorishness to press her.

The lined and radiant face of this old lady at Wargnies-le-Grand has remained with me over the half century. Its expression of intense gratitude and joy had a transcendent quality as if it were radiating from another world. I later wished that I had kept in touch with this old lady, for I have never in my life been the recipient of more intense goodwill from a stranger.

The Battalion was occupied the next morning in cleaning up the yard and outhouses of the chateau where, again, the filth had to be seen to be believed. And that evening we moved forward to Bavay, starting in the afternoon and planning to get in after nine. It was a slow and tiring march with many stops along a congested road which led east from between Wargnies-le-Grand and Wargnies-le-Petit and passed through a place called St. Vaast-la-Vallé where the congestion was at its worst. A bridge had been blown up and the traffic jammed in the roads on both sides was solid, an unmoving block of vehicles and horses.

When we reached Bavay about midnight, the streets were deserted and the place seemed dead. No sound; no lights; little destruction visible in the darkness except that two crossroads had been blown up. The craters were massive. All nearby windows had been blown in, roofs were damaged, and the adjacent streets were littered with tiles. A street had been assigned as Headquarter's objective on the east side of the village. Thither we marched – past the church which, in the darkness, seemed intact. Our street was near the church.

Two of us opened the door of a good-sized house and entered a dark hall. A streak of light was visible under a door at the end of a short passage. I opened the door. Below me were stairs leading into a basement. Out went the light when I opened the door. I switched on my Orilux. The sight I saw has remained one of my most vivid pictures of the first war. Three frightened women's faces, clustered together and brightly lit by my torch were craning their necks upwards from the bottom. They looked like nestling birds with open mouths. I shouted to them to come up. '*Montez. Rien à craindre. Nous sommes Anglais.*' Shrill squeals of excitement. A stream of people, mostly neighbours who had taken refuge in the capacious basement, swarmed up, tumbling over each other in excitement. They wrung our hands and danced about us. An old woman fell sobbing on my neck: '*Après quatre ans, quatre ans, quatre ans.*' There were cries of '*Vive les Anglais.*' A pandemonium of excitement and joy. They produced coffee and baked potatoes which we accepted gratefully, being decidedly hungry. They produced other food which they insisted on our eating because, they said, they had saved it for this moment. They called us '*Sauveurs, Libérateurs, Bienfaiteurs.*' They insisted on my going downstairs to say '*Bonjour*' to the proprietor of the house, a bed-ridden old man who was nearly speechless with emotion. Our limbers did not get in till after midnight having had a tough time getting through the traffic jam at another stream south of the town.

The next morning (8 November) I was woken up early by a tremendous chatter in the street outside. Voluble chopped French in men's and women's voices reached us, some of it with an unfamiliar mixture of clipped German words. Then I heard the strains of a piano. The instrument, found in a house opposite, had been carried into the street. Bentley, one of our orderlies who could play, was performing. Troops from Headquarters and some of the companies lustily raised their voices and were joined by civilians of all ages and both sexes. The most popular air was: 'The Bells are Ringing for me and my Girl,' which had a good lilt which the French soon picked up. Then a dramatic thing happened. Bentley struck up the first bars of the *Marseillaise*. A Frenchman with a raucous voice gave tongue and the tune was caught up by women. More men joined and it was not long before the whole street – indeed the whole town – were singing the *Marseillaise*. A volume of triumphant sound rose in a vibrating ecstasy of fierce happiness. It was the first time for four years that this rousing song had been heard. '*Le jour de gloire est arrivé.*'

Jimmie Coats having returned I became nominally assistant adjutant. In fact I was a supernumerary Captain attached to Headquarters and had no definitely prescribed job. I made myself useful not only to Headquarters but also to the Companies as a sort of liaison officer and interpreter. I spent the morning walking about Bavay having made contact with the civil authorities. The place was decorated with flags and full of rejoicing. Everyone behaved well. No sign of drunkenness. It came through in the afternoon that next morning we were to take Maubeuge. It may have been then that a declaration from General Foch was made known. It was to the effect that – 'When the British Army reaches the Mons-Maubeuge Road, they may leave the rest to me.'

In the afternoon there were conferences and scrutiny of maps; at 11.30 pm, primed with cake and tea, we set out on a nine-mile march to Maubeuge. On the road Headquarters were in good spirits and good voice. They swung along cheerfully in the darkness. Someone next to whom I was marching remarked that the British soldier revealed an important part of himself in his singing during marches – an exuberant, nostalgic and fatalistic side. It occurred to me to wonder how, in the matter of singing on the march, we compared with the French and the Germans. The Belgians, I knew from four years before, were good.

After covering about a third of the way we marched through the small town of Longueville. There singing was stopped, and we trudged on in silence. We reached a farm by the roadside where a discreet light was visible. We were to relieve our First Battalion and it was at this farm that a rendezvous had been made. Here was waiting E.K.Digby who was commanding the First Battalion.

He had been its adjutant during the Battle of Loos (at the time Robin was killed). A handsome and energetic man about a year older than myself, much respected and with something of the aura of a veteran.

Digby, Bullough and Coats sat at a lamplit table in the parlour of the farmhouse. Outside everything was quiet except for occasional bursts of distant machine-gun fire. Digby thought that the Germans had retired and that they would probably move out of Maubeuge without offering resistance. Indeed they might have done so already. While we were talking, the faint high-pitched sound of an approaching shell became unexpectedly audible. The sound rose in the familiar crescendo and the shell burst within a hundred yards of our window. Digby, who was talking at the time, stopped for a moment, said 'Damn,' and then finished the sentence which had been interrupted. A few more whizz-bangs came down near, one close enough to light up the room with its burst. But no harm was done.

The conference over, Brassey and Coats rode ahead to a school at a crossroad some 600 yards further along the route to Maubeuge, and I waited behind with Headquarters at the farm. The shelling stopped. We had been lucky. The Germans might well be retiring. It was not long before a message came for us to move ahead. We marched along silently in the darkness. We skirted a large mine-crater in the road, newly exploded. (Commendably soon afterwards it was filled by a section of good old Fourth Battalion.)

Further on we came to an estaminet where Brassey and Coats were in conference with the O.C. of the First Battalion Irish Guards who were advancing on our right. A beaming old lady kept us supplied with coffee. Here we stayed till zero hour (5 am) when the companies began their advance in artillery formation through the position held by our First Battalion. The big road from Longueville to Maubeuge formed the boundary between the Irish Guards and ourselves.

The forward movement was slow. It was beginning to get light when we reached the outskirts of Maubeuge. A comic incident was then enacted. A fat and moustached Frenchman making signs stood in the road in front of Headquarters as we approached. When within speaking distance he asked in a loud voice if any of us could speak French. He had something important to say. I fell out and he led me into his roadside house. He shouted for his family, formed them up behind him, and, in a dramatic stage whisper, told me that he had stolen from the departing Germans – from a high-ranking officer, in fact – a map showing their artillery positions. He produced the map. He hoped that I could obtain some recognition of his action, and would I take his name? I asked him to write his name and address on the map and assured him that it would be forwarded at once with a report. I remember that it was difficult to get away from this excited man – which I was keen to do since Headquarters had been steadily moving away from us along the road since I had entered his house. The stolen map and a report were quickly sent on to the Brigade; but I doubt if the German gunners continued to occupy for long the positions shown on the map. I heard no more of the matter.

When I caught up with Headquarters, I found five German prisoners tagging along behind them. Three had been sent along by our No.4 Company and two had come from the Irish Guards. They were under-sized, unshaved, dazed and broken men who hardly spoke. The Regimental Sergeant Major had turned them into a carrying party and they were laden with our officers' mess kit.

Maubeuge was captured without a battle. We moved forward slowly without opposition in brightening daylight. Cautiously at first, civilians began to emerge from their houses, and, as we moved eastwards into the old fortified town, the crowds became denser. Their reactions were the same as those of the civilians of Bavay. We were hailed with unrestrained enthusiasm. Most of the men were wearing hats. They took them off and held them at arm's length high over their heads as we passed, straining to hold them as high as possible. The women clapped their hands. Some stood in the street with coffee pots and baskets of bread and cakes. The whiteness of the bread and its apparent abundance surprised me. I later confirmed that we were being offered reserves of food which had been saved for this occasion. The civilian population had expected our arrival within a day or two and several had baked bread in anticipation.

As soon as the onlookers beheld our five German prisoners, their demeanor instantly changed. In the middle of their exuberance they would suddenly fix and point: '*Regardez. Des Allemands!*' They would then burst into derisive laughter. Some bent forward and pointed with contorted faces. Others put their thumbs to their noses and spat. Most clapped their hands exclaiming: '*Ah! Très Bien! Très Bien!*!' Two women burst into paroxysms of rage and shook their fists: '*Ah! Les Brigands! Les Voleurs! Assassins! Pilleurs!*!' Or – '*Vaches! Chameux! Crapules!*' We stopped in front of a house with iron railings. A crowd formed round the five cowed prisoners, jeering and hurling insults. The R.S.M. ordered the five men to get behind the railings. There they stood, pale, silent, exhausted, looking at their feet as if in a trance. A crone with dishevelled hair approached to within a yard of the railings where she screamed and spat like a mad woman. '*Oh! Les Voilà, Les Bêtes, Les Cochons! Oh La Vermine!*' She foamed through her toothless gums and became incomprehensible. The word '*Arracher*' was repeated with a clawing gesture directed at the men behind the railings and at her own face, as if she wanted to tear out their eyes.

With a stream of civilians keeping up with us on the pavements we marched through the town which was quiet. No shelling. Headquarters finally settled itself in a tolerably comfortable house on the eastern side where an orderly room was established; and the companies dug in on the high ground east of the town. Some posts were established in a cemetery on that side. My diary tells me something that I have wholly forgotten – that from 8.30 p.m. to midnight on Saturday 9 November, feeling under-employed, I took a watch for Yam Eccles, part of which was spent in this cemetery. Not a good place to get shelled in, Yam and I had earlier agreed. No humour in having tombstones come down on one's head.

It was also, I think, on the morning of 9 November that two formidable personalities met and conferred in our Orderly Room. They were the Divisional Commander (Torquil Matheson) and the Brigadier (Champion de Crespigny). For some forgotten reason I sat in during part of the time. My recollection is that Torquil, a dark handsome man, did most of the talking. The Brigadier (Crawley to most of us), a powerful athlete who has been mentioned before in this story, listened expressionlessly without moving or saying much. Indeed he gave the impression of being acutely bored. The question of a further advance was not raised. We had, after all, reached the Mons-Maubeuge road; the Generalissimo had spoken; and it might be that the rest was being left to him.

On Sunday 10 November I had a strong desire to see again No.3 Company of the old Fourth Battalion. I visited them briefly in the morning and had a word with Clive Piggott. He told me that the drums were going to beat the retreat during the afternoon. Could I come? I could and did.

I retain a clear image of the scene which was both incongruous in its immediate context and yet fitting as the end of a fine and creditable story. The population of Maubeuge turned out in force in their best Sunday clothes and, in a public square, a delegation of citizens presented to George Edwards no less than three large bouquets of flowers. There he stood in front of a detachment of the Fourth Battalion, tall, handsome, immaculate, composed and austere, somehow out of place amid the flowers and applauding civilians; yet, as judged by those who had served under him during the war years, no recipient of floral or other honours could have been more deserving.

George, who could not speak French, may have felt an embarrassment he did not show; and some people may have felt that his incomprehension of what the French were saying, coupled with the three large bouquets which an orderly was holding for him, combined to produce an element of humour. I found the occasion deeply moving and would have liked to tell the assembled populace, who knew nothing about the man standing before them, how well-deserved their gifts were.

I quote from a letter which I began on the evening of 11 November and finished next evening: 'Today is the reddest of red-letter days. We had, in fact, been expecting what has happened. The news about the German plenipotentiaries passing through our lines at Guise was wired round quickly. Also the news about the abdication of the Kaiser and the Crown Prince and about the mutiny in the German Navy. When therefore we heard last night that the time limit for the ultimatum would expire at eleven this morning, we were prepared.

'We had got up after a night on the floor in our clothes and were dressing when the telephone buzzed. Jimmie Coats picked up the receiver and addressed a character call Jim-Jack Evans, our Brigade-Major. Coats said: 'Hullo Jim-Jack' and listened. When, while listening, his face suddenly lit up we knew that the moment had come. Hostilities, he told us, were to cease at eleven; we were to adopt a defensive position; and there was to be no fraternization or intercourse of any sort with the enemy.' I added in my letter that I could now say that we were in Maubeuge which we had taken in a bloodless battle two days before. I added: 'The news about the armistice ran round like fire. Runners, signallers etc. were asleep nearby, rolled up on the floor. Jimmie gave them the news. Faces radiating joy emerged from blankets and everyone struggled to their feet. Pandemonium! A rush among the orderlies for the job of taking the news round to the Companies. Five minutes later we heard in the distance a faint sound of cheering coming from the cultivated fields beyond the town.'

There is little left to tell. Later in the morning I went up to the 'defensive position' east of the town where exuberance reigned. Gas helmets had been discarded and, as if prison doors had been opened, a spirit of liberation reigned. Gaiety and abandon. While I was chatting with people in No.1, a lively sound of horses' hooves reached us and, along a major road leading east from Maubeuge, a detachment of cavalry appeared. When they trotted past, the infantrymen standing by the roadside gave vent to mixed feelings. The mounted men looked fine, spick and span, their horses in splendid condition. Someone remarked 'Good to see you at last,' or some such remark which implied that more might have been seen of them earlier. But all the exchanges were friendly. The dapper horsemen quickly disappeared in an easterly direction towards (I think) Beaumont and Philippeville. It was while I was watching the trot-past with No.1 that Eleven O'Clock struck. The war was over.

On the evening of Monday 11 November (Armistice Day) our Headquarters moved billets. The new area comprised the northern outskirts of the town including the road to Mons which General Foch had named as the final objective of the British army. Here we were unexpectedly well-housed. I spent most of my spare time that day writing a long letter home.

One last memory, which, though not mentioned in my diary or letters, has remained firmly fixed: after dark, Overton-Jones and I paid a visit to the cathedral hoping to attend some sort of service. Though not particularly given to prayerfulness, we would both have liked a quiet moment. But we were too late for the service. So we made our way to the east side of the town and stood there for a few minutes in silence looking to the south. For the last four years the eastern horizon had been intermittently lit up by gun-flashes and Very lights. Many times had we looked forward to the moment when, after sunset, the horizon would extend on each side permanently silent and dark. Now the moment had come.

I ought, I realized, to be feeling exultant. But I did not. The quiet late-evening sky looked as if it had never reverberated and flickered. After the excitement of the day a sad mood settled on us both. What did the world hold for the countries which had ceased fighting? What did it hold for our two selves? Hopes were combined with misgivings. But I recall one strong feeling – thankfulness that the anxieties of my parents, to whom I had just been writing, were over. My mother had several times said how far beyond reasonable hope seemed the moment when the haunting anxieties of recent years would be permanently lifted. This moment had now come. I wondered what my father and mother were doing at that precise moment. I seemed to see them standing close to each other looking over the estuary of the Rance, giving thanks that at last the end had come without the dreaded catastrophe. I was simultaneously aware of happiness on their behalf, of responsibility to them for what I was later going to do with my life, and, underlying the rest, misgivings about what was going to happen to the world.

EPILOGUE

I conclude my personal story with a last word about myself. I spent the early days of 1919 in the occupation of Cologne. It was not a happy period. The civilian population among whom we were billeted were suffering from the effects of increasingly severe food shortages and our own troops were in a fever to get back to their homes and jobs which, now the war was over, could not for ever remain as secure as they had been when it started.

Colonel Edwin Brassey, who then commanded the Second Battalion, appointed me as the Battalion's demobilization officer so that it became my duty to compose and deal with this fever of restlessness. My main job was to take into account priorities and to allocate accordingly the available places for demobilization. To everyone was assigned a demobilization code number, depending on the pre-war job held by each man in civilian life. I was personally assigned to category no. 42, which comprised students (my career at Oxford having been interrupted early in the war). This category had priority, and I was back in England by February 1919. I returned to Balliol, and proceeded to take degrees first in zoology and then in medicine. The medical curriculum was long, and involved many examinations.

Immediately after leaving Cologne, I joined my parents in Jersey. We spent about three weeks at St. Brelade's Bay Hotel, which gave them a change from Dinard. Seeing that the war was over, that I was safe and that my parents' anxieties on my account were at an end, this post-war period should have been one of memorable relief and equanimity, but it was not. My parents could for the first time take stock of what had irrevocably been lost by my brother's death; and the challenge which had sustained their poise and prevented their spirits from sinking and drooping as the war continued was no longer present on their horizon. But the pervasive question remained: what would be the outcome of the Armistice?

As we passed out of the twenties into the thirties, conditions in Germany deteriorated and the stage was set for the fulfilment of my father's prediction about the consequences of a dictated peace. During the winter of 1919 my father nearly died in Florence of an attack of Spanish 'flu, from which he never properly recovered. After a period of fluctuating invalidism, he finally died a somewhat disillusioned man in 1928. My mother, a staunch Catholic to the last, followed in 1934. Thus my father never knew Germany under Hitler. What would he have thought of this scarcely human being? And how would Hitler's appearance on the European scene, and the tortuous role he played from 1933 onwards, have affected my father's feelings for Germany, which had their origins in Freiburg two decades before? I shakily infer from his strong hostility to Mussolini, when the latter embarked during my father's lifetime on his adventures in Abyssinia and Corfu in the twenties, and from the intense revulsion of my father's friends – among whom were many Jews – against the Nazis and their politics, that my father, who had conducted a vigorous part in the defence of Dreyfus during the 1890s, would have found himself compelled to make what later came to be called an 'agonizing reappraisal'.

I now finish my personal story which began in 1914. When I was demobilized in 1919, I became a member of the Coldstream's Special Reserve of Officers, in which I continued to hold a commission until the Second World War broke out in 1939. But I was then too old for active service in a combatant battalion. A way, however, of avoiding a long period of service in a holding battalion was to make use of the medical degrees which I had by then obtained, and to get myself posted as a regimental medical officer (RMO) to one of the regimental combatant battalions. This is exactly what, in the event, I did. I first got myself transferred, with the modest rank of Captain, to the RAMC. After a rather unhappy spell with a general hospital in Dieppe, I got myself posted as regimental medical officer to my old unit, the regiment's Second Battalion, which was commanded in England and on its transit to France, by my old friend Colonel Lionel Bootle-Wilbraham, D.S.O., M.C. (later Lord Skelmersdale) with whom it was my privilege and joy to serve during the first part of the Second War. I need say no more about this second period of service in the army beyond stating that it was one of the happiest periods of my life, and that I count myself to have been exceptionally fortunate in having had in the two wars this uniquely duplicated experience of army life in the same battalion of the same regiment in closest association with several old and valued friends. I was married in 1923 and have had three children – now grown-up.

Appendix 1

ROBIN'S NOTEBOOK;
LAST LETTERS AND DEATH.

Among Robin's effects which were found after his death was a leather-bound notebook in which he had set down his thoughts after leaving England on 26 August 1915. Some of them are reproduced here.

The opening page of the notebook reads:

Notes on the events which occurred to me and the impressions which I underwent commencing from Aug. 26th 1915, the day of my departure for France, to partake in that universal lapse into barbarism and inhumanity (not to say imbecility and madness) which we call the Fight for Freedom and Peace against tyranny and militarism.

He crossed the channel to Boulogne, and from there went by train to Lumbres, where he spent a few days and where all the remaining entries in the notebook were made.

Monday, August 30th.
Life here is uneventful and I have much time for meditation. It is in a way a period of initiation as I have to accustom myself thoroughly to the idea of the things I am about to go through. What is in store for me? I don't care. I will take what comes and think only that most comforting of thoughts in times of doubt and uncertainty – the thought which brings home the realization of our own stupendous smallness; of the unimportance of whether our life ends today or tomorrow, in the general scheme of things. For fifty years hence and tomorrow are one and the same when compared with the great lapses of time in nature.

There is one subject on which I try not to let my mind dwell as it irritates and disturbs me: that I, a human being, eighteen years old, the product of untold ages of evolution in humanity, should be in this place with the sole intent of putting to death other human beings – equally civilized, with similar ideals and similar beliefs. And with what object? To crush militarism and tyranny from the face of the earth, when the same object would have been achieved by the cession of a few colonies to a nation expanding and desiring space for further progress. And will that end be achieved in this manner which I am practising at the moment? Never!

The whole thing is pitifully humorous in its imbecility, in its hopelessness. If ever I live to see another war, then will I have sufficient moral courage to proclaim my sentiments and to wash my hands of a pack of idiots of which I regret to say I am at present one – unhappily.

Sept. 4th 1915.
During these days I feel very strongly that the expression (or attempted expression) of one's own thoughts and feelings will do more to educate and relieve the mind than any amount of reading. For, as I think Schopenhauer says (into whose writings I have dipped but slightly) too much reading stifles the imagination and causes one's thoughts to run in channels – to be formulated from without instead of from within. One should read a little at a time, and then proceed thoroughly to digest that little, and to form one's own conclusions. The result of other people's thoughts should but act as a suggestion, as a stimulant, of one's own. One's attitude should be both critical and sceptical from the outset, and extremes should be avoided. That is a lesson I have learnt from this war. Those who wholly condemn and wholly exonerate are both equally in the wrong. There is something to be said for each side and each side is in a measure to blame. This appears to me to be the commonsense attitude. For is it conceivable, (taking this war as a particular instance), that of civilized Europe, divided into two halves, one part should be entirely right and the other utterly wrong? Let us at least hope not, for if such were the case, there would exist no measure of security in life. Germany is foremost in art, music, in science and in industry. If, with these tokens of civilization stamped deeply upon her, she is capable of wilfully committing a crime from which not one of the individuals composing her could be wholly exonerated, then civilization is a farce and we would do well to revert to the natural law of prehistoric times. No. There is right and there is wrong on both sides, in pretty equal portions, and – above all – there is misunderstanding.

There, in my opinion, the matter ends. If each side chooses to juggle with facts and to look upon an obvious situation from directly opposite points of view, one conclusion alone is possible. Human beings, taken in general, are childlike in their simplicity. Also nationality, by means of which this simplicity manifests itself, with such terrible results, is a curse and a scourge. May the religion of patriotism perish, and perish quickly!

It fundamentally is the worship of a fetish, whether abstract or concrete, just as in the case of ordinary religions, and whatever may have been the good results of these religions, they have at all events brought (and are bringing) a vast deal of misery and suffering on the heads of us poor animals.

Sunday, Sept, 5th, 1915. *[Last entry in the notebook]*
This is the first really fine day I have experienced out here. At this spot and at this moment it is exquisite. I brought a book out here after lunch, and am now lying in a small and secluded opening in the woods, looking out over the broad valley.

Evening is approaching, the light is mellow and there is a light mist hanging over the hills in the distance. The effect is beautiful, and my repose, both mental and physical, is complete. I am enjoying, but in a semi-apparent and unreal form, that pleasure which will be pregnant with acute happiness when all this madness is over.

*   *   *   *

Robin's last two letters.

The move from Lumbres towards the front line probably began on 21 or 22 September. The place names given in his last letters are garbled, possibly for security reasons, but more probably because he was reproducing phonetically names which he only heard spoken. The letter dated 25 September was the last to be posted and was received by his parents in Torquay before the news of his death.

Arrouange [Allouagne?]
Saturday, Sept. 25th 1915.

Dearest Parents,

Yesterday we were warned that the big effort was going to take place to-day. I went to the C.O.'s conference, as being in charge of the bombers, and he told us the general plan. All yesterday, last night and up to 8 o'clock this morning, the bombardment has been stupendous – a continuous roar. Last night we received orders to move this morning at 4.30, and so I went right to bed and got in some sleep. We marched off early and have just arrived here – about 8 miles. We are on an hour's notice to get moving, and have been warned that there may be no food for 36 hours. If the attack is successful (and reports that come in one after the other state that it is succeeding, that the front trenches have been captured etc.) – we will move before long – through the gap.

I shall spend the short time here preparing my equipment and deciding exactly what to carry, as I shall not see my valise again and we will be bivouacking (if we are not marching and fighting) during the nights. The bombardment has ceased now, and I don't know what it portends. It may be

290

that the Germans are retreating and the guns moving up. We are about 10 miles from the line here and there are thick clouds of smoke in the direction of the battle.

As for myself I am well and very interested. I have been marching heavy these days in order to get accustomed to it and am now in pretty good training. I shall probably need all the energy I possess during the next days. I will do my utmost to write to you daily, if it is only a line. A letter and some cigarettes arrived yesterday, for which many thanks. The cigarettes will travel in my haversack. Whether posts will be delivered regularly or not if we get on the march I don't know, but if all goes well I think they should be.

We have unquestionably got the pleasantest and most interesting task in this attack. Going over the parapet, of course, is the worst, and we escape that. It seems funny to think that at this very moment the phase of warfare which lasted a whole year is perhaps drawing to an end.

Excuse this disconnected scribble, but I am rather pressed for time, as my things must be seen to. Best love, dearest, ever your own loving and devoted ,

Robin

Nobody better![1]

The last letter dated 27 September (the day before he was killed) was found on his body when it was recovered from no-man's-land on 14 October and was among the parcel of possessions delivered to CPB at Ham-en-Artois (see p. 51).

(see p. 51)

German Fire Trench
S.E. of Vermelles.
Monday, Sept. 27th 1915.

Dearest Parents,

I am writing this in the German front line trench, captured from them on Saturday, nearly opposite Vermelles. Let me tell you what has happened since I wrote last. (I could not send a line yesterday, as there was no post -- and there may not be today.) We left the place called Allouangne *[Allouagne]* at a moment's notice, at 2 p.m. on Friday. There I said good-bye to my valise, and from that point carried everything on me. The weight was not small, but I am getting accustomed to it. It rained hard, and we marched from 2 to 9.30. On the way up we passed a few wounded coming back in motor-ambulances, and allowed several regiments of cavalry to ride by us (going up), which cheered the men greatly, as it seemed to point to a real advance.

There were continual checks on the road, and I was very tired when we dragged into a village called Ouchin *[Houchain]*, in pouring rain and with the

---

[1] When Robin was a child, he used to say to his mother, when she kissed him goodnight, 'Nobody better!' – i.e. than her.

roads in a very bad state. The place was seething with troops, and I rushed about and after much swearing and arguing succeeded in getting a couple of sheds with some straw for my platoon. Again my French was of assistance to me. After this I had something to eat in an estaminet with the others, and then went and lay down in the cottage we had procured for the night. No beds, of course, but I managed to get a little sleep on the brick floor, with the aid of my air cushion and overcoat.

Yesterday morning we had some breakfast, and as we were on a moment's notice to move, I lay down again and slept. Besides I was feeling far from well, my stomach was out of order and I was generally. . . . At two we marched off again, and marched as a division towards the firing-line. Immediately opposite us things were comparatively quiet, but on our right the French were doing their attack, by the sound of the bombardment which was in progress. Nothing but troops and lines of transport as we approached the line, and villages full of slightly wounded, still able to walk. At length we got into the zone of fire, where hardly a house was intact, and most of them battered to bits. About dusk we worked in towards Vermelles, and shells began to drop occasionally, mostly near some houses where guns were concealed. All this served to prove that there had been no very great advance, and that things were more or less as they had been. As dusk came on, the scene became quite picturesque as the Germans were sending up their flares – just like bright fireworks – which illumined the country round. At a given moment a red flare went up, some way off to the left and immediately there were sounds of an attack – machine-gun and rifle fire in one continuous burst, with a bombardment and accompaniment of flares and lights. We pushed on gradually in the darkness until we reached a place behind some ruins – the country here is as flat as a billiard table – and there we halted by the side of the road – 9 p.m, First of all it was for an hour's halt, but then the order came that we had to bivouack. I was very tired, and it was a relief to shed my pack., wrap up in my 'trench-coat' and a waterproof sheet, and go to sleep. First, however, there was an issue of tea, which seemed like nectar to me.

At 2.30 a.m. we were roused again (I must have got in three hours sleep) and pushed on in the darkness. We heard we were to occupy the trenches taken from the Germans, and we stumbled on through barbed wire and over our own unoccupied trenches until we came to the once German lines. Into these we filed (we were not under fire) and as it got light we set our men to digging a firing-step on the back of the trench. Before the attack, our trenches had been 800 yards from the German ones – a very long way – and the British had had to run all that way under a terrific fire. The scene is not pleasant, and I will not describe it. You see, the battle-field has not been touched since the attack, and there are many, many dead. Myself and the four other officers are sitting in the German dug-out, which is not very good. Of course there is a lot of German equipment, rifles, and even a few newspapers and letters. I think we will move out of here soon; I hope so. It is a blighted and poisoned land, and makes one sick to look at it. The Germans have retreated two or three miles, and rumour has it that there have been big successes in other parts.

Your most welcome letter has come, and one from Granny too. You have no idea what pleasure they bring here and what a veritable joy they are. Your rusks are a great success, and they are the only food we have now. Good-bye till tomorrow, dearest parents (that is if the posts go regularly).

Ever you own devoted and loving,

Robin

Nobody better.

★   ★   ★   ★

The Battle of Loos lasted basically for four days – 25 to 28 September 1915 – and, from the British standpoint, was a disastrous failure. Apart from the horrendous casualties, it entirely failed in its overall objective of breaking through the German line and putting an end to the period of static trench warfare, which is what Robin was referring to in the penultimate paragraph of his letter of 25 September. The British attacked along a six-mile front from Lens in the south to La Bassée in the north. It was a mining area with numerous pit shafts, or 'puits', which had been fortified by the Germans. The area comprising the Chalk Pit, Chalk Pit Wood and Puit 14 bis, in which both Robin and John Kipling (see below Appendix 2) died, lies about a mile north-east of the village of Loos, which gave its name to the battle. It had been taken and retaken in attacks and counter-attacks during the battle.

Among the papers preserved by CPB's parents was the following account of the actions leading up to Robin's death, written by Captain E.B.Hopwood, who had commanded Robin's company (No. 1) in their attack on the Chalk Pit on 27 September, just after the above letter was written. It had evidently been sent to them by Lt.-Col. Drummond Hay, the Lieutenant-Colonel of the Coldstream Guards.

1st Battalion Coldstream Guards: 27th, 28th and 29th September, 1915.

On the morning of the 27th the Battalion entrenched in the old German trenches east of Lone Tree and west of the Loos – La Bassée road.

The Battalion was ordered to support the attack on the Chalk Pit and Chalk Pit Wood by the 2nd Battalion Irish Guards. The Irish Guards advanced at 4 p.m. and gained the Wood. The 1st Battalion sent up two Companies to support them, and these Companies advanced in perfect order, and gained the Loos – Hulluch Road, where they entrenched.

At 6.30 p.m. the order came for the Battalion to take the Chalk Pit and hold it, so the same two Companies (Nos. 1 and 2) advanced and achieved their objective without any difficulty. By this time it was quite dark, but touch had been gained with the Irish Guards' Company south of the Wood, and the position round the southern edge of the Chalk Pit consolidated.

The remainder of the Battalion then moved up and dug themselves in along the Lens – La Bassée Road for 100 yards, and then back to the Loos – Hulluch Road. The next morning, 28th, our trenches were heavily bombarded by the enemy's guns. At 3.15 p.m. the order came for the Battalion to attack *Puit 14 bis* and establish themselves on the Railway immediately south of it.

At 3.45 p.m. Nos. 1 and 2 Companies, under 2nd Lt. O. Style and Lt. C. Riley left their trenches and assaulted the *Puits*. They at once came under a tremendous enfilade fire from heavy guns and at least three machine-guns – these latter being in the Bois Hugo. Lts. Riley and Style[2] with eight men only managed to reach the objective – the remainder of the attacking lines were swept away by machine-gun fire.

Lt. Riley who was wounded, and two men managed to regain their trenches later on. All ranks behaved magnificently. Our casualties were heavy, amounting to nine officers (including 2nd Lt R. Blacker and three other officers who were reported missing) and over 200 other ranks. The whole of that night was spent in consolidating our position and getting in wounded, and the next day our trenches were heavily bombarded by the enemy's heavy guns.

At 11 a.m. on the 29th an 8-inch shell struck the entrance to Battalion Headquarters (a deep cellar in the Chalk Pit) instantly killing Lt-Col. A. Egerton and Lt. & Adj. Hon. D. Browne. Half the cellar was destroyed and five men buried under the debris – two of them were eventually dug out and rescued. The total casualties sustained by the Battalion during these three days amounted to 13 officers and 258 N.C.O.'s and men.

(Signed) E.B.Hopwood, Capt.,
1st Bn. Coldstream Guards

---

[2] Style was in fact taken prisoner. Among the documents preserved by Carlos and Caroline Blacker was a telegram (unfortunately undated) from Style's parents saying that they had just received a postcard from their son who was 'now a prisoner'.

Appendix 2

THE FINDING OF ROBIN'S BODY; LETTERS FROM GEORGE BERNARD SHAW, CAPTAIN LLOYD, PRIVATE WRIGHT AND RUDYARD KIPLING

As told above, Robin was killed on 28 September 1915, the fourth day of the Battle of Loos. He was reported as 'missing' in the casualty lists issued on 3 October, and his parents hoped desperately that he had been taken prisoner. Indeed on 6 October Carlos wrote to his sister Carmen in Freiburg urging her to do all she could to find out where he was: 'I really do not allow myself to think that Robin is other than alive . . .' He was clearly deeply depressed at the time: 'I wish I could find relief in my old tempestuous rages, but now I feel accablé, and the days seem very long.'

Robin's body was then found in no-man's-land by a party of South Wales Borderers, which included Private Wright, on 14 October; the news, in the form of the letter from Captain Lloyd reproduced below, reached his parents in their house Vane Tower in Torquay on 19 October. George Bernard Shaw was in Torquay at the time, and the following letter and postcard which he wrote to CPB (who was himself on the Western Front only a few miles from where Robin had been killed) describe what happened. This hitherto unpublished letter reveals a compassionate side of GBS's character which has not always been fully appreciated.

The Hydro, Torquay.   19th Oct. 1915

My dear Pip,

The worst is over at Vane Tower. The news arrived this morning; and by good luck Robbie Ross had arrived the night before, just the right man at the right time. We were to have lunched; and when a telephone message came to put us off, I knew at once what had happened; for I had seen the day before in one of Philip Gibbs's letters in the Daily Chronicle a passing description of the chalk pits 'still full of dead'; and this knocked on the head my assumption that all the bodies had been recovered and identified. I said nothing about it; but it prepared me to some extent. I went over to the Tower at once and saw Olive and Robbie.

What happened was that when Olive and your mother came down to breakfast they saw a letter which they at first thought was from you. Carlos came down; opened it; collapsed; and rushed out of the room, bursting into tears as he did so. Your mother made Robbie go in to him. Robbie took the letter from him and read it, and stuck to it, finally sealing it up and making Carlos promise not to read it for a month or so, his reason being that it contained nothing to bear out Robbie's assurance that Robin had been killed instantly, and that it was rather cruelly dry in its statement of the facts. It contained a careful sketch of the place where Robin was found. Consequently neither Carlos nor your mother have read the letter through.

When I arrived, they were walking in the garden. Carlos had promised Robbie to take a walk with him. Robbie, after some talk with me, went and told Carlos I was there. Carlos came in presently and said 'Don't say anything.' But of course I said a lot, not consolatory, but comminatory, damning the universe generally, and insisting that we should kill somebody – anything by way of a stimulant – trying to make him cry for a moment and then to switch him off and make him laugh or have a little raging brainstorm. He said it was impossible to come out when I prescribed Nature as the Healer [it was most fortunately a heavenly day]; but he at last consented to venture through the wood with me and Robbie. In the wood he declared that he would never part with Vane Tower, but would shut it up with all its memories of Robin, and let it rot. I took this in very bad part, and declared that everything connected with Robin should be blazing with life and triumph, whereupon Carlos's morbidezza vanished, and he declared he would never leave it. He then relapsed and said that but for your mother he would kill himself. I assented, but insisted on his killing all the bores in Torquay first. He got led at once into giving us biographies of the worst of them. He came right on to Daddy Hole Plain, stopping three times in the road to deliver picturesque and dramatic descriptive orations in his best style. We stood a long time on the plain talking, <u>laughing</u>, philosophising; and from time to time execrating the folly of drilling three or four unfortunate recruits which was going on. I proposed that we should charge them and trample them down. I played all my stage tricks to keep things going; and when at last we returned to the Tower and I left him, I felt that the back of the black day was broken, and that he would come through valiantly. I put off my return to London by a day so as to be with him a little longer. But I <u>must</u> go the day after tomorrow, my London engagements being imperative.

At teatime I returned to the Tower, Charlotte having in the meantime taken Olive Chetwynd off in the car. Then I saw you mother. She, like me, had been somewhat prepared by something she had heard the day before. She had been crying a good deal; and I had to go gently at first, and even press the Blessed Virgin into the service. But you mother has real quality in her – grit and good sense – and she does not force herself to be miserable: her grief is quite natural and free from the conventional adulterations. Mrs Price was there, and for a moment, Payne, who had been called in to give Carlos bromide, against which I rather protested as a fraud on Robin. I pulled out my High Spirits stop as far as it would go; made Robbie laugh; made Carlos laugh; finally made your mother laugh and got quite a new expression into her face. Robbie looked on at this scandalous exhibition with some amazement; but we really fought off the sorrow until it was getting on for seven o'clock, when Charlotte and I rose to go. I proposed to Carlos that he should come to London with me and have a spree. And so we broke up, half laughing and half crying: Captain Price and Sir John having just arrived.

I feel quite sure that it is virtually all over now: they will recover quite rapidly. The worst time was when the first news came: the really brutal, stunning effect was exhausted then. And Robbie has been worth his weight in gold. Olive's week at the Tower has also been very opportune. She is a very good sort (she and I became pals at once) and her touch never hurts.

I suppose it would not be playing the game to tell your Colonel that you are now an only son, and that your sight is second sight, and will, if applied to military purposes, lead to the destruction of the whole blessed battalion; but I sometimes ask myself whether the salvation of the world does not depend on us all refusing to play the game until the stakes are a little nobler.

I write in haste so as to get this to you as soon as possible.

I find that Robbie, like Charlotte, is greatly interested in you. So I daresay, if he knew I was writing, he would desire to be remembered.

Do not bother to acknowledge this. Carlos shows me your letters. Devilish good letters they are too; but they must take all the writing capacity out of you, and make all other letters drudgery. Perhaps, however, that is a senile delusion on my part. I used to be able to write a frightful lot at your age.

Auf wiedersehen.

Yours ever
G.Bernard Shaw

This letter was followed by a postcard written the next day.

Torquay.   20th October 1915

My letter of yesterday needs a postscript. This evening Carlos took me into the study; produced the letter which Robbie had sealed up; and asked me to read it. He was tortured with the idea that there was something horrible about Robin having crawled into the chalkpit and died a lingering death there. To my great relief, I found that the letter was not only quite perfect in its tone, but that the little sketch map which the writer (Lloyd) had carefully made, showed clearly that Robin had dropped just as he had charged out of the wood, and gave not the slightest reason to fear that he had moved. I urged Carlos to read the letter, which gave me a very favourable opinion of the good sense and genuine consideration of the writer. He just gave the necessary information carefully and exactly and finished with a grave gesture of sympathy: nothing could have been better done. Carlos was enormously lightened by my assurance, though he still could not face the letter.

I spent nearly two hours with him this morning, just listening whilst he let himself rip. He worked off a tremendous head of steam; and I think it did him good. Ross and Payne relieved guard at one, when I left him. He presented me with two pairs of braces!

Your mother was much happier this afternoon. She talked a great deal about you and Robin, and showed me your earliest efforts in fiction. I bade them farewell quite reassured as to the worst being well over, though Carlos kissed Charlotte and broke down a little at parting.

G.B.S.

Captain Lloyd's letter read as follows:

Somewhere in France

16-10-15

Dear Sir,

As your son's papers were recovered by a man of my Coy. you will certainly want to hear where he was found and where he now lies.

My Coy. was holding the new English Front line on the morning of 14.10.15. The morning was misty and the men went out to look to our dead and also no doubt to hunt for souvenirs; one of them found your son and brought me his watch and papers and I have handed them over to our Headquarters.

The same evening I sent out some men and brought your son in and buried him in the spot indicated. It is just North of the sap at <u>present</u> nearest the Chalk Pit and just on the edge of the wood; a rough wooden cross marks the spot. I was burying a man of my Coy. the same night and by error two crosses were made and the S.W.B.'s man's name put on both. As time was short, I just crossed his name out and had your son's put underneath. I tell you this detail as should weather destroy the lettering it may help you to recognize the spot.

> With my sincere sympathy,
> Yours,
> J. Conway Lloyd
> Capt.
> 'A' Coy.
> 1st S.W.B.

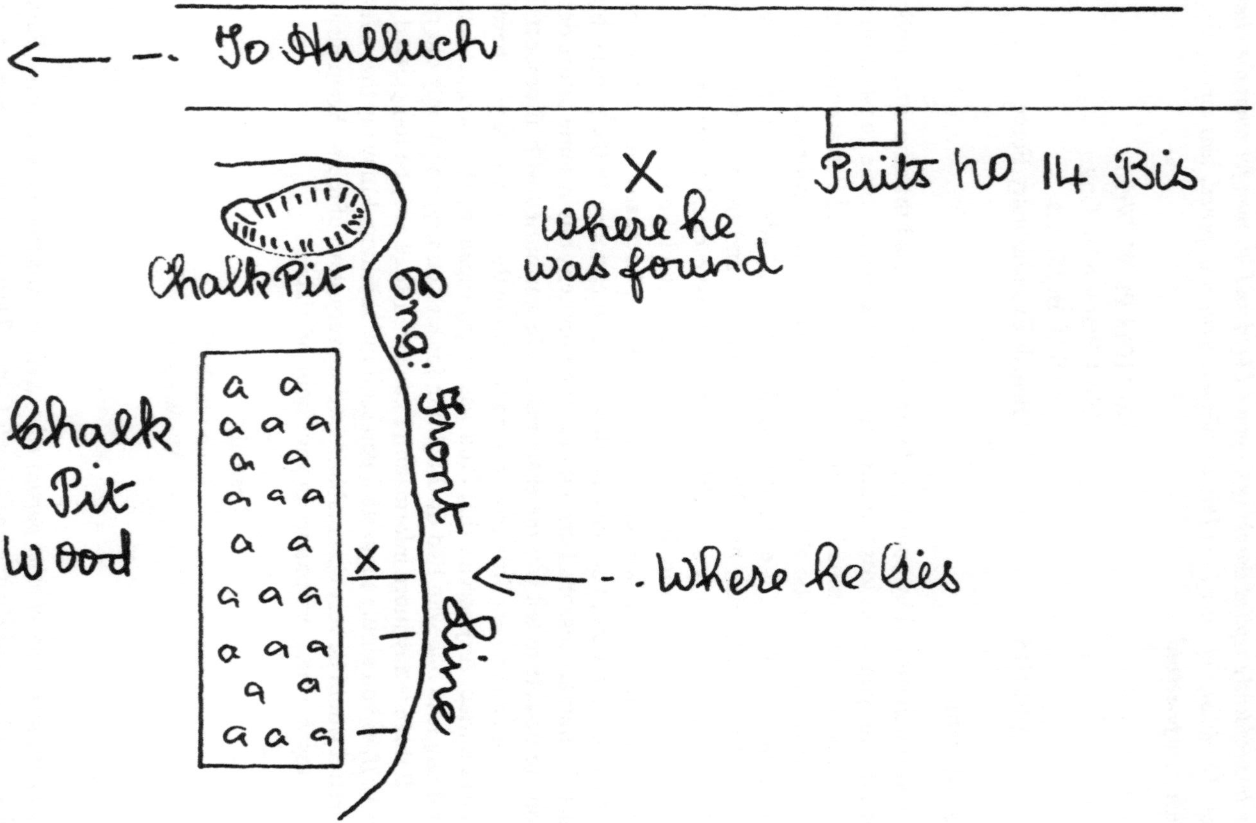

To Hulluch
Puits no 14 Bis
X
Where he was found
Chalk Pit
Eng: Front Line
Chalk Pit Wood
X
Where he lies

Caroline evidently replied thanking Captain Lloyd and his men for what they had done. The following letter from Private Wright, written in pencil, was among those which were preserved.

No 11044 Pt. W. Wright
No 1 Platoon 'A' Coy.
1ˢᵗ S.W.Borderers
British Expeditionary Force

18/11/15

Dear Madam,

I was much moved by your kind letter, and I am glad that the little service that I did for your dear lost son after his death has been a little consolation to his parents, and my sympathies go out to you in your sad bereavement, and any information I may be able to give to help you to bear your sorrow I shall be very pleased to give. We found his body about 200 yds in front of our own lines, and his death must have been instantaneous and from his wounds we gathered that the enemy's machine-gun must have caught him as he was advancing with his men to the attack. One bullet had hit him in the face, but had not disfigured him. We carried him behind our lines, and buried him near the chalk quarries that you have no doubt seen mentioned in the papers, but which for military reasons I cannot describe minutely, but at some future date I hope to be able to tell you the exact place. He was buried with all respect in his uniform, and a neat little cross placed to denote the spot where your heroic son was buried. Any service that I did was amply repaid by the thought that I was doing it to one who had died fighting for his country, and I only did my duty. If there is any more information I can give I shall only be too pleased to give it. If, as you kindly suggested, you send me anything, I may say that a few cigarettes would be very acceptable, as we are very short of them. Again please accept my warmest sympathies in your hour of trial.

I remain
Yours faithfully,
W. Wright

*   *   *   *

Among the thousands of other parents who received shattering news after the Battle of Loos was Rudyard Kipling and his wife Carrie. Their son John[1] was killed on the day before, and probably within a few hundred yards of the spot where Robin met his death; he was in the Second Battalion of the Irish Guards who had spearheaded the

---

[1] See Tonie and Valmai Holt, *My Boy Jack. The Search for Kipling's Only Son*, Leo Cooper 1998

attack on the Chalk Pit Wood. John Kipling had also been a close friend of Oscar Hornung, who had been one of CPB's best friends at Eton, and of Oliver Baldwin (son of Stanley Baldwin, Prime Minister 1923-31 and 1935-37)) who was his, John Kipling's, cousin, and with whom CPB had an encounter on the evening of 27 September 1918 during the Battle of the Canal du Nord (see p. 265). Like Robin, John Kipling was initially posted as 'missing' and his body was never recovered and identified with certainty. On hearing that he was missing, CPB wrote to Rudyard Kipling as follows:

4th Btn. Coldstream Guards,
Guards Division,
B.E.F.
Oct. 13th 1915

Dear Mr Kipling,

I wonder if you will accept from a complete stranger an expression of the deepest sympathy in the loss that has come upon you.

I only knew your son very slightly, having met him in the ship coming back from Engelberg [*a Swiss ski resort frequented by the Kiplings*] with Oscar Hornung and having travelled up in the train with him. But this I can tell you that his death is deeply felt out here by all who knew him. Everyone admired him, and everyone liked him, officers and men alike. I, myself, have always thought that those who stay at home in perpetual anxiety and fear are more to be pitied than we who are actually engaged out here and have other things to disturb our thoughts.

You are fighting a battle of thoughts more severe and more unremitting than we, and now you, yourself, are fighting the hardest battle of all.

I send you all the sympathy and encouragement that I can.

Yours sincerely,
C.P.Blacker

The Kiplings were clearly touched by this letter. Carrie wrote on the bottom of the letter 'These boys are so nice. Could anything be more delightful than this.' *Rudyard replied as follows:*

Bateman's,
Burwash,
Sussex.
Oct.17, 1915

Dear Blacker,

I am more grateful to you than I can well say for your letter about John. I heard dark rumours of his trip from Engelberg with Oscar Hornung and an adventure with a seasick passenger, a basin and a fifty centime piece. It must have been a merry passage.

I expect you are quite right about the harder on those who stay behind; but it is a pride and a consolation to know that the lad in his short life was liked and didn't do his work badly. His Company Commander has written me how he handled his platoon. The Brigade training makes men and I'm thankful I've been allowed to give a man to the work.

When you are back in England we want you to come down here if you can. It's a peaceful part of the world and you'll be more than welcome.

Wishing you all good fortune.
Ever sincerely yours,
Rudyard Kipling

CPB never took up the invitation to visit the Kiplings at Bateman's. Had he done so he would have found himself out of sympathy with Rudyard Kipling's venomous Germanophobia, which was so diametrically opposed to the attitude taken by his father.

Appendix 3

EDITOR'S POSTSCRIPT.

Having spent several months intermittently working on the editing of these memoirs, I developed a strong urge to visit some of the places described. Thus in early May 1998 I crossed the Channel and drove straight to Corbie, which, as CPB states, is about 15 km east of Amiens. I arrived there about 7 pm, and, having booked into a small hotel, went in search of the tow-path. The main road to Amiens crosses the Somme at a point where there is also a lock. There are paths down both sides of the river east of the lock, and the path on the south side is lined with poplars. It is of course possible that in 1917 there were poplars on the north side as well, and the path on that side extends further than that on the south, where it had been recently been re-made for a distance of about two kilometres and then peters out. But the path on the south side corresponds so closely with my mental picture that I have little doubt that it was on this side that my father had had his strange experience.

Next day I was joined by a friend who came by train from Paris and whom I met in Amiens. We returned to Corbie and went to look for the wood. A range of hills runs along the north side of Corbie with woods along the crest. There were two possibilities, but whereas that on the north-east of Corbie had no flowers at all, the other to the north-west was filled with bluebells. It was also substantially closer to Corbie. We reached it, as had CPB, by a chalky path bordering ploughed fields. We climbed over a fence into the wood and found a path which eventually led us past what appeared to be a hunting lodge. Bluebells and other wild flowers were everywhere.

In the evening the skies, which had been overcast since my arrival, suddenly cleared, and after dinner, the moon being nearly full, we walked along the tow-path. It was the 7th of May, and an old diary for 1917 tells me that in that year the moon was full on that very date. But our moon did not convey the feeling of being 'personalized and observant' as had CPB's. It was very peaceful, and at one point where the tow-path crossed a side stream which left the main canal we paused to watch and listen to the water tumbling over the weir. But we saw no luminous bodies and heard no music.

The following day was a beautiful spring morning and we drove to the scene of the events of 15 September, 1916, beginning with a walk in Bernafay Wood, where the Fourth Battalion had assembled on the night before the attack. Needless to say Bernafay Wood presented a very different aspect to that which CPB had seen. It was no longer an 'insalubrious place, where . . . the sustained din of our own artillery, the fairly regular German shelling, the pervasive malodours of gas and putrefaction formed a background to anticipations of what lay ahead.'

We then drove past Trônes Wood[1], and stopped at a war cemetery bordering the road near Guillemont. These war cemeteries are kept in immaculate condition, and a register of the names of those buried there can generally be found in a recess near the entrance. Here, to our excitement and satisfaction, we found Treffry's name, and so his grave (see illustration). The grave next to his was that of Raymond Asquith (the son of H.H. Asquith who was then Prime Minister) also killed on 15 September 1916.

We continued to Ginchy, and parked the car on the road from there to Longueval which runs along the crest of the 'ridge' which had been regularly shelled with 'five-nines' and which my father had crossed and re-crossed several times that day. As he had found on his subsequent visits, this 'ridge' is only slightly raised above the surrounding countryside, now covered with wheat fields. We skirted the east side of Delville Wood, and then walked along a track which brought us on to the Flers-Ginchy road, and so back into the village of Ginchy. In the course of this brief circuit we must have been close to the place where the 'whizzbangs' had come down and Treffry was mortally wounded.

I have little doubt that this incident had a more profound effect on my father than any other of the war. It was something he never talked about; once, when I was a boy, I asked him what he had done to earn his Military Cross, and I got a very short answer: 'I brought some wounded back.' On the evening of 15 September he began a letter to his parents: 'I have got through the morning of the great 15th safely, and have had experiences that shall never be effaced from my memory as long as I live.' When he came to the whizzbangs he wrote: 'What occurred, I am not going to describe to you; I scarce dare to think of it. Suffice it that Treffry was killed . . . Some time or other when the war is over, I will tell you what took place if you want to know.' But in a paradoxical way it also seemed to boost his morale. 'It is a curious thing,' he wrote in the same letter,

---

[1] We were somewhat puzzled by the fact that on the large-scale French map which I had obtained, the wood was named 'Bois des Troncs', and some local farmers whom we met confirmed that this was the correct name. Yet in all the histories of the Battle of the Somme, at least those in English, it is invariably named 'Trônes'.

'but I have a strange conviction that I am coming through this show all right. It is, of course, absolutely illogical, but it is none the less insistent.' He finished the letter the next day and ended: 'There is one thing. I think that my experience of yesterday has given me the worst that the war can provide. I feel that I am now immuned in a way, as I can never possibly have anything happen to me again that can touch that.'

Returning to my own visit to the area, we walked into Ginchy as the church clock was striking eleven; it was the anniversary of VE Day, and a small ceremony was being performed at the war memorial by the church. We stopped to watch it, and when it was over we were warmly welcomed by the local inhabitants, who invited us into a nearby schoolroom where we were given champagne. In an adjoining office there was a memorial plaque to the grandson of Charles Dickens, another victim of the Battle of the Somme.

After visiting Delville Wood (where there is one tree, and only one, which has survived from World War I) we drove along the road from Ginchy to Les Boeufs, stopping at the memorial to the Guards Division. Some farmers were harrowing the fields opposite; we asked one if they still found relics of the war in the fields and he indicated an unexploded shell lying by the side of the road. It must have been very close to this spot that Harold Macmillan (Prime Minister 1957–1963) was severely wounded on the same epic day of 15 September 1916, when he was in the Grenadier Guards. Shot in the thigh and pelvis by machine-gun bullets, he lay for several hours in a deep shell hole where he read Aeschylus's *Prometheus* in Greek. He was found after dark by his sergeant and carried back to his battalion's trenches near Ginchy.

The next day we went to the Canal du Nord. Leaving the car in Demicourt we walked east along what must have been the same sunken road which CPB had taken on 27 September 1918. After about a mile the road petered out, and, skirting a ploughed field, we reached the crest of the high ground to the west of the canal. We must have been close to the place where Gratridge, the studious-looking guardsman who resembled President Wilson, had had his face blown off.

The canal is, of course, now full of water, and we reached it just north of the lock where the dressing station had been established. We walked north along the bank and crossed the canal by the iron girder bridge where Mouse Post had been and Frisby had earned his Victoria Cross; then we turned south along the east bank of the canal. At about the point where Carey Trench joined the canal bed a small cottage has been built. We rang the bell and spoke to the woman who lived there, but she knew of no remains of a trench, and was clearly ignorant of the cataclysmic events which had happened there eighty years before. We must have been within yards of the spot where my father was knocked unconscious and wounded in the head.

There is a British war cemetery on the crest of the high ground to the east of the canal, and cannot be far from the location of Summer Lane; Sark Post, where Geoffrey Howard had earned his M.C. by the capture of the German machine-gun post, must have been somewhere in the fold of the hillside just to the north of us. Many of the graves in the cemetery are of men killed on 27 September 1918, and if one stands on the walls one can get a good view over the surrounding country. The smooth featureless agricultural fields give no indication that this was the site of the Hindenburg Support Line. Bourlon Wood was clearly visible to the north-east, but it needed imagination to see it as had CPB that day, when 'it had been bombarded from zero hour by guns of every calibre. . . . The crowns of the trees only could be seen; the boles were hidden by a mist of yellow smoke. . . . Towering columns of smoke were shooting upwards, overtopping the trees. Parts of the wood were on fire; and, from a few yards above, the tree-tops were being spat upon by bursts of shrapnel.'

We walked into Graincourt, and then back to Demicourt by the iron girder bridge. Between the bridge and Demicourt we again saw a shell lying at the side of a field. From Demicourt we drove south to Hermies, then west to Havrincourt, and then north, skirting the western edge of Bourlon Wood, where I cannot say that I sensed a sinister *genius loci*. I then dropped my friend in Lille, and drove on to Clairmarais Forest.

I was unable to find any place to stay in Clairmarais itself, so I drove into St Omer, where I booked into a hotel. The next morning I drove back to Clairmarais. The church and the monastery were easily identified; the cottage where the *estaminet* had been (which I take to have been on the corner of the road leading to Coin Perdu) had been rebuilt, and is no longer an *estaminet*. Coin Perdu itself, as CPB found to his surprise in 1949, does not overlook the forest; one must go well beyond it before one reaches higher ground which would afford such a view.

The forest itself is intersected with numerous roads and paths. I drove up a road leading into the forest from the north side near the monastery, and then walked up a path which led to the highest point of the forest. There are still some splendid beech trees there, though I doubt if any of them date back to 1916, and perhaps they are now outnumbered by oaks. But I saw no sign of the heron colony. It was a wonderful spring morning and there was a great feeling of peace. Perhaps I was able to absorb some of the spirit of the forest which helped to sustain my father's morale during the traumas of the ensuing months.

DRAMATIS PERSONAE

Allan, J.L. ('Woggs'), officer in No.3 Coy., 4th Bn.C.G.; Australian; wounded 29 May 1917.

Atkinson, G.C.L., M.C., officer in No.1 Coy., 2nd Bn. C.G.; wounded in the battle of St Leger, August 1918.

Bain-Marais, Colin, officer in 4th Bn. C.G.; wealthy South African.

Baldwin, Oliver, officer in Irish Guards; Etonian.

Barnard, Tom, officer in No.1 Coy., 2nd Bn. C.G.; later fellow zoology student at Oxford.

Batten, Nat, driver with the Belgian Field Hospital whose dismissal precipitates CPB's resignation.

Beck, Corporal, post corporal in No.3 Coy., 4th Bn. C.G.; friend of Corporal Neasham.

Beck, John, officer in No.1 Coy. 2nd Bn. C.G.; with CPB in the battle of the Canal du Nord, September 1918.

Biddulph, M.W.J., officer in No.1 Coy., 2nd Bn. C.G.; Etonian and runner.

Bisseker, F.D., officer in No.1 Coy. 2nd Bn. C.G.; with CPB in battle of Canal du Nord, Sept. 1918.

Blacker, Carlos, CPB's father; gentleman of leisure; b.1865, d.1928.

Blacker, Caroline, CPB's mother; American; daughter of Gen.Daniel Frost.

Blacker, Robin, CPB's younger brother; killed at battle of Loos, Sept., 1915.

Bloxham, Bert, driver with the Belgian Field Hospital

Blundell, E., ('The General') elderly officer in No.1 Coy, 4th Bn. C.G.

Bootle-Wilbraham, Lionel (later Lord Skelmersdale), officer in No.3 Coy., later Company Commander of No.2 Coy., and then Adjutant 4th Bn. C.G.; Commanding officer of 2nd Bn. C.G. in 2nd World War. One of CPB's closest life-long friends.

Bosanquet, W.S.B., officer in No.1 Coy., 4th Bn. C.G.; wounded November 1915.

Bower, Leonard, ('Bolo'), officer in No.3 Coy., 4th Bn. C.G.; Etonian.

Boycott, H.C., middle-aged officer in No.3 Coy. 4th Bn. C.G.; South African; died of wounds 21 March 1918.

Brassey, Col. Edwin, D.S.O., M.C., Commanding Officer, 2nd.Bn. C.G.

Brassey, Gerard, officer 2nd Bn C.G.; nephew of Col.E.Brassey; killed at battle of St Leger, August 1918.

Bruorton, W., middle-aged officer in No.3 Coy., 4th Bn. C.G.; 'choleric' South African.

Bullough, Ian, M.C., Second-in-Command, 2nd Bn. C.G.; commands the battalion in the battle of the Canal du Nord, Sept. 1918 and in the battle of Villers Pol, Nov. 1918.

Bulteel, W.G., officer at Windsor, summer 1915; later in 2nd Bn., C.G.; Cornishman.

Burton, Stephen, Second-in-command 4th Bn.C.G.; killed July 1917.

Caldwell, G.R.M. ('Scotty') officer in 2nd Bn. C.G.; accompanied CPB on short leave to Le Treport, June 1918; killed October 1918.

Carnham, Guardsman, orderly with CPB when he was wounded in the Battle of Canal du Nord, November 1918.

Cartwright, W.H., ('Canada'), officer in No.1 Coy., 4th Bn. C.G. 'An almost non-stop talker with a scarred chin who had been wounded at Neuve-Eglise with the Canadians in early 1915. Everybody liked this man, myself included.'

Champion de Crespigny, Brig.-Gen. C.R. ('Crawley'), officer commanding Guards Brigade; distinguished athlete.

Chard, W.W., officer from the Somerset Light Infantry, with CPB on wood-cutting detachment in Clairmarais Forest, spring 1916.

Chitty, Frederick, officer in No.1 Coy., 2nd Bn. C.G.; Etonian.

Churchill, E.J., Eton master who arranged CPB's appointment as courier for the Belgian Field Hospital

Coats, Jimmie, M.C., company commander no.1 Coy., 4th Bn. C.G.; later adjutant 2nd Bn. C.G.; '. . . a good-looking and rich young man . . . he was cheerful and outspoken, liked by everyone and a good soldier'.

Colby, Dr., American head of an ambulance unit working near the Belgian Field Hospital.

Collins, H.E.C., officer in No.3 Coy., 4th Bn. C.G.

Corbould, W.H., officer in No.1 Coy., 4th Bn. C.G.

Cordingly, T.R., officer in No.1 Coy., 4th Bn., C.G.

Cross, A.D., ('Archie'), officer in 2nd Bn., C.G.

Davis, Miss, matron at the Belgian Field Hospital.

Dawglish, M.J. ('Doggie'), CPB's headmaster at Cothill School 1905-09.

Dean, Corporal in 4th Bn. C.G.; boxer.

Dickinson, Alan, M.C.('Dickie'), Company Commander of No.3 Coy., 4th Bn. C.G. in succession to 'Bingo' Packenham. 'Dickie was a truly admirable man. As I understood him his three salient qualities were modesty, gentleness, and a sense of duty'.

Dorman, Capt. Mark, M.C., officer in 4th Bn. C.G.; transferred from 3rd Bn. after severe experiences; implication that the 4th Bn. is a soft option provokes CPB to apply for a transfer to the 2nd Bn.

Drummond Hay, Col. Richardson, Lieutenant-Colonel of the Coldstream Guards.

Drury, Col. William, senior padre at G.H.Q., St Omer; visited CPB in Clairmarais Forest, spring 1916.

Eccles, Capt.L.W.G. ('Yam'), Company commander, No.4 Coy., 2nd Bn. C.G.

Edwards, Guy, ('George'), Adjutant, later Commanding Officer, 4th Bn. C.G.

Espin, C.E., officer in No.3 Coy., 4th Bn. C.G.; later transferred to 2nd Bn. and wounded at battle of St Leger, Aug. 1918. Tall South African.

Farquhar, G.W.J., officer in 2nd Bn. C.G.; Etonian with a habit of glowering.

Feerich, Mlle., Belgian girl, secretary to Dr Willems at the Belgian Field Hospital; nicknamed 'Clytemnestra' by CPB.

Firbank, G.C., M.C. ('Firks'), officer in No.1 Coy, 2nd Bn. C.G.; had been wounded three times, including loss of an eye.

Fletcher, F.W.P., ('Boggles'), officer in 2nd Bn. C.G.; Etonian.

Forrester, Joe, Quartermaster, later second-in-command No.1 Coy., 4 Bn. C.G.; became lifelong friend of CPB. 'Joe was among the least jealous, malicious and egotistical of men. I never heard him say a disparaging or unkind thing of anyone. I never heard him grouse or ventilate grievances. He was always cheerful.'

Frere, Bartle, friend of CPB at Eton; killed in war.

Frere, Sir Bartle, Commandant of the Belgian Field Hospital; cousin of Eton friend.

Fricker, Regimental Quartermast Sergeant, 4th Bn. C.G., 'authoritarian figure'.

Frisby, Capt.C.H., V.C., officer in 1st Bn. C.G.; earned V.C. for his capture of Mouse Post in the battle of Canal du Nord, Sept. 1918.

Furze, G., Company commander of No.4 Coy., 4th Bn. C.G.

Grayston, G.A.,M.C., ('Graybags'), officer in 4th Bn. C.G.

Greene, Quincey, officer in No.3 Coy, 4th Bn. C.G.; American and an 'irrepressible talker'; later transferred to 3rd Bn. and killed in the second battle of Arras 28 March 1918.

Hamilton, Baillie, London secretary of the Belgian Field Hospital.

Handley, G.F.B., M.C. and Bar, middle-aged officer in 2nd Bn., C.G.; mortally wounded in battle of St Leger, Aug. 1918.

Havilland, Hugh de, ('The Man'), CPB's housemaster at Eton, 1909–1914.

Hay, Tom, driver with the Belgian Field Hospital.

Hayes, J.C., officer in 2nd Bn. C.G.; 'a competent, cheerful and companionable South African'.

Hodge, Harold, chairman of the Belgian Field Hospital.

Hornung, E.W., father of Oscar H.; novelist; ran a tea stall for troops near Arras in January 1918.

Hornung, Oscar, friend of CPB's at Eton; killed 7 July 1915.

Howard, A.N., M.C. ('Geoffrey' or 'Longshanks'), officer first in 4th and later in 2nd Bn. C.G.; awarded M.C. for his capture of Sark Post in battle of Canal du Nord, 27 Sept. 1918.

Kelsey, A.R., M.C., officer in 4th Bn. C.G.; mathematician who was 'without jealousy, malice or personal ambition'. Awarded M.C. his actions on 15 September 1916.

Kirk, 2nd Lt., officer from Lincolnshire Regiment with CPB on wood-cutting detachment in Clairmarais Forest, spring 1916.

Leahy, Father, Roman Catholic priest who celebrated an open-air mass in Flanders, July 1916.

Liddell, Major, commanding officer of wood-cutting detachment in Clairmarais Forest, spring 1916.

Lumsden, D.S., officer in No.3 Coy., 4th Bn. C.G.; South African.

Mackensie-Rogan, Major J., Director of Music, C.G.

Marshall,Lt., officer on the wood-cutting detachment in Clairmarais Forest, spring 1916.

Mayne, Sister Cora, theatre sister at the Belgian Field Hospital.

Morris, Dr, surgeon and anaesthetist at the Belgian Field Hospital; wife of Dr Shaw.

Morrison, (no name or title recorded), Sir Bartle Frere's unpopular successor as Commandant of the Belgian Field Hospital, whose dismissal of Batten provokes CPB's resignation.

Neasham, Corporal, No.3 Coy., 4th Bn. C.G., killed by a shell near Proven.

Overton-Jones, E., M.C., officer in 4th Bn. C.G.; artist and naturalist; became life-long friend of CPB.

Pakenham, Hon.E.M. ('Bingo'). Company Commander of No.3 Coy., 4th Bn. C.G., 1915–16. Mumbling and incompetent when sober; snarling and irascible when primed with *vin ordinaire*.

Paterson, R.J., officer in 4th Bn. C.G.; Etonian who accompanies CPB to Fourth of June dinner in St Omer, 1917.

Patterson, Romaine, Railway Transport Officer who accompanied CPB from Arras to Le Treport, June 1918; distinguished linguist and scholar.

Pearce, C.M.H., officer in No.3 Coy., 4th Bn. C.G., until deafened by a shell in December 1915.

Peck, Sergeant, acting sergeant-major in No.1 Coy., 2nd Bn. C.G., in battle of Canal du Nord, Sept. 1918.

Peto, Mike, Company commander of No.2 Coy., 4th Bn. C.G.

Piggott, Clive, officer in No.3 Coy., later Adjutant, 4th Bn. C.G.; lifelong friend of CPB: 'I see him now as one of the best men I have known'.

Philimore, Rev., padre 4th Bn.C.G.

Prior, E.F., Eton master; officer in Rifle Brigade; killed 15th Sept. 1916.

Raffle, Wilfred, Medical Officer to 4th Bn. C.G.

Rean, Lt., Adjutant to wood-cutting detachment in Clairmarais Forest, spring 1916.

Richards, E.G.C., ('Bon'), officer in No.1 Coy., 4th Bn. C.G.

Secker, driver at the Belgian Field Hospital; boxer.

Sharp, Sergeant, heavyweight boxer in 4th Bn. C.G., formerly in Australian police.

Shaw, Dr, surgeon at the Belgian Field Hospital.

Sheridan, Sergeant, Treffry's platoon sergeant in No.3 Coy.,4th Bn. C.G.; with CPB when Treffry was mortally wounded, 15 September 1918.

Skeffington-Smyth, Col.R, D.S.O. ('Skeff'), Commanding officer, 4th Bn. C.G. until October 1918.

Spencer, Capt. T.D., Company commander of No.3 Coy., 2nd Bn. C.G., in battle of Villers Pol, Nov. 1918.

Sorrel,H.A.G., officer at Windsor, who told CPB that Robin was 'missing'.

Sprigge, Cecil, friend of CPB from Eton, and later one of his best lifelong friends; officer in 1st Bn., C.G.; later joined the Navy.

Streatfield, Rev.S.F., padre at the Belgian Field Hospital.

Tate, Guardsman, CPB's servant after the death of Temple; with CPB in battle of Canal du Nord.

Temple,Guardsman, CPB's servant 1915–16; died in hospital (cause unknown), October 1916.

Thompson, H.C.St J., ('Tommy'), officer in No.1 Coy., 4th Bn. C.G.; later transferred to 3rd Bn., and mortally wounded in battle of Cambrai, Nov. 1917.

Treffry, D.K., middle-aged officer No.3 Coy., C.G.; mortally wounded near Ginchy, 15 September 1916.

Van Briel, Joseph, Belgian soldier in charge of the Belgian Field Hospital's depot in Dunkirk.

Watson-Smyth, E.J., Company commander, No.1 Coy., 2nd Bn. C.G.; killed in battle of St Leger, August 1918.

Wells, Philip, Medical Officer, 2nd Bn. C.G. in battle of Canal du Nord, Sept.1918.

Wilkinson, Alex, Company commander of No.1 Coy., 2nd Bn. C.G., in battle of Villers Pol, Nov. 1918; lifelong friend of CPB.

Willems, Dr., eminent Belgian surgeon at the Belgian Field Hospital.

INDEX